Social Work with Adults

Social Work

with

Adults

Edited by

Martin Davies

Policy

Law

Theory

Research

Practice

palgrave
macmillan

First published 2012 by
PALGRAVE MACMILLAN

Palgrave Macmillan in the UK is an imprint of Macmillan Publishers Limited, registered in England, company number 785998, of Houndmills, Basingstoke, Hampshire RG21 6XS.

Palgrave Macmillan in the US is a division of St Martin's Press LLC, 175 Fifth Avenue, New York, NY 10010.

Palgrave Macmillan is the global academic imprint of the above companies and has companies and representatives throughout the world.

Palgrave® and Macmillan® are registered trademarks in the United States, the United Kingdom, Europe and other countries.

ISBN-13: 978–0–230–29384–7

This book is printed on paper suitable for recycling and made from fully managed and sustained forest sources. Logging, pulping and manufacturing processes are expected to conform to the environmental regulations of the country of origin.

A catalogue record for this book is available from the British Library.

A catalog record for this book is available from the Library of Congress.

10 9 8 7 6 5 4 3 2 1
21 20 19 18 17 16 15 14 13 12

Printed and bound in the UK by Charlesworth Press, Wakefield, West Yorkshire

For Mr Edwin T S Ho, consultant surgeon, without whose skill and tenaciousness this book would not have been conceived, let alone taken to completion

Brief contents

Full contents

List of figures, tables and boxes

Figures

Tables

Boxes

The authors

Michael Bamber, Practice Consultant Social Worker, Norfolk County Council

Alison Brammer, Senior Lecturer in Law, Keele University

Suzy Braye, Professor of Social Work and Social Care, University of Sussex

Jenni Brooks, Research Fellow, Social Policy Research Unit, York University

Paul Clarkson, Research Fellow, Personal Social Services Research Unit, Manchester University

Shirley Cusack, Director, Keys to Inclusion, Edinburgh

Jane Edwards, Independent Analyst, North Yorkshire

Sherrill Evans, Senior Lecturer, Centre for Social Work and Social Care Research, Swansea University

Donald Forrester, Professor of Social Work Research, Tilda Goldberg Centre for Social Work and Social Care, University of Bedfordshire

Sarah Galvani, Assistant Director, Tilda Goldberg Centre for Social Work and Social Care, University of Bedfordshire

Mary Gardner, Direct Payments Manager, Self-directed Support Team, Sheffield City Council

Tony Gilbert, Deputy Head, School of Social Science and Social Work, Plymouth University

Georgia Glynn, Research Fellow, Tilda Goldberg Centre for Social Work and Social Care, University of Bedfordshire

Nick Gould, Professor of Social Work, Bath University

Kate Gridley, Research Fellow, Social Policy Research Unit, York University

Liz Howard, Senior Practitioner, Self-directed Support Team, Sheffield City Council

Susan Hunter, Senior Lecturer in Social Work, Edinburgh University

Aisha Hutchinson, Honorary Research Fellow, University of Bedfordshire

Peter Huxley, Professor, Centre for Social Work and Social Care Research, Swansea University

Rhiannon Jones, Senior Lecturer in Social Work, Manchester Metropolitan University

Caroline Leah, Lecturer in the School of Community-Based Medicine, University of Manchester

Janet Leece, Independent Researcher, Staffordshire

Michelle McCann, Research Fellow, Tilda Goldberg Centre for Social Work and Social Care, University of Bedfordshire

Ann McDonald, Professor of Social Work, University of East Anglia, Norwich

Gillian MacIntyre, Lecturer in Social Work, Strathclyde University

Niki Marshall, Support Planning Coordinator, Adult Social Care, Sheffield City Council

Debbie Martin, Director of approved mental health professional training, southwest England, and PhD student at Bath University

Jack Nathan, Lecturer in Social Work, Institute of Psychiatry, Kings College, London

Jonathan Parker, Professor of Social Work and Social Policy, Bournemouth University

Jason Powell, Professor of Social Sciences, University of Central Lancashire

Michael Preston-Shoot, Professor of Social Work and Dean of the Faculty of Health and Social Sciences, University of Bedfordshire

Liz Salmon, Professional Social Work Lead, Community Learning Disability Teams, Sheffield City Council

Jerry Tew, Senior Lecturer, Institute of Applied Social Studies, Birmingham University

Angela Thurnham, Research Fellow, Tilda Goldberg Centre for Social Work and Social Care, University of Bedfordshire

Michael Titterton, Director of HALE (Health and Life for Everyone), Edinburgh

Sarah Wadd, Research Fellow, Tilda Goldberg Centre for Social Work and Social Care, University of Bedfordshire

Martin Webber, Lecturer in Social Work, Institute of Psychiatry, King's College London

Judith Wood, Senior Skills Tutor, Scope, Royston

Preface

The world of social work is not a static system but one that is always evolving. This book is designed to explore the elements that have influenced and continue to influence that evolutionary process: policy, law, theory and research all contribute to the end product – what the frontline social worker does in practice.

One of the best pieces of advice I was given when I was an undergraduate at Liverpool University was:

> Always remember when you are reading an academic textbook, it is not like a detective story. You are not meant to read it steadily through from page 1 to page 267. Rather, you should 'manage' it in such a way that it serves your own personal interests.

This advice is especially appropriate for this book. It has a strong internal structure that enables it to be used in different ways depending on what each reader wants.

	Part I Personalization	Part II Mental health	Part III Substance use	Part IV Old age
Policy	Chapter 1	Chapter 6	Chapter 11	Chapter 16
Law	Chapter 2	Chapter 7	Chapter 12	Chapter 17
Theory	Chapter 3	Chapter 8	Chapter 13	Chapter 18
Research	Chapter 4	Chapter 9	Chapter 14	Chapter 19
Practice	Chapter 5	Chapter 10	Chapter 15	Chapter 20

How to use this book

First, this book can be used in order to explore any or all of the four topics that are introduced – the personalization agenda, mental health, substance use or old age. The four parts provide comprehensive coverage of each subject. The reader who approaches it in this way will quickly experience the differences in background and style between the authors who write on the five academic spheres. Policy, law, theory and research each have their own intellectual heritage, and these are well reflected in the various contributions to this book. The practice chapters, by contrast, are down to earth and tell a number of real-life stories. By following the advice of my erstwhile teacher in Liverpool, the reader could usefully read each practice chapter first before turning to the weightier material that, in chapter order, precedes it. Ask yourself, then, how does the policy, law, theory or research material relate to the real world of practice that my authors have recorded for you?

A second approach that I myself tackled with fascination is to read in sequence all four chapters on each of the five relevant spheres – policy, law, theory, research, practice. For example, you can ask yourself: What are the similarities and differences between the theoretical perspectives that are outlined in respect of the four fields of social work – personalization, mental health, substance use and old age? You will find some similarities and some clear differences in each of the spheres. For example, in the sphere of law, the author of Chapter 17 begins by saying 'there is no body of law separately identifiable as relating exclusively to older people', which cannot be said in respect of mental illness.

Alternatively, a concentrated reading of all four practice chapters will give the reader an illuminating glimpse of the challenges that confront the social worker every day – and how they are being tackled.

A third approach to the book, as with all academic works of reference, is simply to go to one or more chapters in order to receive an up-to-date, state-of-the-art précis of where our subject is at in the second decade of the twenty-first century. For example, with an essay to write on the emergence of the personalization agenda, the recovery model in mental health, the feasibility of therapeutic intervention in cases of substance use, or the challenge of an ageing society, you would be home and dry. Well, almost! Each author has provided a note about three books or papers suggested as being suitable 'for further reading'; if you tackle those with an inquiring mind, you really will be able to call yourself an up-to-date expert in that field.

You should bear in mind that this book has a companion volume, *Social Work with Children and Families*, which has an identical internal structure, covering family support, child protection, adoption and fostering, and residential child care. By using the two books together, you will get a synoptic view of eight different areas of contemporary social work practice. There may be a growing distance between the various specialist fields in social work, but the work that is done shares many common features, and the two books together accurately reflect the extent to which poverty remains a powerful common factor in the majority of cases.

The authors of this book and its companion volume are based in all parts of the UK and the Republic of Ireland. This wholly desirable fact has, however, presented the editor with a problem – especially in respect of the policy and law chapters. There are some clear and many slight differences in legislation and policy to be found in the five countries, and if this had been designed as a comprehensive textbook, they would have had to be punctiliously identified. But, as I explain in the Introduction, the book is not intended to cover every aspect of social work. My interest and, I hope, that of the book's readers is concentrated on the conceptual differences between policy, law, theory, research and practice – and these are capable of intelligent interpretation, whatever the national context to which they apply.

Martin Davies

Acknowledgements

From the moment of its conception, almost exactly two years before publication, this book has benefited from the intellectual imagination of a great many people. Although the component parts of the book represent familiar territory, the idea of presenting them synoptically and, to a certain extent, deconstructing them involved a degree of risk, and I am immensely grateful to my many colleagues for responding to the idea so enthusiastically.

I owe a particular debt to two people who encouraged me to move forward with the original idea. Catherine Gray of Palgrave Macmillan is one of a rare breed of publishers' editors who responds to her authors' embryonic creations with a powerful mixture of critique and inventiveness and I like to think that she brings out the best in me. Viv Cree in Edinburgh is like me in that she inhabits that dangerous and difficult territory of being a social scientist within the essentially ideological field of social work. I greatly admire her writing, and she was generous in her response to my original outline; more than that, she played a major part in the process of lining up a cast of potential authors.

Several other people helped me with the book's early development, possibly more than they realized at the time: among them, David Howe, Cathy Humphreys, Nigel Parton, Gill Schofield and June Thoburn all enabled me to clarify my ideas. Lucy Brims gave invaluable help to the author of the Introduction to Part I.

But, of course, a book like this owes everything to its authors, and I have been blessed with an amazingly positive and committed team of colleagues. I have shared their good humoured online company for the past two years, and they have tolerated my persistence with a level of forbearance that time and again took me by surprise. Together, we have shared the highs and lows of ordinary life – theirs and mine. I thank them.

Martin Davies

Introduction

Social workers have, for more than a century, been a significant and increasingly substantial occupational group in the UK and other parts of the world. From their beginnings within the framework of voluntary societies, they have moved steadily, as public employees, towards the hard centre of our democratic welfare economy. They grow accustomed to the fact that members of society who have no need of their services may view them and their profession with some ambivalence. Thirty years ago, in *The Essential Social Worker,* I argued that they play a crucial part in the maintenance of our complex community in a state of approximate equilibrium. This remains true.

The scale and the cost of social work have risen in line with our growing population; practitioners face ever more complex problems as family structures fracture, people live longer, substance misuse disturbs the surface of people's lives, and the state commits itself to reliance on community-based, rather than institutional-based, support systems.

Against this background, and reflecting the way in which, from time to time, policy wheels turn full circle, there has been a gradual shift away from the idea of 'generic' social work – the conventional wisdom in the second half of the twentieth century. Social workers still do their basic training together, but the scale of public and political concern about the primacy of child welfare has led to a clear policy division now between 'social work with children and families' and 'social work with adults'. This book, together with its companion volume, reflects that development.

The division between the two books is not clear-cut, because families and indeed communities as a whole are made up of children and adults, young and old, who freely interact with and depend on each other. In this volume, for example, the chapters on substance use cannot avoid the fact that the phenomenon has clear implications for the practice of child protection.

Authors were invited to tackle the question: 'How does policy/law/theory/research affect social work practice in each of the four chosen fields – the personalization agenda, mental health, substance use, and old age?' And, in parallel to that, different authors were asked to provide material outlining the reality of practice in those same fields.

It should be said at the outset that the two volumes together are not designed to be encyclopedic or comprehensive guides to the whole field of social work practice; there are a number of other books that fulfil that aim. The intention, rather, is to see what happens when you 'deconstruct' the five elements. What are the differences of emphasis between them? How do the four 'academic' spheres feed in to the practice chapters? Through a series of questions – one in each chapter – readers are invited to join in the task of 'Making connexions'. There are very few certainties in social work, but a thoughtful and reactive reading of this text will enable the reader to form a judgement on what weight should be placed upon a whole range of probabilities.

In this Introduction, I will briefly touch on some of the thoughts and ideas that have been prompted in me as a result of working with the 20 chapters. I will do so by briefly reflecting in turn on each of the five 'key elements'.

Policy

Social work's aims and functions cannot be unidirectional. In the past, arguments about care or control, change or maintenance, therapy or welfare have been debated as though each one precluded the other. But as the authors of the policy chapters identify, such is not the case. The management of risk and the pursuit of recovery and wellbeing are independent policy objectives, but both are part of the social worker's remit.

Social work itself has played only a small part in the identification of policy objectives in respect of work with adults. Clinical medicine, psychiatry, psychology and the criminal justice system all loom large in the discussions and debates that precede any policy changes that impinge on practice; and the case for attention to the social context, traditionally associated with the social worker's role, sometimes struggles to gain a hearing.

The most significant policy development of recent years has been the emergence of the personalization agenda, but Leece (in Chapter 1) argues that the origins of it lie in pressure, not from social work, but from the disabled people's movement, from feminist thinking and from the strength of the neoliberal dynamic across the political board. In their discussion of the significance of personalization as a policy development, Gilbert and Powell (Chapter 16) identify what they call three trajectories:

1 independent self-managing consumers with private means and resources
2 people in need of some support to enable them to continue to self-manage
3 people who are dependent and unable to commit to self-management.

Although they apply this classificatory scheme to 'older people', it is clearly applicable in all areas of social work with adults. The first trajectory doesn't impact on social work, but the second and third trajectories feed into the social worker's caseload, and the distinction between them helps to explain the nature of the apparently conflicting policy objectives that social workers are expected to pursue.

Law

Because social workers are operating in a predominantly public sector field of practice, many of their roles are prescribed by law: legislation and statutory guidelines are the formal means by which policies that originate in government are put into operation.

Medicine and legal authorities exert a powerful influence on much of what social workers do in the field of mental health, and they have to balance their awareness of political anxiety about risk with their professional commitment to patient autonomy and wellbeing. As Gould and Martin reflect, this goes to the heart of the care and control tension that characterizes the social work function (Chapter 7).

Moreover, the language of the law – as illustrated in the familiar verb 'to section' meaning 'to arrange for the compulsory admission to hospital' – is a socially powerful determinant of the mental health world and of the part that social workers play in it.

In the other areas of work with adults covered by this book, the influence of the law tends to be more indirect. Social workers need to understand the relevant statutes, and service users will expect them to be knowledgeable about the law, to work within it, and to be able to give guidance on how its benefits can be maximized and its restrictions be challenged.

Legislation is always evolving. Even as this book is being written, major changes in the law affecting the field of adult social care are anticipated; and the rapidly developing personalization agenda is likely to demand new statutes to accommodate concerns about the potential conflict between the principle of user autonomy and risk. Indeed, the ongoing need to balance ideas of 'safeguarding' with principles of human rights will continue to challenge the skill of legislators, although no more powerfully than it challenges the social worker on the ground.

Theory

For the most part, social work does not have the characteristics of a science. Thus, when we speak of theory in social work, we are not normally referring to testable propositions, and we are usually drawing on work done in one or other of the mainstream human disciplines – sociology, psychology, biomedicine.

This does not invalidate the importance of theory, but it does mean that different kinds of theories will have different roles to play as they are absorbed by the practising social worker. Parker (Chapter 18) draws a distinction between macro-, mezzo- and micro-levels of theory. In the context of old age, he suggests that, at the macro-level, 'social policies determine welfare provision in response to questions of ageing; mezzo-level theories help us to understand the particular situations older people find themselves in; and micro-level theories set out how social workers may practise with individuals, their families and communities'.

The intellectual background of each of the three levels can be approximately pinpointed. At the macro-level, social and political theory, with relevant inputs from economics and demography, play a large part. The mezzo-level tends to be informed by empirical sociology and anthropology. The micro-level draws principally on various branches of psychology, although it is a strange fact that social psychology, which has a track record of empirically proven effectiveness at micro-levels in fields such as marketing, advertising and other areas of persuasion, is conspicuous by its near-absence from contemporary social work theory in the UK.

A frequently recurring theme within the framework of social work theory concerns the unease said to be felt by social workers at any mention of the medical model – 'something of a "boo" word in social work and the social sciences', say Forrester and Hutchinson in Chapter 13. (The contrasting 'hurrah' word is *psychosocial*.) It is, of course, true that the historical and continuing role of social work is to build bridges between the service user and the environment, but it is equally true that it is not possible to work effectively in the fields of mental health, substance misuse or old age without some awareness of the biomedical dimensions affecting those whom the social worker is serving.

A powerful dimension in what we do is political: social work is the product of political debate, and it is therefore not surprising that social workers – like doctors, nurses, police officers and teachers – feel the need to fight their professional corner. Whether that contributes to a smooth running welfare and healthcare system is, of course, open to debate. But it reflects the fact that social work's perspective, while not atheoretical, owes as much – perhaps more – to ideology and an asserted value base as it does to empirically based theory.

Research

Research can take many forms, but the politicians and policy-makers who commission it tend to want it to tell them whether identified forms of social work intervention achieve the results that are desired. They look at the benefits that have accrued in healthcare from pharmaceutical or orthopaedic research, and feel that it is reasonable to look for similar achievements in the field of social welfare.

As Evans and Huxley argue in Chapter 9, there *are* areas of social work research in the field of mental health where gains have indeed been made. But, in three respects, it has to be acknowledged that research in social work presents problems:

1 The level of financial investment in it has been exceedingly modest, and there is little scope for private sector commercial interest, which is what has largely driven pharmaceutical developments.
2 The behavioural and social sciences have always presented particular problems of methodology, especially with regard to experimental designs – this fact affects not only social work and education, but other behavioural fields like economics and criminal justice.
3 In much of social work, there is a massive conceptual problem because of a lack of clarity in or agreement about the system's objectives. These factors generally make it difficult for practitioners to do more than regard research as providing useful background information or stimulating thought.

The authors in this book provide examples of many different kinds of research. For example:

■ The early development of the personalization agenda has been closely monitored in a form of operational research: seeking verbal feedback from service users, carers and social work staff. But, says MacIntyre in Chapter 4, 'it shows little evidence of cost savings', and if that is a major policy objective, such a research-based conclusion could have a significant impact on its future, notwithstanding the broadly positive views of those involved.

■ Research can help to improve the quality of social work assessments. Referring in Chapter 19 to a rare example of a randomized controlled trial in an experimental study, Clarkson reveals that social workers who took advantage of access to health information from specialist clinicians were more likely to detect important difficulties affecting the old people under their care. But that finding has to be viewed against a backdrop of tribal resistance in social work to anything or anyone associated with clinical perspectives.

■ Describing a project in the field of substance misuse that employed mixed research methods to monitor the use of intensive social work contact and a prescribed method of intervention, Forrester et al. (Chapter 14) claim that the outcomes were positive and led to cost savings.

Research has been active within social work for more than 60 years. Although, in the UK, some of the work is initiated and carried out by academic social scientists, there has been a growing tendency for qualified social workers to play an active part. But there remain two problems before research can begin to have a fruitful impact on practice:

1 Within the social work research community, there needs to be recognition that the scientific tradition is based on the idea of the cumulative and incremental expansion of knowledge; too often, naive researchers imagine that each single, self-contained project will make a major impact on theory or practice.

2 There is a need for social work education to teach research-based practice skills – as and when they become available and are confirmed as having the desired effect in respect of clearly defined objectives.

Practice

Policy, law, theory, research – they all contribute to our understanding of the nature of the work done by the social worker in practice. But, conversely, without some exploration of the reality of practice, policy, law, theory and research are of no more intellectual significance than the solving of a crossword puzzle.

So what is the nature of social work practice in the twenty-first century? So far as work with adults is concerned, the evidence is quite clear:

■ Social workers are employed very largely in the public sector. They put government-defined policy into practice, adapting their approach as policy evolves. Their objectives are the objectives of their employer: they can be varied and complex, but often they revolve around the concepts of risk, resilience and/or recovery, although the language employed may vary in different contexts.

■ They specialize in trying to see the whole picture – working 'holistically', if you like. They acknowledge the power of intergenerational factors; they recognize the impact of the social and physical environment on service users' lives; and, when necessary, they work with professionals from other disciplines in order to achieve their specified objectives.

■ They operate within a framework of legislation and system procedures, interpreting them according to their professional value base.

■ They function within a framework of available resources.

In our accounts of social work, there are elements of assessment, welfare guidance, counselling, gatekeeping, policing and therapeutic intervention. But the primary focus is on the attempt to enable service users to gain or regain control over their own fortunes. As Leah says in Chapter 10: 'It is part of a social worker's role and responsibility to enable service users to believe in a better future and to assist them to identify and make the changes they want to happen.'

Martin Davies

Part I
Social Work and the Personalization Agenda

Personalization has been a hot topic in social care in recent years. It has prompted mixed emotions in social workers, but offers rewards to service users and practitioners when it is correctly implemented. In terms of policy, the personalization agenda may be said to have united service users and politicians. The goal of delivering services in partnership with service users and empowering vulnerable adults to determine their own care provision has become a focal point for reformers.

The Department of Health publication, *A Vision for Adult Social Care* (2010), identified personalization as a core principle, indicating that 'individuals not institutions' should control care and that personal budgets, preferably delivered through direct payments, should form the primary method of delivering services to vulnerable adults. Part I of this book aims to guide readers through what may at first appear to be a maze of disparate views, legislation, theory, perspective and practice and help them to gain an understanding of personalization in practice.

In Chapter 1, Janet Leece, using a historical perspective, reviews the trend towards allowing individuals to have an increased say in how their care is delivered. Charting how state provision for social care has changed over time, she suggests that more recent influences such as feminism, the disability rights movement and, in politics, liberal and market agendas have shaped the development of policy.

In Chapter 2, Suzy Braye and Alison Brammer provide an overview of the law surrounding personalization, even though, as they say, 'as yet, there is no statute law on personalization'. They introduce us to the foundations and components of the legal framework that inform practitioners and affect service users, and they consider to what extent the many different pieces of legislation might be strengthened in the future. They are in no doubt that 'legal, policy and practice sea change lies ahead'.

Chapter 3 explores some of the theoretical perspectives that inform the personalization agenda. Susan Hunter and Mike Titterton examine the key influences that have shaped its development. Among these are the idea of 'normalization' and the social model of disability; but, in the end, they argue, building a theoretical structure for the personalization agenda will be likely to draw on person-centred planning, management of personal welfare, positive risk-taking and the concept of resilience.

In Chapter 4, Gillian MacIntyre summarizes the findings from three major research inquiries into personalization: the first evaluated the use of individual budgets in England, and the other two reviewed the early development of self-directed support programmes in Scotland. Of particular interest is the comparison drawn between how different parties – service users, carers, staff – viewed the initiative. MacIntyre goes on to summarize what the research reveals about the impact of personalization on different user groups and briefly explores the extent to which it has been shown to be cost-effective or not.

Chapter 5 offers case examples from practitioners, carers and service users in order to illustrate how personalization works in practice. We see how the flexibility brought by direct payments and self-directed support has allowed service users to become empowered to gain better support and receive bespoke care packages, often becoming employers of personal assistants. The experience of those practitioners who have embraced the personalization agenda appears to be positive, as imaginative care plans demonstrate how user-led services can massively improve on previous provisions. Concerns have been raised, however, because of the argument that personalization may not be suitable in all circumstances or that agency restrictions may not always allow best practice to prevail.

Throughout Part I, there is a sense that the movement towards a universal personalized service is gaining momentum. Some authors express concern about the extent to which the personalization agenda is motivated by the need to cut costs or to shift responsibility for risk management from the local authority to the service user. But the overriding message is that there are now remarkable opportunities for social workers and service users to work together to create care plans inspired by 'individuals not institutions'.

Michael Bamber

Reference

DH (2010) *A Vision for Adult Social Care: Capable Communities and Active Citizens.* London: DH.

undertook many domestic tasks, such as helping people to wash and dress in their own homes, which would later be considered legitimate work for local authority home care services.

Social researchers such as Charles Booth and Seebohm Rowntree completed surveys of poor areas, statistically showing the full extent of health and social deprivation in Britain. These studies demonstrated the lack of health and fitness of army recruits, high infant and child death rates, and disadvantages for children from poor families in terms of their weight, height and general health (Rowntree, 1901). It became apparent that the arguments for a lack of state involvement in family life were not acceptable in the new industrialized way of life.

The Second World War (1939–45) had an enormous impact on family life, with increasing numbers of women working in factories, on the land and in the armed forces, leaving fewer women at home to care for family members. In response to this, new powers were given to local authorities, under the Defence Regulations, to enable them for the first time to establish domestic support services (home helps) to elderly infirm people. The welfare state, which developed at this time, was the result of a great change in social policy. It brought the bulk of health, social care and welfare benefits into central government responsibility and control. This new structure, with its system of social security benefits, brought about an end to social workers in England and Wales making cash payments to people in need, as the National Assistance Act 1948 made direct payments by local authorities illegal. In Scotland, the situation differed slightly, in that the Social Work (Scotland) Act 1968 allowed social workers to make cash payments in exceptional circumstances, although this provision was rarely used.

The expansion of the British welfare regime continued up to the mid-1970s, fuelled by the international postwar economic boom. Demographic trends – a combination of a baby boom and growing numbers of older people – increased the demand for welfare services alongside growing prosperity and technological advances, and this encouraged greater expectations of care provision. Together with this, a critique of the support provided in institutions had been developing, following a study by Townsend (1962) that gave evidence of poor conditions in residential homes for older people. At about the same time, the view was gaining ground of the desirability of people living independently in the community, with support provided by a network of care, expected to be mainly female relatives.

The 1970s also brought political uncertainty, disillusionment and a heightening of social and political conflicts. The Keynesian view of the economic responsibilities of government and the way economic policy was managed came increasingly under attack, with fears that the welfare system could not be sustained in the form in which it had been developed. There were concerns about the spiralling cost of residential care for older people, despite the push to greater support in the community, the fear of unsustainable demographic and expenditure trends, higher and higher wage demands by trade unions, rising unemployment and escalating inflation. There were increasing claims made on the government in the form of state welfare and questions were raised about whether the state should actually assume the major responsibility for the provision of support (Means and Smith, 1998).

In 1974, the Labour Party was elected on the promise of a 'social contract', an agreement between government and the unions to 'preserve welfare services in return for restraining demands for wage increases' (Cochrane and Clarke, 1993, p. 46). In the two years following Labour's return to power, real wages fell, as the unions complied with the social contract and inflation soared. In an attempt to stem the nation's economic deterioration, the government was obliged to seek help in the form of a loan from the International Monetary Fund. The terms of this loan required a cut in public expenditure on welfare, causing widespread protest and provoking union action in what became known as 'the winter of discontent'. The social demo-cratic consensus of support for the welfare state began breaking down and a neoliberal critique of the welfare state started to emerge.

Neoliberalism and the market economy perspective

In neoliberal economics, public sector provision is seen as highly bureaucratic, unre-sponsive, inefficient and operating as a monopoly rather than being controlled by market forces. Private provision, on the other hand, is considered likely to free market forces to operate competitively, so encouraging new alternative sources of welfare to develop, which in turn would lead to more efficient services and greater consumer choice, what became known as the three Es – efficiency, economy and effectiveness. In this perspective, there is emphasis on individual behaviour, where individuals, when left to their own devices, are active, innovative, responsible, rational people who are the best judge of their own interests and seek to provide for themselves and their families (Clarke, 2004). Individuals are thus transformed from being passive subjects of welfare, provided by a benevolent state, into active consumers able to make their own choices and decisions.

With the election in 1979 of Margaret Thatcher as prime minister, policies based on ideas of neoliberalism came to dominate the 1980s and 90s. This philosophy became known as the 'New Right' and can be seen in various government publications of the time. A report by Sir Roy Griffiths, *Community Care: Agenda for Action* (1988), had a number of key objectives reflecting market ideology, and this went on to form the basis of the NHS and Community Care Act 1990, putting the ideas of the market discourse into practice in social care. The implementation of the Act required enormous changes in the social care market. Local authorities in England and Wales, while retaining the responsibility of assessing an individual's needs, were required to separate the function of service purchasing from that of service provision, and to spend the majority of their new funding for community care in the independent sector. The intention was to develop a mixed economy of social care or 'quasi-market', which involved the private, public, voluntary and the informal sector: 'internal trading systems within public sector organizations that are intended to mimic the behaviour of real markets by creating internal trading between different sections' (Cochrane et al., 2001, p. 87).

ment of the market economy perspective, with its focus on market ...ndividual as a rational decision-maker, signalled a shift away from ...r by the state and made the reintroduction of cash payments for social .pport more likely. Although it was still illegal for local authorities to make direct payments at this stage, the philosophy of the New Right placed the possibility of cash payments in social welfare squarely back on the agenda.

Informal care and the feminist perspective of care

As well as the distinction made in welfare policy between the 'deserving and unde-serving poor', much of the thinking behind social welfare in Britain has been heavily associated with ideas of the family, and particularly women's role in providing infor-mal (unpaid) support for their relatives. The debate about the impact of the 'burden' of informal care on women was influenced enormously by feminist research in the 1980s, which was critical of the role expected of female carers, especially the increased responsibilities required by the community care reforms of the 1990s. Feminist scholars argued that the state was effectively transferring its responsibilities for care onto the shoulders of women: care by the community rather than care in the commu-nity (Dalley, 1988). Feminist research emphasized the negative impact on women of undertaking care for their family, in terms of their ability to participate equally in the labour force. This can cause financial disadvantages for women throughout their lives, and lead to or increase women's financial dependence on men (Arber and Ginn, 1991). In response to this, the International Wages for Housework campaign argued that women should receive state payment for the unpaid domestic tasks they perform for their family.

The proliferation of research into caring was mirrored in the political arena by the emergence of organizations for informal carers, which began to agitate for better state support for people providing informal care. Government reaction to this was the introduction of the invalid care allowance in 1975, a social security benefit paid to single women who were providing significant levels of support. It was assumed by the government that married or cohabiting women would be at home and available to provide care without payment. After a long struggle by the Association of Carers, in 1986 this benefit was additionally made available to married women and men. This highlights an important change in welfare policy, as the invalid care allowance was a cash payment paid by the state to individuals for the care they provided.

The carers' lobby went on to suggest that they were being exploited as family members, and argued for improved support through central taxation, social security and health and welfare systems, and pressed for public recognition of the unpaid work performed by carers. A number of pieces of legislation followed, highlighting the importance of informal care and emphasizing the priority of family care over that provided by paid workers, while making attempts to help informal carers to continue looking after their relatives. The pressure from carers' organizations and the work of feminist academics did much to raise awareness of informal carers' experiences and bring about greater emphasis on the roles and rights of carers. It revealed the many disadvantages faced by women who provide care and raised the notion of payment for the unpaid care these women provide. It was another step along the road towards the personalization of social welfare.

Independence and control: disabled people's perspective

Disabled academics and activists have strongly challenged the ideas of the feminist analysis of care. They argue that its focus on the oppression of able-bodied women coping with the 'burden of care' for their families fails to acknowledge the contributions of disabled adults in providing support and of men caring for their partners. The disabled people's movement suggests that feminist research ignores the rights of disabled adults to go to work and be economically independent, to live independently within the community and to have children and care for them in the way that able-bodied people may do (Morris, 1989).

Organizations set up and run by disabled people in Britain, inspired by the independent living movement in the USA, began to campaign in the 1980s for the right to live independently at home rather than in residential care. There was a focus on notions of independence, with disabled activists rejecting the commonly held view in society that achieving independence requires the ability to be self-reliant, and redefining it as having control over the decision-making processes in a person's life (Barnes, 1991). The disabled people's movement tried to create a human rights discourse based on citizenship and rejecting the segregation and exclusion of disabled people from society. They argued strongly for control over the way in which support is provided and demanded the right to receive the cash to purchase it themselves.

In 1986, following sustained pressure from disabled activists, the government launched a means-tested benefit, the independent living fund (ILF), to be paid via social security. This was the first large-scale provision of substantial cash payments in recent times, paid directly to disabled adults to meet their support needs, and can be seen as the forerunner of direct payments. The government had been concerned that loss of the domestic assistance payment (paid through supplementary benefit), which had been removed by the Social Security Act 1986, would result in some disabled adults having to go into residential care (Kestenbaum, 1993). The ILF scheme was more popular than had been anticipated and, in 1993, worried about the financial implications, the government changed the system to exclude new claimants over the age of 65. As a result, ILF payments became a top-up for younger people receiving large support packages from local authorities.

In 1989, the British Council of Disabled People and the Spinal Injuries Association, two organizations representing disabled people in the UK, began to campaign for the legislation to be changed to enable local authorities to make direct payments for the purchase of support. As part of this campaign, they commissioned research to produce evidence about the cost implications of cash payments. This research

it the costs and benefits of direct payments for personal assistance, and
ed them with traditionally provided services. The study concluded that direct
nts could offer a higher degree of choice, reliability, control and user satisfaction than service provision, and could be 30–40% cheaper than equivalent
service-based support (Zarb and Nadash, 1994).

Zarb and Nadash's research findings were to prove crucial in the campaign for
direct payments. While the arguments for cash payments by disabled activists were
born from a desire for greater control and independence, the research evidence of
their cost-effectiveness was especially persuasive. In 1996, the Community Care
(Direct Payments) Act was passed by Parliament, giving local authorities in
England, Wales and Scotland the power (but not the duty) to make cash payments
to disabled people aged under 65. The legislation was amended in 2000 to include
older people and in 2001 to encompass parents of a disabled child, disabled young
people and carers.

The direct payment legislation was in place and its implementation just starting
when, in 1997, a Labour government was elected into office, bringing with it a new
philosophy of social welfare.

New Labour and personalization

The Labour government came to power in 1997 having declared in its election manifesto: 'We will be the party of welfare reform' (Labour Party, 1997, p. 5). This brought
a new perspective to social policy, and one with clear continuities with Thatcher's
conservatism. Combining ideas from Old Labour and the New Right, it became
known as the Third Way. This new philosophy built on the 1980s' legacy of neoliberalism, fusing the individualistic focus on independence with notions of
responsibility, a strong work ethic and conditionality of welfare benefits (Jordan,
2005). It sanctioned values of autonomy and choice, rather than collectivism, as a
basis for public services, with local authorities expected to adopt a style based on
commercial enterprise.

The managerial agenda of a business-oriented social care system was already well
underway following the community care reforms, and New Labour embraced the
public sector management agenda. Many of the welfare reforms made by preceding
Conservative governments were left in place, and the early years of the new government saw a number of policy proposals that were underpinned by a discourse of
modernization. Central themes of the modernizing agenda for social care were:

- the promotion of independence linked to a requirement for services to be more
responsive to the needs of the people using them
- the reduction of dependency on service provision through rehabilitation and
prevention.

We can see from this that New Labour's vision of a welfare state based on rights,
duties and responsibilities, with consumers as creative negotiators rather than

passive recipients of services, is compatible with the focus of the disabled activists on independence, choice and control over service provision via the right to receive direct payments.

The new government thus welcomed the concept of 'cash for care', actively encouraging local authorities to increase the number of people using direct payments. Nine million pounds were pledged over three years to promote the take-up of cash payments, and in 2003 the government made them a mandatory responsibility for local authorities in England and Wales. To further persuade local authorities to extend their schemes, direct payments were made an indicator of their performance. In 2005, the government published its strategy for disabled people, a document that went a stage further by introducing a new structure, whereby several funding streams would be brought together in the form of 'individualized budgets' (Prime Minister's Strategy Office, 2005).

Determined to bring about a radical and substantial shift in the way services are delivered, the White Paper *Our Health, Our Care, Our Say: A New Direction for Community Services* was published (DH, 2006). This presented proposals for the whole health and social care system, and reiterated the expansion of cash payments, including the introduction of individualized budgets. The term 'personalization' first appeared the following year in the concordat *Putting People First: A Shared Vision and Commitment to the Transformation of Adult Social Care* (HM Government, 2007). This agreement between central and local government and the social care sector set the direction for the next 10 years, and made it clear that a personalized system that put people at the heart of things was to be the future for adult social care.

Personalization into practice

Systems of cash payments for disabled and older people exist throughout Europe, Australia, Canada and the USA. It is, however, difficult to make comparisons between countries, as schemes tend to vary in the way they are organized and funded. For example, in some countries, cash payments are financed in the same way as in the UK from central taxation, while in others, such as in Holland and Germany, funding comes from long-term care insurance. There are also differences in the way schemes operate; for example, in Austria, the 'Pflegegeld' (cash allowance) system can be used to pay for permanent residential provision, but this would not be defined as a direct payment in the UK.

Table 1.1 reveals that take-up was slow in the early stages of the implementation of direct payments. There are a number of possible explanations for this. For example, research suggests that social workers often lacked the relevant information or training about cash payments, and consequently did not feel confident about offering them to service users. There are also regional variations in the number of people using cash payments: in the main, the north of England has reported a lower take-up than the south, which has been attributed to local authorities' ideological positions, with

Labour-controlled local authorities being less likely to develop direct payments than Conservative-controlled authorities (Riddell et al., 2005).

Table 1.1 Use of direct payments in England

Date of calculation	Number of people using direct payments in England	Notes
Autumn 1998	1,404	
Summer 2000	3,612	Includes Wales
September 2001	5,423	
September 2002	7,882	
September 2003	12,585	
September 2004	21,912	
September 2005	24,744	
2007–2008	67,000	
2008–2009	86,000	
March 2009	92,878	Personal budgets including direct payments
May 2010	140,000	Personal budgets including direct payments

Sources: Auld, 1999; Jones, 2000; CSCI, 2004, 2005; Community Care Statistics 2008–09; ADASS, 2009, 2010

Table 1.1 also shows the impact of government pressure on local authorities to extend and develop their schemes. We can see that between September 2003 and September 2005, when direct payments became a mandatory responsibility and an indicator of performance, the numbers of people using them almost doubled. Since then, usage has continued to grow steadily, with 140,000 people receiving a personal budget or direct payment in 2010, although regional disparities continue to occur. In 2009, the Department of Health published a set of milestones to chart local authorities' progress towards achieving a personalized system. One of these targets required at least 30% of eligible service users or carers to be receiving a personal budget by April 2011. In a survey to look at their progress, eight out of nine local authorities in the East Midlands said they were very confident that they could reach this target, while only four of the fifteen authorities in the southwest were able to say the same (ADASS, 2010). Jeff Jerome, the national director for social care transformation, expressed his concern, saying that while local authority progress towards personalization is steady, there is still 'a worrying group of stragglers regarding personal budgets' (ADASS, 2010, p. 3).

There have been disparities in take-up rates between groups of disabled people too. We can see in Table 1.2 that proportionally fewer people with learning disabilities or mental health needs access direct payments than people who have a physical disability. This probably reflects the conflict between risk-taking and safeguarding for social work professionals, who may hesitate to offer cash payments to people perceived as having difficulty in managing them (Mind, 2009). There have also been issues around the area of consent for people with cognitive impairments, as the direct payment legislation requires an individual to have the capacity to consent to receiving their care in this way. Yet there are a number of methods that can be employed to support people so that they can access personalized provision. For example, a 'suitable person' can receive a direct payment on behalf of someone who lacks metal capacity, or advocates, support brokers, family and friends can help people to articulate their requirements and manage their care. Older people have also been slow to opt for cash payments, and despite being the largest single group of people using community care services, they made up only half of the numbers using personal budgets in 2010 (ADASS, 2010). It has been suggested that older people may find the process of planning and managing their support burdensome.

Table 1.2 Categories and number of people using direct payments at 31 March 2006

Category of user	Number of people using direct payments at 31 March 2006
Older people (65+)	9,733
People with a learning disability (18–64)	4,750
People with a physical disability (18–64)	13,690
People with a sensory disability (18–64)	963
People with mental health issues (18–64)	1,477

Source: CSCI, 2006

In terms of the future of personalized support in social welfare, it is hard to predict what will happen. Given government commitment, it is probable that in the short term, numbers using direct payments/personal budgets will continue to grow, but in the longer term, this commitment is less assured. In its quest to find ways to contain expenditure on care, government interest in personalization appears to have been fuelled by a belief that it is cheaper than traditional service delivery. However, there is no robust evidence yet to show whether the large-scale implementation of personal budgets will be more or less cost-effective than traditional service provision. Furthermore, recent evidence suggests that while personal and individual budgets can improve outcomes for users, they are unlikely to result in significant savings for local authorities (Glendinning et al., 2008; Audit Commission, 2010). If personalized systems fail to make the anticipated savings, it seems likely that government allegiance will falter.

To increase this uncertainty, the Conservative/Liberal Democrat coalition government, formed in May 2010, has pledged continued support for personal budgets while instigating wide-ranging spending cuts in public services in an attempt to reduce the UK budget deficit. In the Comprehensive Spending Review, announced in October 2010, the chancellor made cuts of over 28% to local authority budgets for the period 2011–15, and this may place local authority spending on personal budgets in jeopardy.

As well as doubts about future funding for personalization, and the cost of an expanded system, concern has been expressed about whether there will be an adequate supply of personal assistants available to be employed by personal budget holders. From 2009 to 2010, it has been estimated that the personal assistant work-force increased by 35% to account for one-fifth of all jobs in social care (Fenton, 2011); it remains to be seen whether this expansion is sustainable. Most of the people who have a personal budget receive it in the form of a direct payment, with the majority spending the money on employing a personal assistant to meet their needs (ADASS, 2010). Direct payment users can employ almost anyone they choose as their personal assistant, although the legislation currently prevents them from employing their spouse, partner or a close relative living in the same house, unless there are exceptional circumstances. Research has shown that many users do employ friends and relatives to provide their support, but significant numbers experience problems in recruiting personal assistants, and one of the reasons for this appears to be the low wages they are able to offer (Leece, 2010). The reduction in local author-ity funding from central government may exacerbate this, as it influences the rate that can be given to direct payment users, and this in turn influences how much users can pay their personal assistants. On the other hand, unemployment has been rising since 2007, and in May 2010 stood at 8%, with 2.51 million unemployed people (www.statistics.gov.uk), which may help direct payment users to compete more effectively in the job market for personal assistants.

Conclusion

An exploration of the history and policy of social welfare in Britain reveals that cash payments are part of that history and are at the core of the personalization agenda. Their prevalence and usage have fluctuated depending on circumstances in society, such as demographic movements, changing female working patterns and prevailing ideology. Cash payments have been a feature of social welfare policy and are part of an evolving process. The impetus for their recent reintroduction, via the Community Care (Direct Payments) Act 1996, has several strands, which have come together to bring personalization to the forefront of adult social care:

■ the long campaign by the disabled people's movement focusing on social justice and rights in their demand for independent living and control of their social support
■ the ideas of the market economy perspective and neoliberalism that have influ-enced government thinking and led to a reduction of state involvement in social welfare, while increasing consumer power and choice
■ the need for government to find a cost-effective method of providing social care for the increasing numbers of older people in the population
■ feminist research that highlighted the disadvantages and costs for informal carers of supporting their relatives.

We are in the midst of what can arguably be described as the most radical transformation of social welfare since the introduction of the welfare state in the 1940s. The number of people using personalized support was predicted to rise to 376,000 by March 2011 (ADASS,

> **Making connexions**
>
> The personalization agenda is described as 'the most radical transformation of social welfare since ... the 1940s'.
>
> What are its implications for social work practice?

2010), and while this forecast may turn out to have been optimistic, an upward trend in the short term does seem likely.

As for the future, only time will tell whether government support for personalization will continue, with personal budgets becoming a mainstream option, or whether they are destined to be a fleeting episode in social welfare.

Further reading

■ Gardner, A. (2011) *Personalization in Social Work*. Exeter: Learning Matters.

Up-to-date consideration of the practical implications of the personalization agenda.

■ Glasby, J. and Littlechild, R. (2009) *Direct Payments and Personal Budgets: Putting Personalization into Practice* (2nd edn). Bristol: Policy Press.

Details the history of personalization, its impact on social work and the practical considerations involved.

■ Leece, J. and Bornat, J. (eds) (2006) *Developments in Direct Payments*. Bristol: Policy Press.

Edited collection of research studies that charts the changes, critically evaluating progress, take-up, inclusion and access to direct payments by different user groups.

References

ADASS (Association of Directors of Adult Social Services) (2009) *Putting People First: Measuring Progress.* London: ADASS/LGA.

ADASS (2010) 'Progress in the delivery of personal budgets 2010', www.adass.org.uk/index.php?option=com_content&view=article&id=328, accessed 20 September 2010.

Arber, S. and Ginn, J. (1991) *Gender and Later Life: A Sociological Analysis of Resources and Constraints.* London: Sage.

Audit Commission (2010) *Financial Management of Personal Budgets: Challenges and Opportunities for Councils*, http://www.audit-commission.gov.uk/nationalstudies/localgov/personalbudgets/Pages/default.aspx, accessed 16 November 2010.

Auld, E. (1999) *Community Care (Direct Payments) Act 1996: Analysis of Responses to Local Authority Questionnaire on Implementation, England.* London: DH.

Barnes, C. (1991) *Disabled People in Britain: A Case for Anti-discrimination Legislation for Disabled People*. London: Hurst/BCODP.

Borsay, A. (2005) *Disability and Social Policy in Britain Since 1750: A History of Exclusion*. Basingstoke: Palgrave Macmillan.

Clarke, J. (2004) *Changing Welfare, Changing States: New Directions in Social Policy*. London: Sage.

Cochrane, A. and Clarke, J. (eds) (1993) *Comparing Welfare States: Britain in International Context*. London: Sage.

Cochrane, A., Clarke, J. and Gewirtz, S. (2001) *Comparing Welfare States*. London: Sage.

CSCI (Commission for Social Care Inspection) (2004) *Direct Payments: What are the Barriers?* London: CSCI.

CSCI (2005) *Social Care Performance 2004–2005*. London: CSCI.

CSCI (2006) *Delivery and Improvement Statement*, August, London: CSCI.

Community Care Statistics (2008–09) *Social Services Activity Report*, http://www.ic.nhs.uk/statistics-and-data-collections/social-care/adult-social-care-information/community-care-statistics-2008-09-social-services-activity-report-england, accessed 2 October 2010.

Dalley, G. (1988) *Ideologies of Caring*. London: Macmillan.

DH (Department of Health) (2006) *Our Health, Our Care, Our Say: A New Direction for Community Services,* White Paper. London: DH.

DH (2010) *Prioritising Need in the Context of Putting People First: A Whole System Approach to Eligibility for Social Care – Guidance on Eligibility Criteria for Adult Social Care*, http://www.dh.gov.uk/en/Publicationsandstatistics/Publications/PublicationsPolicyAndGuidance/DH_113154, accessed 2 October 2010.

Fenton, W. (2011) *The Size and Structure of the Adult Social Care Workforce in England*, http://www.skillsforcare.org.uk/research/research_reports/size_and_structure_2011.aspx, accessed 12 September 2011.

Glendinning, C., Challis, D., Fernandez, J.-L. et al. (2008) *Evaluation of the Individual Budget Pilot Programme: Summary Report*. York: Social Policy Research Unit.

Griffiths, R. (1988) *Community Care: Agenda for Action*. London: HMSO.

HM Government (2007) *Putting People First: A Shared Vision and Commitment to the Transformation of Adult Social Care*, http://www.thurrock.gov.uk/socialcare/publications/pdf/dh_people_first.pdf.

Jones, R. (2000) *Getting Going on Direct Payments*. Trowbridge: Wiltshire Social Services, on behalf of the Association of Directors of Social Services.

Jordan, B. (2005) 'New Labour: choice and values', *Critical Social Policy,* **25**(4): 427–46.

Kestenbaum, A. (1993) *Making Community Care a Reality: The Independent Living Fund 1988–1993*. London: RADAR.

Labour Party (1997) *New Labour Because Britain Deserves Better,* manifesto. London: Labour Party.

Leece, J. (2010) 'Paying the piper and calling the tune: power and the direct payment relationship', *British Journal of Social Work*, **40**(1): 188–206.

Leece, J. and Leece, D. (2010) 'Personalization: perceptions of the role of social work in a world of brokers and budgets', *British Journal of Social Work*, doi: 10.1093/bjsw/bcq087.

Means, R. and Smith, R. (1998) *From Poor Law to Community Care: The Development of Welfare Services for Elderly People 1939–1971*. London: Policy Press.

Mind (2009) *Personalization in Mental Health: A Review of the Evidence*, http://www.bristol. ac.uk/norahfry/research/current-projects/evidence.pdf, accessed 24/9/2010.

Morris, J. (ed.) (1989) *Able Lives: Women's Experience of Paralysis*. London: Women's Press.

Prime Minister's Strategy Office (2005) *Improving the Life Chances of Disabled People*. London: Cabinet Office.

Riddell, S., Pearson, C., Jolly, D. et al. (2005) 'The development of direct payments in the UK: implications for social justice', *Social Policy and Society*, **4**(1): 75–85.

Rowntree, B. (1901) *Poverty: A Study of Town Life*. London: Macmillan.

Townsend, P. (1962) *The Last Refuge: A Survey of Residential Homes for the Elderly in England and Wales*. London: Routledge & Kegan Paul.

Zarb, G. and Nadash, P. (1994) *Cashing in on Independence: Comparing the Costs and Benefits of Cash and Services*. London: Policy Studies Institute.

2
Law on personalization

SUZY BRAYE AND ALISON BRAMMER

As yet, there is no statute law on personalization. It has emerged within a context of policy development relating to older people, disabled people and those with health or mental health-related needs. While it can be seen as a response to the pressure to find a way of delivering adult social care that is value driven, accountable and recognizes dignity, it is arguable that individualization, responsibilization and the privatization of risk also are discernible drivers (Ferguson, 2007). Clements (2011, p. 47) notes that 'in contrast to the many statutory duties and the fanfare of regulations that underpin community care law, personalization is based on no law whatsoever'. Nevertheless, legal rules from a range of sources, including statute, guidance and case law, are highly relevant to personalized practice. Sometimes, they provide mandates (duties and powers, principles and procedures) on aspects of practice that help achieve the goals of personalization. Sometimes, they provide guidance on the balance to be struck when dilemmas arise. Occasionally, they place constraints on what can be done to personalize services. Equally, there are core legal principles and concepts that underpin the whole notion of personalization and are influential in shaping our approach to the wellbeing of those who require support to achieve their goals and ambitions.

This chapter considers how legal rules shape and guide social work practice in the context of personalized services. First, it explores how the law contributes the foundations that inform and, to some extent, could be argued to provide a rationale for personalization; these are concepts such as human rights, adult autonomy and a duty of care. It then considers the core components of personalization as manifested in government policy – first, choice and control, and second, personal dignity and individual safety – and demonstrates how, in relation to each of these, legal rules support or otherwise drive approaches to practice that can achieve personalization.

Finally, the chapter anticipates changes that are the subject of consultation and recommendation by the Law Commission (2010, 2011a, 2011b) in its consideration of the need for reform of adult social care law, and looks forward to further development of the legal framework to support personalization practice.

Overarching frameworks for personalization

The development of personalization within existing legal frameworks

Clements (2011, p. 47) argues that, 'like "community care", it is difficult to say with any precision what the government means by personalization, apart from at the rhetorical level'. There is confusion in the new terminology, with 'personalization', 'personal budgets' and 'self-directed support' being used interchangeably, yet none of these terms are defined in law. It is perhaps best understood as a further policy development in the assessment and delivery of adult social care services. To understand fully the legal basis for personalization, it is necessary to review how the law relating to adult care services has developed.

The legal basis for adult social care can be traced back to the National Assistance Act 1948, and a subsequent raft of legislation providing a range of duties and powers by which local authorities can support adults who may be old, or have physical or learning disabilities or mental health problems, and are sometimes described as 'vulnerable'. Key legislation was introduced in 1990 in the form of the National Health Service and Community Care Act (NHSCCA). This placed on a statutory footing the emphasis on services in the community to promote individual independence. The Act signalled a change in the role of local authorities from direct provider to coordinator of services, but a duty to carry out an assessment of need is central to its operation (s. 47) and is accompanied by a statutory definition of what constitute community care services (by reference to earlier legislation). Thus the local authority retains control, albeit with greater choice for the service user by the inclusion of voluntary and private sector service providers, and an emphasis on participation in assessment and decision-making.

Since 1990, further law and policy have cemented the commitment in favour of care in the community and away from institutional provision. Notable developments included three pieces of legislation recognizing the need to support unpaid carers – Carers (Recognition and Services) Act 1995, Carers and Disabled Children Act 2000 and Carers (Equal Opportunities) Act 2004, with the 2004 Community Care Assessment Directions providing a clear mandate for participation by both service users and carers in decision-making. The policy emphasis on rights, independence, choice and inclusion has gathered pace; such principles are central, for example, to the learning disability strategy enunciated in *Valuing People* (DH, 2001) and developed in *Valuing People Now* (DH, 2009a). Government policy in the form of the personalization agenda was formally set out in a cross-government concordat *Putting People First* (DH, 2007), followed a year later by a specific definition of personalization:

> What it means is that everyone who receives social care support, regardless of their level of need, in any setting, whether from statutory services, the third and community or private sector or by funding it themselves, will have choice and

Law

control over how that support is delivered. It will mean that people are able to live their own lives as they wish, confident that services are of high quality, are safe and promote their own individual requirements for independence, well-being and dignity. (DH, 2008a, p. 4)

The coalition government remains consistent to this in setting out its vision for adult social care (DH, 2010a, p. 8):

Individuals not institutions take control of their care. Personal budgets, preferably as direct payments, are provided to all eligible people. Information about care and support is available for all local people, regardless of whether or not they fund their own care.

While there is no 'Personalization Act' that gives statutory expression to this policy drive, a number of key legal principles provide highly relevant foundations.

Human Rights Act 1998

A core legal concept underpinning personalization is that of human rights. The Human Rights Act 1998 (HRA) and articles of the 1950 European Convention on Human Rights (ECHR) have a discernible impact on practice. Importantly, this is due to the status of local authorities as public bodies under section 6 of the HRA, who are thereby obliged to act in a way that is compatible with the terms of the ECHR. As a result, all actions of the local authority within adult social care, including the assessment and delivery of services, must be compliant with the human rights of the service user. The courts have addressed human rights arguments in a range of decisions, which vary in the extent to which individual choice and control are promoted. It is clear that the courts recognize that Article 8 (ECHR), the right to respect for private and family life, may be engaged in many aspects of adult social care law. The ambit of Article 8 is potentially wide; for example, in *A* v *East Sussex CC* [2003], the court noted that:

embraced in the 'physical and psychological integrity' protected by Article 8 is the right of the disabled to participate in the life of the community and to have what has been described as 'access to essential economic and social activities and to an appropriate range of recreational and cultural activities'. (para. 99)

A local authority was found to have breached Article 8 when it failed to provide the community care services identified in its assessment of need (*R (Bernard)* v *Enfield LBC* [2002]), although the circumstances were fairly extreme. Statements from the judiciary have also made it clear that the state has a positive obligation to take steps to promote Article 8 rights, which goes beyond responding to violations (Munby LJ, 2011).

The role of the Equality and Human Rights Commission (EHRC) includes overseeing the application and impact of the HRA 1998 as well as the Equality Act 2010, which addresses a range of types of discrimination. The EHRC has powers under section 16 of the Equality Act 2006 to make formal inquiries into particular areas of practice. In addition to its first triennial overview report (EHRC, 2010), in 2011 it published the findings of an inquiry, of direct relevance to personalization, into the effectiveness of the systems protecting and promoting the human rights of older people, specifically in relation to Articles 3 and 8 (ECHR), who receive home-based care and support. The report (EHRC, 2011) points to areas of real concern in the treatment of some older people and identifies a significant legal loophole, in that the independent home care providers and unregulated providers, such as personal assistants who provide the majority of care in individuals' own homes, do not have any direct duties under the HRA 1998.

Autonomy in decision-making, personal choice and control

A further core concept embedded within the legal infrastructure, and which informs understandings of the overarching legal frameworks for personalization, is the concept of adult autonomy in decision-making, and the related issue of how mental capacity mediates that principle in relation to the exercise of choice and control. Related to this is the question of the state's duty of care and how that is expressed in decisions on personal welfare and wellbeing, while observing the principles of individual choice and control associated with personalization.

Adult autonomy

The principle of personal autonomy, referring to the right to make one's own decisions on personal matters, free from interference by the state, is embedded in UK law. It is strengthened by the requirements of the ECHR, in particular Article 5 (right to liberty and security of the person) and Article 8 (right to respect for private and family life). Adult autonomy includes the right to make decisions that may seem risky or unwise by others; this is spelled out clearly in the principles set out in section 1 of the Mental Capacity Act 2005 (MCA). This underpinning principle of autonomy can be seen to be essentially supportive of choice and control within personalization policy.

Mental capacity is a key consideration in determining the extent to which autonomy of decision-making may be exercised. The MCA 2005 makes it clear that capacity is a function-specific concept, that is, it varies according to the complexity of the decision to be made. Importantly, the Act establishes a presumption of capacity, and the right of an individual with capacity to make even unwise and risky decisions. This could be seen as tantamount to strong support for choice and control.

Autonomy is not, however, absolute. Individual autonomy may be limited, and interference with individual rights lawful. Article 5 of the ECHR is a *limited* right and thus may be subject to interference in circumstances that have a clear legal basis, for example following criminal conviction. Article 8 of the ECHR is a *qualified* right and may be subject to interference in certain circumstances, such as for the protection of the rights and freedoms of others. In both cases, interference with the right must be proportionate. Furthermore, there may be statutory curtailment of autonomy, where intervention is required in order to protect either the individual or others in their immediate environment, as, for example, when compulsory admission to psychiatric hospital is effected under the rules set out in the Mental Health Act 1983 (MHA; as amended in 2007). But where power *is* exercised through intervention in citizens' lives, administrative law expressing the principles of natural justice stands between the individual and the state. Its principles require decisions made by those with power to be made transparently, fairly, rationally, lawfully and impartially, in ways that demonstrate control of discretion, consistency, participation, efficiency, equity and equal treatment.

It is also important to note that there are circumstances in which the courts will engage in decision-making in respect of an adult who nonetheless has mental capacity. In so doing, courts are exercising their inherent, protective jurisdiction, which extends to vulnerable adults regardless of whether they have mental capacity. The definition of vulnerable adult is found in *No Secrets* policy guidance on adult safeguarding (DH, 2000, p. 8), which refers to a vulnerable adult as someone

> who is or may be in need of community care services by reason of mental or other disability, age or illness; and who is or may be unable to take care of him or herself, or unable to protect him or herself against significant harm or exploitation.

Thus mental capacity may be present. In *Re SA (Vulnerable adult with capacity: Marriage)* [2005], the court determined that

> the inherent jurisdiction can be exercised in relation to a vulnerable adult who, even if not incapacitated by mental disorder or mental illness, is, or is reasonably believed to be, either (i) under constraint or (ii) subject to coercion or undue influence or (iii) for some other reason deprived of the capacity to make the relevant decision, or disabled from making a free choice, or incapacitated or disabled from giving or expressing a real and genuine consent. (para. 77)

This has been applied on an interim basis in an adult safeguarding case, *A Local Authority* v *DL, RL and ML* [2010], in which the court responded to a local authority's application for a non-molestation order to prevent aggressive and violent behaviour towards an older couple by their adult son who lived with them, where the couple had taken no steps to protect themselves. While awaiting a full hearing, the court made an order requiring the son not to behave unlawfully. The court also concluded that in addition to its inherent jurisdiction, it had alternative authority under section 222 of the Local Government Act 1972 to make an injunction that would prevent the son from continuing to impede the local authority in fulfilling its statutory function of providing community care services.

A more circumspect view about inherent jurisdiction, however, was expressed in *LBL* v *RYJ and BJ* [2010], where, in relation to a young woman judged by the Court of Protection to have capacity to decide where she wished to live, the local authority

Law

requested the exercise of inherent jurisdiction to overrule her mother's views on the matter. Here the judge considered that inherent jurisdiction in relation to an adult with capacity was restricted to circumstances in which they were prevented from making decisions by external pressure or constraint that impeded the exercise of free will. These were not the circumstances of this case.

Thus the extent of court powers in determining matters that relate to adults with capacity is not, as yet, fully determined, and is clearly an area in which there will be further development. In the meantime, it is important to recognize that there are circumstances, notwithstanding the principle of adult autonomy, in which the courts will see fit to intervene in decision-making.

There are further legal rules relating to people who do not have mental capacity, which are explored below, with an evaluation of the extent to which they can be seen to support personalization principles.

Duty of care

The common law 'duty of care' owed by the state towards its citizens is sometimes experienced as, or assumed to be, in conflict with the principle of personal autonomy, and its expression through choice and control. Established in *Donoghue* v *Stevenson* [1932], this duty is owed to anyone who may be affected by an action taken where injury might be foreseen, and particularly high standards are expected of people with professional expertise. The duty of care encompasses the requirements both to protect from harm (*Z* v *UK* [2000]; *Keenan* v *UK* [2001]) and to take positive action to promote ECHR rights. A duty of care is an essential prerequisite in claims of negligence, which require the claimant to demonstrate that the duty existed and was breached and that damage ensued. Court decisions on whether a duty of care is owed by public authorities to those in whose lives they intervene (or choose not to intervene) have increasingly established that it *is* owed, and have eroded the earlier assumed immunity enjoyed by local authorities in the public interest of having freedom to exercise their statutory duties without interference (Preston-Shoot et al., 2001).

The duty of care exists regardless of whether there is also any statutory duty or power in relation to any particular matter. This is often most tellingly exemplified in adult safeguarding, where there is no statutory duty to investigate actual or suspected significant harm, yet a duty of care to vulnerable adults may be argued to exist, and underpins the interagency arrangements for investigation and intervention. Research into professionals' views on and responses to self-neglect, for example (Braye et al., 2011a), indicates that a duty of care is seen as justifying information-sharing and intervention, particularly in circumstances where a refusal of services by people with capacity is associated with severe and life-threatening self-neglect. The courts have endorsed the local authority's role in at least investigating the circumstances in which an adult who might be deemed vulnerable appears to be choosing a self-harmful path, while stopping short of legitimizing intervention to prevent a mentally competent adult from carrying through such actions. The case of *Re Z (Local Authority: Duty)* [2004] concerned an injunction sought to prevent the husband of a woman with an incurable degenerative brain disease, who wished to travel to Switzerland to commit assisted suicide, from committing a criminal offence by removing his wife from England. The court determined that there was no basis in law for preventing a mentally competent person from taking their own life. However, the local authority retained a duty to investigate the position of a vulnerable adult to identify their true intention, to consider whether they were legally competent to make the decision, whether they were subject to any undue influence and to identify any potential criminal offence.

The developing centrality of a duty of care as a driver for intervention, aside from any considerations of capacity and consent, is traced by Brammer's (2010) commentary on relevant cases, from which she concludes that liability in negligence may be more readily established when operational decisions have departed from the broad policy environment in which decision-making takes place. In the context of personalization, it is appropriate to see the duty of care as a continuing obligation that extends beyond immediate assessment. Even where an individual purchases their own support services with direct payments, the duty would extend to a requirement for transparent, proportionate monitoring and review of the individual's support plan.

Legal underpinnings for core components of personalization: choice and control

Recognizing that there is an absence of statutory backing for personalization, this section sets out existing legal rules that can be seen as supportive of it. They perhaps provide key 'building blocks' for choice and control that, while not amounting to a right to decide, do support aspects of the decision-making process. Considered here will be legal rules on access to information, participation in assessment and care planning, advocacy and accountability, together with mechanisms for self-directed support such as direct payments and individual or personal budgets, lasting powers of attorney and advance decisions. Crucially, however, the legal constraints on personalization will also be explored.

Access to information about services

Access to information about social care provision is one of the core building blocks of personalization, and the legal rules are supportive here. Local authorities have a duty to publicize information about the services they offer; this is required by the Chronically Sick and Disabled Persons Act 1970 (s. 1(2)(a), as amended by s. 9, Disabled Persons (Services, Consultation and Representation) Act 1986), and by the NHS and Community Care Act 1990, its associated policy and practice guidance (DH, 1990, 1991a) and subsequent requirements on the single assessment process for older people (DH, 2002). There are requirements for information to be accessible and easily available, giving clear guidance on services, eligibility, costs and timescales. The whole purpose is to help people make informed choices (DH, 1991b); information should 'enable users and carers to exercise genuine choice and participation in the assessment of their care needs' (DH, 1990, p. 26). Equally, the local authority must provide information on the financial contribution they are likely to require the service user to make (Community Care Assessment Directions 2004).

Legal rules also exist on information for carers. Section 1 of the Carers (Equal Opportunities) Act 2004 confers a duty to inform carers of their right to an assessment under the Carers (Recognition and Services) Act 1995. The HRA 1998 strengthens rights to information via Article 10 (ECHR), the right to freedom of expression, which includes the right to receive and impart information (*Open Door Counselling and Dublin Well Woman* v *Ireland* [1992]). A further effect is that information should be published in a format accessible to its likely readership, for example to reflect different languages and the impact of disability.

In its proposal for law reform, the Law Commission (2011b) envisages a general statutory duty for local authorities to provide information, advice and assistance about adult social care as part of its universal remit, this being seen as particularly important in a context where high eligibility thresholds may exclude larger numbers of people from more targeted service provision.

Participation in assessment and self-assessment

The principle of participation by individuals in decision-making about their use of adult social care was embedded within the policy and practice guidance that underpinned implementation of the NHSCCA 1990: 'The individual service user and … any carers should be involved throughout the assessment and care management process. They should feel that the process is aimed at meeting their wishes' (DH, 1990, p. 25). There was recognition of the power imbalance between professionals and service users, but it 'can be corrected by sharing information more openly and by encouraging users and carers … to take a full part in decision-making' (DH, 1991c, p. 14). The theme was similarly central to the later Community Care Assessment Directions 2004, which clearly specify the requirement for consultation with the individual being assessed and with their carer(s), and for reasonable steps to be taken to reach agreement with the individual and, where appropriate, with their carer(s) on the services being considered.

The code of practice to the Mental Health Act 1983 (DH, 2008b) promotes the involvement of patients in formulating plans and using care and treatment services. Indeed, the Mental Health Act itself, as amended by the Mental Health Act 2007, now has statutory principles of participation embedded (s. 118(2B)). These include the requirement for decisions to be informed by respect for patients' past and present wishes and feelings, by their involvement in planning, developing and delivering care and treatment appropriate to them, and by the views of carers. Showing a similar trend for statutory principles, the MCA 2005 articulates the right to receive support to exercise capacity and the right to make one's own decisions, even where these might be eccentric or unwise.

The participation principle in relation to carers has been clearly articulated (DH, 2010b), signalling a change of status:

> Family members and carers, other than in very specific circumstances, have to be regarded as experts and care partners. (p. 5)

> To recognise carers as expert care partners is to value both their role in providing support and the wider knowledge and skills they possess as individuals. (p. 7)

Case law has reinforced this principle. In *G* v *E* [2010], a local authority removed a young man with learning disabilities from the home of his long-term carer without sanction by the Court of Protection. The carer was not involved in the decision to remove the young man and had no contact with him for several months. The court noted that Article 8 (para. 88) gives 'not only substantive protection against any inappropriate interference with their family life but also procedural safeguards including the involvement of the carers in the decision-making process'. The failure to involve the carer contributed to the court's finding that there had been a breach of the young man's Article 8 (ECHR) rights.

But the legal rules on participation in assessment cannot be described as conferring control of the assessment process, or even choice on how it is carried out. Under the NHSCCA 1990, the assessment is to 'be carried out in such a manner and take such a form as the local authority consider appropriate' (s. 47(4)). The legality of self-assessment remains questionable. The current legal position is that the duty to carry out a community care assessment clearly rests with the local authority, and there is no express provision that allows the local authority to delegate that statutory duty. The Law Commission (2010, p. 34) notes that 'relying on a self-assessment alone to assess a person's needs without any validation or review of the assessment would effectively amount to a delegation of this statutory duty'.

In its final recommendations for law reform, the Law Commission (2011b, p. 26) explicitly recognizes the tension between professional assessment and personalization: 'We must find a way of reconciling the broader perspective of personalization with the continued existence of a legal right to a low-threshold assessment process, which acts as a gateway to state funding.' Rather than embedding self-assessment in statute, thus potentially compromising the state's duty to assess, it recommends guidance on how self-assessment should be integrated within the assessment process where appropriate, referring to these arrangements as *co-produced* assessment. Recognizing the importance for personalization of being able to refuse assessment, it also proposes that statute should specify the circumstances in which a local authority can deem its assessment duty to have been discharged, for example when assessment is declined by a person with capacity in situations without risk of harm.

A further example of ways in which the legal rules may constrain assessment prac-

Law

tice is the legal requirement for separate assessments of a carer and the person they care for, leading the Princess Royal Trust for Carers (2009, p. 18) to advocate that 'where families wish to, they should have the option of being assessed for eligibility as a whole family, rather than having to negotiate separate assessments and eligibility for each individual'.

As will be seen later, the limitations that the legal rules place on choice and control in assessment are only part of the picture; when it comes to decision-making following assessment, the law can be seen as equivocal in its support for personalization. But there is more supportive provision to consider first.

Advocacy

Advocacy for users of adult social care provision has been promoted since the introduction of community care in the early 1990s. Practice guidance (DH, 1991a) calls for service users and carers to receive information about advocacy services that might support them in disputes about needs and services. More substantially, the MCA 2005 and the MHA 2007 (amending the MHA 1983) require advocates to be involved in certain prescribed circumstances where support may be required to ensure that wishes and feelings are identified and made known to decision-makers. An independent mental capacity advocate (IMCA) must be appointed for a person who lacks capacity but has no one to speak for them where it is proposed to provide serious medical treatment, NHS accommodation or local authority accommodation and where deprivation of liberty is being proposed. An IMCA can also be appointed for reviews, and in abuse investigations. An independent mental health advocate (IMHA) must be appointed for all patients detained under the MHA 1983 (except those held on 72-hour detentions) and for those under guardianship or supervised community treatment and for those in respect of whom certain far-reaching treatments (under s. 57) are being considered. Their role is to promote the patient's understanding of their circumstances, and to provide information about, and support in exercising, rights.

But some potentially empowering legal rules relating to the representation of service users' views have remained unimplemented. Sections 1–3 of the Disabled Persons (Services, Consultation and Representation) Act 1986 gave disabled people the right to appoint representatives to support them and act on their behalf in dealing with local authority assessment and service provision. These sections were, however, never implemented. The Law Commission (2011b) recommends that this statutory right be retained, with powers for it to be modified and implemented in line with contemporary understandings of advocacy. Equally, advocacy is included within the proposed statutory definition of community care services.

Accountability

The opportunity to challenge aspects of practice is an important aspect of personalization. Concerns about the assessment or delivery of community care services may be raised under the Local Authority Social Services and National Health Service (England) Complaints Regulations 2009. Complainants who remain unsatisfied with the resolution offered through local authority channels may subsequently apply for judicial review of the matter, or raise their concern with the local government ombudsman. Particularly significant in the context of personalization is the extension from October 2010 of the remit of the local government ombudsman, with the introduction of new powers to investigate complaints relating to providers of self-funded care. The effect of this development is to introduce consistency between adults who purchase their own care – with an individual budget, direct payments or their own money – and adults whose care has been directly arranged and funded by the local authority, who have had access to this independent complaints service for many years.

While complaints and redress fell outside the Law Commission's remit in reviewing adult social care law, its final report (2011b) nonetheless recommends that the system be reviewed and the need for the introduction of a community care tribunal be considered.

Direct payments, individual budgets and personal budgets

There are a number of legal and policy initiatives that support the development of self-directed care, all of which make important contributions to personalization.

The Community Care, Services for Carers and Children's Services (Direct Payments) (England) Regulations 2009 (made under the authority of the Health and Social Care Act 2001, s. 57) permit local authorities to make direct payments to people to whom they have a duty to provide a service under the Chronically Sick and Disabled Persons Act 1970 (s. 2). This duty is discharged by the monetary payment as long as the local authority is satisfied that the service user's own arrangements will meet the need that calls for the provision of the service. Direct payments are a central element of personalization policy, and have been available since 1996; however, take-up remains low and there is substantial regional variation in provision (Fernandez et al., 2007). Initially, direct payments were only available if the individual could consent to the payment and was deemed capable of managing the payment. This effectively excluded some people with learning disabilities. The Health and Social Care Act 2008 remedied this inequality by allowing payments to be made to a 'suitable person' to receive and manage the payment on behalf of the individual lacking capacity; this could be a relative or friend.

Closely related to direct payments are personal budgets, but they do not have the same degree of legal clarity. Mitchell (2011) points out that while direct payments are mandatory if certain conditions are met, 'the legal framework surrounding personal budgets is surprisingly obscure' (p. 8) and that 'the precise legal nature of a "personal budget" is elusive' (p. 9). A personal budget is not in itself mandatory; it is essentially an allocation of funding to meet eligible needs following assessment. The charity In Control (Tyson et al., 2010, p. 38) defines it as money that is available to a person who needs support. The money comes from their local authority social services. The person controlling the budget (or their representative) must know how much money they have for their support, be able to spend the money in ways and at times that make sense to them and know what outcomes will be achieved with the money.

The personal budget can be taken as a direct payment, or used by the council to commission services on the user's behalf, or a combination. A further option is for the service user to engage a budget broker (Carr and Robbins, 2009). The budget can be used flexibly to cover the cost of equipment, adaptations, transport, personal care and so on, although flexibility is limited to the extent that the budget must be used to meet the objectives in the care plan, which itself should have been agreed with the service user.

The budget should be sufficient to meet the assessed need; practice guidance (DH, 2009b) calls for transparency of decision-making and for the employment of a resource allocation system in setting indicative allocations, although 'it is important for councils to ensure that their resource allocation process is sufficiently flexible to allow for someone's individual circumstances to be taken into account when determining the amount of resources he or she is allocated in a personal budget' (p. 41). Evaluations of personal budget arrangements (Tyson et al., 2010) have shown positive impacts in terms of budget holders feeling in control of their support and overall quality of life.

Individual budgets work on the same principle of allocating funding for eligible needs, but bring together a more diverse range of funding streams, including social care, housing, health and disabled facilities grants. Like personal budgets, they currently lack any legislative basis. Outcomes have again been positive in terms of the impact on feeling in control but have been more mixed for different user groups (Glendinning et al., 2008).

Under the Law Commission's (2011b) proposals for law reform, direct payments remain and are no longer restricted to nonresidential services. The report, however, recognizes the rather different legal status of personal budgets, which it recommends should be dealt with outside the statutory framework through granting the secretary of state (England) and Welsh ministers (Wales) powers to make regulations, should they choose to for policy reasons, that would require local authorities to allocate personal budgets.

Lasting powers of attorney and advance decisions

The MCA 2005 introduced key mechanisms for the autonomy of decision-making to be preserved even beyond the loss of mental capacity. These allow someone who has capacity to appoint representatives with a lasting power of attorney (LPA) to make decisions on their behalf. An LPA can be held in relation to finances or personal welfare (including healthcare and treatment) and it enables the donor to give decision-making power to someone they trust to carry out their wishes once they no longer have capacity, or in the case of a financial LPA, while capacity is still retained.

nd this, choice and control can be expressed as an advance decision
ried treatment; such a decision must be respected once a need for the
question arises, even if the individual has by then lost capacity, provided
dence that the advance decision exists, is valid, and applies to the treat-
question. As Brammer (2010, p. 485) comments, 'the greatest autonomy in
adv.ce decision making will be secured by an individual utilising both procedures'
(an LPA and advance decisions). Even so, an LPA and advance decisions regarding
medical treatment are not unassailable. They may be overruled, for example, by use
of the MHA 1983 to effect compulsory admission to hospital or guardianship.

Provision for adults who are deemed not to have capacity

The emphasis of the MCA 2005 is on presuming and promoting capacity, enabling
individuals to take first-hand decisions wherever possible and, if not, to participate
as fully as possible in decisions taken on their behalf. Where capacity is deemed not
to exist, then decisions made by others must be in the individual's best interests. This
is a different concept from that of choice and control. Assessing best interests must
involve a range of diverse factors, set out in the code of practice to the Act (Department for Constitutional Affairs, 2007), and, while the individual's wishes and feelings
must be taken into account by the decision-maker, they are not determinative.

An intervention carried out in the best interests of an adult lacking capacity is
permissible and protected under the MCA 2005 (s. 5), provided it does not contra-
vene an advance decision, or the wishes of anyone holding an LPA, or a court-appointed
deputy, and provided it does not amount to deprivation of liberty. If deprivation of
liberty is deemed necessary in order to promote the individual's best interests, then
additional deprivation of liberty safeguards must be observed. These were inserted
into the MCA 2005 through an amendment under the MHA 2007, made necessary
by the European Court of Human Right's ruling in the case of *HL* v *UK* [2004]
(known as the Bournewood case), in which the detention as an informal patient of
a man without capacity, without procedural safeguards, was deemed to breach his
right to liberty under Article 5, ECHR. The determining factor is the degree and
continuity of control exercised over residence, treatment and social contacts (Ministry of Justice, 2008). The additional safeguards, comprising a range of assessments
and consultations, including the involvement of an IMCA, provide a counterbalance
and a protection against the arbitrary exercise of power in interventions where it
might appear that choice and control are most lacking.

It is important to note the MCA 2005 does not provide for interventions with
people lacking capacity that are for the protection of others rather than in the best
interests of the individual involved. In such circumstances, recourse may be to the
MHA 1983 (amended in 2007), provided the criteria for admission to hospital or
guardianship are met.

Relevant in the context of personalization is guidance from the Court of Protection on the relationship between the wishes and feelings of an adult who does not have

capacity, and the principle of best interests that applies in professional decisions on their behalf. In *ITW* v *Z & M* [2009], the court considered the validity of a will made by a woman of 87, who had changed previous wills that left her money to charity, leaving it instead to a man with whom she had more recently been living. The court decided that she did not have capacity to make the will, and thus it made a will on her behalf, reinstating the beneficiaries of her earlier wills. It held that the wishes and feelings of a person who lacks capacity are not determinative, and that where they do not accord with best interests, then best interests must prevail. While wishes and feelings are a significant factor, the weight to be attached to them will vary from case to case, and (in relation to each individual) from issue to issue. In considering the weight to be attached, all the relevant circumstances must be considered, including the degree of incapacity, the strength and consistency of the wishes expressed, the impact of departing from them, the extent to which they are rational, sensible, responsible and capable of being implemented, and the extent to which they would be compatible with best interests.

In a case more directly related to a decision about personal welfare, *PCT* v *P & AH* [2009], the Court of Protection considered where a young man with learning disabilities should live – in supported housing with limitations on contact with his mother, or with his mother. The court determined that he did not have capacity to decide for himself, as he could not 'use or weigh' relevant information as part of the decision-making process, in part because of the enmeshed relationship with his mother, which restricted his perspective in thinking about his future. The court then had to use the principle of best interests in determining where he should live, and thus had to decide what weight to place on his wishes and feelings, which were to live with his mother. Because the court had doubts about the extent to which his wishes and feelings were self-generated, it placed less weight on them than it might otherwise have done, and concluded that it was not in his best interests to live with his mother, because his mother's care had hampered the development of his independence and raised concerns about his access to necessary medical treatments. Requiring him to live in supported housing with restrictions on contact with his mother, although interfering with his and his mother's right to respect for private and family life under Article 8 of the ECHR, was a proportionate response to the need to secure his best interests. The restrictions constituted a deprivation of liberty, which the court duly authorized.

Constraints on choice and control

Despite the positive contributions to personalization identified above, there are aspects of current legislation that can be seen to impede personalization. An unusual example is the Choice of Accommodation Directions 1992, which allow individuals who require residential accommodation to exercise choice over the actual placement. The Law Commission (2010) suggests that these represent early examples of personalization and self-directed support. In contrast to direct payments, however, which allow the individual to directly arrange services, the local authority must still arrange accommodation on the person's behalf.

The role of local authority discretion

While the policy rhetoric of choice and control is strong, the courts are reticent about challenging local authorities' prerogative to determine how eligible needs will be met, despite strong user preferences. The Supreme Court case of *R (McDonald)* v *Kensington and Chelsea RLBC* [2011] demonstrates the limits to choice and control within the law as it currently stands. The original needs assessment in this case referred to a *need for assistance to use the commode during the night*; the council had originally supplied a night carer, but subsequently proposed replacement of that service with incontinence pads, which the user, who was not incontinent, referred to as an affront to her dignity. However, in a later review of needs, the council had rephrased the need in much more general terms, referring to the *need to urinate safely at night*. The Appeal Court determined that while the original change of provision had breached the council's duty, from the review point onwards, the provision of incontinence pads no longer did so because it met the redefined need to urinate safely. The Supreme Court upheld this view, although not unanimously (LJ Hale dissenting). It confirmed that the council had not interfered with the service user's rights to private and family life under Article 8 (ECHR) and that, even had they done so, such interference would have been justified because the change of provision represented a proportionate response to the individual's needs, ensured her safety and independence, and (in securing cost savings) promoted the equitable allocation of limited care resources. Equally, the council's action did not constitute unlawful disability discrimination.

Local authority discretion was reinforced in a decision by the High Court (*R (Broster & Others)* v *Wirrall MBC* [2010]), which concluded that there is no duty on a local authority to provide a personal budget and a refusal to do so does not constitute a breach of Article 8 (ECHR) or disability equality legislation. The decision related to a claim by 16 people with learning disabilities, living as tenants of an organization providing accommodation and services under contract to the council. The court was concerned that the tenants would be unduly influenced by the organization in deciding how to spend their budget allocation, that is, they would be influenced to continue to purchase the organization's services after the council withdrew from the contract. It drew on statutory guidance (DH, 2010c) that does not make personal budgets mandatory.

Such judgments reinforce longstanding case law that upholds the discretion of the local authority to determine how eligible needs should be met, and to take resource considerations into account when making decisions (*R* v *Lancashire CC, ex parte Ingham & Whalley* [1995]).

Resources

One of the key challenges of the interface between legal rules and personalization lies in the question of how resources impact on decision-making. Since the introduction of the NHSCCA 1990 (and even before), the allocation of resources in adult social care has been contentious. The landmark decision of *R* v *Gloucestershire CC ex parte Barry*

[1997] confirmed resources to be a relevant factor that councils could take into account when assessing need. For this to happen in a fair and transparent way, local authorities employ eligibility criteria as a means of rationing resources. Guidance entitled *Prioritising Need in the Context of Putting People First* (DH, 2010c), replacing *Fair Access to Care Services* (DH, 2003), identifies four eligibility bands – critical, substantial, moderate and low – that are applied to individuals' needs and risks to independence at the assessment stage when allocating a personal budget, just as they have done for more traditional provision of services. A very real constraint on individual choice and control is in the application of these eligibility bands. Many authorities will only provide support to individuals whose needs fall in the critical or substantial bands – a practice confirmed as lawful in *R (Chavda)* v *Harrow LBC* [2007].

The resource allocation system (RAS), a national framework employed by local authorities, sets indicative allocations for the cost of meeting specific types of need. In the case of *R (Raphaela Savva)* v *Kensington and Chelsea* [2010], a disabled woman with serious health problems challenged the lawfulness of the council's method of calculating personal budgets and complained that the council had not provided adequate reasons for its allocation to her. Initially, the court did not uphold her claim that the council had acted unlawfully in its calculation method, but did agree that the council had not provided adequate reasons for its calculation. Both parties appealed, and the Court of Appeal upheld both decisions of the lower court. Thus, it was not unlawful for the council to use the RAS as a starting point for its determination of the personal budget, although assessors must decide in each individual case whether this is sufficient. Importantly, under common law (in the absence of any statutory or regulatory duty to give reasons), the local authority was, in the interests of fairness, required to give an adequate explanation of how a personal budget allocation is determined, although it could in future consider this duty discharged by an offer of the provision of reasons on request, and the court did not anticipate this being an onerous duty. For example, in this particular case, it was suggested that it would be 'adequate to list the required services and assumed timings … together with the assumed hourly cost' (para. 21).

The use of the RAS as a starting point for budget allocation was confirmed in *R (KM)* v *Cambridgeshire CC* [2010], provided practitioners check that the result is sufficient to meet the council's obligation to provide services, and modify it if necessary. In this case, the council had commissioned an independent assessment of needs but did not accept the higher funding level recommended by the independent assessor, raising the allocation instead to the level determined by its own employees' assessment; this was judged lawful by the court.

Other cases have similarly limited the legal avenues for challenging decisions in which resources play a part. In *R (Domb and others)* v *Hammersmith & Fulham LBC* [2009], the Court of Appeal rejected a challenge to the council's decision, following a substantial consultation exercise, to start charging for care services rather than raising the eligibility threshold. The service users argued that the council had not paid due regard to disability equality considerations in introducing the charges, but the court held the council's decision to be entirely rational. The court did, however, imply in its judgment that although in this case it was too late to bring a challenge to the council's budget once that budget had been set, it might in theory be possible at an earlier point to challenge the setting of a budget that would provide insufficient resources for the council to meet its obligations in law.

The impact of resources and eligibility criteria on personal dignity are also made acutely clear in the case of McDonald, discussed earlier.

Legal underpinnings for core components of personalization: personal dignity and safety

When expressed as giving 'choice' and 'control' to the individual, personalization is difficult to argue against and assumed to be beneficial (Boxall et al., 2009). Certain consequences of personalization may, however, include an element of unacceptable risk. Safeguarding adults work has developed alongside personalization, the common feature between the two areas being the lack of a clear statutory framework, although various elements of existing law have an impact on safeguarding, for example the criminal law. *No Secrets* guidance (DH, 2000) gives some direction to local authorities and other agencies on their safeguarding responsibilities, and there exists a complex system of interagency arrangements to ensure that local safeguarding interventions are timely and effective (Braye et al., 2011b).

The government's consultation (DH, 2009c) on the review of *No Secrets* (DH, 2000) asked respondents to comment on the interface between personalization and safeguarding. Personalization as a practice has largely developed since the introduction of this guidance and is one of the policy changes that prompted its review. For the purposes of the consultation, personalization is referred to as 'choice and control in services and support'. A theme to emerge from respondents noted that 'a balance needs to be established between empowerment and protection and between the rights for self-determination and the duty to ensure safety of people and safety of public money' (DH, 2009c, p. 30). Carr (2010) makes the point that safeguarding and personalization share the same underlying principles of empowerment, autonomy and independence.

As noted in best practice guidance (DH, 2010d, p. 7), 'personalisation does not replace the need for adult safeguarding systems and procedures'; rather, it may be seen as part of a range of activities designed to uphold fundamental rights to safety, and self-directed support processes should incorporate good risk analysis. Case law (*Local Authority X* v *MM and KM* [2007]) has sought to establish an appropriate balance:

> The emphasis must be on sensible risk appraisal, not striving to avoid all risk, whatever the price, but instead seeking a proper balance and being willing to tolerate manageable or acceptable risks as the price appropriately to be paid in order to achieve some other good – in particular to achieve the vital good of the

Law

elderly or vulnerable person's happiness. What good is it making someone safer if it merely makes them miserable? (para. 120)

But personalization creates new challenges that must be addressed in order to ensure that safeguarding principles are considered alongside those of choice and control, and here the legal rules are less well developed, or less overtly applied.

Regulation of the workforce

Many people with a personal budget will choose to employ a personal assistant to carry out caring and other tasks to meet their assessed needs. A personal assistant does not have to be employed by any sort of agency and may simply respond to a direct advertisement placed by the individual, who effectively becomes the personal assistant's employer. The risk of abuse to individuals receiving care in their own homes is well recognized and was one of the reasons for the introduction of closer regulation of domiciliary care agencies. Carers employed by registered care providers are subject to Criminal Records Bureau (CRB) vetting and barring checks under the Safeguarding Vulnerable Groups Act 2006. Personal assistants who are employed directly are, however, unregulated, despite concerns expressed when the legislation was being introduced that this afforded a lower level of protection (Hanson and Hamilton, 2006). There is no reason to assume that individuals who are appointed directly by the person requiring care are any less likely to pose such a risk than those appointed by registered care providers; indeed, the potential risk may be compounded by a recruitment process less rigorous than that practised by an agency, and not supported by the requirement for CRB checks or by the regulation and inspection framework.

Employment liability

A perhaps unexpected consequence for service users receiving direct payments is that as soon as these are used to employ an individual, as a carer for example, the service user becomes an employer bound by the complex raft of employment legislation. Such a situation was illustrated in the case of *Roberts* v *Carlin* [2010]. Direct payments were made to meet the assessed needs of an 18-year-old man with cerebral palsy. The payments were made to his mother who entered into contracts to employ carers. A carer was dismissed by the mother and the employment tribunal had to decide whether

Making connexions

The personalization agenda contains three key elements:

1. the encouragement of choice and control to be exercised by the service user

2. the need for adult safeguarding systems and procedures to be maintained

3. resource allocation constraints.

How can the social worker manage the sometimes conflicting relationship between these three elements?

the reason for dismissal was an incident of poor caring or the carer's pregnancy. As the carer had been employed for less than a year, she brought a claim of sex discrimination, rather than unfair dismissal, arguing that the real reason for her dismissal was her pregnancy. The mother claimed that she had dismissed the carer because on one occasion the carer had got the son out of bed and left the house without telling the mother that her son was up. The mother was ill in bed on that day. A couple of weeks after this incident, the mother informed the carer that she was dismissed because of the incident and followed this with a solicitor's letter of dismissal. The carer claimed that the dismissal was actually because she had just revealed to the mother that she was pregnant. The tribunal found that the reason for the dismissal was the pregnancy, and that if the real reason was the caring incident, the dismissal would have occurred earlier.

Conclusion

This chapter is written at a time of turbulence and change in the legal structures that support adult social care. There are indications of the direction of travel, signalled by the Law Commission's (2010) consultation paper on adult social care law reform, the government's response (DH, 2010e), the Law Commission's (2011a) report on consultation responses and its final proposals (Law Commission, 2011b).

While the Law Commission recognizes the government's espousal of personalization, it notes that Wales takes a more cautious approach, committing instead to self-directed care (Welsh Assembly Government, 2011), and remains sceptical about the extent to which personalization should be embedded in statute law:

> While we accept the importance of our scheme being able to accommodate personalization, we maintain our view that it would be a mistake to bind our recommendations to a particular philosophy or policy ... the history of adult social care law is littered with examples of statutes which have attempted to implement prevailing policies but which now look increasingly out of date. (Law Commission, 2011b, p. 5)

The Law Commission's proposals do not depart substantially from the established process of local authority assessment, determination of eligibility and provision of a flexible range of care and support to meet eligible needs. This is in line with the explicit approach adopted: 'Underpinning this framework are the core entitlements and rights that are crucial to the existing legal framework' (p. 5).

Adult wellbeing (rather than personalization) is the core underpinning principle recommended for recognition in statute. But there is much that recognizes and reflects personalization principles too. While not explicitly badged as personalization, the proposed statutory principles for adult social care include the requirement to 'follow the individual's views, wishes and feelings wherever practicable and appropriate' (Law Commission 2001b, p. 24). The proposed definition of community care services takes a hybrid approach, specifying both the broadest possible range of service inputs and the sought outcomes of provision, to allow for personalization within the choice and selection of services.

Safeguarding also remains firmly on the agenda, and complements rather than contradicts the objectives of personalization, recognizing the need to balance the commitment to choice and control with the need to ensure that individuals with self-directed care are not at greater risk of abuse. Proposals include a statutory safeguarding adults board[1] under the leadership of the local authority and a statutory duty to investigate where an adult is at risk, with local authority power to request cooperation from others in doing so. Section 47 of the National Assistance Act 1948, under which people can be removed from their homes on public health grounds, is recommended for repeal on the grounds that it is incompatible with rights contained within the European Convention on Human Rights, thus further reinforcing autonomy and self-determination.

It is clear that personalization has emerged against a backdrop of community care law that can largely accommodate the change in policy. The current legal rules do much to support the emphasis on choice and control, through the core principles and the specific provisions outlined in this chapter. Equally, they place constraints on the prioritization of personal choice above all else, offering guidance that assists in balancing conflicting imperatives, and at times a more collective vision that recognizes social justice alongside individual rights. Indeed, even government rhetoric has recognized that rights to self-determination will be 'constrained by the realities of finite resources' (DH, 2007, p. 2). Nonetheless, the principle of personalization has cross-sector commitment and support (Think Local, Act Personal, 2011) and clearly underpins the direction of travel.

Later in 2011, the government (DH, 2011b) launched a consultation on the priorities for adult social care to inform a 2012 White Paper, bringing together the Law Commission's (2011b) report on the reform of law, the Dilnot Commission's (2011) report on the funding of care, and the government's own adult social care policy vision (DH, 2010a). Personalization is identified as one of six areas that have the greatest potential to bring improvements to the care and support system. At the same time, outcome measures for adult social care (DH, 2011c) include several that specifically target key markers of personalization:

- the proportion of service users who have control over their daily life
- the proportion of service users who receive self-directed support, and those receiving direct payments
- the proportion of people who find it easy to find information about support
- the proportion of carers who say they have been included or consulted in discussions about the person they care for.

There is also recognition that the mechanisms of personalization will profoundly affect the social care market:

> Self-directed support, such as personal budgets, are allowing people to design their own care and support packages, and buy services from whomever they see fit to meet their needs. This will inevitably lead to further growth in non-regulated services and micro-providers, as people look for more specific, less traditional services. (DH, 2011d, p. 12)

It is thus beyond doubt that legal, policy and practice sea change lies ahead.

Note

1 Shortly after publication of the Law Commission's report, the government committed itself to placing safeguarding adults boards on a statutory footing (DH, 2011a).

Appendix 2.1 Table of cases

A Local Authority v DL, RL and ML [2010] EWHC 2675 (Fam)

A v East Sussex CC [2003] EWHC 167 (Admin)

Donoghue v Stevenson [1932] AC 562

G v E [2010] EWHC 621 (Fam)

HL v UK [2004] 40 EHRR 761

ITW v Z & M [2009] EWHC 2525 (Fam)

Keenan v UK [2001] 33 EHRR 913

LBL v RYJ and BJ [2010] EWHC 2665 (COP)

Local Authority X v MM and KM [2007] EWHC 2003 (Fam)

Open Door Counselling & Dublin Well Woman v Ireland [1992] 15 EHRR 244

PCT v P & AH [2009] EW Misc 10

R (Bernard) v Enfield LBC [2001] EWHC 2282

R (Broster & Others) v Wirral MBC [2010] EWHC 3086 (Admin)

R (Chavda) v Harrow LBC [2007] EWHC 3064 (Admin)

R (Domb and others) v Hammersmith &Fulham LBC [2009] EWCA Civ 941

R (JL) v Islington [2009] 12 CCLR 322

R (KM) v Cambridgeshire CC [2010] EWHC 3065 (Admin)

R (McDonald) v Kensington and Chelsea RLBC [2011] UKSC 33.

R (Raphaela Savva) v Kensington and Chelsea [2010] EWCA Civ 1209

R v Gloucestershire CC ex parte Barry [1997] 2 All ER 1

R v Lancashire CC, ex parte Ingham & Whalley [1995] CO/774/95

Re SA (Vulnerable adult with capacity: Marriage) [2005] EWHC 2942 (Fam)

Re Z (Local Authority: Duty) [2004] EWHC 2817

Roberts v Carlin [2010] UKEAT 0183 09 1712

Z v UK [2001] 2 FLR 612

Further reading

■ Brammer, A. (2010) *Social Work Law* (3rd edn). Harlow: Pearson Education.

Accessible, clear and comprehensive guide to the legal frameworks within which social work is practised.

■ Braye, S. and Preston-Shoot, M. (2010) *Practising Social Work Law* (3rd edn). Basingstoke: Palgrave Macmillan.

Practitioners' guide to negotiating the complexity of legal rules, dealing with professional practice dilemmas within a rights-based framework.

■ Clements, L. and Thompson, C. (2011) *Community Care and the Law* (5th edn). London: Legal Action Group.

Scholarly and comprehensive exploration of community care law, integrating key legal detail with commentary on, and analysis of, its complexity.

References

Brammer, A. (2010) *Social Work Law*. Harlow: Pearson Education.

Boxall, K., Dowson, S. and Beresford, P. (2009) 'Selling individual budgets, choice and control: local and global influences on UK social care policy for people with learning difficulties', *Policy and Politics*, **37**(4): 449–515.

Braye, S., Orr, D. and Preston-Shoot, M. (2011a) *Self Neglect and Adult Safeguarding: Findings from Research*. London: SCIE.

Braye, S., Orr, D. and Preston-Shoot, M. (2011b) *The Governance of Adult Safeguarding: Findings from Research*. London: SCIE.

Carr, S. (2010) *Enabling Risk, Ensuring Safety: Self-directed Support and Personal Budgets*. SCIE Report 36. London: SCIE.

Carr, S. and Robbins, D. (2009) *The Implementation of Individual Budget Schemes in Adult Social Care: Research Briefing 20*. London: SCIE.

Clements, L. (2011) 'Social care law developments: a sideways look at personalization and tightening eligibility criteria', *Elder Law Journal*, **1**(1): 47–52.

Department for Constitutional Affairs (2007) *Mental Capacity Act 2005: Code of Practice*. London: DCA/TSO.

DH (Department of Health) (1990) *Community Care in the Next Decade and Beyond: Policy Guidance*. London: HMSO.

DH (1991a) *Care Management and Assessment: Practitioners' Guide*. London: DH.

DH (1991b) *Getting the Message Across: A Guide to Developing and Communicating Policies, Principles and Procedures on Assessment*. London: DH.

DH (1991c) *Care Management and Assessment: Summary of Practice Guidance*. London: DH.

DH (2000) *No Secrets: Guidance on Developing and Implementing Multi-agency Policies and Procedures to Protect Vulnerable Adults from Abuse*. London: DH.

DH (2001) *Valuing People.* London: DH.

DH (2002) *Guidance on the Single Assessment Process for Older People,* LAC(2002)1. London: DH.

DH (2003) *Fair Access to Care Services*, LAC 2003 12. London: DH.

DH (2007) *Putting People First: A Shared Vision and Commitment to the Transformation of Adult Social Care.* London: DH.

DH (2008a) *Transforming Adult Social Care*, LAC(DH)(2008)1. London: DH.

DH (2008b) *Code of Practice: Mental Health Act 1983.* London: TSO.

DH (2009a) *Valuing People Now.* London: DH.

DH (2009b) *Guidance on Direct Payments for Community Care, Services for Carers and Children's Services.* London: DH.

DH (2009c) *Safeguarding Adults: Report on the Consultation on the Review of No Secrets.* London: DH.

DH (2010a) *A Vision for Adult Social Care: Capable Communities and Active Citizens.* London: DH.

DH (2010b) *Carers and Personalization: Improving Outcomes.* London: DH.

DH (2010c) *Prioritising Need in the Context of Putting People First: A Whole System Approach to Eligibility for Adult Social Care.* London: DH.

DH (2010d) *Practical Approaches to Safeguarding and Personalization.* London: DH.

DH (2010e) *The Government Response to Law Commission Consultation Paper 192: Review of Adult Social Care Law.* London: DH.

DH (2011a) *Statement of Government Policy on Adult Safeguarding. Gateway Reference 16072.* London: DH.

DH (2011b) *Caring for Our Future: Shared Ambitions for Care and Support.* London: DH.

DH (2011c) *Transparency in Outcomes: A Framework for Quality in Adult Social Care. The 2011/12 Adult Social Care Outcomes Framework.* London: DH.

DH (2011d) *Transparency in Outcomes: A Framework for Quality in Adult Social Care. A Response to the Consultation and Next Steps.* London: DH.

Dilnot Commission (2011) *Fairer Care Funding: The Report of the Commission on Funding of Care and Support.* London: Commission on Funding of Care and Support.

EHRC (Equality and Human Rights Commission) (2010) *How Fair is Britain? Equality, Human Rights and Good Relations in 2010: The First Triennial Review.* London: EHRC.

EHRC (2011) *Close to Home: An Inquiry into Older People and Human Rights in Home Care.* London: EHRC.

Ferguson, I. (2007) 'Increasing user choice or privatising risk? The antinomies of personalization', *British Journal of Social Work*, 37, 387–403.

Fernandez, J.-L., Kendall, J., Davey, V. and Knapp, M. (2007) 'Direct payments in England: factors linked to variations in local provision', *Journal of Social Policy,* 36, 97–121.

Glendinning, C., Challis, D., Fernandez, J. et al. (2008) *Evaluation of the Individual Budgets Pilot Programme: Final Report.* York: Social Policy Research Unit.

Hanson, K. and Hamilton, T. (2006) 'Private family arrangements and the welfare of adults who lack capacity: an analysis of the safeguarding vulnerable groups bill', *Journal of Adult Protection,* **8**(3): 16.

Law Commission (2010) *Adult Social Care.* London: Law Commission.

Law Commission (2011a) *Adult Social Care: Consultation Analysis.* London: Law Commission.

Law Commission (2011b) *Adult Social Care Law.* London: Law Commission.

Ministry of Justice (2008) *Mental Capacity Act 2005: Deprivation of Liberty Safeguards: Code of Practice to Supplement the Main Mental Capacity Act 2005 Code of Practice.* London: MoJ/TSO.

Mitchell, E. (ed.) (2011) 'Personal budgets', *Social Care Law Today,* 79.

Munby LJ (2011) 'Dignity, happiness and human rights', *Elder Law Journal,* **1**(1): 32.

Preston-Shoot, M., Roberts, G. and Vernon, S. (2001) 'Values in social work law: strained relations or sustaining relationships?', *Journal of Social Welfare and Family Law,* **23**(1): 1–22.

Princess Royal Trust for Carers (2009) *Putting People First without Putting Carers Second.* London: PRTC/Crossroads Caring for Carers.

Think Local, Act Personal (2011) *Think Local, Act Personal: A Sector-wide Commitment to Moving Forward with Personalization and Community-based Support.* London: Think Local, Act Personal/SCIE.

Tyson, A., Brewis, R., Crosby, N. et al. (2010) *A Report on In Control's Third Phase: Evaluation and Learning 2008–2009.* London: In Control.

Welsh Assembly Government (2011) *Sustainable Social Services for Wales.* Cardiff: Welsh Assembly Government.

Law

3
Conceptual foundations and theory-building in personalization

SUSAN HUNTER AND MIKE TITTERTON

In this chapter, we discuss what we consider to be the principal theoretical approaches that have influenced and informed the concept of 'personalization'. In addition to reviewing the main conceptual foundations, we lend critical attention to the challenge of building a robust 'theory' to support the development of this notion by emphasizing selected theoretical elements, which we feel have particular potential for this task.

There has of late been a lively and growing interest in personalization in research, policy and practice. Duffy (2010, p. 203), who advocates forcefully on behalf of the notion, admits that it is 'rather vulnerable to being used and interpreted in different ways'. The term has tended to be used in rather broad and vaguely specified ways by those recommending its adoption, such as the Department of Health (2007). That said, it usually entails two dimensions: the individual level, providing cash, in lieu of public services, directly to eligible service users who then plan, purchase and manage their own support needs (Wood, 2010); and at the service level, designing systems that create commissioning and provider environments that are responsive to choice and control by service users and reach out beyond services into mainstream resources and universal solutions to the problems of daily living (Sang, 2009). Here, we define personalization as:

> personalization embodies the development of welfare strategies that incorporate self-managed and individualized forms of support, based on the expressed needs and wishes of the person, and subject to their control.

This definition covers recent trends in policy and practice in health and social care in the UK, including initiatives involving the management of personal welfare, self-directed support, self-management, and individual and personal budgets. These trends are common to the four countries of the UK, although diverse policy trajectories, welfare mixes, regulatory regimes and legislative bases can be found when England, Scotland, Wales and Northern Ireland are compared (Titterton et al., 2010). There have been accompanying criticisms of personalization by those concerned that it simply represents a shift of the responsibilities of the welfare state to the individual in a time of increasing austerity; thus risk is transferred from public services to the person in a process of 'responsibilization' or 'individualization' (see, for example, Kemshall, 2002; Taylor-Gooby, 2006).

Theoretical influences

The growth of interest in personalization in the literature has not been matched by a concern with its conceptual foundations. Of those writers who do comment on this, there are a diversity of opinions about influences. Beresford (2010a) claims that key influences are independent living, normalization and social role valorization (Wolfensberger, 1972; Tyne and Williams, 1988; Oliver, 1989; Barnes and Mercer, 2010). Other writers like Sang (2009) pinpoint the influence of social policy theorists such as Richard Titmuss (1960), with his views about citizenship and universalism. Duffy (2010) points to more contemporary influences such as the likes of Demos (Leadbeater and Lownsbrough, 2005).

The thinking has found expression in the Department of Health's *Putting People First* (2007), a major programme to 'transform' adult care services that has four key elements, one of which is personalization, This has been a UK-wide initiative, albeit with different routes being followed throughout. For example, in Scotland, there have been more radical moves to introduce legislation to make self-directed support the default option for service users (Scottish Government, 2009, 2010). Not only is there intercountry variation, but there is also huge intracountry variation, with different local authorities pursuing self-direction with differing enthusiasms, perceptions and interpretations (see, for example, Manthorpe et al., 2009; Jenkins and Hay, 2010).

Nonetheless, it is clear that personalization remains rather underdeveloped in terms of concept and theory-building. It is equally evident that a variety of diverse conceptual strands have come together and have become intertwined to form 'personalization'. Figure 3.1 provides an outline of the main notions that have influenced its development.

In this chapter, three main theoretical bases are identified: person-centred and participatory approaches; theories relating to citizens as consumers and producers of welfare; and risk and resilience theories. These theoretical bases are interdisciplinary in nature and include perspectives from sociology, psychology, economics, social policy and social work. While some may be recognizable to students of social work, it is our intention to encourage the reader to take into account theories that may be less familiar and to make connections with practice issues.

Theory

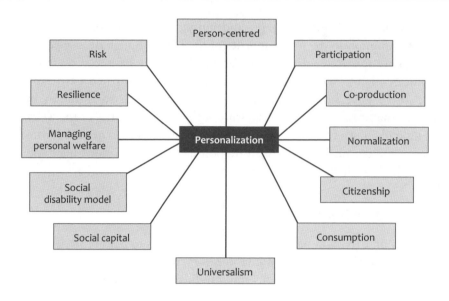

Figure 3.1 The contributory elements behind personalization

Person-centred and participatory approaches

Notable themes in the research and policy literatures since the 1960s have drawn attention to the need for greater emphasis to be placed on consultation and involvement and greater participation by the beneficiaries of welfare. In line with this, there have been arguments for shifting the terminology for these beneficiaries – from passive recipients to active participants, from client to service user and citizen. Universalism and citizenship theories of the sort favoured by Titmuss (1960) have come back into play for professionals through policy initiatives such as *Valuing People* (DH, 2001) and *The Same as You?* (Scottish Executive, 2000), in part bolstered by human rights approaches under the impact of the 1950 European Convention on Human Rights legislation, now embodied in UK law under the Human Rights Act 1998.

At the heart of what have become loosely known as person-centred approaches is the cluster of interventions known as 'person-centred planning', developed in the field of learning disabilities over the last 25 years. What is distinctive about person-centred planning and its array of associated planning tools, compared with 'traditional' and expert approaches to planning, is the emphasis placed on:

- capacity and 'gifts' of the service user rather than deficiencies
- improving lifestyle and quality of life, not simply receiving services
- putting the individual at the centre of the process
- shifting power from professionals to users and their chosen 'significant others'
- 'inclusion' in the sense that no one is excluded on the basis of severity of disability and that family and community resources are mobilized as well as those of the state.

In essence, person-centred planning is about 'working with' people rather than 'doing unto', about ownership and sharing decision-making powers with those who rely on services, and about aiming for community inclusion (Snow, 1994; Sanderson et al., 1997; Mount and Lyle O'Brien, 2002; O'Brien, 2004).

Such aspirations resonate well with the social work values of respect, self-determination and choice. Their theoretical underpinnings, sometimes overlooked, are numerous and eclectic. Sanderson et al. (1997, p. 39) offer one helpful representation of person-centred planning's conceptual DNA, depicting it as the trunk of a robust palm tree with an extensive root system comprising 'normalization' and 'five accomplishments':

- the social model of disability
- 'good practice in social work assessment'
- individual planning
- individualized funding
- the inclusion movement.

The focus here will be on normalization and the social model of disability; we conclude with a comment on individualized funding and the management of personal welfare.

Normalization

Scandinavian writer Bengt Nirje (1982) formulated one well-recognized and supported definition of normalization:

> making available to all people with disabilities patterns of life and conditions of everyday living which are as close as possible to the regular circumstances and ways of life or society.

In other words, it involves a recognition and indeed an assertion of the rights of people with learning disabilities to have not only access to 'a good life', however defined, on an equal basis to non-disabled people, but to one that would also be valued by non-disabled people.

Seen through a retrospective lens of 30 years, this now seems uncontentious. However, in order to understand its extraordinary impact on service development and the accompanying, sometimes heated, debates (Brown and Smith, 1992; Jackson, 1994), it is important to appreciate its historical backdrop. Normalization evolved as an alternate worldview to the eugenics movement that was pre-eminent in the early part of the twentieth century. The eugenics movement gained notoriety for its assertion that people with learning disabilities (and other 'degenerates') were a menace to the gene pool, and for its association with the Holocaust (Race, 2007). Indeed, the technology of the Nazi concentration camps was perfected on people with disabilities. In the period immediately preceding Wolfensberger's initial important writings on normalization (Wolfensberger, 1972, 1999), the persisting influence of eugenic ideas was evident in segregated services, sterilization and contraception without consent, and ultimately in the scandals of ill-treatment documented in English and Welsh 'mental handicap' hospitals (Morris, 1967; Martin, 1984).

Wolfensberger's development of what is called the 'normalization' framework explicitly set out to counter such negative perceptions within mainstream society at all levels – the individual, family/neighbourhood and society. His key contribution was to take the idea applied in Scandinavia to modernize institutional care through more homely patterns of living, and to develop it into a coherent conceptual framework that also had relevance in community settings and across domains of practice. By marrying these practical innovations with sociological theories of deviance, Wolfensberger (1983) developed the concept of valued roles for people with learning difficulties and other marginalized groups, and argued their importance in 'offsetting' social devaluation – this became known as 'social role valorization'.

Embedded within theories of social deviance and devaluation, of stigma, and within an understanding of the dynamics of congregated and segregated institutions described by Goffman (1961), Wolfensberger proposed that reversing these vicious circles of experience and service delivery required a different kind of engagement between service providers and service users. This invited practitioners to consider what was a 'valued' life for themselves and how that matched the experience of people who use services; and by using what he termed the 'cultural analogue', he asked them to identify what kinds of services might not only remedy these experiences but also create more positive lifestyles.

The reframing of his original ideas as 'socially valued roles' and 'normative' lifestyles for people was, in part, a response to the unjustified, as he saw it, 'perversion' that he was advocating 'normalizing' people rather than services (1983). Reworked by John O'Brien (1987), the definitive, and today the most referenced, version of normalization is commonly known as the 'five accomplishments'. These 'accomplishments' derived from stakeholder discussions that identified their importance in underpinning quality of life, and in achieving inclusive lives for people with learning disabilities. It is argued that services should be judged on the following outcomes:

- sharing ordinary places – people should be in the community
- developing skills or competences to survive well
- making choices and being in control of the support provided
- being treated with respect and having a socially valued role
- participating in community activities.

In the UK, these ideas ultimately led to the independent living movement (King's Fund, 1988) and a radical overhaul of conventional service development, with a 'paradigm shift' in favour of community living, often referred to as 'supported living' (Kinsella, 1993).

However, the framework has not been without its critics. The language of normalization was open to misinterpretation as 'something done to people' rather than services. It was criticized from a feminist and cultural standpoint (Brown and Smith,

1992; Emerson and Hatton, 2005) and in particular from the service user/carer perspective. Whose ordinary life? Whose norms? These were questions that were often raised. Particularly contentious was the added value given to integrating people with learning difficulties/disabilities with non-disabled people at the expense of recognizing the importance of 'affiliation' and collective strength between people with disabilities. Nonetheless, these ideas continue to have a profound impact on the thinking of professionals across disciplines. It is not difficult to see how these dimensions of 'accomplishment' informed the emergence of person-centred approaches and the policy and practice of personalization.

That said, it is the importance of affiliation and the collective voice of service users themselves that brings us to the next theory in which personalization is rooted, namely the social model of disability.

Social model of disability

The social model of disability was developed during the 1980s by activists with physical disabilities belonging to the 'disability movement' to counteract what they termed the 'personal tragedy' (and medicalized) model of disability. It distinguishes between 'impairments' that are found in individuals and the 'disability' that arises from the barriers within society, such as inaccessible buildings and prejudicial attitudes, which limit the participation and achievements of people with disabilities. In drawing attention to the process whereby individual identity becomes subsumed within a medical label, the theory challenges services to see people with disabilities as people first with varying needs for support at varying times, and as citizens with rights and expectations to participate on an equal basis with fellow citizens. Put simply, the social model of disability locates the 'problem' in the interaction with the person's social and physical world, rather than within the person themselves. The impact of the movement is reflected in legislative successes such as the Disability Discrimination Act 2005 and in service innovation such as independent and supported living.

In traditional models of professional assessment, it is argued, individuals are seen as passive recipients of expert treatment, to be 'cured', 'fixed' or 'rehabilitated' in some way as measured against 'normality'. Proponents of the social model of disability argue that this is a form of social oppression that ignores the economic, environmental and cultural barriers faced by people with disabilities. The dependence of service users and their lack of control over life choices has been the major focus of this writing, which found practical expression in the independent living movement that provided support to people in their own homes rather than allocating them to services, usually congregated ones, provided by professionals.

The social model of disability has not been without its critics, who draw attention to the absence of consideration within the model of the 'lived experience' of individuals, such as being in constant pain. Nonetheless, it has been an effective movement in politicizing and increasing the confidence of people with disabilities to have their voice not only heard but acted on. Among its political achievements, it can count the

Theory

establishment of the independent living fund, which was the precursor of direct payments and individual budgets that offer individuals greater control over their service support through the provision of money (an agreed budget from local authorities) instead of arranged services. Questions of choice, control and individual funding as developed by the disability movement have been fundamental in informing the evolution of personalization policy and person-centred practice.

Individualized funding and the management of personal welfare

The idea and, indeed, the provision of individualized funding in lieu of services, whether in the form of direct payments, individual budgets or personal budgets, evolved through the independent living movement and has constituted possibly the most empowering social policy and practice initiative in recent years. However, its implementation is not without problems.

Designed as an attempt to develop a new paradigm for welfare research, the 'management of personal welfare' model is based on a critique of assumptions about the homogeneity of vulnerable groups and coping responses, and the failure to take account of those who are vulnerable but not necessarily in contact with welfare services (Titterton, 1992; Williams et al., 1999). It is based on multidisciplinary perspectives, embracing a wide range of literature to strengthen its conceptual and empirical foundations. It posits that professionals can learn much from the informal coping repertoires, resources and strategies of vulnerable persons, such as persons with disabilities. Personal narratives about how adverse risks and threats to welfare are perceived and how these are managed and dealt with form an important resource for welfare researchers and practitioners. They can use these to achieve a much better understanding of the need for the fashioning of more individual and personally tailored forms of support, attuned to the strengths, assets and coping strategies of the person. This supplies a powerful theoretical and empirical basis for the development of personalization strategies in health and social care settings

Consumption and co-production theories

There has been a distinctive shift throughout the public sector towards treating the recipients of public goods and services as consumers or even customers. This was seen, in part at least, as an effort to shift power towards the recipients; however, various writers have questioned the consumerization of service users, and argued instead for notions of the latter as producers or co-producers of welfare. This point is picked up below.

Consumption

There has been a fruitful strand of theory about the role of 'consumption' in modern capitalist societies. Here it is contended that the consumption of public goods and services, such as welfare, education and housing, has become an increasingly important component of capitalist and corporatist societies, and the concentration on production by theorists has failed to capture this new phenomenon (Castells, 1977). This is particularly so in the case of understanding the development of urban public services and urban forms of living. The growth of urban social movements, prepared to push and shove for a change in services, has also become a central aspect of modern society (Pickvance, 1976; Castells, 1978; Dunleavy, 1980; see also Thompson, 2002 and Anyon, 2005 on social movements, social justice and welfare).

There has been much commentary on the construction of 'disability' in Western societies and the rise of a 'disability movement' pushing for more rights and more responsive services from the state (Oliver, 1989; Barnes and Mercer, 2010). This consumption-based approach provides a rich vein of theory to draw on – especially to gain a critical purchase on issues such as the role of the state and public services in the era of advanced capitalism. In addition, at the present time, where there has been another crisis of international capitalism, with excessive consumption and credit (O'Toole, 2009), another layer of critical appraisal can be added.

In social welfare theory and in accounts of the development of the modern welfare state, the issue of consumption has been sidestepped in favour of the question of markets and the potential of the latter for bringing about the transformation of public services. On the political right, the enthusiasm for the development of market relations is not unexpected. Perhaps the most articulate advocacy of this approach from a more central, social democratic viewpoint can be found in the writings of Julian Le Grand (Bartlett and Le Grand, 1993). More ambiguous interventions in this fraught area have been made by Taylor-Gooby et al. (2004). Yet others remain much more hostile to any notion of the 'marketization' of public goods and services, concerned by what they see as the constant threat of the privatization of the welfare state (see, for example, Wilding, 1986).

In their wide-ranging survey of trends in social services across the UK, Titterton et al. (2010) noted that the promise of welfare pluralism has never quite been fulfilled. Welfare pluralism theory was intended as a critique of state welfare and a recognition of the role of independent sector players (Beresford and Croft, 1983). However, the great mixed economy of welfare trumpeted by the Griffiths Report (1988) had difficulties from the outset and has not been realized. Those purchasing care, either as individuals or local authorities, do not behave as consumers in other types of market, lacking complete information and/or being closely interconnected with provision in a way that limits the motivation to spend rationally. There have been some experimental efforts, as well as attempts to introduce 'quasi-markets' into some areas of social policy, particularly in England (Bartlett and Le Grand, 1993).

Reliance on informal care remains highly significant; families remain the biggest provider of care within the UK, followed some way behind by the state, and then the independent sector. The HALE survey found that, even though the UK is a unified entity, there is diversity within it, and, in some intriguing instances, some significant

Theory

differences in policy and practice within the UK itself (Titterton et al., 2010). There are divergences and there are commonalities in the welfare mix throughout the four countries of the UK. The upshot in terms of personalization is that implicit assumptions about a ready marketplace for negotiating and purchasing services are far from justified. Criticisms have also been made about assumptions of a readily available supply of carers or personal assistants for purchase by such market-based means as direct payments (Scourfield, 2005).

If personalization means anything, it must mean more than simply purchasing and arranging services. This brings us to a consideration of co-production theory.

Co-production

'Co-production' has been defined as a new term, used in the context of personalization, that recognizes people who use social care and support as having assets and expertise to bring to the table (Beresford, 2010b). This means more power and resources being shared on the front line, so that people who use services and carers are empowered to co-produce their own solutions alongside social workers and other social care practitioners. Hunter and Ritchie (2007, p. 12) have offered an elaboration that pitches co-production as:

> an approach to service design and delivery which is informed by a distinctive world-view and which demands particular skills and methods to make it work. It is one way to tackle some of the deep-rooted malaise in contemporary society.

Taking a step back, however, it is not unusual to see a cross-reference to co-production in accounts of partnership and collaboration that set out the increasing complexity of service delivery at a time of emphasis on citizenship, efficiency and effectiveness. These two associated ideas are discussed first.

'Partnership' is probably the most familiar of these terms. Historically, the term referred to shared activity between the voluntary and statutory sectors (Marsh and Fisher, 1992), but has evolved more recently into a focus on multi-agency and multidisciplinary activity (Øvretveit, 1993; Hunter and Wistow, 1997) and, most recently, into the involvement of users of services and carers. This aspiration towards user participation and partnership has become so pervasive as to be reasonably described as a service development mantra. Close examination, however, reveals a continuum of interpretations of the term from consultation, to representation, to having a vote at the table. These discussions occur and relate equally to decisions about individual care as they do to strategic and developmental planning. As social work students know well, user involvement in course planning and teaching is now a requirement for professional accreditation of training courses (Scottish Social Services Council, 2003). The landing point on this continuum of partnership is usually mediated by considerations of control and power, and how much or how little effective say users have in the decisions made. Arnstein's ladder of participation offers a well-known conceptualization of this process, although some recent critics have suggested that the model is too static to accommodate the nuances of power and knowledge between professionals and services users (Tritter and McCallum, 2006).

'Collaboration' made a later appearance in the literature, and while it is suggested that the terms are used interchangeably, some distinctions have been elaborated. Essentially, these boil down to partnership, with its 'working together' strapline tending towards formal, agency and professionally driven agendas, whereas collaboration is the active process and outcome of these organizational arrangements. One elaboration of the idea, particularly significant for the consideration of co-production, was developed by Huxham (1996), who proposed that the purpose or point of collaboration was to achieve what she called 'collaborative advantage'. In other words, agencies that worked in true partnership with each other could expect to achieve outcomes or solutions they could not achieve separately. It is not hard to see that the needs or requirements for support of an older person with dementia and their carer cannot easily be met by one agency. That 'collaborative advantage' or 'synergy', as it is sometimes called, could produce an enhanced or value-added solution to the challenges of, for example, dementia and caring was an important conceptual development. We argue that while co-production relates to partnership and collaboration, it is not simply another subset of the lexicon of partnership.

We understand co-production to be a particular form of partnership between professionals and service users, in which the 'problem owners' have a greater role in both defining and developing the solutions. The idea behind co-production is that neither the government, public services, nor charities, however seamless the operation, can 'deliver' welfare services: families, individuals and communities have to be co-producers of welfare alongside professionals, and not merely recipients. This is where the significance of collaborative advantage to co-production lies – in its application to the idea of the user as 'expert' in their own problem and with a contribution to make to problem-solving that may involve arranged services or not. This requires a different way of thinking from

> traditional public provision models … in which the professionals are powerful experts and the service users are grateful recipients, and from the consumerist model where the state is the funder and market-maker, the provider agencies are competing suppliers and the service user is a free and informed shopper. (Hunter and Ritchie, 2007, p. 15)

This is a dynamic process that resonates with Leadbeater and Lownsbrough's (2005) concept of 'deep personalization', in which service users become co-designers and co-producers of services rather than consumers of standardized services. While service users may choose to use arranged state-sponsored services, it is likely that community and family resources may be 'contracted', especially if the service user has an individual budget, or direct payment, to use to meet their needs in lieu of an arranged service.

At the core of both these concepts is a dialogue between stakeholders and a transfer of power that is recognized and respected by professionals. It is critical to bear this in mind

Theory

> **Making connexions**
>
> Two separate ideas are introduced by this chapter:
>
> 1. The idea of the service user as a consumer.
> 2. The idea of the service user as a co-producer, 'with assets and expertise to bring to the table'.
>
> Which idea do you think is closer to the reality of practice?

when consulting a literature that contains diverse strands with different consequences. For example, the public management literature contains discussions that conceptualize co-production as a 'missing piece of the puzzle for reforming democracy and the welfare state' (Pestoff, 2006, p. 205). Greater involvement in local initiatives and proposals for the creation of a 'national service' for providing welfare services are reported. The argument goes beyond that of promoting the renewal of local democracy to a strategy for responding to citizens' needs for services that the state can no longer meet (Pestoff, 2006). Some of these discussions resonate with current ideas of the Big Society but derive from a different philosophical base.

The concept of co-production could make a significant contribution to the development of personalization. However, there is a risk of personalization being colonized by these public management ideas in a way that dilutes the core concept of transfer of power and control for making decisions that affect individuals' own lives. It is vital that practitioners remain alert to the possibility of an 'unholy' alliance between ideology, technology and austerity that neutralizes the impact of these ideas.

Risk and resilience theories

In many ways, the strand we end with, namely theories associated with risk and resilience, may seem an unusual angle from which to view personalization, as often 'risk' can seem to be the uninvited spectre at the feast. Discussions of personalization are often enthusiastic and tend to minimize issues to do with risk, which, when it does feature, appears as something of an afterthought. Yet it should be at the heart of these discussions, as the assessment and management of risk by professionals and service users take on new dimensions when personal budgets and supports are considered.

It is helpful to consider two strands here, risk literature and resilience literature. Sometimes the two concepts are brought together and, at times, not very satisfactorily, but there are two distinctive types of literature.

Risk theory has come a long way, particularly in the past two decades. The most influential approach has been that fashioned by Ulrich Beck (1992) with his notion of the risk society, which has helped shape much of the theoretical discussion about risk in modern societies or 'late modernism' (Giddens, 1998; Adam et al., 2000). Overviews of the risk literature in relation to health and social care, and the complex issues raised, can now be found (Alaszewski et al., 1998; Titterton, 2005; Manthorpe, 2007; Alaszewski, 2009; Clarke, 2009). A rigorous critique of negative definitions and understandings of risk has been forged (Titterton, 2005), while the complex dilemmas that welfare professionals face in their decision-making have also been explored (Titterton and Hunter, 2011).

One of the most interesting strands to emerge from risk theory relates to the notion of positive risk-taking (Titterton, 2011). Positive risk-taking is an approach that promotes the taking of risks as a deliberate and planned strategy designed to enhance health, welfare and educational outcomes. This approach encourages a focus on capacity-building, in terms of skills, knowledge and understanding, of service users, informal carers and professionals alike. It is an approach that has enormous potential for developing strategies for personalization where individuals can be their own risk managers.

Resilience theory has not developed in the same manner and has nothing similar to the risk society thesis. It has largely been the reserve of clinical psychopathology, but has gradually been breaking out into other fields. Much valuable insight can be forged from studies of, and deliberations on, how children and young people in difficult and challenging circumstances have overcome their disadvantages and proved resilient in adverse contexts (Rutter, 1987; Luthar and Zigler, 1991; Wolff, 1995; Luthar, 2003). At long last, an effort is being made to link the two theoretical approaches of risk and resilience: explicit bridges should be made between the two, for example in looking at the potential of boosting and building on the resilience of adults and older people for dealing with ill health and life stresses.

In respect of personalization, resilience theory has much to offer, particularly for those looking for directions about the importance of working with the strengths of individuals and groups. Notions of supporting social capital and social networks, other key ideas for personalization, are also relevant here. In risk theory, the notion of positive risk-taking should form a vital component of the values and conceptual basis of personalization.

Conclusion

In our examination of the major theoretical approaches that have influenced and shaped the emergence of personalization, we have critically discussed the three main strands of person-centred and participatory approaches, theories to do with citizens as consumers and producers of welfare, and theories relating to aspects of risk and resilience. We have presented a range of rich theoretical resources for welfare researchers and practitioners in supporting the development of personalization strategies. To build a more coherent theoretical basis for the latter, it has been suggested that person-centred planning, management of personal welfare, positive risk-taking and resilience theories hold out the greatest promise.

In order to bolster the building of theories and concepts, it is evident that a more self-aware and reflexive examination is required. Greater clarity and awareness of the roots of these building blocks, such as resilience theory, will provide directions for researchers and practitioners about how the potential of personalization can be developed.

Further reading

■ Barnes, C. and Mercer, G. (2010) *Exploring Disability.* Cambridge: Polity.

Explores key issues in disability studies, including the politicization of disability and its representation in the media and in culture.

■ Kemshall, H. and Wilkinson, B. (eds) (2011) *Good Practice in Assessing Risk: Current Knowledge, Issues and Approaches.* London: Jessica Kingsley.

Third in a series of volumes on risk in social care settings, it provides a topical and lively overview of the current state of thinking on this challenging topic.

■ Wolfensberger, W. (1975) *The Origin and Nature of our Institutional Models.* New York: Center on Human Policy, Syracuse University.

In this seminal text, Wolfensberger explores how service design and delivery are moulded by the images, historical and contemporary, that society holds of the individuals who use and rely on these services. Much of the professional thinking that underpins contemporary ideas, such as inclusion and personalization, was built on Wolfensberger's analysis.

References

Adam, B., Beck, U. and van Loon, J. (2000) *The Risk Society and Beyond: Critical Issues for Social Theory.* London: Sage.

Alaszewski, A. (2009) 'The future of risk in social science theory and research', *Health, Risk and Society,* **11**(6): 487–92.

Alaszewski, A., Harrison, L. and Manthorpe, J. (1998) *Risk, Health and Welfare.* Buckingham: Open University Press.

Anyon, J. (2005) *Radical Possibilities: Public Policy, Urban Education and a New Social Movement.* New York: Taylor & Francis.

Barnes, C. and Mercer, G. (2010) *Exploring Disability.* Cambridge: Polity.

Bartlett, W. and Le Grand, J. (1993) 'The theory of quasi-markets', in J. Le Grand and W. Bartlett (eds) *Quasi-markets and Social Policy.* Basingstoke: Macmillan – now Palgrave Macmillan.

Beck, U. (1992) *Risk Society: Towards a New Modernity.* London: Sage.

Beresford, P. (2010a) 'Personalization, brokerage and service users: time to take stock', *Journal of Care Services Management,* **4**(1): 24–31.

Beresford, P. (2010b) *Personalization in Brief: Implications for Social Workers in Adults' Services.* London: SCIE.

Beresford, P. and Croft, S. (1983) 'Welfare pluralism: the new face of Fabianism', *Critical Social Policy,* **3**(9): 19–39.

Brown, H. and Smith, H. (1992) *Normalisation: A Reader for the Nineties.* London: Routledge.

Castells, M. (1977) *The Urban Question.* London: Edward Arnold.

Castells, M. (1978) *City, Class and Power.* London: Macmillan.

Clarke, C.L. (2009) 'Risk and long-term conditions: the contradictions of self in society', *Health, Risk and Society,* **4**(11): 297–302.

DH (Department of Health) (2001) *Valuing People: A New Strategy for Learning Disability for the 21st Century.* London: TSO.

DH (2007) *Putting People First.* London: DH.

Duffy, S. (2010) 'The future of personalization', *Journal of Care Services Management,* **4**(3): 202–16.

Dunleavy, P. (1980) *Urban Political Analysis.* London: Macmillan.

Emerson, E. and Hatton, C. (2005) 'Deinstitutionalisation', *Tizard Learning Disability Review,* **10**(1): 36–40.

Giddens, A. (1998) 'Risk society: the context of British politics', in J. Franklin (ed.) *The Politics of Risk Society.* Cambridge: Polity.

Goffman, E. (1961) *Asylums: Essays on the Social Situation of Mental Patients and Other Inmates.* New York: Doubleday.

Griffiths, Sir R. (1998) *Community Care: Agenda for Action.* London: HMSO.

Hunter, S. and Ritchie, P. (eds) (2007) *Co-production and Personalization in Social Care.* London: Jessica Kingsley.

Hunter, D.J and Wistow, G. (1997) *Community Care in Britain: Variations on a Theme.* London: King's Fund.

Huxham, C. (ed.) (1996) *Creating Collaborative Advantage.* London: Sage.

Jackson, R. (1994) 'Normalisation principle: Back to basics?', *British Journal of Developmental Disabilities,* **40**(9): 175–9.

Jenkins, L. and Hay, M. (2010) 'Journeying towards personalization: from pilot to implementation: the learning and experiences of introducing self-directed support in Cambridgeshire', *Journal of Care Services Management,* **4**(3): 236–49.

Kemshall, H. (2002) *Risk, Social Policy and Welfare.* Buckingham: Open University Press.

King's Fund Centre (1988) *Ties and Connections: An Ordinary Community Life for People with Learning Difficulties.* London: KFC.

Kinsella, P. (1993) *Supported Living: A New Paradigm.* Manchester: National Development Team.

Leadbeater, C. and Lownsbrough, H. (2005) *Personalisation and Participation: The Future of Social Care in Scotland.* London: Demos.

Luthar, S.S. (ed.) (2003) *Risk and Vulnerability: Adaptations in Changing Times.* Cambridge: Cambridge University Press.

Luthar, S.S. and Zigler, E. (1991) 'Vulnerability and competence: a review of research on resilience in childhood', *American Journal of Orthopsychiatry,* **61**(1): 6–22.

Manthorpe, J. (2007) 'Managing risk in social care in the United Kingdom', *Health, Risk & Society,* **9**(3): 237–9.

Manthorpe, J., Stevens, M., Rapaport, J. et al. (2009) 'Safeguarding and system change: early perceptions of the implications for adult protection services of the English individual budgets pilots – a qualitative study', *British Journal of Social Work,* **39**(8): 1465–80.

Theory

Marsh, P. and Fisher, M. (1992) *Good Intentions: Developing Partnerships in Social Services*. York: Joseph Rowntree Foundation.

Martin, J. (1984) *Hospitals in Trouble?* London: Routledge.

Morris, P. (1967) *Put Away: A Sociological Study of Institutions for the Mentally Retarded*. London: Routledge & Kegan Paul.

Mount, B. and Lyle O'Brien, C. (2002) *Building New Worlds*. Amenia, NY: Capacity Works.

Nirje, B. (1982) 'The Basis and Logic of the Normalization Principle', paper presented at the Sixth International Congress of IASSMD, Toronto.

O'Brien, J. (1987) *Frameworks for Accomplishment*. Litonia, GA: Responsive Associates.

O'Brien, J. (2004) 'If person-centre planning did not exist, *Valuing People* would require its invention', *Journal of Applied Research in Intellectual Disabilities,* 17, 11–18.

Oliver, M. (1989) 'Disability and dependency: a creation of industrial societies', in L. Barton (ed.) *Disability and Dependency*. Lewes: Falmer.

O'Toole, F. (2009) *Ship of Fools: How Stupidity and Corruption Sank the Celtic Tiger*. London: Faber and Faber.

Øvretveit, J. (1993) *Coordinating Community Care: Multidisciplinary Teams and Care Management*. Buckingham: Open University Press.

Pestoff, V. (2006) 'Citizens and co-production of welfare services', *Public Management Review,* **8**(40): 503–19.

Pickvance, C. (1976) 'On the study of social movements', in C. Pickvance (ed.) *Urban Sociology: Critical Essays*. London: Tavistock.

Race, D. (2007) *Intellectual Disability: Social Approaches*. Maidenhead: Open University Press.

Rutter, M. (1987) 'Psychosocial resilience and protective mechanisms', *American Journal of Orthopsychiatry,* **57**(3): 316–31.

Sanderson, H., Kennedy, J., Ritchie, P. and Goodwin, G. (1997) *People, Plans and Possibilities*. Edinburgh: Scottish Human Services Trust.

Sang, B. (2009) 'Personalization: Consumer power or social co-production?', *Journal of Integrated Care,* **17**(4): 31–8.

Scottish Executive (2000) *'The Same As You?' A Review of Services for People with Learning Disabilities*. Edinburgh: Scottish Executive,

Scottish Government (2009) *Personalization: A Shared Understanding. Commissioning for Personalization*. Edinburgh: Scottish Government.

Scottish Government (2010) *Proposals for a Self-Directed Support (Scotland) Bill: Consultation*. Edinburgh: Scottish Government.

Scottish Social Services Council (2003) *The Framework for Social Work Education in Scotland*. Dundee: Scottish Social Services Council.

Scourfield, P. (2005) 'Implementing the Community Care (Direct Payments) Act: Will the supply of personal assistants meet the demand and at what price?', *Journal of Social Policy*, 34, 469–88.

Snow, J. (1994) *What's Really Worth Doing and How To Do It: A Book For People Who Love Someone Labeled Disabled (Possibly Yourself)*. Toronto: Inclusion Press.

Taylor-Gooby, P. (2006) 'Social and public policy: reflexive individualization and regulatory governance', in P. Taylor-Gooby and J.O. Zinn (eds) *Risk in Social Science*. Oxford: Oxford University Press.

Taylor-Gooby, P., Larsen, T. and Kananen, J. (2004) 'Market means and welfare ends: the UK welfare state experiment', *Journal of Social Policy*, 33, 573–92.

Thompson, N. (2002) 'Social movements, social justice and social work', *British Journal of Social Work,* **36**(6): 711–22.

Titmuss, R. (1960) *The Irresponsible Society*, Fabian Tracts 323. London: LSE online archive.

Titterton, M. (1992) 'Managing threats to welfare: the search for a new paradigm of welfare', *Journal of Social Policy*, **21**(1): 1–23.

Titterton, M. (2005) *Risk and Risk Taking in Health and Social Welfare*. London: Jessica Kingsley.

Titterton, M. (2011) 'Positive risk taking with people at risk of harm', in H. Kemshall and B. Wilkinson (eds) *Good Practice in Assessing Risk; Current Knowledge, Issues and Approaches*. London, Jessica Kingsley.

Titterton, M. and Hunter, S. (2011) 'Risk, professional judgement and the law: antimony and antagonism in an age of uncertainty', in J. Gordon and R. Davies (eds) *Social Work and the Law in Scotland* (2nd edn). Basingstoke: Palgrave Macmillan/Open University.

Titterton, M., Pelling-Deeves, S. and Nolan, P. (2010) *Social Services and Welfare Institutions in the United Kingdom: Report for the Polish Government Ministry of Labour and Social Policy*. Edinburgh/Warsaw: HALE & WZROS.

Tritter, J. and McCallum, A. (2006) 'The snakes and ladders of user involvement: moving beyond Arnstein', *Health Policy,* 76, 156–68.

Tyne, A. and Williams, P. (1988) *Normalisation: A Foundation for Effective Services*. London: Campaign for Mentally Handicapped People.

Wilding, P. (ed.) (1986) *In Defence of the Welfare State*. Manchester: Manchester University Press.

Williams, F., Popay, J. and Oakley, A. (eds) (1999) *Welfare Research: A Critical Review*. London: UCL Press.

Wolfensberger, W. (1972) *The Principle of Normalisation in Human Services*. Toronto: National Institute on Mental Retardation.

Wolfensberger, W. (1983) 'Social role valorization: a proposed new term for the principle of normalisation', *Mental Retardation*, 21, 234–9.

Wolfensberger, W. (1999) 'The origin and nature of our institutional models', in R. Kugel and W. Wolfensberger (eds) *Changing Patterns in Services for the Mentally Retarded*. Washington, DC: President's Committee on Mental Retardation.

Wolff, S. (1995) 'The concept of resilience', *Australian and New Zealand Journal of Psychiatry,* 29, 565–74.

Wood, C. (2010) *Personal Best*. London: Demos.

Theory

4
Personalization: what the research tells us

GILLIAN MACINTYRE

This chapter will identify the key messages emerging from research with respect to the personalization agenda within social work and health across the UK.

According to Carr (2008, p. 3), personalization is about

> starting with the individual as a person with strengths and preferences who may have a network of support and resources, which can include family and friends ... Personalization reinforces the idea the individual is best placed to know what they need and how those needs can be best met. It means that people can be responsible for themselves and can make their own decisions about what they require, but that they should also have information and support to enable them to do so.

On the other hand, Ferguson (2007) has argued that personalization involves the tacit acceptance of the marketization of social work and involves the deprofessionalization of the social work role.

Clearly, personalization has its starting point in two very different camps. On the one hand, it can be viewed as promoting individual choice and control via the provision of individually tailored services that aim to achieve goals that have been identified by individuals. On the other hand, it can be viewed as being primarily about cutting costs and reducing the responsibility of the state towards its citizens.

The language used adds another layer of complexity to the issue, with terms such as 'direct payments', 'self-directed support' and 'individual budgets' being used, often interchangeably. Mackay and MacIntyre (2011) have suggested that if personalization is viewed as a broad concept, then self-directed support (the terminology primarily used in Scotland) involves an individual or personal budget with some form of self-assessment of need. Direct payments are one way of exercising such choice and control, but should be viewed as part of a broader system of self-directed support, in which an individual might also take all or part of the identified resource and place it with a third party to exercise on their behalf. Or they might simply be aware of it as a 'virtual' budget within traditional services.

The parameters of this research review incorporate the terms 'personalization', 'self-directed support' and 'individual or personal budgets'. The studies included have been conducted within the UK since 2000 – in recognition of the infancy of the personalization agenda. Studies focusing on direct payments only, published prior to 2000, have been excluded. This acknowledges the rapid speed with which developments relating to personalization have occurred.

Evaluation of the individual budget pilot scheme in England

Across the UK, a number of pieces of research have been commissioned in order to evaluate the effectiveness of personalization while identifying barriers to implementation. In England in 2005, the Department of Health piloted an individual budget scheme across 13 pilot sites. All sites were expected to offer individual budgets between April 2006 and December 2007. The pilot had a number of features that differed from direct payments. These included a greater role for self-assessment, greater opportunities for service users to determine their own outcomes, and greater opportunities to determine how the outcomes should be achieved. Individual budgets brought together funding from a range of funding streams and, importantly, individuals should know how much money they were to receive and how much services cost. The Department of Health commissioned an evaluation of the individual budget scheme in 2005, the findings of which were reported by Glendinning et al. in 2008.

The evaluation adopted a multi-method approach drawing on a range of qualitative and quantitative methods. A randomized controlled trial method was adopted in 12 of the 13 pilot sites in order to provide a comparison group. This enabled the researchers to more robustly determine the implications of receiving an individual budget or not. In addition, in-depth qualitative work was carried out with a range of service users around three months after receiving a personal budget. The research also identified process issues for the local authorities involved in implementing the pilot.

Service user perspectives

The evaluation identified a number of successes in relation to service users' experiences. Individual budgets were thought to have a positive impact on the lives of service users. This was particularly true where imaginative and flexible care plans had been put in place. People with mental health problems were found to benefit most from the flexibility offered by having an individual budget. This was not universal across user groups, however, with older people being less likely to manage their own budget or to use it to pursue leisure activities. The researchers suggest that this might be a result of the relatively low level of spend on older people. In addition, older

Research

people were found to experience a reduced quality of life: it appears that the introduction of an individual budget had a negative impact on their wellbeing, with carers
reporting higher levels of anxiety among older people. In contrast, people with learning disabilities had the highest resource expenditure, although they were more likely
to spend this on traditional services. Those with physical disabilities exercised most
control over their budget. They were also more likely to access funding from alternative sources such as the independent living fund. Despite the positive outcomes
reported by those with mental health problems, they remained the smaller user group
of individual budgets. Overall, it would appear that the majority of those who participated in the pilot continued to purchase traditional services.

For a more in-depth appreciation of the experiences of service users and carers,
Rabiee et al. (2009) interviewed fourteen service users from 6 of the 13 pilot sites.
Participants were asked about their previous support arrangements, their experiences
of self-assessment, and the potential impact of receiving an individual budget. The
research identified a number of positive features around the use of individual budgets.
Participants found the self-assessment process to be user-friendly and valued the flexibility provided by individual budgets, in terms of what the money could be spent
on and how this flexibility could contribute to the quality of their life (Rabiee et al.,
2009). Participants particularly valued being able to choose their own carers, although
a range of concerns were identified around the additional burdens and strains that
this might place on individuals and their family members. This was particularly true
where the overall value of the individual budget was likely to be less than the cost of
a traditional support package:

> Where the disabled person had high support needs and the level of the IB [indi-
> vidual budget] was lower than the value of their previous support arrangements,
> there were concerns that this would place additional burdens on family members
> because of the implicit expectation that more unpaid, informal care would be
> required. (Rabiee et al., 2009, p. 928)

Service users emphasized the importance of ongoing support as crucial to the
success of individual budgets. Indeed, it is understandable that freedom to make
decisions might well be a daunting task after having little choice or control over services received for many years. Those with good support networks were best placed to
benefit from individual budgets. However, all service users and carers mentioned
terms such as 'mentoring' and 'advocacy'. Such support was considered essential in
order to alleviate the potential of unwanted administrative burdens and responsibilities (Rabiee et al., 2009).

Carer perspectives

Glendinning et al. (2009) undertook further research to build on the national evaluation, which focused on the impact of individual budgets on the family and carers
of individual budget recipients. The research involved carrying out structured and

semi-structured interviews with the carers of people within the individual budget evaluation who had been allocated an individual budget and with carers from the control group. The research also involved telephone interviews with council officers with responsibility for carers' services and support, as well as a reanalysis of data from the main evaluation.

The study found that individual budgets could impact positively on carers' quality of life, social care outcomes (see Glendinning et al., 2009) and psychological outcomes. Interestingly, two-thirds of the carers interviewed had changed their views of what they could achieve in their lives after their family member received the offer of an individual budget. A range of new options were perceived to be available. These included paying someone else to do tasks they had traditionally undertaken themselves. Yet despite this, carers whose relative received an individual budget undertook more caring tasks than those in the control group, in terms of involvement in assessment and helping the service user to plan how to use the budget and manage the financial aspects involved. In addition, they were unlikely to receive payment from the individual budget for undertaking these roles.

The research identified a significant variation in terms of carer satisfaction. This can probably be explained by the nature, level and scope of carers' involvement in the various processes associated with having an individual budget. Those who expressed less satisfaction were likely to have felt that their views and the views of the person they care for were taken less seriously in assessment and support planning. In addition, carer satisfaction was closely linked to service user satisfaction. Put simply, if the service user was happy, the carer was also likely to report high levels of satisfaction (Glendinning et al., 2009).

Staff perspectives

The individual budget pilot was felt to re-energize care managers, resulting in renewed engagement with the voluntary sector and greater flexibility among service providers (Glendinning et al., 2008). On the other hand, there were a number of reported difficulties around the attitudes of frontline staff regardless of which user group was being offered an individual budget. Manthorpe et al. (2009) explored the issue of training for frontline care managers and social workers with respect to individual budgets. The aim was to identify any possible changes in the role of professionals. Eighteen telephone interviews were conducted across the 13 pilot sites with training and development managers. The interviews suggest that the role of the social worker and care manager had changed as a result of the personalization agenda: it involved advocating or brokering service provision for service users and providing support when things did not go as planned, and protecting people from harm. This dilemma lies at the heart of the personalization agenda: promoting the right of adults to exercise choice and control, while protecting their right to remain as safe as possible (Manthorpe et al., 2009).

Such complex issues highlight the need for good quality, timely training that

Research

needs to be provided in-house and within professional education. Training will need to enable social workers to develop their existing skills while providing them with the confidence to challenge existing cultural resistance (Mackay and MacIntyre, 2011). Manthorpe et al. (2009) argue that initial training might help to determine whether the role of the social worker will be supportive or will tend more towards monitoring and scrutiny.

Glendinning et al. (2008, p. 156) drew attention to a number of questions about decision-making and supporting individuals to make choices:

> This is not simply a technical issue: political and ethical questions about the level of public support provided for different kinds of lifestyles, and what represents good quality of life for whom at different points in the life course.

The research identified an inherent tension between the task of meeting clearly assessed and identified needs and the philosophy of a personalized approach that focuses on individually defined outcomes.

A number of challenges relating to the difficulties of implementing individual budgets while maintaining traditional forms of service delivery were identified (Glendinning et al., 2008). Alongside this, a number of important process issues were noted. These related to difficulties in determining a model of resource allocation as well as integrating budgets from a range of different sources. There was limited evidence to suggest the use of non-social work funding streams during the pilot. Nor did the evaluation find evidence of cost savings, with individual budgets costing around the same as the traditional packages of care received by the comparison group. Indeed, within the pilot, there was evidence of increased costs with respect to care management time, although this was thought to be likely to decrease as confidence in the processes increased.

Self-directed support

In Scotland, parallel developments are ongoing under the banner of 'self-directed support'. Two major evaluations of progress have been undertaken. Homer and Gilder undertook a review of self-directed support that was published in 2008. The work involved interviews with 24 service users who were in receipt of self-directed support and their carers, and 14 telephone interviews with council officers from three local authorities who formed part of a self-directed support pilot.

Service user perspectives

The research found that, overall, service users were positive about the impact that self-directed support had made to the quality of their care and when they received it. Self-directed support was thought to offer more flexibility, particularly for those who wished to receive their care away from home. Service users reported greater choice, control and independence, but they also identified a number of challenges, which related primarily to the levels of bureaucracy involved in negotiating with funders and managing employees. The need for adequate support to enable service users and their families to manage these processes was identified as crucial. To this end, each of the three pilot authority areas had introduced support mechanisms to assist with the implementation of self-directed support. Two councils had developed in-house support services, while the other had employed a local service to provide support and monitoring.

At the time of the study, a number of areas of confusion continued to exist with respect to self-directed support. These related to eligibility criteria – only those whose needs were assessed as critical were eligible for the scheme – that left little scope for preventive or anticipatory work. An added layer of complexity related to the different rules governing eligibility for different funds. Service users also identified a lack of clarity with regard to how the level of their funding had been determined, and few were confident that they understood fully what the money could be spent on (Homer and Gilder, 2008).

A more recent study carried out by Manthorpe et al. was published in 2011. The review aimed to identify the range of barriers and facilitators to the implementation of self-directed support in Scotland. The study took the form of a literature review of published literature on self-directed support that was carried out in order to inform an evaluation of the three test sites. Within the literature, a number of barriers to the take-up and use of self-directed support were identified. These are broadly similar to those identified in Glendinning et al. (2008) and Manthorpe et al. (2009) with respect to the English experience of implementing individual budgets.

In terms of barriers for service users and carers, these related primarily to the administrative burden of self-directed support. Indeed, it seems likely that many service users do not want the responsibility of managing their own service. Employing one's own personal assistant or family member is not always straightforward and brings with it the responsibilities that come with being an employer, such as managing holidays or sick leave. Closely linked with this are issues around accountability and blame, and, in particular, the management of risk (Manthorpe et al., 2011). The review identified concerns that there are no mechanisms in place for registering or screening personal assistants. There is a lack of clarity around who is responsible for monitoring and safeguarding against risk. Similarly, in a review of the evidence base as it relates to risk and self-directed support, Carr (2010) highlights the tension between promoting choice and safeguarding from harm. She has highlighted a number of concerns:

- the possibility of increased risk to those already shown to be at risk of abuse or neglect
- the possibility that service users and carers may be reluctant to use self-directed support due to fear of potential risks
- organizational and professional risk aversion.

There is a lack of specific research focusing on how people who use self-

Research

directed support perceive and manage risk. Despite the lack of research evidence, it seems clear that risk enablement and safeguarding training for staff, service users and carers is crucial. Risk-averse cultures might result in frontline staff becoming overly concerned with fraud prevention when administering self-directed support (Carr, 2010). This results in less focus on positive risk-taking to the detriment of service users. To this end, social work skills are essential to promote risk enablement and detect and prevent abuse. This might also help to prevent decisions being taking based on generalized views of capacity or the likely risky behaviour of particular service user groups. In addition, the provision of information and advice for service users about a range of issues, including employment and support, should enable them to make informed choices, thus reducing the risk of harm (Carr, 2010).

In order to facilitate self-directed support, Manthorpe et al. (2011) highlighted the need for good quality, accessible information for service users and carers, alongside the provision of comprehensive support from professionals. In addition, the establishment of social networks would enable service users to share their ideas and experiences of using self-directed support. The literature review suggests that independent support from brokers or advocates can help where it is necessary to challenge the local authority.

Carer perspectives

Carers reported being reassured about the care that their family member was receiving and several spoke of an easing of the burden of care (Homer and Gilder, 2008). Manthorpe et al. (2011) identified some of the issues faced by the small number of carers who received payment under the new self-directed support arrangements for undertaking the caring role. This raised a number of concerns and ethical dilemmas:

> The use of family carers to compensate for a lack of services ... can institutionalize a system of low paid care and make family members dependent on the service user for whom they are caring. (Manthorpe et al., 2011, p. 29)

Staff perspectives

There was felt to be a lack of clarity about how self-directed support links to other parts of the welfare state and how it can be funded at the same time as traditional social care and health services. The literature reveals a lack of understanding generally about how funds are calculated and how various sources of funds are accessed (Manthorpe et al., 2011). In addition, at the time of the review, self-directed support was not sufficiently publicized. This might relate to preconceptions about which service users are an appropriate client group for self-directed support but might also be a result of staff concerns about their job and role. The literature identified concerns that self-directed support might be more expensive, rather than less costly, as a result of the reduction of block contracts (Manthorpe et al., 2011).

Manthorpe et al. (2011) identified a number of facilitators of good practice from a staff perspective. They highlighted the importance of training and skill development for staff to enable them to become better equipped to work within the new systems and explain them to others. There is a need for greater leadership in order to disseminate messages about good practice and knowledge and to encourage and support those who are starting up or who need help with addressing later problems.

Personalization for specific service user groups

Since the onset of the personalization agenda, there has been growing recognition of the particular support needs of certain service user groups in order to maximize the potential benefits of personalization. This is epitomized by In Control, a national charity whose philosophy recognizes that all groups should have the right to exercise control over their lives regardless of age, disability or illness. In 2003, In Control began working in six local authority areas in England, with the initial focus on people with learning disabilities. Since then, it has supported more than 400 organizations nationally to transform their services and deliver personalization. The first phase was evaluated in 2005 (Poll et al., 2006) and the second phase in 2007 (Hatton et al., 2008). The evaluation aimed to highlight the early experiences of people who received a personal budget. It sought to explore whether using self-directed support had made a difference to people's lives, what support they had to do this, and whether there were differences in terms of take-up across care groups and in the way money was spent. Interviews were carried out with 196 people who had been using self-directed support in 17 local authorities. For the purposes of the evaluation, a person was deemed to have had self-directed support if they (or their carer) knew:

- the amount of money available to them to meet their needs and the outcomes to be achieved with the money
- that they or their carer had been given control over the money, to the extent that they could spend it on things, in ways and at times that were right for them.

Variations in the numbers of people across local authorities and the fact that most participants had been using self-directed support suggested that implementation across the country was variable. However, those questioned suggested that the essential characteristics of self-directed support were present – feeling in control, understanding what self-directed support is for, and changing the way money is spent as a result (Hatton et al., 2008). Participants were also asked to make judgements as to whether particular aspects of their lives had got better, worse or had stayed the same since receiving self-directed support.

Research

Service user perspectives

The vast majority (97%) of respondents felt that they had control over how their individual budget was spent and felt that they understood what outcomes they were hoping to achieve. The majority reported some change in their support package (in either content or delivery) since receiving self-directed support. Almost half reported some improvement in their health or wellbeing. This was more likely to be the case if they had been using self-directed support for over a year and if they had family or friends to support them in planning their self-directed support (Hatton et al., 2008). It appears that having support from multiple sources was a major indicator of greater satisfaction. Benefits were not felt uniformly across all service user groups: older people were less likely to report improvements to their general health and wellbeing. In terms of quality of life, almost all respondents reported positive changes and there was no significant difference across different service user groups here (Hatton et al., 2008).

A majority of participants reported improvements in the choice and control they had over their lives, as well as improvements in their personal dignity and economic wellbeing since starting on self-directed support. Only a minority of people reported improvements in their feelings of safety and security at home since starting on self-directed support.

The evaluation suggests that self-directed support appears to offer a mechanism to increase social inclusion, with 64% of respondents reporting improvements in the extent to which they participated in community activities. It is important to note, however, that a small minority reported things getting worse since starting self-directed support (Hatton et al., 2008). This could perhaps be explained by a movement away from traditional services such as day centres, resulting in greater isolation. Older people were less likely to report improvements in community participation when compared with people with learning or physical disabilities.

Despite the inclusive nature of the In Control philosophy, there is some concern that those with the most complex or profound disabilities might miss out on the opportunities offered by an individual budget. In a review of learning disability services in England, Mansell (2010) suggests that this is particularly likely to be the case if packages do not result in cost savings for local authorities. He argues that there is a need for effective leadership to ensure that self-directed support is extended to all user groups, including those with multiple and profound disabilities. This will need to involve independent advocacy services, as not everyone will have family members who will be able to support them in planning and maintaining self-directed support. Relating to this are workforce issues. Providing personal assistance for people with multiple or profound disabilities is a demanding job that involves particular qualities and skills. Training will be required to upskill the workforce and this will need to be recognized when determining the value of self-directed support packages (Mansell, 2010).

People with mental health problems and, to a certain extent, older people have been underrepresented in the move towards personalized services. Newbronner et al.

(2011) undertook interviews with ten national organizations and five local authority case study sites were identified. Within each case study site, individual interviews and focus groups were conducted with service users in receipt of a personal budget and their carers. Interviews were carried out with council officers, frontline staff and local support provider organizations – 69 service users and carers, 40 practitioners and managers and 12 support provider organizations participated in the research. In common with the other studies reported on in this chapter, service users and carers identified the need for good quality, accessible information as crucial to the success of personal budgets. Importantly, it was identified that psychiatric nurses as well as social work staff need to have knowledge about the processes involved in accessing a personal budget (Newbronner et al., 2011).

> **Making connexions**
> Pivotal to the success of the personalization agenda is the high-quality training of frontline staff. What should this training consist of?

Older people and people with mental health problems generally felt that there was a lack of support with respect to the assessment process. It was felt that assumptions were made about what people could or could not do in relation to self-assessment, and there was little evidence of risk and safety issues being explicitly discussed with people. In addition, the ways in which resources were allocated appeared to be inequitable, with older people with higher level care needs being particularly disadvantaged (Newbronner et al., 2011). Those with mental health problems, on the other hand, reported being happy with the level of resources received. It appeared that if greater support had been available with respect to care planning and setting up services, more flexible and innovative packages could have been purchased. Indeed, there was some concern that many personal budget holders were being steered towards third party managed accounts or services commissioned by the local authority rather than being given the opportunity to manage their own budget (Newbronner et al., 2011). This illustrates the assumptions being made about particular service user groups' ability to manage the process, potentially resulting in less choice and control.

Discussion

The research studies discussed within this chapter have adopted a number of methods in order to evaluate the personalization agenda. These methods have ranged from literature reviews, interviews and focus groups with service users, carers and a range of professionals to randomized controlled trials. Perhaps reassuringly, the messages revealed by each of the studies are remarkably similar. It is clear that, for service users and carers, personalization offers a number of benefits. These relate primarily to a greater sense of choice and control alongside greater independence and an increase in perceived general health and wellbeing. In certain cases, personalization was also thought to offer the potential for greater social inclusion as well as the opportunity to reduce carer stress and burden.

Research

These benefits were not universally experienced and certain groups of service users and carers reported greater benefits than others. Those with physical disabilities reported the greatest take-up of self-directed support and the greatest satisfaction. They were most likely to have chosen the option of an individual budget (or direct payment) and were most likely to employ innovative support packages. They were closely followed by people with learning disabilities who have probably benefited from the initial focus on their needs as part of the In Control programme (Poll et al., 2006). Older people, those with mental health problems and those with multiple or profound needs have been less likely to take up a personalized service. Among those who do, older people in particular are likely to report lower levels of satisfaction. It appears that these groups have been subject to institutional discrimination in the form of negative assumptions about their desire, ability and capacity to take up a personalized service. These assumptions may have some basis in truth, as Glendinning et al. (2008) report, because service users are more interested in the outcomes they can achieve than in the process of getting there. In addition, the cumbersome levels of bureaucracy and new levels of responsibility placed upon individual service users and their families can be off-putting.

In order to offset these negative features, the research evidence highlights the need for adequate support at all stages of the process, from self-assessment, through care planning to service planning and maintenance. Local authorities have adopted a number of ways of doing this, often commissioning third sector providers to take on this role. They have a clear role in supporting service users and their families to commission innovative support packages and services, although this assumes that such services already exist. The research suggests that peer support through the development of social networks will also empower service users to more creatively use their budget.

The creative use of budgets will not necessarily result in cost-effectiveness, and within the research there was little evidence of cost savings (Glendinning et al., 2008; Manthorpe et al., 2009). Many of the studies were unable to provide this information for a number of reasons, but the best calculations available do not suggest significant savings to either health or social care budgets. There is concern that this will have implications for the roll-out of personalized services to other service user groups, particularly for those with higher level care needs (Mansell, 2010). There is concern that self-directed support will not be offered to those for whom it is not possible to identify significant savings. As it stands, resource allocation models appear to discriminate against some service user groups: older people with more complex needs appear to fare less well (Newbronner et al., 2011).

Despite these difficulties, the personalization agenda seems to be here to stay. Pivotal to its success is the high-quality training of frontline staff alongside strong leadership from those at policy and management level. The difficulties faced by staff in implementing the agenda have been well documented (Manthorpe et al., 2009) and staff have had to overcome the perceived threat to their role and to refocus their energies on building relationships and managing risk. It is here that perhaps the biggest tension and dilemma underpinning the concept of personalization lies. On the one hand, the philosophy centres on individual need and outcomes encouraging choice and independence, which suggests staff taking a light touch approach. Yet this leaves service users who are already potentially at risk of harm more exposed to risk than ever before. For staff, whose responsibility it is to safeguard and manage risk, this raises a number of difficulties. The research suggests that information-sharing and shared decision-making is perhaps the best way to overcome these difficulties. Carr (2010) suggests that risk enablement needs to be at the core of the self-directed support process, involving the concepts of person-centred planning, choice, control and autonomy.

Clearly, these are akin to social work values, all of which suggests that self-directed support and the social work role and task should go hand in hand. In these times of economic uncertainty, however, where it is incumbent upon local authorities to reduce budgets, the success of the personalization agenda, which, when done according to the principles of good practice identified in this chapter, shows little evidence of cost savings, remains to be seen.

Further reading

■ Ferguson, I. (2007) 'Increasing user choice or privatising risk? The antinomies of personalization', *British Journal of Social Work*, **37**(3): 387–403.

Accessible discussion of some of the main concerns arising from the personalization agenda.

■ Hunter, S. and Ritchie, P. (2007) *Co-production and Personalization in Social Care: Changing Relationships in the Provision of Social Care.* London: Jessica Kingsley.

Useful overview of key developments in relation to social work and social care. Particularly useful for newly qualified workers.

■ Mackay, D. and MacIntyre, G. (2011) 'Personalization and the role of the social worker', in R. Taylor, M. Hill and F. McNeill (eds) *Early Professional Development for Social Workers.* Birmingham: Venture Press.

Comprehensive overview of different forms of personalization in relation to adult services.

References

Carr, S. (2008) *Personalization: A Rough Guide*, SCIE Report 20. London: SCIE.

Carr, S. (2010) *Enabling Risk, Ensuring Safety: Self Directed Support and Personal Budgets.* London: SCIE.

Ferguson, I. (2007) 'Increasing user choice or privatizing risk? The antinomies of personalization', *British Journal of Social Work,* **37**(3): 387–403.

Glendinning, C., Challis, D., Fernandez, J. et al. (2008) *Evaluation of the Individual Budget Pilot Programme: Final Report.* York: SPRU.

Research

Glendinning, C., Arksey, H., Jones, K. et al. (2009) *The Individual Budgets Pilot Projects: Impact and Outcomes for Carers*, Working Paper 1902. York: SPRU.

Hatton, C., Waters, J., Duffy, S. et al. (2008) *A Report on In Control's Second Phase 2005–2007*. London: In Control Publications.

Homer, T. and Gilder, P. (2008) *A Review of Self Directed Support in Scotland*. Edinburgh: Scottish Government.

MacKay, D. and MacIntyre, G. (2011) 'Personalization and the role of the social worker', in R. Taylor, M. Hill and F. McNeill (eds) *Early Professional Development for Social Workers*. Birmingham: Venture Press.

Mansell, J. (2010) *Raising our Sights: Services for Adults with Profound and Multiple Disabilities*. London: DH.

Manthorpe, J., Jacobs, S., Rapaport, J. et al. (2009) 'Training for change: early days of individual budgets and the implications for social work and care management practice: a qualitative study of the views of trainers', *British Journal of Social Work*, **39**(7): 1291–305.

Manthorpe, J., Hindes, J., Martineau, S. et al. (2011) *Self Directed Support: A Review of Barriers and Facilitators*. Edinburgh: Scottish Government.

Newbronner, L., Chamberlain, R., Bosanquet, K. et al. (2011) *Keeping Personal Budgets Personal: Learning from the Experiences of Older People, People with Mental Health Problems and their Carers*. London: SCIE.

Poll, C., Duffy, S., Hatton, C. et al. (2006) *A Report on In Control's First Phase 2003–2005*. London: In Control Publications.

Rabiee, P., Moran, N. and Glendinning, C. (2009) 'Individual budgets: lessons from early users' experiences', *British Journal of Social Work*, **39**(5): 918–35.

5
Personalization in practice

Michael Bamber, Jenni Brooks, Shirley Cusack, Jane Edwards, Mary Gardner, Kate Gridley, Liz Howard, Niki Marshall, Liz Salmon and Judith Wood

There has been a venerable tradition in social work of 'starting where the client is' as a counterbalance to the temptation for professionals to superimpose their own preconceptions on the service user's situation; the personalization agenda is a logical and imaginative progression from that principle. It pays respect to the idea that every individual is an expert in their own life. Although the social worker bears responsibility for the appropriate use of public resources, the service user may often be the best judge of how those resources may most efficiently be employed.

There follow nine examples of how personalization has worked in practice. The range of possible applications is potentially limitless, and we would need to provide a hundred, or more, examples to get a full sense of how the agenda is impacting on the social worker's role. One thing, however, is clear: that role is certain to be affected by the evolutionary development of personalization in practice.

Some accounts of personalization in practice

Practice example 1 Mary

The solution to Mary's needs was found on her own doorstep

Mary was a 78-year-old lady, recently widowed and suffering from bipolar disorder and dementia. She had two sons: one who lived abroad and one who lived in Scotland. Because of her condition, Mary was not always comfortable with or trusting of people she didn't know. Consequently, finding the right sort of care and carer could have been problematic for her and her family.

The answer to Mary's care needs was found, literally, on her own doorstep. Her long-time next-door neighbour Kathy, a woman in her fifties who had recently given

Practice

77

up work due to her own health issues, became Mary's carer. The family's suggestion that Kathy should become her carer was greeted with delight by Mary herself but met some resistance from her social worker who was concerned about Kathy's health. However, an agreement was reached and Kathy and Mary embarked on their successful and mutually beneficial relationship.

Because of her close proximity, Kathy was able to visit Mary several times a day and pop in at lunchtime to prepare a snack, in addition to providing her with a freshly cooked hot meal each evening. Mary had someone who knew her likes and dislikes and who she knew well and trusted implicitly to look after her, and her life and her sense of wellbeing wasn't disturbed. Kathy was able, for example, to go with Mary to their local hairdressers where both women would get their hair done at the same time and come home via a teashop.

Mary's son in Scotland and his wife had known Kathy for many years and were confident not only in her ability to care for Mary but also knew that she cared about Mary – to them, a vital quality for Mary's carer. They phoned Kathy frequently to see how Mary was and to support her in her caring role.

Because Kathy was known to many of Mary's friends and family, it meant that she and they could liaise regarding their visits. If, for example, Kathy had a hospital appointment, she would arrange for one of Mary's friends or church members to visit while she was out. Kathy had a teenage son who had grown up living next door to Mary and who would sometimes bring her meals in. He would chat to her while she ate, offering a different type of conversation and a young person's perspective on the world.

The relationship continued for over three years and had many positive aspects to it for both women. For Kathy, it provided a sense of purpose, a part-time job she could cope with despite her illness, a formalization of what she was, on a lesser scale, already doing for Mary, and job satisfaction. Mary received the care she needed from someone she knew and trusted and could continue her life with very few changes. She and her family also felt secure knowing Kathy would respond rapidly in an emergency at any time of day or night. The relationship had a synergy that nobody had anticipated and only ended when Mary's health began to deteriorate and she went to live with her son in Scotland, where she died a year later.

Practice example 2   Maud

A fully rounded cost-effective package of care

Maud, aged 83, lives in a village near a market town. The social worker was asked to complete a reassessment of her needs as her daughter was concerned that she was socially isolated and needed a break from caring for her husband Stan. She was also dependent on him to assist her with her orientation as she had mild cognitive difficulties.

Maud had been provided with a standard care package. Agency carers visited three times a day to help her to wash and dress in the morning and evening and complete a weekly hygiene clean in her bathroom and kitchen. She was pleased with this service but her daughter Rachel, aged 52, felt this could be better organized and more could be done to assist her mother.

The social worker visited the family and spent time with Maud and Rachel. Stan did not engage with the assessment. They talked about Maud's need to have a break from caring for Stan, to experience her community and to give Stan a break from supporting her. The social worker completed the personal budget questionnaire to supplement the review. Maud was asked what was most important to her. She said that she had been adopted by 'good Christian people' who had died many years ago and it saddened her that she had been unable to tend to their grave. She also expressed a desire to feel part of her community. While she was unimpressed by the idea of going to a day centre, she said that she would much prefer to go to a local supermarket where she might see people she knew, enjoy a meal in the café and do a spot of shopping at the same time. Working together with Maud, the social worker completed a support plan that incorporated these ideas.

Permission was sought to action the plan. It was agreed that, by enabling her to access social and spiritual services, the social worker had achieved outcomes that had been inspired by this woman's identified needs. She was able to employ a local personal assistant (PA) through a direct payment, rather than use agency carers. She made regular social trips to the supermarket and quarterly visits to her parents' grave with her PA. As the nature of the delivery of services had changed, the cost of the complete package was actually less than the more restrictive package that she had previously had. At review, she was delighted at how her life had changed and the social worker was astonished to hear her previously resistant husband request a care package to help with his personal care. The assessment process was started immediately.

By considering all Maud's requests, the social worker felt able to offer a fully rounded cost-effective package of care that was individually tailored to achieve her desired outcomes. Maud was a much happier woman whose wishes and feelings had been fully recognized.

Practice example 3 ˙ Les

When the past impacts on the present

Les, aged 68, lives in a market town. He asked the department to increase his home care provision and enable him to attend a day centre because he said he felt socially isolated and at risk of depression. The social worker was asked to complete a reassessment of Les's needs in order that his request could be considered. The social worker was concerned that Les's computer record indicated that he was considered a 'risk to children', but this was not initially investigated further because it did not seem to relate directly to Les's request.

The social worker and Les discussed his current care package. He said he was happy with the morning support from his agency carer who, it was agreed, could also

Practice

provide him with evening care as he was no longer safe to prepare for bed. The social worker considered the possibility of assisting him with his social isolation. Les was a keen sports fan who followed his local stock car racing team. He had become friends with some of the drivers and crew, but was unable to travel to local meetings because of his poor health and his concern about how he might cope with potential race crashes. Les wondered if he might be able to use money to access a premium TV channel that would allow him to watch his friends at the race meeting in the comfort of his living room. The social worker suggested that he invite a friend round to enjoy the race. Les was awarded extra funds for this subscription; it was felt that it achieved the outcome of allowing him to access his community and prevent him from becoming socially isolated.

Then Les requested that he employ someone to take him away for a weekend using his personal budget. At this point, the social worker investigated his file and, following discussion with a manager, decided that Les would not be able to employ a PA as he had a conviction for a crime against a child. The social worker visited Les to explain the decision to him. He was unimpressed, saying that a lawyer had tricked him into a guilty plea to avoid prison. He talked of mounting a campaign to clear his name of crimes that had occurred 20 years previously. He was unhappy with the decision but accepted that he would not be able to access the support that he wanted. Alternatives were discussed, but Les was not interested in spending a short break in institutional care.

A few weeks later, the social worker received a call from a nursery worker. Les had visited the nursery to try to fill out an application for a parking badge. The caller suggested that the social worker had not done enough to help Les. Following advice, the police were informed of this inappropriate choice of assistance. Les then withdrew from social services, commissioning his own care privately.

The social worker reflected on what could have been done to improve the interaction and to avoid what was felt to be an unfortunate consequence. It seemed that entering into a more personalized approach with this man had forced the social worker to confront Les with his past. Had a more superficial approach been employed, it might simply have led to an extension of his care package without considering the bigger picture. However, Les was able to achieve his aims, privately employing a carer and enjoying his televised sport without statutory support. The social worker felt that he had fulfilled his professional responsibilities, acting to safeguard others, and offering Les adequate services to meet his needs – even though some were rejected.

Practice example 4   Claire

A good arrangement – now under threat

Claire is a 54-year-old mother of two. Until nine years ago, she worked as a nursery nurse and Sunday school teacher, and her husband John travelled widely for work. Then she had an episode of encephalitis (acute inflammation of the brain), which left her with a brain injury affecting her memory, balance and coordination. She now uses a wheelchair, experiences sudden bouts of fatigue and has regular epileptic seizures.

Encephalitis has had a huge impact on Claire's life, but her identity and independence are as important to her now as they ever were. After her encephalitis, Claire didn't feel the standard social care assessment gave her the opportunity to fully convey who she was, so instead she and John wrote their own care plan, detailing their life before and after the encephalitis, with photographs illustrating the things that were important to them.

It took several years and a great deal of effort to obtain, but Claire now has an individual budget that she uses to fund a team of PAs and pursue her interests. She explains that having control over the budget has enabled her to regain her independence and sense of self:

> Because for the past nine years, I fought very hard with the system, and kicked and screamed and done everything I can to keep myself as John's wife and Paul and Callum's mum, and keep that family unit and keep it going. And now I've got my individual budget, it's given not only that aspect of it, but a 'Claire' aspect to it. So that now, with my individual budget, it allows me to say, not social services to come in and say, 'Right, you need to get up for a shower. It takes you two hours to shower. It takes you an hour for your lunch, and it takes you two hours to go shopping. That's what you need for your care.' No, it doesn't. I'm Claire. Some mornings, I don't feel well and I don't want to get up till 12 o'clock. And I'll get up at 12 o'clock, and I'll feel like this is heaven, because my carers are here.

Unfortunately, this setup is now under threat. She and her husband moved to a new local authority area where the rules about the use of personal budgets appear to be different. Her needs have not changed but she has been told that this authority is short of money and she cannot therefore retain the package of care she has. In particular, she cannot use her budget to fund help with domestic cleaning. Claire currently uses some of her budget to pay one PA to clean while another helps with personal care. She sees these as two separate, but equally important roles:

> If they're ironing and they've got a steam iron on, they can't just suddenly drop that if I shout, if my catheter's full or something's happened they can't come to me. Whereas if they're doing my care side, they're here for 'Claire', and they're by my side and they're part of me and they're an extension to me. And they do things in our home and make our home tick the way I would have had it nine years ago.

Nine years ago Claire was a house-proud mother and an active, self-determined woman. Individual budgets have enabled her to continue to be that person, but it remains to be seen whether this will continue. The restrictions imposed on the use of budgets by this local authority may save money, but they could also reduce disabled people's independence and sense of self.

Practice

Practice example 5   George

'It's like having a friend around'

George is 19 years old, and has autism with learning difficulties. He lives at a residential college, going home in the holidays and for one weekend each term. He has verbal dyspraxia – he can speak, but people often have difficulty understanding him if they do not know him well. He needs a lot of one-to-one attention, and help with travelling and facilitating communication with other people. George also needs support to make decisions.

At college, he has a team of staff and a one-to-one support worker who is helping him to learn skills to live independently. When he is at home, his mum and dad take it in turns to be with him, and occasionally his younger brother helps out after school too. Since George has been going to college, he and his family have been having discussions with George's care manager about the most appropriate way for him to be supported when he is at home. His mum works and cannot spend all her annual leave with him, and both she and George feel it would be better for him to have someone nearer his own age to give him support.

George's mum heard about direct payments through other parents at George's college, and asked the care manager about them. The care manager suggested that George could have a direct payment to employ someone to support him with the independence skills he had been learning at college. The direct payment was awarded close to George's holiday, and while they originally intended to look for a PA for George, the family felt there was not time to advertise and employ someone in time for George's holidays. Instead, the family decided to employ someone through an agency.

To begin with, this was not entirely successful. The first agency did not have workers available when George was at home, and the second sent two different workers in two days. While George did not seem too bothered by the situation, his family felt it would be more appropriate for him to have a consistent worker who could build a relationship with him. The third agency sent a young man to work with George. Tom was a student at the local college, a similar age to George and both like music. George likes the fact that Tom drives, and they go out together in Tom's car. For George, it is like having a friend around; they share the same college holidays, so the pairing suits both of them.

Using the direct payment to pay an agency means that George cannot be as flexible in the hours of support he receives as perhaps he might if he employed someone directly. However, his family appreciates that the agency holds and manages the direct payment money for them, and that the agency has backup staff available if Tom cannot work on a particular day. George's mum can use her annual leave when it suits her, rather than being restricted to George's college holidays. Tom is happy because George needs support during the times that Tom needs work, so they can build a relationship together. And George is happy because he gets on well with Tom, and looks forward to seeing him in the holidays.

Practice example 6 | John

A remarkable improvement in health and happiness

John, who is now 22, has severe learning disabilities, is bilaterally deaf, has curvature of the spine, is hypotonic and has complex health needs, which have meant that he has had a tracheotomy in place since he was two years old. John does not communicate verbally and has epilepsy. He needs his suction machine and other medical equipment with him wherever he goes.

The social worker was working in the transition team when she first met John. He was 19 years old then and in his final year at school. At the time, the transition team were piloting self-directed support as a way of helping all young adults to plan for their own support and services after leaving school. John was living at home with his mum, a single parent, and two younger brothers, both of whom have severe learning disabilities. There were only two people in John's life who were trained in his care needs – his mum and his teaching assistant, both middle-aged women.

John's needs were assessed in order to draw down an indicative budget for him to use to plan his support and services. His mother was extremely worried and afraid – she felt that no one would ever be able to care for John, his options were limited and that he would need nursing care on a 2:1 ratio. The social worker encouraged her to feel more positive and explained that self-directed support might be able to offer more choice and opportunity to John. Despite her initial scepticism, John's mother soon got into the swing of things and, following the assessment, the team laid on a couple of person-centred planning sessions to help John and his mum pull together a support plan of how John's needs might be met.

While the support planning was happening, a bombshell descended in the form of continuing healthcare. The legislation had just changed, and the responsibility for John's care was placed with the primary care trust. John's mother felt that his familiar world had come to an abrupt end. She had seen the support plan taking shape and had come to accept that it gave hope for John's future. Now, with the legislative and organizational change, this no longer looked like an option under continuing healthcare. However, everyone worked hard to ensure that this didn't impact on John's opportunity to choose and direct his own support and services. An agreement was reached that social care would case manage John's care and that he could use his support plan to agree with health a package of support that they could fund.

John chose and trained four PAs, two of them male, with the support of his mother and the children's hospital. All his PAs were trained in epilepsy, Makaton (a language programme using signs and symbols to help people communicate), Ambu bag resuscitation, tracheotomy care and the administration of rescue medication. A protocol for managing emergency healthcare was set up with the hospitals and the ambulance service. With these formalities out of the way, John and his mother could get on with the day-to-day stuff of what young men like to do after school. John chose a place to go every day that he liked very much: he tried a number of options and chose everything himself. He decided with his PAs what he would like to do with his time, including employing a teenager his own age to do 'lad's nights' – watch DVDs, order pizzas, play computer games, have a laugh and all this without his mother.

Four years down the line, John is incredibly happy; he still has the same team of PAs and is very much in control of his own life. What is more remarkable is the improvement in his health. John is more active and fitter than he has ever been, he has not been admitted to hospital once in the four years since leaving school and he hasn't had flu or a chest infection.

From the point of view of social care, he is a young man with complex needs that ordinarily the team would have expected to see regularly. They would have often needed to arrange emergency overnight accommodation if his mother was unwell or was struggling; or provide a lot of ongoing support sorting out the nightmare of agencies and staff turnovers, missed calls or changes in the 'right' person to contact. John and his mother organize their PAs well to cover more difficult times and his mother is amazed at how well her son is doing and his improved confidence, health and ability to control his own life.

Practice example 7   Mrs Hakeem

The provision of support that respects cultural principles

Mrs Hakeem is a 79-year-old lady from the Muslim community. Her daughter Shameen contacted social care services three years ago when she was struggling with the task of caring for her mother, whose health was deteriorating with numerous age-related conditions, including arthritis, memory difficulties, diabetes, blood pressure and failing eyesight. Shameen had two young children and was finding it hard to juggle her mother's care with being a parent.

Mrs Hakeem was really upset at the thought of having to 'be cared for' by anyone other than her daughter. Her cultural and religious needs were important to her and, being from an older generation, there was no compromising these strong principles. This placed Shameen in a difficult position: she felt that, by approaching social care, she was asking her mother to accept something that would cause her distress.

At the time Mrs Hakeem was referred to the team, self-directed support was being piloted. The self-directed support team were approached to consider the possibility of Mrs Hakeem taking part in a pilot to see if she and her daughter could be supported in a way that meant that Mrs Hakeem would not have to compromise her cultural needs. Mrs Hakeem was mistrustful and reluctantly agreed to have an assessment carried out. Her daughter and the social worker attended a live planning session to put together a support plan on Mrs Hakeem's behalf. Shameen was really impressed at the possibilities and solutions that self-directed support might be able to offer.

Shameen managed to convince Mrs Hakeem to attend the next two planning sessions; with her daughter's support, she put together an idea of how she would like to be supported. As a result, Mrs Hakeem was able to employ two people from her own community to help her with all her personal care needs and with the management of her own home, including preparing meals that were culturally appropriate. She could arrange for the support to be given at times that made sense to her, including additional support with personal care for prayer time. She chose to have support from her PAs to enable her to attend mosque, something she hadn't been able to do for a long time; she also chose to have support from her PAs to allow her to join in with community activities. Her PAs helped Mrs Hakeem with her shopping and doctor's appointments. Shameen was thus able to be part of her mother's life as her daughter rather than her carer and could devote more time to her young children as they started school.

Mrs Hakeem used her budget to purchase a bed that would rise and recline so that she was able to get herself in and out of bed without needing PA support; this was a much better option because it supported Mrs Hakeem to be more independent in her own home and not reliant on care at all times. Referrals were made for equipment such as grab rails and a walking frame.

Altogether, the equipment and the PAs from the Muslim community meant that Mrs Hakeem was able to continue her life in a way that did not compromise her strong religious and cultural beliefs, and without her daughter having to provide care that was exhausting her and impacting on her ability to be a good mother to her two girls.

Practice example 8   Nicole

The family also needs support

Nicole is married with two children aged 8 and 10. She spent over 18 months in a psychiatric unit following a serious breakdown in her mental health while in her early forties. The social worker was invited to a review that was considering Nicole's discharge plans.

She talked to Nicole's family and the professionals involved in her care about self-directed support and how she would assess and plan with Nicole. Nicole's family reacted positively, and her husband Matthew pointed out that, as a family, they too felt fragile because Nicole's breakdown had had a significant impact on all of them. Matthew felt they would need regular breaks to enable them to continue providing good support to Nicole at home. Nicole did not join in with her review and the social worker was told that Nicole would participate in any meetings, assessments or planning sessions. Everyone felt it would be a real challenge getting Nicole to have any say in what she wanted.

Nicole was discharged from the unit shortly before she was 44. The social worker visited the home to do the assessment; she commented that Matthew and the two children contributed more than Nicole, but was nevertheless pleased that Nicole stayed all the way through and did actually join in the discussion from time to time.

Before the social worker left, she spent some time talking to Nicole about what a support plan was and how they could do it together with her family.

The next time the social worker visited, Nicole was keen and had lots of ideas about what she wanted to include in her support plan. The social worker was careful to go at Nicole's pace, and they had four sessions in all. Matthew said they were moved and surprised at how much insight Nicole had into herself and her needs, and how she engaged in choosing the things she would like to do. The children were pleased and said they felt like they were getting their mother back. Matthew said he felt it was the first time Nicole had been supported to have a say in her own life since the breakdown; previously, it had seemed to him that other people were making decisions for Nicole, whether she liked them or not.

Nicole chose to go horse riding, to have piano lessons, aromatherapy and support from an agency that she chose. Nicole and her family also selected some regular breaks through the 'shared lives' service. One of the most important things to Nicole was the provision of support over the summer holidays. The family had their own caravan and spent several weeks of every year there. Nicole felt that her family needed some time out – to have a holiday that focused on what they wanted to do. Nicole also wanted to have time to do the things she liked doing, which she said were keeping her well. Her family said that, at times, they felt frustrated and tied. So they used Nicole's budget to purchase support from an agency in Cumbria where they had their caravan, which meant that Nicole could go off on her own a couple of times a week, either to go swimming, horse riding or just to go on a shopping spree.

> **Making connexions**
>
> Under the market economy perspective, according to Janet Leece in Chapter 1, 'individuals are transformed from being passive subjects of welfare, provided by a benevolent state, into active consumers able to make their own choices and decisions'. Does this suggestion fit the circumstances of the service provided for Nicole and her family? Can you see any shortcomings in the social work process?

Nicole continued to remain at home with all the support she chose. She started a college course and her confidence grew. She gradually got back into being a wife and a mother, and the social worker came to see her as a woman who had benefited enormously from the support she received and the love of her family. Neither Nicole nor her family had to tap back into mental health crisis teams or psychiatric units.

Practice example 9   David

The value of having one's own space to return to

David is 25 years old. He has cerebral palsy, significant learning difficulties, and is a wheelchair user. He communicates verbally but needs assistance to understand what is going on around him, to meet his care needs and to keep him safe. A mental capacity assessment concluded that David did not have the capacity to choose where he should live.

David finds unexpected noise – particularly noise made by other people – disturbing and upsetting. When he is upset, his behaviour can be of concern in relation to his own and others' safety. Because of this, he has to be monitored closely at all times when with his peers.

David lived at a transition service for four years and initially shared a flat with nine other young people. During his time at the service, David worked with staff to assemble a portfolio, which included information about his likes and dislikes, how he wanted to spend his time, up-to-date assessments from therapists, physical programmes, his detailed care plan and a description of his dreams and aspirations for the future. This was used to support David to plan his move to a permanent home.

David said consistently, and demonstrated through his behaviour, that he wanted to live on his own with his own team of staff. When it was time for David to move from the transition service, he was enabled to make his view known. His social worker and family were understandably concerned about him living alone as this was not something he had ever experienced. They felt that he would be isolated and lonely. The transition service proposed converting an onsite flat to make it accessible for David and that they would provide him with an opportunity to live on his own, with 24-hour staffing in place, to see if that was what he really wanted. David's family were reassured, as they felt he would still be close to the people and places he knew. His social worker considered this a positive action to take and he put David's view forward at a panel in order to obtain funding.

David was delighted to have the chance to live in the flat and to shop, cook and clean for himself. He worked with staff to plan a weekly schedule that included these activities, exercise opportunities, sessions in the skills centre at the transition service and a day practising independence skills at a local regional college. Gradually, David began to demonstrate that he was more able to cope with other people's noise because he had his own space to return to when it all became too much. This resulted in him being more sociable than he had been in the past. His concerning behaviour reduced significantly and his confidence grew.

At review, David talked about what he had been doing and how he felt about living on his own. He was enthusiastic about the experience, and his family, social worker and staff team agreed that he was thriving in this environment. The service David attended had recently bought some flats locally and his social worker sought funding for him to move into one of these. Staff worked with David to establish that he had capacity to enter into a tenancy and he was involved in interviewing a team of staff to support him in his new flat.

David is now enjoying life in his own home and is keen to welcome visitors. He has a full weekly schedule that keeps him active in the local community. He is a frequent visitor to the transition service where he is able to catch up with friends. His family and his social worker are pleased to see him settled, happy and well supported.

Practice

Personalization: what do the professionals think?

We have seen in this chapter how some instances of personalization have worked in practice. What about the experiences and feelings of those who are tasked with taking forward the personalization agenda?

In 2011 in Scotland, at a conference of professional practitioners (mainly working with children with disabilities and their families), advantage was taken of the opportunity to explore participants' opinions. Most were positive about the personalization agenda, although some wanted more clarity or more information about how it should be done and what considerations needed to be taken into account.

Workers are generally positive about personalization

The majority of social workers are enthusiastic about the personalization agenda and want to create a society where families have more control. They envisage families being supported by services working *with* them rather than *for* them. They talk of things like contributing, choice and control, belonging and 'being someone': 'The needs of the whole family can be better met and they have full control over their lives, supported by the government.'

They believe that families will have greater flexibility as they will have more control over the workforce. They make the link between self-directed support and inclusion, with people living less segregated lives, sharing ordinary places and being genuine and active members of their communities. They emphasize their belief in 'inclusion for all'. Personalization will mean an increase in opportunities for young people to grow, develop and contribute to their community and enhance community networks. Social workers feel that a personalized approach helps to make connections so that disabled people can be 'known' and have 'witnesses to their lives'.

Personalization encourages needs-led services, with the needs being identified by the service user, rather than prescribed by the providers. This approach provides greater flexibility, more choice and is more responsive, because it replaces rigid, resource-led services, in which 'one size fits all – take it or leave it'. Personalized support is more likely to meet the needs of the whole family. Life for children with disabilities and their families will become more positive and 'normal'. Personalization can also offer enhanced support to the black and minority ethnic community, as it is person centred and thus can more easily take account of cultural, language and social perspectives. Personalization offers more creative and innovative solutions.

Some workers highlight the risks and have concerns about personalization

There are fears that a more personalized model may be used to 'do the same with less money', or that money may be misused.

If not managed properly, transferring responsibility to families might mean that some could feel unable to manage. It would be a mistake to assume that all parents and carers are fully aware of or are in a position to manage the responsibilities that might be involved. What if the family wants something different from the child? Support needs to be planned in partnership, and the relationship between the lead worker and the family is critical.

If traditional services close, there is a fear that there would be nothing available if or when things go wrong; for example, traditional respite can provide a safe place during crises that other forms of respite may not. There needs to be some backup if self-directed support arrangements break down. There are huge complications in managing and coordinating all the different supports in times of crisis. Workers have concerns for families who lack confidence and about support for those who may choose not to take up self-directed support. In rural communities, there may be a lack of availability of people to employ as PAs.

In the development of direct payments, the length of time involved in the process for allocating the payment can be too long; thus a streamlined, simple sequence for allocating individual budgets is needed. Personalized support must be fair and equitable and should improve on the past rather than merely replicating it.

Making it work in practice

Good quality personalization practice requires one clear approach that will ensure consistency, equity and transparency.

There needs to be strong support for families to take them through the self-assessment process, together with support and information available for people who are on the receiving end of the personalization policy. The whole family needs to be taken into consideration, with the possible need for independent advocacy for children and young people, particularly for children in transition and young carers.

Workers need to develop better partnership working with local organizations; and planners and managers need to consider how the workforce will be trained in personalized approaches.

If the risks are acknowledged and safeguards put in place, it should be possible to move forward using the personalization agenda to make a positive difference to the lives of those who rely on social workers to provide a life-enhancing service.

Further reading

■ Gardner, A. (2011) *Personalisation in Social Work*. Exeter: Learning Matters.
Practical guide to the application of personalization.

■ Glasby, J. and Littlechild, R. (2009) *Direct Payments and Personal Budgets: Putting Personalization into Practice*. Bristol: Policy Press.

Practice

Sets out the background and context for the implementation of direct payments and personal budgets, and explores the implications of personalization for social work practice.

■ Scourfield, P. (2007) 'Social care and the modern citizen: client, consumer, service user, manager and entrepreneur', *British Journal of Social Work*, 37(1): 107–22.

Offers a more cautionary look at the difficulties faced by personalization, with an emphasis on the employment relationship between service users and PAs, questioning the movement towards a market-based system of care provision.

Part II
Social Work and Mental Health

Mental health social work is one of the most challenging, dynamic and engaging aspects of the profession. Often working alongside colleagues from health professions in multidisciplinary teams, mental health social workers practise amid contested paradigms and exemplify the tension between 'care' and 'control' that is inherent in social work.

The following five chapters discuss multiple influences on mental health social work practice. Several common themes emerge, which represent key dilemmas for practitioners. For example, in Chapter 7, Nick Gould and Debbie Martin discuss how mental health social workers undertaking statutory functions under mental health law walk a tightrope between 'care' and 'control' when assessing someone for compulsory admission to hospital. Although often referred to as a dichotomy, 'care' and 'control' are not mutually exclusive, as compulsory treatment *is* a form of care, albeit in the context of restricted civil liberties.

Mental health policy also has a dual concern with ensuring public safety and promoting the recovery of people with mental health problems. As explored by Martin Webber and Jack Nathan in Chapter 6, risk aversion in policy and practice, and the dominant influence of research evidence in mental health policy, has contributed to the retrenchment of mental health social workers to statutory roles rather than leading on social interventions. However, we must remember that some important features of contemporary mental health services originated in social work. For example, as explored by Sherrill Evans and Peter Huxley in Chapter 9, the US principles of social work case management permeate care coordination in the UK, and the strengths model underpins contemporary recovery models. The challenge for mental health social work is to develop its own evidence base to influence mental health policy and strengthen practitioners' positions in multidisciplinary teams.

Empowerment and recovery discourses are resurgent in mental health services. Social workers can readily engage in these discussions as they are close to our value base. As Caroline Leah illustrates in Chapter 10, challenging stigma and discrimination, promoting social inclusion and supporting normal life opportunities are core aspects of the mental health social work role. However, creative practice that has the potential to enhance an individual's wellbeing, such as positive risk-taking, can be stifled by an overly prescriptive system of risk management, exemplifying the challenge of working within mental health services.

The contested theoretical underpinnings of mental health practice are discussed by Jerry Tew in Chapter 8. The biopsychosocial model is commonly referred to in discussions about community mental health practice, although there is limited consensus among and within professional groups about approaches to mental health practice. Some psychiatrists fear that mental health services have become too psychosocial and call for a return to biomedical approaches, but others disagree. Some clinical psychologists are concerned about the widespread use of psychological therapies in primary care, as cognitive behavioural therapy should not be seen as a panacea for common mental disorders such as depression and anxiety. Social workers, meanwhile, bemoan the loss of social approaches.

Mental health problems are rarely verifiable by biological indicators, although research to identify them is continuing apace. They are caused by a complex mixture of psychological, biological and social factors, with different factors taking prominence for different people at different times. Biological and psychological approaches to treatment are currently dominant and it can be a challenge for mental health social workers to focus on the social perspectives. The case studies in Chapter 10 represent the complexity of social work practice in mental health services, and the interplay of the competing, and sometimes complementary, approaches.

These chapters are written by mental health social work experts and open a window to the challenging field of mental health social work. They provide a valuable introduction for students or anyone interested in learning more about this exciting field of social work.

Martin Webber

6
Social policy and mental health social work

MARTIN WEBBER AND JACK NATHAN

Contemporary mental health social work practice is a fusion of statutory functions, therapeutic interventions and care management. In multidisciplinary mental health services, social workers play an important role in promoting social perspectives as a counterbalance to the dominant psychiatric paradigm.

Social policy has helped to shape social work practice in mental health services. On the one hand, mental health policy is underpinned by a strong concern for public safety, which has resulted in a bureaucratic system of risk management that somewhat stifles innovation in mental health social work. On the other hand, contemporary mental health policy embraces the notion of personal recovery, as opposed to clinical recovery or the absence of symptoms. This supports social work practice that seeks to enable individuals to achieve their life goals, irrespective of the mental health problems they may be experiencing. This chapter will explore these dynamics in the context of the relevant policy themes and competing influences that have helped to shape policy and, ultimately, social work practice in mental health services.

Social work in mental health services

Mental health problems are common. In a national survey in 2007 (McManus et al., 2009):

- almost one in four (23.0%) people in England met the diagnostic criteria for a mental health problem
- 15.1% of adults suffered from depression or anxiety
- the prevalence of psychosis was 0.4%
- 5.6% of people reported that they had attempted suicide at some point in their lives.

Mental health problems are more common in developed Western countries (WHO World Mental Health Survey Consortium, 2004) and in urban areas in particular (Ayuso-Mateos et al., 2001). It is possible that the diagnostic criteria for depression may artificially inflate prevalence estimates (Horwitz and Wakefield, 2007), but depression is widely recognized as a significant global health problem (Murray and Lopez, 1997).

Mental health problems have a social dimension (Tew, 2005). In the UK, for example, high rates of psychosis in migrant and ethnic minority populations can be attributed, in part, to their high levels of social disadvantage (Morgan and Hutchinson, 2010). Further, in a review of international studies on the incidence and prevalence of depression, Lorant et al. (2003) found that adults in the lowest socio-economic group are twice as likely to be depressed than those in the highest socioeconomic group at any one time. Intervening to mitigate the social influences on mental health problems, and manage the complex social circumstances of many sufferers, provides a clear rationale for the involvement of social workers in mental health services.

Mental health services in the UK and many other developed countries have largely adopted a biopsychosocial approach to address the complex interplay of biological, social and psychological factors in the aetiology and course of severe mental health problems. To provide holistic care and treatment as required by this model, mental health services typically bring together social workers, psychiatrists, clinical psychologists, mental health nurses, occupational therapists, support workers and a range of other specialist practitioners such as employment specialists into multidisciplinary teams. Social workers practise primarily in secondary or tertiary NHS mental health services, although some are prominent in primary care (see, for example, Firth, 2010).

Within multidisciplinary teams, concerns have been expressed by social workers (for example Nathan and Webber, 2010) and psychiatrists (for example Craddock et al., 2008), among others, that role identities have become blurred and a slide towards genericism has diluted the perspectives that the respective professions bring. Role tensions are evident within mental health social work itself, as there are divergent perspectives about the extent to which social workers should become embedded within NHS structures (McCrae et al., 2004). But this is nothing new. The creation of unified local authority social services departments in 1971 brought together mental welfare officers, who undertook statutory functions under the Mental Health Act 1959 and primarily performed a 'sectioning service' (Rolph et al., 2003), and psychiatric social workers, who had psychodynamic training and worked closely with psychiatrists in the aftercare of people discharged from hospital. The evolution of mental health social work as a discipline has witnessed these 'care' and 'control' functions being merged into one role.

The Mental Health Act 1983 created the role of approved social worker (ASW), who had more power and greater professional autonomy to exercise an independent opinion than their predecessors. Their role was to conduct a social assessment of an individual's circumstances and investigate the possibility of using other services to avoid the need for a hospital admission. ASWs provided important safeguards against unnecessary infringement of the civil liberties of people with mental health problems by psychiatrists, and social workers earned respect for undertaking the role. The opening up of the role to nurses, occupational therapists and psychologists by the Mental Health Act 2007, as approved mental health professionals, has fuelled concerns about the unique contribution that social work can make to mental health services.

During the quarter of a century in which social workers undertook the ASW role, they witnessed the culmination of a long process of deinstitutionalization of mental health care in the UK. The number of psychiatric inpatient beds declined from about 150,000 in 1955 in England (Rogers and Pilgrim, 1996) to about 30,000 in 2005 (Winterton, 2007). Mental health policy hastened the development of community care for people with mental health problems, although it was also influenced by the mounting costs of institutional care (Scull, 1977), moral critiques of asylums (Goffman, 1961), the development of new drugs (Busfield, 1986), and a shift in the psychiatric discourse towards 'mental health' and psychological interventions (Rogers and Pilgrim, 1996).

Contemporary mental health policy embraces notions of 'recovery' and 'social inclusion' in clear contrast to the era of institutional care. The UK coalition government's mental health strategy (DH, 2011, and see Box 6.1) is oriented towards prevention, wellbeing and enhancing public mental health as it builds on the 10-year *National Service Framework for Mental Health* (NSF) (DH, 1999a). As such, the policy environment is increasingly conducive to social workers adopting leadership roles in mental health services, although practitioners remain constrained by bureaucracy and, ironically, a medicalization of their role (Nathan and Webber, 2010). These tensions are explored in the following sections, which address three underpinning influences on contemporary policy: evidence, risk and recovery.

Box 6.1

Six objectives of mental health strategy

1 *More people will have good mental health:* More people of all ages and backgrounds will have better wellbeing and good mental health. Fewer people will develop mental health problems – by starting well, developing well, working well, living well and ageing well.

2 *More people with mental health problems will recover:* More people who develop mental health problems will have a good quality of life – a greater ability to manage their own lives, stronger social relationships, a greater sense of purpose, the skills they need for living and working, improved chances in education, better employment rates and a suitable and stable place to live.

3　*More people with mental health problems will have good physical health:* Fewer people with mental health problems will die prematurely, and more people with physical ill health will have better mental health.

4　*More people will have a positive experience of care and support:* Care and support, wherever it takes place, should offer access to timely, evidence-based interventions and approaches that give people the greatest choice and control over their own lives, in the least restrictive environment, and should ensure that people's human rights are protected.

5　*Fewer people will suffer avoidable harm:* People receiving care and support should have confidence that the services they use are of the highest quality and at least as safe as any other public service.

6　*Fewer people will experience stigma and discrimination:* Public understanding of mental health will improve and, as a result, negative attitudes and behaviours to people with mental health problems will decrease.

Source: DH, 2011

Evidence-based mental health policy

The mental health NSF (DH, 1999a) aimed to improve the quality and consistency of mental health services in the UK by the setting of national standards. It was developed through a largely rational model of policy-making. An external reference group, consisting of academics, psychiatrists, GPs, service users, social workers and mental health voluntary sector organizations, examined and validated research evidence to inform the policy. The seven standards it set were explicitly based on research evidence about which interventions and service configurations are most effective. However, the chair of the external reference group acknowledged that the quality and quantity of evidence varied considerably between the standards, for example with little evidence being available about effective work with carers (Thornicroft et al., 2002). The *NHS Plan* (DH, 2000) implemented the NSF through the creation of new types of mental health team:

1　Multidisciplinary *community mental health teams* (CMHTs) were already established in many areas of the UK by the time of the publication of the NSF. Although these teams form the bedrock of community mental health care, they have been surprisingly underevaluated. For example, a systematic review of evidence of their effectiveness included only three randomized controlled trials (Malone et al., 2007). The only consistent difference was that CMHTs were more effective at keeping people out of hospital than other types of mental health team. Many of the presumed benefits of CMHTs, such as lower cost, improved social functioning, greater user and carer satisfaction, have not been found in randomized controlled trials.

2　The NSF drew on evidence from the USA about the effectiveness of assertive community treatment (Marshall and Lockwood, 1998), which led to the establishment of *assertive outreach teams* (AOTs) throughout England and Wales. The assertive community treatment model of care, which promotes assertive engagement with reluctant service users who pose serious risks to themselves or others if their mental health problem is untreated, found its origins in 'hands-on' social work practice (Test, 1998). Subsequent UK studies of AOTs (Burns et al., 1999; Killaspy et al., 2006) have, however, found that they are no more effective than CMHTs at keeping people out of hospital or improving their health or social functioning. In a challenging fiscal environment, and with an increasing emphasis on outcomes (DH, 2010a), the future for AOTs appears bleak (Burns, 2010).

3   The *NHS Plan* (DH, 2000) also introduced *crisis resolution and home treatment* (CRHT) teams to provide treatment to people in their own homes when acutely unwell. In comparison with inpatient care, they reduce the need for repeat hospital admissions (Joy et al., 1998) and reduce the length of stay in hospital (Burns et al., 2001). Since their introduction in the UK, the rate of inpatient admissions has fallen (Glover et al., 2006). However, social workers report that, by assessing people for home treatment prior to a Mental Health Act assessment, CRHT teams may increase the likelihood of a compulsory admission because the individual's mental health has deteriorated further and an informal admission can be difficult to negotiate due to the reduction in number of beds (Furminger and Webber, 2009). CRHT teams are founded on the premise that care and treatment must be provided in the 'least restrictive' environment, but this can be counter to the principle that hospital treatment is in the 'best interests' of some people at certain times, creating a dilemma for social workers (Nathan and Webber, 2010).

4   *Early intervention in psychosis* (EIP) teams were established, as there is evidence that people with a shorter period of untreated psychosis have better outcomes (Marshall et al., 2005; Perkins et al., 2005). These multidisciplinary teams work with young people experiencing their first episode of psychosis and engage them in treatment using flexible and occasionally innovative methods. Evidence from a randomized controlled trial in London found that those receiving support from an EIP team were more likely to regain or establish new social relationships, spend longer in vocational activity, have better social functioning, have a better quality of life and be more satisfied with their service than the comparison group, but there was no improvement in their psychotic symptoms (Garety et al., 2006). Similarly, in a recent study, cognitive behavioural therapy and family intervention were found to have no effect on the rate of remission and relapse in psychosis (Garety et al., 2008). As confirmed by clinical guidelines, the key predictor of relapse remains ceasing medication (National Collaborating Centre for Mental Health, 2010).

The roles of practitioners within these different types of community mental health services, including social workers, are mostly determined by the nature of the team in which they reside, but their practice is also influenced by clinical guidelines produced by the National Institute for Health and Clinical Excellence (NICE). These guidelines review evidence about interventions for specific mental health problems and recommend their implementation on the basis of their effectiveness. As psychological and pharmacological interventions are the most prevalent forms of evidence-based treatments, clinical guidelines recommend their use above social interventions, which rarely feature in them. In the depression guidelines (National Collaborating Centre for Mental Health, 2004), for example, only one social intervention – befriending – is recommended because a randomized controlled trial has reported its beneficial effect (Harris et al., 1999). As social interventions (particularly 'messy' social work practice) are less amenable to randomized controlled trials, practice within mental health services is biased towards psychiatry and psychology. Space precludes a more in-depth discussion of the role of evidence in mental health policy, but this can be found elsewhere (for example Webber, 2011).

Risk-averse mental health policy

The care programme approach (CPA) (DH, 1990) has underpinned the delivery of care to people with mental health problems since 1991. Later integrated with parallel care management procedures in social services, the CPA ensures that each person has a care plan that is reviewed regularly. Coordination of care delivery within the CPA is shared between mental health professionals, although social workers hold the most complex cases and work with the people with the most social problems (Huxley et al., 2008). The CPA provides a structure in which responsibility for individuals is clearly defined. With the integration of risk assessment and management procedures into the CPA in 1999 (DH, 1999b), practitioners have arguably become more risk averse in their practice for fear of being held responsible for any major adverse incidents.

Concerns about public safety are explicit within mental health policy. Homicides committed by people with a diagnosis of schizophrenia in the early 1990s, such as the stabbing of Jonathan Zito by Christopher Clunis at a London underground station (Ritchie et al., 1994), were picked up by the media as illustrative of inadequate community care policy. Subsequent public anxiety about the management of people with mental health problems prompted the introduction of supervision registers and supervised discharge (Mental Health Act 1983, s. 25a, as amended by the Mental Health (Patients in the Community) Act 1995) in the mid-1990s to help ensure closer monitoring of people at risk of relapse on discharge from hospital. However, supervision registers were not consistently applied and did not identify a homogeneous group of people at risk (Bindman et al., 2000). Further, supervised discharge was applied disproportionately to people of African Caribbean origin (Hatfield et al., 2001), who typically first encounter mental health services via the police or compulsion (Morgan et al., 2004). In what is now a classic early study of pathways to care for people of black or minority ethnic origin, Cole et al. (1995) found that police involvement and compulsory admissions in first episode psychosis most often happened when there was no GP involvement and the absence of help-seeking by a friend or relative.

Community treatment orders (CTOs), introduced in England and Wales by the Mental Health Act 2007, replaced supervised discharge. A feature of mental health law in many jurisdictions throughout the world, such as Scotland, Australia, Canada, New Zealand and the USA, there is no robust evidence that CTOs either have a positive or a negative effect (Churchill, 2007). This suggests that their introduction in England and Wales was motivated more by a concern for public safety than by evidence of their effectiveness. Since their introduction, CTOs have been used more frequently than supervised discharge and people from black and ethnic minority groups are disproportionately placed under their restrictions (Evans et al., 2010).

A managerial approach to people with mental health problems, and a predominant focus on biomedical treatment, has created the 'bureau-medicalization' of mental health care in the UK (Nathan and Webber, 2010). Social workers have become subsumed within the hegemonic infrastructure of the NHS and they are finding it increasingly difficult to articulate psychosocial perspectives, although there are many to draw upon (see Webber and Nathan, 2010). Ironically, perhaps, it is social policy that may provide an opportunity for social work to redefine its role within mental health services, as the recovery paradigm becomes resurgent.

Recovery-oriented policy

At the heart of contemporary mental health policy are the discourses of wellbeing and recovery (DH, 2011). These acknowledge that while people continue to experience symptoms of mental distress, they should be supported to work towards their goals and take responsibility for their lives (Slade, 2009). It represents a shift in thinking away from eradicating 'disease' to supporting individuals to recover their personal and social identity. For social workers, it represents a less radical shift in thinking and practice as, without using the language of recovery, the profession has always held a psychosocial view that has promoted 'the empowerment and liberation of people to enhance wellbeing' (IFSW, 2000).

Paradoxically, the recovery discourse has created an unexpected practice tension for social workers. This arises from the institutionalization of the term 'recovery' itself, as there is now an organizational pressure for service users 'to recover'. This can mean practitioners are minded to terminate work with a person on grounds more related to organizational strictures, rather than careful assessment of their need. This perspective is reinforced by the introduction of 'support time and recovery workers' in mental health services whose role is to 'promote recovery'. CMHTs have been configured to include a 'support and recovery' focus where support time and recovery workers and mental health professionals support people to develop life skills and pursue educational, social and vocational opportunities according to their needs and life goals. In their own terms, such laudable expectations are precisely what any practitioner would want for the people they work with and are, again, not something new to social workers. There has also always been an understanding that some people need long-term support – in that sense, not everybody recovers. It is not without reason that CMHTs have had a 'continuing care' function. Needs for ongoing care have not disappeared as a result of government policy or a change of designation. Recovery seems to have been conflated with enabling people to maximize their potential.

A 'maximizing potential' model would forestall other dangers inherent in the recovery discourse. Primary among those are that the recovery model individualizes people's problems. What if they don't 'recover'? Are they to be blamed for their 'deficiency'? In this way, the recovery model, perhaps inadvertently, decontextualizes the environment of poverty, deprivation and unemployment, let alone the long-term sequelae of a childhood marked by abuse, parental mental health problems and so on.

Taking the international definition of the profession, social workers also bear a responsibility to 'intervene at the points where people interact with their environments' (IFSW, 2000). Nathan and Webber (2010, p. 23) suggest that this means that social workers have, uniquely among the professions, the key task of enabling service users to have 'a voice in relation to the dominating institutions in which they live'. This will inevitably involve not only, as suggested above, arguing for a hospital bed, but also for the continuing provision of social work or other professional support. This is a form of 'social inclusion as citizen', where people are able to access a key welfare provision. The recovery model must not result in exclusion from the services set up to provide them with the help they need.

The notion of social inclusion is central to the recovery discourse and was a core component of Tony Blair's vision for a 'New Britain'. He established the Social Exclusion Unit in 1997 to promote cross-government initiatives to tackle the social ills associated with poverty. As people with mental health problems were one of the most excluded groups in society, it started a programme of work designed to provide them with access to opportunities routinely available to others in society (SEU, 2004). The government's discourse of social inclusion predominantly focused on inclusion in paid work. As a result of this, mental health day services came under scrutiny and have since been transformed or, in many cases, closed down. In their place, vocational services were established to support people to enter education, training or employment (DWP/DH, 2006). They were encouraged to follow a model of 'individual placement and support', in which an individual is placed in competitive employment and supported by employment specialists. This model has been found to be more effective than pre-vocational training at helping people with mental health problems stay in employment (Bond and Drake, 2008), but has rarely been implemented in England (Rinaldi et al., 2010).

Social inclusion policy has encouraged the participation of people with mental health problems in the arts, which has increased levels of empowerment (Hacking et al., 2008). It has also reminded mental health professionals that adults with mental health problems can also be parents. Social Care Institute for Excellence (SCIE, 2009) guidance has renewed the call for stronger collaboration between children's social care services and mental health services, although professional tunnel vision remains a challenging barrier to joint working. Social workers, trained to view people holistically and across the life course, are well placed to lead these initiatives. But the social policy they are perhaps best placed to lead is the personalization agenda.

The personalization of adult social care (HM Government, 2007) is transforming the organization and delivery of services to people with social care needs. The piloting of personal health budgets (DH, 2009) may lead to a similar transformation of the delivery of health services, particularly to those with long-term mental health problems. Personalized care, facilitated by personal budgets, has the potential to improve the quality of life and wellbeing of people with mental health problems (Glendinning et al., 2008). The take-up of personal budgets is currently modest, but is expected to rise as health and social care funding streams become increasingly merged. The coalition government places personalization at the heart of its social care policy (DH, 2010b). This has the potential to challenge current models of service delivery, empowering users to make increased choices about their care that may be at odds with professional or societal views about what is 'good for them'.

A quick review of comments made in *Community Care* magazine illustrate the extent to which social workers feel overwhelmed by the bureaucracy involved in setting up personal budgets for mental health service users. There are also political sensitivities about what service users can and cannot purchase with their personal budgets, which practitioners are aware of. Ironically, a system designed to liberate service users is tying professionals up in red tape. Although they may support the policy in principle, in practice it is often unworkable and social workers feel reluctant to champion it.

Policy influences on mental health social work

There are a number of competing tensions and interests that shape mental health policy, most outside the sphere of social work. These include a drive towards evidence-based policy (as in the NSF and NICE guidelines), which is led by

> **Making connexions**
>
> 'Mental health policy has provided social work with an important role to fulfil in working with people with mental health problems.'
>
> What is that role, and what qualities does it call for in the mental health social worker?

the dominant mental health professions of psychiatry and psychology. However, public concern about the perceived dangers of people with severe mental health problems, fuelled by a series of homicide inquiries and stoked by a hostile media, hastened the introduction of policy in the absence of evidence. Promoting personal recovery is anathema to risk-averse mental health services, a tension that policy prescriptions alone cannot resolve. Some tentative steps have been taken towards promoting social inclusion, but policies such as this, which encompass the values of social work, are yet to be championed by the profession.

Social work in mental health services has been shaped by the evidential world of psychiatry and psychology; social workers are trained to provide the core 'control' functions under mental health law, and they help service users to have more of a say in their own care and treatment. They are small in number in mental health services and their voice is often not heard. They rarely have a seat on NHS trust executive boards and, at the time of writing, their fledgling professional college (in England) is in the early stages of its development. However, mental health policy has provided social work with an important role to fulfil in working with people with mental health problems. This is enhanced by the values, knowledge and skills that practitioners bring to the role. The perceived threat that the approved mental health professional role poses in practice represents an opportunity for social workers to take a leadership role in the training of the other professions engaging in this task. As instanced by the Reclaim Social Work initiative in the London Borough of Hackney's children's services, with appropriate leadership and support, social workers will be able to take a leading role in other policy domains close to the profession's value base.

Appendix 6.1 Abbreviations frequently used in the field of mental health

ACT	assertive community treatment
AMHP	approved mental health professional
AOT	assertive outreach team
ASW	approved social worker
CMHT	community mental health team
CRHT	crisis resolution and home treatment
CTO	community treatment order
EIP	early intervention in psychosis
IPS	individual placement and support
NICE	National Institute for Health and Clinical Excellence
NSF	National Service Framework

Further reading

■ Lester, H. and Glasby, J. (2010) *Mental Health Policy and Practice* (2nd edn). Basingstoke: Palgrave Macmillan.

Accessible and engaging overview of mental health policy and mental health services; provides an introduction to working within them.

■ Rogers, A. and Pilgrim, D. (2001) *Mental Health Policy in Britain: A Critical Introduction* (2nd edn). Basingstoke: Palgrave – now Palgrave Macmillan.

Offers both a historical perspective and an exploration of mental health care in the post-institutional era.

■ Webber, M. (2011) *Evidence-based Policy and Practice in Mental Health Social Work* (2nd edn). Exeter: Learning Matters.

Provides an overview of contemporary mental health policy in the UK and the evidence base that underpins it.

References

Ayuso-Mateos, J.L., Vazquez-Barquero, J.L., Dowrick, C. et al. (2001) 'Depressive disorders in Europe: prevalence figures from the ODIN study', *British Journal of Psychiatry*, 179, 308–16.

Bindman, J., Beck, A., Thornicroft, G. et al. (2000) 'Psychiatric patients at greatest risk and in greatest need: impact of the supervision register policy', *British Journal of Psychiatry*, 177, 33–7.

Bond, G.R. and Drake, R.E. (2008) 'Predictors of competitive employment among patients with schizophrenia', *Current Opinion in Psychiatry*, 21, 362–9.

Burns, T. (2010) 'The rise and fall of assertive community treatment?', *International Review of Psychiatry*, 22, 130–7.

Burns, T., Creed, F., Fahy, T. et al. (1999) 'Intensive versus standard case management for severe psychotic illness: a randomised trial', *The Lancet*, 353, 2185–9.

Burns, T., Knapp, M., Catty, J. et al. (2001) 'Home treatment for mental health problems: a systematic review', *Health Technology Assessment*, **5**(15): 1–139.

Busfield, J. (1986) *Managing Mental Illness*. London: Hutchinson.

Churchill, R. (2007) *International Experiences of Using Community Treatment Orders*. London: Institute of Psychiatry, King's College London.

Cole, E., Leavey, G., King, M. et al. (1995) 'Pathways to care for patients with a first episode of psychosis: a comparison of ethnic groups', *British Journal of Psychiatry*, 167, 770–6.

Craddock, N., Antebi, D., Attenburrow, M.-J. et al. (2008) 'Wake-up call for British psychiatry', *British Journal of Psychiatry*, 193, 6–9.

DH (Department of Health) (1990) *Caring for People: The Care Programme Approach for People with a Mental Illness Referred to Specialist Mental Health Services*. London: DH.

DH (1999a) *National Service Framework for Mental Health: Modern Standards and Service Models*. London: DH.

DH (1999b) *Effective Care Co-ordination in Mental Health Services: Modernising the Care Programme Approach – A Policy Booklet*. London: DH.

DH (2000) *The NHS Plan: A Plan for Investment, A Plan for Reform*. London: DH.

DH (2009) *Direct Payments for Health Care: A Consultation on Proposals for Regulations and Guidance*. London: DH.

DH (2010a) *Equity and Excellence: Liberating the NHS*. London: DH.

DH (2010b) *A Vision for Adult Social Care: Capable Communities and Active Citizens*. London: DH.

DH (2011) *No Health Without Mental Health: A Cross-Government Mental Health Outcomes Strategy for People of All Ages*. London: DH.

DWP/DH (Department for Work and Pensions/Department of Health) (2006) *Vocational*

Services for People with Severe Mental Health Problems: Commissioning Guidance. London: Care Services Improvement Partnership.

Evans, R., Makala, J., Humphreys, M. and Mohan, C.R. (2010) 'Supervised community treatment in Birmingham and Solihull: first 6 months', *The Psychiatrist*, 34, 330–3.

Firth, M.T. (2010) 'Not just talk: what a psychosocial primary care mental health service can do', *Practice: Social Work in Action*, 22, 293–307.

Furminger, E. and Webber, M. (2009) 'The effect of crisis resolution and home treatment on assessments under the Mental Health Act 1983: an increased workload for approved social workers?', *British Journal of Social Work*, **39**(5): 901–17.

Garety, P.A., Craig, T.K., Dunn, G. et al. (2006) 'Specialised care for early psychosis: symptoms, social functioning and patient satisfaction: randomised controlled trial', *British Journal of Psychiatry*, 188, 37–45.

Garety, P.A., Fowler, D.G., Freeman, D. et al. (2008) 'Cognitive-behavioural therapy and family intervention for relapse prevention and symptom reduction in psychosis: randomised controlled trial', *British Journal of Psychiatry*, 192, 412–23.

Glendinning, C., Challis, D., Fernández, J.-L. et al. (2008) *Evaluation of the Individual Budgets Pilot Programme: Final Report*. York: SPRU.

Glover, G., Arts, G. and Babu, K.S. (2006) 'Crisis resolution/home treatment teams and psychiatric admission rates in England', *British Journal of Psychiatry*, 189, 441–5.

Goffman, E. (1961) *Asylums: Essays on the Social Situation of Mental Patients and Other Inmates*. Harmondsworth: Pelican Books.

Hacking, S., Secker, J., Spandler, H. et al. (2008) 'Evaluating the impact of participatory art projects for people with mental health needs', *Health and Social Care in the Community*, 16, 638–48.

Harris, T., Brown, G.W. and Robinson, R. (1999) 'Befriending as an intervention for chronic depression among women in an inner city: 1: randomised controlled trial', *British Journal of Psychiatry*, 174, 219–24.

Hatfield, B., Shaw, J., Pinfold, V. et al. (2001) 'Managing severe mental illness in the community using the Mental Health Act 1983: a comparison of supervised discharge and guardianship in England', *Social Psychiatry and Psychiatric Epidemiology*, 36, 508–15.

HM Government (2007) *Putting People First: A Shared Vision and Commitment to the Transformation of Adult Social Care*. London: DH.

Horwitz, A.V. and Wakefield, J.C. (2007) *The Loss of Sadness: How Psychiatry Transformed Normal Sorrow into Depressive Disorder*. New York: Oxford University Press.

Huxley, P., Evans, S., Munroe, M. and Cestari, L. (2008) 'Mental health policy reforms and case complexity in CMHTs in England: replication study', *Psychiatric Bulletin*, 32, 49–52.

IFSW (International Federation of Social Workers) (2000) *Definition of Social Work*, http://www.ifsw.org/en/f38000138.html, accessed 9 February 2011.

Joy, C.B., Adams, C.E. and Rice, K. (1998) 'Crisis intervention for people with severe mental illnesses', *The Cochrane Library*, 4.

Killaspy, H., Bebbington, P., Blizard, R. et al. (2006) 'The REACT study: randomised evaluation of assertive community treatment in north London', *British Medical Journal*, 332, 815–19.

Policy

Lorant, V., Deliege, D., Eaton, W. et al. (2003) 'Socioeconomic inequalities in depression: a meta-analysis', *American Journal of Epidemiology*, 157, 98–112.

McCrae, N., Murray, J., Huxley, P. and Evans, S. (2004) 'Prospects for mental health social work: a qualitative study of attitudes of service managers and academic staff', *Journal of Mental Health*, 13, 305–17.

McManus, S., Meltzer, H., Brugha, T. et al. (eds) (2009) *Adult Psychiatric Morbidity in England, 2007: Results of a Household Survey*. London: NHS Information Centre for Health and Social Care.

Malone, D., Marriott, S., Newton-Howes, G. et al. (2007) 'Community mental health teams (CMHTs) for people with severe mental illnesses and disordered personality', *Cochrane Database of Systematic Reviews*, 3.

Marshall, M., Lewis, S., Lockwood, A. et al. (2005) 'Association between duration of untreated psychosis and outcome in cohorts of first-episode patients: a systematic review', *Archives of General Psychiatry*, 62, 975–83.

Marshall, M. and Lockwood, A. (1998) 'Assertive community treatment for people with severe mental disorders', *The Cochrane Library*, 2.

Morgan, C. and Hutchinson, G. (2010) 'The social determinants of psychosis in migrant and ethnic minority populations: a public health tragedy', *Psychological Medicine*, 40, 705–9.

Morgan, C., Mallett, R., Hutchinson, G. and Leff, J. (2004) 'Negative pathways to psychiatric care and ethnicity: the bridge between social science and psychiatry', *Social Science and Medicine*, 58, 739–52.

Murray, C.J. and Lopez, A.D. (1997) 'Alternative projections of mortality and disability by cause 1990–2020: Global Burden of Disease Study', *The Lancet*, 349, 1498–504.

Nathan, J. and Webber, M. (2010) 'Mental health social work and the bureau-medicalisation of mental health care: identity in a changing world', *Journal of Social Work Practice*, 24, 15–28.

National Collaborating Centre for Mental Health (2004) *Depression: Management of Depression in Primary and Secondary Care. National Clinical Practice Guideline Number 23*. London: British Psychological Society/Royal College of Psychiatrists.

National Collaborating Centre for Mental Health (2010) *Schizophrenia: The NICE Guideline on Core Interventions in the Treatment and Management of Schizophrenia in Primary and Secondary Care*, updated edition. London: NICE.

Perkins, D.O., Gu, H., Boteva, K. and Lieberman, J. A. (2005) 'Relationship between duration of untreated psychosis and outcome in first-episode schizophrenia: a critical review and meta-analysis', *American Journal of Psychiatry*, 162, 1785–804.

Rinaldi, M., Miller, L. and Perkins, R. (2010) 'Implementing the individual placement and support (IPS) approach for people with mental health conditions in England', *International Review of Psychiatry*, 22, 163–72.

Ritchie, J.H., Dick, D. and Lingham, R. (1994) *The Report of the Inquiry into the Care and Treatment of Christopher Clunis*. London: HMSO.

Rogers, A. and Pilgrim, D. (1996) *Mental Health Policy in Britain*. Basingstoke: Palgrave Macmillan.

Rolph, S., Atkinson, D. and Walmsley, J. (2003) '"A pair of stout shoes and an umbrella": the role of the mental welfare officer in delivering community care in East Anglia: 1946–1970', *British Journal of Social Work*, **33**(3): 339–59.

SCIE (Social Care Institute for Excellence) (2009) *Think Child, Think Parent, Think Family: A Guide to Parental Mental Health and Child Welfare*. London: SCIE.

Scull, A. (1977) *Decarceration: Community Treatment and the Deviant – A Radical View*. Englewood Cliffs, NJ: Prentice Hall.

SEU (Social Exclusion Unit) (2004) *Social Exclusion and Mental Health*. London: Office of Deputy Prime Minister.

Slade, M. (2009) *Personal Recovery and Mental Illness: A Guide for Mental Health Professionals*. Cambridge: Cambridge University Press.

Test, M.A. (1998) 'The origins of PACT', *The Journal of NAMI California*, 9, 5–6.

Tew, J. (ed.) (2005) *Social Perspectives in Mental Health: Developing Social Models to Understand and Work with Mental Distress*. London: Jessica Kingsley.

Thornicroft, G., Bindman, J., Goldberg, D. et al. (2002) 'Creating the infrastructure for mental health research', *Psychiatric Bulletin*, 26, 403–6.

Webber, M. (2011) *Evidence-based Policy and Practice in Mental Health Social Work* (2nd edn). Exeter: Learning Matters.

Webber, M. and Nathan, J. (eds) (2010) *Reflective Practice in Mental Health: Advanced Psychosocial Practice with Children, Adolescents and Adults*. London: Jessica Kingsley.

WHO World Mental Health Survey Consortium (2004) 'Prevalence, severity, and unmet need for treatment of mental disorders in the World Health Organization World Mental Health Surveys', *Journal of the American Medical Association*, **291**(21): 2581–90.

Winterton, R. (2007) *Mental Health Services: Hospital Beds*, House of Commons written answers, 6 Feb, Col. 805W, *Hansard*.

Policy

7
Mental health law and social work

NICK GOULD AND DEBBIE MARTIN

It might be surprising to many people in the UK that mental health is the area of practice in which social workers have the most direct power in relation to the restriction of liberties of citizens. This is despite the raised public profile of child protection work and the prominence of statutory social work in that arena. Since the Mental Health Act 1959 (MHA), social workers have carried the primary responsibility for applying for admission to hospital of people with a mental disorder, although, as we shall see, the Mental Health Act 1983, as amended by the 2007 Act (hereafter referred to as the MHA 1983) has broadened the role to incorporate other professionals. This chapter will consider:

- the social and institutional factors that have shaped the law in relation to people living with mental health problems
- how in modern times the legal context has influenced the social work role
- the part played by social workers in relation to people detained in mental hospitals or treated compulsorily in the community
- the role of social workers in the deprivation of liberty of individuals by virtue of mental incapacity
- the social work contribution to safeguarding, with particular regard to the tribunal system
- some potential trends for the future.

The intention of the chapter is not to replace comprehensive textbooks on mental health law (for example Barber et al., 2009; Jones, 2011), but to signpost the main implications for social workers, and the tensions and controversies relating to their role.

The socio-legal context

All developed countries have some form of statute that defines the conditions under which individuals can be considered mentally unwell and their rights to self-determination overridden in order to detain, and possibly treat, them against their will (Hatfield, 2008). Sociologists and social theorists locate this impulse to intervene authoritatively in the lives of people with mental health problems in various explanatory frameworks. Social theorists such as Foucault (1965) have situated the origin of this impulse to segregate and detain those deemed to be mentally abnormal in the eighteenth-century Enlightenment, a philosophical movement that promoted rationality as the defining characteristic of humanity, and consigned those considered to be 'other' to regulatory systems of confinement and control. Some historians and sociologists contest this perspective, drawing on Marxist analyses of class structures formed under industrialization and the emergence of capitalism and its need to regulate members of the 'lumpenproletariat' who were unable to participate in waged labour (Garland, 1985). Social constructionists see confinement as a form of social control by which 'rule-breakers' or deviants are labelled and coerced into moral careers as patients (Spector and Kitsuse, 1977). Other, more functionalist commentators take a more benign view of the development of psychiatry as a form of therapeutic intervention, which evolves as scientific inquiry produces new forms of treatment.

It is clear that the role of compulsion in relation to people with mental health problems is a contested arena and has led some analysts to question whether the very category of mental health law is not an inherently discriminatory and repressive construct. For example, Campbell and Heginbotham (1991) argue that singling out people with mental health problems as in need of specific forms of legal intervention presumes that they present uniquely high forms of risk to others, whereas research evidence indicates that, overall, they present levels of dangerousness that are not elevated above the general population, and the primary risk they represent is to themselves. A historical overview of the development of mental health law in England suggests that control of people who are mentally unwell is an arena within which medicine and the law compete to extend their power and influence. Within this struggle, social work has come to occupy a position as an arbiter between the medical paternalism of 'doctor knowing best' and legalism, which asserts that the welfare of people with mental health problems is best adjudicated through judicial procedure (Peay, 1989). In modern times, this pendulum between medical paternalism and legalism has swung in an arc that alternates roughly every 25 years. The MHA 1959 reflected medical ascendancy as represented by the development in the 1950s of a new generation of psychotropic drugs, while the MHA 1983 gave patients additional legal safeguards against forcible detainment and treatment in the face of criticism from European human rights jurisdictions and civil libertarian mental health reformers. The 2007 reform of the MHA 1983 arguably signals a revalidation of medical influence, by broadening the legal definition of mental disorder to permit greater medical discretion and introducing supervised treatment in the community (see below).

Law

The role of social workers in the mental health arena

A paradigmatic change in the care of people with mental health problems began in the 1950s and early 1960s, with pharmacological developments in the treatment of major psychoses, fiscal pressure to reduce spending on large hospitals, and continuing scandals concerning standards of care in those institutions (Fawcett and Karban, 2005; Gould, 2010). Eventually, these pressures would coalesce in the emergence of community-based care as the preferred model to hospitalization. The MHA 1959, based on recommendations of the 1957 Percy Commission on the law relating to mental illness, created the role of the mental welfare officer (MWO), an employee of the local authority who was authorized to make applications for compulsory detention in hospital for assessment and treatment, or for guardianship where protective supervision in the community was deemed to be appropriate. The application had to be supported by the recommendation of approved doctors, but the MHA 1959 institutionalized the role of an independent non-clinician (MWOs were usually social workers) to assess and determine whether an application for hospitalization was necessary in the interests of the health or safety of the individual, or for the protection of others. This role evolved in the MHA 1983 (and the 1984 equivalent in Scotland) and was further professionalized with the replacement of MWOs by approved social workers (ASWs). ASWs were still appointed by the local authority but approval was based on the successful completion of specialist post-qualifying training following a national curriculum laid down by the Central Council for Education and Training in Social Work (CCETSW). The function of the ASW remained broadly as for MWOs – to make applications for hospitalization or guardianship, where this was supported by approved doctors.

The MHA 1983 was revised in 2007 (although the primary legislation remains the MHA 1983) and the ASW became the approved mental health professional (AMHP). The main impetus for reform of the 1983 Act was political ('populist' in the words of Rogers and Pilgrim, 2010, p. 226) anxiety about the supposed dangerousness presented by patients who were unsupervised in the community. However, the opportunity was also taken to address workforce concerns that the ageing demographic profile of mental health social work specialists meant that there could be future problems in meeting demand for professionals to fulfil the assessment, application and supervision functions of the legislation (Huxley et al., 2005). Hence, eligibility was extended from social workers to include other practitioners in allied mental health occupations, namely nursing, psychology and occupational therapy. However, post-qualifying training and approval for AMHP status remains under the aegis of the professional body for social work – the General Social Care Council (GSCC) until the replacement in 2012 of its regulatory functions by the Health Professions Council – and local authorities respectively.

The rationale for the role of the AMHP (and previously MWO and ASW) has remained fairly consistent – there should be a person who can be neutral and independent of medical opinion in determining whether compulsion is necessary.

Although the AMHP operates under the legislation as an independent professional accountable for their own practice (and is therefore directly liable for malpractice), they are also appointed by a local social services authority, which is independent of the NHS mental health services. However, this independence and neutrality is under-cut by apparent contradictions. From 1959 onwards, the legislation has also enshrined the right of the nearest relative to make an application for compulsory powers to be invoked (Rapaport and Manthorpe, 2008). Although codes of practice reinforce the view that it is preferable that AMHPs rather than relatives make applications, critics argue that the law enshrines an archaic echo of the eighteenth-century private madhouses where families could confine troublesome relatives. More recently, under the 2007 amendments, the enlargement of the applicant role to include NHS employees such as nurses to act as AMHPs, and the prevalent situation whereby mental health social workers are seconded to NHS trusts, makes it more difficult to demonstrate that the AMHP's judgement is truly independent of medical practition-ers and health authorities.

Despite these anxieties, the AMHP is in an important position to operate as a countervailing power to that of medical practitioners, in an arena where most would see the dominant paradigm as still being that of the medical model. A study of ASW assessments in six local authorities found that 10.1% of referrals were diverted to voluntary admission to hospital, and 7.2% were provided with community-based alternatives to hospital care (Hatfield, 2008). This study suggests that social workers were doing more than rubber-stamping requests to section individuals. The training of AMHPs remains under the direction of the regulatory body for social work (the GSCC), so that practitioners are educated to bring to their decision-making perspectives drawn from the social sciences, a knowledge of the broad field of welfare law, child protection, and a value base that places a strong emphasis on anti-discrimination (GSCC, 2007). In many ways, the role of the AMHP goes to the heart of the historical tensions in social work between care and control, between the impulse to promote the capacities of the individual to exercise self-determination and judging those circumstances where a concern for risk to self and others justifies the use of compulsion. As Pritchard (2006, p. 200) wrote in relation to ASWs, although it is equally applicable to the AMHP role:

> Fundamentally, it is these 'tensions' that provide the challenge to the ASW – the challenge of making a balanced and reasoned decision in the midst of often chaotic circumstances, often without having all the information one would wish, while always ensuring that there are medical, ethical and legal bases for the deci-sion reached.

Civil admissions to hospital

Civil admissions to hospital under the MHA 1983 require an application by an AMHP or the patient's nearest relative. However, as indicated above, the 'AMHP is usually a more appropriate applicant than the patient's nearest relative, given an AMHP's professional training and knowledge of the legislation and local resources' (DH, 2008, para. 4.28). An application can only be made when the presence of mental disorder has been established, the legal criteria are satisfied, medical recommendations have been given, and there is no suitable alternative to detention. The process of coordinating the assessments to establish whether these requirements are met is the responsibility of the AMHP (DH, 2008). Both the MHA 1983 and the related code of practice set out the statutory obligations and guidance to be followed when undertaking this role.

Before a patient can be detained, or made subject to any of the MHA 1983 provisions, the presence of mental disorder must be established. For civil detentions, this is by two medical practitioners, with the exception of section 4, where only one is required. The amended definition of mental disorder, 'any disorder or disability of the mind' (MHA 1983, s. 1), arguably increases the population that fall within its scope (Fennell, 2007). The code of practice suggests conditions that are regarded as mental disorders, for example affective disorders and personality disorders (DH, 2008, para. 3.3). In addition, disorders such as fetishism and paedophilia fall within its scope (DH, 2007, para. 24). The only remaining exclusion concerns dependence on alcohol or drugs. While this determination falls to medical practitioners, the AMHP must also be satisfied that mental disorder exists. This may, in practice, raise some ethical issues, for example the potential for the MHA 1983 to be used to contain those with deviant behaviours, as opposed to treating mental disorders.

To be detained under section 2 of the MHA 1983 (admission for assessment for up to 28 days), the patient:

- [must be] suffering from mental disorder of a nature or degree which warrants detention ... in a hospital for assessment (or for assessment followed by medical treatment), for at least a limited period; and
- ought to be so detained in the interests of his own health or safety or with a view to the protection of others.

For section 3 (admission for treatment for up to six months), the patient:

- [must be] suffering from [a mental disorder] of a nature or degree which makes it appropriate for him to receive medical treatment in hospital; and
- it is necessary for the health or safety of the patient or for the protection of other persons that he should receive such treatment and it cannot be provided unless he is detained under this section; and
- appropriate medical treatment is available for him.

Section 4 (admission for assessment for up to 72 hours) may be used in cases of urgent necessity, when securing the attendance of the two medical practitioners necessary for a section 2 would involve an undesirable delay.

When establishing whether the grounds are met, the AMHP need only be satisfied that the mental disorder is of a nature *or* degree warranting detention. 'Nature' refers to its chronicity, its prognosis and previous responses to treatment, and 'degree' refers to the current manifestation of the disorder (*R* v *Mental Health Review Tribunal* [1999]). In addition, at least one of the three risk criteria – health (physical and mental), safety, or risk to others – must be identified. For section 3, appropriate medical treatment must be available; this is to 'ensure that no-one is detained ... unless they are actually to be offered medical treatment' (DH, 2008, para. 6.7). However, the case of *MD* v *Nottinghamshire Health Care NHS Trust* [2010] sets a low threshold for this criterion to be met. Finally, when considering legal criteria, the AMHP should consider all the alternatives to detention:

■ for section 2, this includes the possibility of facilitating an informal admission
■ for section 3, they must be satisfied that treatment cannot be provided unless detained under that section.

Indeed, an application cannot be made unless the AMHP is satisfied that detention is the most appropriate way of providing care and treatment (MHA 1983, s. 13).

Where the relevant detention criteria are met, and medical recommendations are given, the AMHP is able to exercise discretion in deciding whether or not to complete an application for detention. This discretion leaves the AMHP with the difficult task of considering the competing demands of social control and patient autonomy (Campbell, 2010), and making a decision based on the individual circumstances of the case.

Supervision in the community

The MHA 1983 contains three civil means of community compulsion: guardianship; leave of absence; and community treatment orders (CTOs). Each provision has distinct criteria, and allows varying levels of compulsion. Each of the provisions will be outlined, with a particular focus on the role of, and dilemmas faced by, AMHPs.

Guardianship: section 7

Guardianship is available to mentally disordered patients who are 16 or over provided that:

■ [their] mental disorder [is] of a nature or degree which warrants reception into guardianship; and
■ it is necessary in the interests of [their] welfare, or for the protection of other persons.

The application is made by an AMHP (or nearest relative) and is addressed to the local authority. Applications must be founded on two medical recommendations, and if accepted by the local authority, a guardian will be named:

Private individuals hardly ever act as guardian. For example, in 2008 there were 410 new cases where the local authority was the guardian and only four where the guardian was a private individual or organization. (Brown, 2009, p. 31)

Guardianship gives the guardian the power to require:

- the patient to reside at a specified place
- the patient to attend at places for the purpose of medical treatment, occupation, education or training
- access to the patient, at any place where they are residing, to any medical practitioner, AMHP or other specified person.

The patient can be taken to the place of residence in the first place, and be returned if they leave with the intention of not returning. The purpose of guardianship is to provide 'an authoritative framework for working with a patient, with a minimum of constraint, to achieve as independent a life as possible' (DH, 2008, para. 26.4). However, there are limitations to the powers:

- a patient required to reside in a specified place has freedom of movement and cannot be deprived of their liberty
- there is no power to enforce medical treatment or to allow forced entry.

Leave of absence: section 17

Leave of absence allows detained patients to be lawfully absent from hospital. Leave may be granted by the patient's responsible clinician (RC), and may be for a specified occasion or indefinitely. If considered necessary in the interests of the patient or for the protection of others, the RC may direct that the patient remain in the custody of a member of hospital staff or anyone authorized by the hospital managers, for example a social worker. Section 17 requires the RC to consider a CTO if leave is granted for more than seven consecutive days. However, section 17 may be used to provide long-term community treatment, provided that a significant component of the treatment plan takes place at a hospital (*R (DR)* v *Mersey Care NHS Trust* [2002]).

Community treatment orders (CTOs): section 17A

CTOs were introduced in November 2008. Their purpose is to 'allow suitable patients to be safely treated in the community rather than under detention in hospital, and to provide a way to help prevent relapse and any harm – to the patient or to others' (DH, 2008, para. 25.2). CTOs are available to patients subject to section 3 or unrestricted part 3 patients, providing they meet the following criteria (MHA 1983, s. 17A(5)):

(a) the patient is suffering from mental disorder of a nature or degree which makes it appropriate for him to receive medical treatment;

(b) it is necessary for his health or safety or for the protection of other persons that he should receive such treatment;

(c) subject to his being liable to be recalled as mentioned in paragraph (d) below, such treatment can be provided without his continuing to be detained in a hospital;

(d) it is necessary that the responsible clinician should be able to exercise the power to recall the patient to hospital; and

(e) appropriate medical treatment is available for him.

It is the role of the AMHP to establish whether:

- they agree with the responsible clinician that the above criteria are met
- it is appropriate to make the order
- any conditions imposed are necessary or appropriate.

If the AMHP does not agree, a CTO cannot be imposed, and 'it would not be appropriate for the responsible clinician to approach another AMHP for an alternative view' (DH, 2008, para. 25.27).

AMHPs are also involved in the revocation and extension of CTOs. Revocation may only follow recall by the patient's RC, and effectively places the patient back on their initial detention section. AMHPs are able to agree to revocation when satisfied that the detention criteria for section 3 are met, and they consider it appropriate to revoke the order. Extension of a CTO requires an AMHP to agree that the criteria are met and that it is appropriate to extend the order.

AMHPs can exercise discretion when deciding whether to agree to a CTO, its revocation or extension. The notion of appropriateness in each of these stages raises a number of practice questions for AMHPs. It is inescapable that the driving force behind CTOs was the management of risk posed by those with a mental disorder (DH, 2000). This results in a balancing act between 'the sometimes competing demands of protective interventions while still trying to preserve the rights of service users' (Campbell et al., 2006, p. 1106).

In the absence of any empirical evidence to support the use of CTOs under the MHA 1983 (see the inconclusive finding of international studies, Churchill, 2007), AMHPs should take care when considering the appropriateness of imposing compulsion on those considered well enough to live within the community.

Mental Capacity Act 2005

The Mental Capacity Act 2005 (MCA), implemented in 2007, 'provides a statutory framework for decision-making on behalf of people who lack capacity to consent to their care and treatment' (Barber et al., 2009, p. 63). The Act was amended to introduce the deprivation of liberty safeguards (DOLS), implemented in 2009. DOLS allow for the lawful deprivation of liberty of incapacitated adults in hospital or care home settings. The MCA 2005 also allows capacitated adults to make preparations for a time when they may lack capacity, and provides for the Court of Protection to make property and affairs and personal welfare orders for those who lack capacity.

The scope of this part of the chapter is limited to two key features of the MCA 2005 that affect social work practice:

1   care and treatment decisions made on behalf of those lacking capacity, under section 5
2   the lawful deprivation of liberty of incapacitated adults, under schedule A1.

Section 1 of the Act sets out principles that underpin the legislation and 'apply to all actions and decisions taken under this Act' (Jones, 2008, p. 9). The principles cover the following points:

■   assume capacity unless incapacity is established
■   take all practicable steps to help the person make the decision
■   a person is not incapable just because they make an unwise decision
■   act in the best interests of the person
■   seek a less restrictive alternative where possible.

To establish whether the Act applies, the decision-maker must determine whether the person lacks capacity in relation to the decision. The decision-maker is not defined by the Act, but the code of practice describes them as 'the carer most directly involved with the person at the time' (Department of Constitutional Affairs, 2007, p. 69). This could be a social worker concerned with the decision to move someone from one environment to another.

To establish incapacity, the decision-maker must apply the following tests. They must establish an 'impairment of, or a disturbance in the functioning of the mind or brain' (MCA 2005, s. 2) affecting the person's ability to make a decision. The decision-maker must then establish whether the person is able to:

■   understand the relevant information
■   retain that information
■   use or weigh that information as part of the process of making the decision
■   communicate their decision.

If one or more of the above points is not satisfied, the person is deemed to lack capacity in relation to the decision and the decision-maker may make a decision in the person's best interests. Section 4 of the MCA 2005 provides a checklist for best interests.

Section 5 acts

Provided the above procedure has been followed, the decision-maker may make decisions on behalf of the incapacitated person. Decisions under this section may cover 'personal care' and 'healthcare and treatment' (Department of Constitutional Affairs, 2007, p. 95). However, there are limitations to acts carried out. For example, restraint may only be used to prevent harm to the person, provided it is a proportionate response to the likelihood of harm and the seriousness of that harm. Care or treatment that amounts to a deprivation of liberty is outside the scope of this

Making connexions

What are the roles expected of the social worker as a consequence of the Mental Capacity Act 2005?

section. Where a deprivation of liberty is occurring, efforts should be made to reduce restrictions, and where this is not possible, DOLS should be considered.

Deprivation of liberty safeguards (DOLS)

DOLS were introduced in response to *HL* v *UK* [2004], where the European Court of Human Rights concluded that HL had been unlawfully detained, as his detention did not meet the requirements of Article 5 of the 1950 European Convention on Human Rights. Article 5, the right to liberty and security of person, requires that detention is in 'accordance with a procedure prescribed by law' and that those deprived of their liberty 'shall be entitled to take proceedings by which the lawfulness of his detention shall be decided speedily by a court'. HL had been detained at common law, therefore neither of these requirements were met.

DOLS conform to Article 5 requirements, in that they provide a statutory procedure and an appeal to the Court of Protection. To ensure compliance with the law, social workers (and others) working with incapacitated people must be able to establish when a deprivation of liberty is occurring. However, it is to be noted that deprivation of liberty under the MCA 2005 does not provide an alternative means of detention to the MHA 1983, where an objecting patient, meeting the criteria for MHA 1983 detention, requires treatment for a mental disorder in a hospital (*GJ* v *The Foundation Trust and Ors* [2009]).

There is no statutory definition of deprivation of liberty, which presents a problem in practice. Guidance can be found in case law judgments and Chapter 2 of the MCA DOLS code of practice (Ministry of Justice, 2008). Where a deprivation of liberty is identified, those responsible for the person (the care home or hospital), as the managing authority, must follow the procedures set out in schedule A1 of the MCA 2005.

These procedures have created a new statutory role, the 'best interests assessor', for social workers (among others). The best interests assessor has to identify deprivation of liberty, and establish whether it is in the person's best interests. In addition, the best interests assessor is responsible for identifying a representative for the person, for suggesting recommendations and the time frame for which a deprivation should occur.

Mental health tribunals and the social work role

This chapter shows that social workers play a range of safeguarding functions in relation to people with mental health problems. A particularly important function is to provide social reports to mental health tribunals (MHTs), although it is important

Law

to emphasize that this duty is not limited to social workers but can be provided by other members of the clinical team. MHTs are judicial hearings that consider appeals against detention or compulsory community provisions by patients who come under the jurisdiction of the MHA 1983, that is, they have been sectioned, are subject to a guardianship order, or are supervised under a CTO.

The work of MHTs has become more prominent, and under the MHA 2007 was extended under continuing pressure, resulting from cases taken to the European Court of Human Rights, and since the incorporation of European standards in the Human Rights Act 1998 to ensure that detained patients had proper access to due legal process to review their loss of liberty. The UK is one of the few jurisdictions where there is no judicial input to the decision to commit an individual to hospital (it is based on the views of the AMHP or nearest relative and doctors) (Hatfield, 2008), and so it was deemed essential to their human rights that they should have recourse to a judicial hearing. Within the court structure for England, the MHT is one part of the Health, Education and Social Care Chamber, a new tribunal framework created by the Tribunals, Courts and Enforcement Act 2007.

Members of the tribunal are appointed by the lord chancellor and fall into three categories: legal members, medical members and other members (previously known as 'lay members'):

1   Members within the 'other' category are appointed for their knowledge of social services or other relevant qualifications or experience, and a significant number have a background in social work.
2   The legal member acts as chair of the tribunal; where the patient has been made the subject of a hospital order by a court, the legal member will be a member of the judiciary of at least equivalent standing to the judge who made the original order.
3   The medical member, invariably a consultant psychiatrist, is a decision-making member of the tribunal but also examines the patient before the tribunal hearing and reports their findings to the other members.

The patient has a right to legal representation and can make an application to a tribunal for discharge or variation of the legal conditions of the MHA 1983 to which they are subject, although not to changes to the conditions attached to a CTO. MHT hearings are conducted either at the hospital where the patient is detained, or some other mental health service facility that is local and accessible. MHTs have the constitutional status of a court but their rules require them to avoid unnecessary formality and to be flexible in the proceedings (Tribunal Procedure Rules 2008, 1.3).

The Practice Direction for tribunals requires that the MHT receive and consider a social report on the circumstances of the patient (Tribunals Judiciary, n.d.). It is not a requirement that the report is prepared by an AMHP, nor does it have to be by a social worker, although most are, and it is a persuasive argument that social workers are best placed and most qualified to provide the content of the social circumstances report as stipulated by the Practice Direction (Tribunals Judiciary, n.d., s. E17), that is:

1   the patient's home and family circumstances
2   a summary of the views of the nearest relative
3   the views of any other nonprofessional person substantially involved in the care of the patient
4   the views of the patient, including the hoped-for outcome of the MHT
5   opportunities for employment and housing available to the patient
6   community support that can be provided to the patient and its likely effectiveness if a discharge is made
7   the patient's financial circumstances (including entitlement to benefits)
8   the patient's strengths and other positive factors that may have a bearing on the tribunal decision
9   an assessment of the risks that might be presented if a discharge is made, and how they could best be managed.

Normally, the social circumstances report will be presented by its author, and social workers have to be prepared to defend their evidence and recommendations under cross-examination from members of the MHT and the patient's legal representative. Periodically, tribunals are criticized for being too sympathetic towards the views of the detaining authority, or compromised in their objectivity by the dual role of the medical member (as assessor and decision-maker) (Peay, 1989). Statistics for 2008–9 show that 14% of MHT applications were successful so, although in most cases the patient fails to persuade the tribunal to discharge them from hospital or lift the relevant order, in a significant minority of cases, the MHT finds against the detaining authority (Administrative Justice and Tribunals Council annual statistics). Although up-to-date evidence is sparse on decision-making in tribunals, it seems reasonable to suggest that social work continues to make a relevant contribution to the MHT's consideration of the social variables influencing detention and the assessment of risk.

Future perspectives

Recent studies of the mental health workforce suggest that social workers undertaking statutory duties are under significant strain. In a study of burnout and job satisfaction among mental health social workers in England and Wales, Evans et al. (2006) found high levels of stress and emotional exhaustion, and low levels of job satisfaction, with levels of symptomatology twice those reported by psychiatrists in equivalent studies. These levels of dissatisfaction and distress were even higher in ASWs. The authors concluded that without greater support and validation from employers, the problems of recruitment and retention would increase. A further study by the same authors concluded that ASWs received less support at work than other mental health social workers, and their role gave them less autonomy in decision-making and, by implication, less job satisfaction (Evans et al., 2005). As we have discussed, the broadening of eligibility to undertake the AMHP role has been a device to compensate for recruitment problems among social workers, but this does not in itself fix the inherent strains of statutory mental health work. One prediction is that this will merely spread burnout and stress to other mental health professionals (Evans et al., 2005). Another study (albeit before the implementation of the MHA 2007) talks of the 'disappearing approved social worker' (Huxley et al., 2005), as numbers of ASWs per 100,000 population halved in England and Wales between 1992 and 2002.

These tensions may increase as social workers, among others, are expected to grapple with the increasing statute, guidance and case law governing decisions made for or on behalf of those considered mentally disordered and those lacking mental capacity to make care and treatment decisions (Hale, 2009). The application of the increased statutes (the MHA 1983 and MCA 2005) highlights the disparity between the capacitated patient's right to refuse treatment. This presents a further dilemma for professionals who cannot avoid the fact that those with capacity are able to refuse treatment for physical ill health, even if it leads to their death, but those considered mentally disordered may have their capacitated refusal overridden, by detention under the MHA 1983. Szmukler et al. (2010, p. 12) argue that these two separate regimes are unacceptable, and advocate the fusing of legislation, stating that:

> this 'two-track' approach is inconsistent with general principles of healthcare ethics and with notions of human rights, particularly the right of people with mental disorders to be free of unnecessary discrimination in law.

Given the recent reform of mental health and mental capacity legislation, it is unlikely that we will see such a change in the near future, and it may be argued that such a 'fusing' of statutes would be untenable, but social workers, when applying legislation, are well placed to use their skills and discretion to minimize discrimination and champion patient choice wherever possible.

Appendix 7.1 Table of cases

| GJ v The Foundation Trust and Ors [2009] EWHC 2972 (Fam) |
| HL v UK [2004] 40 EHHR 761 |
| MD v Nottinghamshire Health Care NHS Trust [2010] UKUT 59 (AAC) |
| R (DR) v Mersey Care NHS Trust [2002] EWHC 1810 (Admin) |
| R v Mental Health Review Tribunal for the South Thames Region ex parte Smith [1999] COD 148 |

Further reading

■ Barber, P., Brown, R. and Martin, D. (2009) *Mental Health Law in England and Wales*. Exeter: Learning Matters.

Includes and explains the Mental Health Act 1983 as amended by the 2007 Act.

Provides guidance to mental health professionals on the operation of law in practice. In addition to the revised statute and explanations of it, it contains appendices detailing tribunal rules, mental health regulations, the Human Rights Act 1998 and a case law summary.

■ Gould, N. (2010) *Mental Health Social Work in Context*. London: Routledge.

Written for social work students and practitioners, it does not address mental health law in detail, but provides a broad discussion of the context of statutory practice.

■ Jones, R. (2011) *Mental Health Act Manual* (14th edn). London: Sweet & Maxwell.

Richard Jones is a qualified social worker and solicitor, so is alert to social work perspectives on mental health law. Colloquially known as 'Jones', this is the standard reference text on mental health law used by legal practitioners; probably regarded as the most authoritative commentary on judicial decision-making.

References

Barber, P., Brown, R. and Martin, D. (2009) *Mental Health Law in England and Wales*. Exeter: Learning Matters.

Brown, R. (2009) *The Approved Mental Health Professional's Guide to Mental Health Law* (2nd edn). Exeter: Learning Matters.

Campbell, J. (2010) 'Deciding to detain: the use of compulsory mental health law by UK social workers', *British Journal of Social Work*, **40**(1): 328–34.

Campbell, J., Brophy, L., Healy, B. and O'Brian A.-M. (2006) 'International perspectives on the use of community treatment orders: implications for mental health social workers', *British Journal of Social Work*, 36, 1101–18.

Campbell, T. and Heginbotham, C. (1991) *Mental Illness: Prejudice, Discrimination and the Law*. Aldershot: Dartmouth.

Churchill, R. (2007) *International Experiences of Using Community Treatment Orders*. London: Institute of Psychiatry, King's College London.

Department of Constitutional Affairs (2007) *The Mental Capacity Act 2005: Code of Practice*. London: TSO.

DH (Department of Health) (2000) *Reforming the Mental Health Act:* Part 1, *The New Legal Framework*. London: TSO.

DH (2007) *Explanatory Notes: Mental Health Act 2007*. London: Office of Public Sector Information.

DH (2008) *Code of Practice: Mental Health Act 1983*. London: TSO.

Evans, S., Huxley, P., Webber, M. et al. (2005) 'The impact of "statutory duties" on mental health social workers in the UK', *Health and Social Care in the Community*, **13**(2): 145–54.

Evans, S., Huxley, P., Gately, C. et al. (2006) 'Mental health, burnout and job satisfaction amongst mental health social workers in England and Wales', *British Journal of Psychiatry*, **188**(1): 75–80.

Fawcett, B. and Karban, K. (2005) *Contemporary Mental Health: Theory, Policy and Practice*. London: Routledge.

Fennell, P. (2007) *Mental Health: The New Law*. Bristol: Jordan.

Foucault, M. (1965) *Madness and Civilisation*. New York: Random House.

Garland, D. (1985) *Punishment and Welfare: A History of Penal Strategies*. Aldershot: Gower.

Gould, N. (2010) *Mental Health Social Work in Context*. London: Routledge.

GSCC (General Social Care Council) (2007) *Social Work in Mental Health Services: Specialist Standards and Requirements for Post-qualifying Social Work Education and Training*. London: GSCC.

Hale, B. (2009) 'Taking stock', *Journal of Mental Health Law*, 19, 1111–16.

Hatfield, B. (2008) 'Powers to detain under mental health legislation in England and the role of the approved social worker: an analysis of patterns and trends under the 1983 Mental Health Act in six local authorities', *British Journal of Social Work*, **38**(8): 1553–71.

Huxley, P., Evans, S., Gately, C. et al. (2005) 'Stress and pressures in mental health social work: the worker speaks', *British Journal of Social Work*, **35**(7): 1063–79.

Huxley, P., Evans, S., Webber, M. and Gately, C. (2005) 'Staff shortages in the mental health workforce: the case of the disappearing approved social worker', *Health and Social Care in the Community*, **13**(6): 504–13.

Jones, R. (2008) *Mental Capacity Act Manual* (3rd edn). London: Sweet & Maxwell.

Jones, R. (2011) *Mental Health Act Manual* (14th edn). London: Sweet & Maxwell.

Ministry of Justice (2008) *Mental Capacity Act 2005: Deprivation of Liberty Safeguards Code of Practice to Supplement the Main Mental Capacity Act 2005 Code of Practice*, London: TSO.

Peay, J. (1989) *Tribunals on Trial*. Oxford: Oxford University Press.

Pritchard, C. (2006) *Mental Health Social Work: Evidence-based Practice*. London: Routledge.

Rapaport, J. and Manthorpe, J. (2008) 'Family matters: developments concerning the role of the nearest relative and social worker under mental health law in England and Wales', *British Journal of Social Work*, **38**(6): 1115–31.

Rogers, A. and Pilgrim, D. (2010) *A Sociology of Mental Health and Illness*. Maidenhead: McGraw Hill.

Spector, M. and Kitsuse, J. (1977) *Constructing Social Problems*. Menlo Park, CA: Cummings.

Szmukler, G., Saw, R. and Dawson, J. (2010) 'A model law fusing incapacity and mental health legislation', *Journal of Mental Health Law*, 20, 1–140.

Tribunals Judiciary (n.d.) Practice Direction: Health Education and Social Care Chamber: Mental Health Cases, http://www.justice.gov.uk/downloads/guidance/courts-and-tribunals/tribunals/mental-health/publications/PracticeDirection.pdf.

8

Theory in mental health social work

JERRY TEW

Perhaps more than in any other field of social work practice, theory within mental health remains a contested area, with medical, psychological and social theories providing radically different accounts of how we should approach the range of strange and unusual experiences that constitute mental distress. Particularly in the 1990s, the biomedical paradigm became increasingly dominant in framing understanding and we were invited to see complex human experiences as if they were just 'symptoms' of supposed underlying disease processes. Although still dominant, this paradigm has become increasingly challenged, not least by service users and survivors themselves.

At the heart of this challenge is an increasingly robust evidence base, which indicates that life events and social experiences are at least as important as genetics in increasing one's susceptibility to mental distress, and that one's prospects of longer term recovery probably depend more on social attitudes, relationships and opportunities than they do on medical treatments (Tew, 2011). Even the notion of 'recovery' itself is contested, with service users and survivors claiming the right to define what it may mean for them. In a shift that is as profound as the development of the social model of disability, people have redefined 'recovery' as a process that is primarily personal and social: it is about 'getting a life' and reclaiming self-worth and valued social roles, irrespective of whether one may still continue to experience certain distress experiences.

Instead of the old rehabilitation paradigm, in which one had to become medically 'well' before one could re-enter mainstream social and economic life, a recovery approach suggests the reverse: it is through finding 'a place in the world' and taking active control over one's life that one makes progress, and this progress towards a more satisfying and connected lifestyle may render any ongoing 'symptoms' more manageable – or even result in their complete remission. This view has support in the research evidence. Although employment is not the be-all and end-all of recovery, it is interesting to note that overall rates, of both 'social' recovery and remission of symptoms, have been shown to correlate with economic cycles (and therefore employment opportunities) rather than any advances in drug or other treatments (Warner, 2004). Similarly, schemes that place people within mainstream work settings (and provide good support to both employee and employer) can result not only in improvements in their wider social functioning but also in a reduced level of 'symptoms' (Burns et al., 2009).

There is a concern that social work practice in mental health has, in some countries, become increasingly reactive (Ramon, 2009), concentrating on issues such as safeguarding and risk without any underpinning understanding of how socially focused interventions and supports may be crucial in enabling people to move forward and recover meaningful lives. Without such theoretically informed approaches to practice, mental health services may inadvertently become part of the problem: a cocktail of firefighting and defensive risk management practice may serve to maintain people within positions of chronic powerlessness, alienation and impoverished social circumstances – paradoxically at greater long-term risk both to themselves and to others.

What is mental distress?

Mental distress can take many forms, including strange or unusual cognitive experiences such as hearing voices or other forms of psychosis, out-of-control emotional states such as depression or anxiety, or behaviours that are harmful to self or others such as self-injury, anorexia or compulsive violence. Forms of mental distress may also be reflected in changes to one's brain physiology, hormone levels and other biological factors, but this does not mean that it is necessarily caused by any underlying disease process. Instead, there is increasing evidence from brain-scanning research that such changes can result from adverse social experiences such as trauma or deprivation (Perry et al., 1995) and can be reversed through more positive social experiences or psychological therapies (Roffman et al., 2005). In this way, the social and the biological may be seen as two sides of the same coin, rather than contradictory modes of explanation where the biological is assumed to have priority (Tew, 2011).

Traditional medical approaches to diagnosis may fail to capture the complexity and the meaning of such experiences (Mezzich et al., 2010) and can provide little 'added value' in areas such as predicting risk (Hiday, 2006) or social potential (Tsang et al., 2000). While each person's experience of mental distress is unique to them, a range of social and psychological theories may be helpful in starting to make meaningful what may otherwise appear a somewhat bewildering experience both for the person and for those around them. Theories may provide pointers as to what the experience may be about, what may have contributed to it, and what may be helpful in enabling the person to work through and resolve it.

Following Szasz (1961), a helpful starting point can be to see a manifestation of mental distress as, in some way or another, a 'last-ditch' or extreme response to a problem of living that one is unable to resolve in any other way. This locates the experience at the interface between the personal and the social: it is just as much about one's relational context as it is about one's inner world. It may start with an acute sense of unease about oneself and one's situation – one that may relate to past as well as current difficulties – but represents an escalation from this to a place where familiar coping mechanisms and rationally based solutions no longer offer any way out.

There are two apparently contradictory 'victim' and 'survivor' perspectives, which may be helpful in unpicking the meanings of distress experiences: to use one but not the other may be to miss the complexity of a person's struggle. At one and the same time, a particular manifestation of mental distress may potentially be seen as:

- a way of coping with (or containing) our underlying unease or problem of living
- a 'cry for help' that may also express (often indirectly) what the unease may be about (Tew, 2011, p. 29; see also Herman, 1997).

Theories that may be particularly helpful in making sense of distress experiences, and the sources of unease that may underlie these, include both psychological and social approaches. However, it is often helpful to use a combination of these so that we can start to build the 'bigger picture' of how internal and external experiences may be interacting to provoke and sustain particular manifestations of mental distress. In this chapter, I explore some key bodies of theory that may be relevant and which address the interface between our personal and social worlds, but this selection is by no means exhaustive.

Crisis theory and crisis resolution

Crisis theory provides an overarching framework within which to understand many (but not necessarily all) manifestations of mental distress – one that may be fleshed out using a range of other theoretical perspectives to make sense of more detailed processes and connections (Loughran, 2011). It has a long history within both social work and social psychiatry (see, for example, Caplan, 1965) and provides a framework within which to apply other theoretical perspectives, such as psychodynamic and systems approaches. In mental health practice, it should provide a theoretical foundation for crisis resolution services (Johnson and Needle, 2008), although in some instances there has been a tendency for such services to become little more than the provision of medical care and treatment in people's homes.

A crisis may be defined as a situation that is moving out of control, where, individually and/or collectively, people no longer have ways of restoring their former equilibrium. It may represent a spilling over of existing but unresolved tensions and/or an encounter with new and challenging circumstances; either way, a dominant feature of most crises is conflict, both internal and external (O'Hagan, 1994), accompanied by a breakdown of personal and social control mechanisms, and a disruption of familiar identities and relationships. It can be a time of risk and fear, but also an

Theory

opportunity for positive change. As Caplan argues, it is not something to be relieved but something to be resolved – a perspective that fits well with recovery-oriented mental health practice.

For many people, their experiences of mental distress feel like crises in a number of different ways that are potentially overlapping. People may find it makes sense to see what they are going through as some combination of:

- *a crisis of personal agency:* no longer feeling fully in control of one's thoughts, feelings or actions
- *a crisis of coping mechanisms:* existing ways of dealing with one's unease or external stresses may no longer be working
- *a crisis of identity:* no longer being comfortable within one's familiar social identities, and/or lacking any secure sense of who one is
- *a crisis of meaning:* previously taken-for-granted assumptions about one's world and one's place within it may start to feel 'up in the air' and one may find oneself trying out alternative forms of explanation, for example conspiracy theories, spiritual or symbolic connections
- *a crisis of social functioning:* no longer being able to sustain or perform one's usual social roles, or finding oneself stripped of such roles if others take over
- *a crisis within key personal relationships:* tensions or conflicts may have escalated to the point where the relationship itself feels threatened (or threatening)
- *a crisis of connection:* no longer feeling connected to familiar people or places or disengaging from social networks.

The sense of crisis may not be confined to the person experiencing mental distress; family, friends or carers may also find themselves bound up into a more collective sense of crisis, in which the routines and familiarities of daily life have become upended and their immediate context in terms of relationships and identities no longer feels stable.

Typically, crises have histories: an insidious build-up of unease and unresolved conflicts or issues in response to particular life events and social circumstances. For some time, this may remain well hidden beneath a surface veneer of apparently unproblematic social functioning. However, this may leave individuals and social groupings vulnerable to, or unable to cope with, particular events or stresses in the here and now that may not, in themselves, seem that significant – the 'straw that broke the camel's back'. Coping strategies may have been developed to contain the unresolved issues and their implications, which may work reasonably successfully for a period of time. However, faced with growing unease or further stresses, they may have to be enforced with increasing desperation, potentially at some cost to individual or collective functioning. Alternatively, they may start to collapse and people may give up trying to uphold existing norms of functioning. It is only by exploring such histories that apparently inexplicable overreactions to everyday adversities may start to make more sense.

In some instances, a crisis may emerge first within the interrelationships of a social grouping, such as a family or a workplace. Within this, some individuals may be more susceptible than others to take on the stresses of the wider group, and may go on to exhibit signs of mental distress. In other instances, a crisis may primarily originate within one individual but then resonate or spill over into the lives of those around them (Figure 8.1).

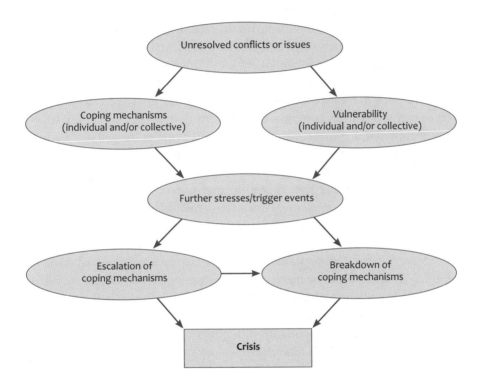

Figure 8.1 Model of build-up to a crisis

When people are desperate – as previous ways of coping have failed – they may be open to trying out new ways of being and relating, and may be more accepting of help from others. Working with people in crisis can be an efficient and effective use of time. This may be the 'window of opportunity' when change is possible, as most crises are resolved (for better or worse) within four to six weeks (Golan, 1986; Kanel, 2003). Effective crisis resolution may involve engaging with problems and difficulties in wider social systems as well as with a distressed individual and their immediate family or friends (Bridgett and Polak, 2003). However, for such change to 'stick', there is a need to focus on how those involved can support each other in sustaining that change in the face of subsequent challenges and adversities, and developing the skills, social networks and problem-solving capacities in order to do this (Healy, 2005).

Power relations, oppression and empowerment

Dealing with the impact of forms of social oppression and finding ways to promote empowerment can be central to many areas of social work practice and can be particularly relevant to working with mental health difficulties. However, this may not always be theorized as clearly as it might be, which is unsurprising, given the different understandings of power within the wider social and psychological literature.

Research findings suggest that being on the receiving end of the oppressive imposition of power by others may often be a precursor of mental distress. The much higher rates of diagnosed schizophrenia among African Caribbean people in Britain (Fearon et al., 2006) cannot be explained by any other factor apart from subjection to racism, and this is mirrored in the experiences of others whose identities lead them to be subordinated or excluded within current social relations (Janssen et al., 2003; Jorm et al., 2003; Williams, 2005). Similarly, an overall review of studies showed that up to 70% of those suffering from psychosis (both men and women) are victims of physical or sexual abuse (Read et al., 2005). A common feature of such oppressive experiences tends to be that victims may have found themselves powerless to resist or challenge what was happening to them, perhaps due to structural imbalances in power at a societal level and perhaps due to more local factors, such as social isolation or cultural expectations, leading to a lack of support or protection. Although mechanisms may vary, it seems clear that such oppressive experiences can be turned inward – and it can be helpful to see many manifestations of mental distress as embodying a combination of internalized oppression and blocked-off anger, fear or sadness relating to this.

Issues of control and loss of control can also be central to many experiences of mental distress, and this is intimately bound up with power relations, both internal and external. Some people describe their repeated self-injury or anorexia as a desperate attempt to reassert control when feeling chronically powerless and out of control. Research with voice hearers has shown that what can matter more than the content of people's voices is people's power relation to them: does the voice have the power to command or dish out derogatory criticism, or does the person have the power to negotiate with or challenge their voices (Birchwood et al., 2000)? Interestingly, a person's power relations vis-à-vis their internal world tend to mirror their external power relations with family, friends and others. Feeling overwhelmed within external relationships tends to lead to being overwhelmed in one's intrapsychic relationships, whereas feeling empowered externally can provide the key to taking more charge of one's internal world and feeling confident to challenge those internal voices that are unhelpful or positively damaging.

In a more general sense, empowerment, both in terms of rediscovering self-efficacy and connecting and developing 'power together' with others, has been seen by many survivors as absolutely central to their personal recovery journeys (Chamberlin, 1997; Nelson et al., 2001; Mancini, 2007). This would suggest that an awareness of and confidence in working with issues of power should be central to social work practice in mental health – so that we can enable people to make the journey from internalized oppression and powerlessness to the point where they are able to reclaim control over the direction of their life and the capability to engage with their social world, no longer as a victim, but as a survivor.

In order to do this, it is helpful to have a clearer theorization of power relations that goes beyond the idea of a competitive 'zero-sum game', in which it is seen as a commodity that one person can only gain at another's expense (Barnes and Bowl, 2001; Masterson and Owen, 2006). In making sense of how power may be impacting on people's lives, it is important to see how power relations may be limiting or productive – closing down or opening up opportunities for them. Potentially, both processes may be intertwined, as accessing certain positions of power may entail accepting other limitations and disciplining oneself so as to present a required level of conformity (Foucault, 1982). Alongside this, power may also operate 'vertically' within hierarchical relationships in which one person has *power over* another, or 'horizontally' as *power together* in connection with others. Although we may associate power over with acting oppressively, this is not necessarily the case: people (most typically women) may often use their power to protect and nurture others (Baker Miller, 1991). Similarly, not all instances of power together are necessarily empowering: people may develop power together in ways that are collusive or exclusionary. Putting this together, Figure 8.2 provides a matrix to distinguish how power may be operating in a particular situation.

	Power over	Power together
Productive modes of power	*Protective power* Deploying power in order to safeguard vulnerable people and enhance their opportunities	*Cooperative power* Collective action, sharing, mutual support and challenge – through valuing commonality and difference
Limiting modes of power	*Oppressive power* Exploiting differences to enhance one's own position and resources at the expense of others, or trying to resist this, if on the 'receiving end'	*Collusive power* Banding together to exclude others or suppress awareness of different perspectives and experiences

Figure 8.2 Matrix of power relations
Source: Tew, 2002, p. 166

Our understanding of power relations must also embrace wider 'structural' differences in power positions (that are often linked to social identities such as gender or race), more localized 'subcultures' of power embedded within the discourses of families, communities and agencies, and the micro-operation of power within personal relationships. These overlapping layers of power relations connect to provide the context in which we operate and experience ourselves. Sometimes, power relations at different levels may be mutually reinforcing, which, if they are productive, may be particularly enabling in terms of opening up possibilities for influence, choice or accessing social opportunities. Alternatively, if they are all limiting, they may be particularly damaging in their effects – and it can be a constellation of structural powerlessness (on the basis, perhaps, of age and gender), linked to powerlessness within family relationships and collusive exclusion by peers that may render a child particularly vulnerable to abuse. Sometimes, there may be complexities and contradictions between levels that may offer possibilities to resist or negotiate potentially limiting forms of power, for example a particularly supportive personal relationship within a family may enable a girl to transcend some of the limitations placed upon her by cultural prescriptions of feminine roles.

People with mental distress are often past or current victims of oppressive power – structural, local and interpersonal – and their distress may serve to reproduce, and trap themselves within, limiting or damaging forms of power relations. Some of this may come from within, in terms of feeling out of control or being dominated by feelings or thought patterns that may relate to unresolved abusive experiences. However, some of this may also come externally from experiences of stigmatization, exclusion or even 'demonization' on the basis of one's mental health status, which may be similar to the sorts of social discrimination faced by other disabled people, but potentially more extreme. In order to understand this, labelling theory may be recast within an understanding of unequal power relations, allowing us to explore how collusive power may operate within the social mainstream to define certain groups and identities as 'other'.

It is also important to analyse the implications of professional interventions in terms of power. For example, can compulsory powers be used in a way that feels like the use of protective rather than oppressive power? Unfortunately, research evidence suggests that the oppressive impact of insensitive or excessive use of coercion can be far-reaching, potentially damaging people's sense of self and personal relationships (Barnes et al., 2000; Hughes et al., 2009).

While managing crises may depend on the appropriate use of protective power by professional helpers and informal carers, recovery depends on a different sort of power relationship – a shift from providing support to building partnerships based on cooperative power. This may entail a degree of risk-taking and letting go – both for professional helpers and family or friends (who may no longer need to see themselves as carers) – but this may be essential if people are to be enabled to take charge of their lives again (see Topor et al., 2006).

Systems theory and social capital

Both breakdown and recovery occur within social and relational contexts, but these can tend to be neglected within the individualistic focus of much mental health practice, including the practice of social workers. Systems theories in their various guises have provided the most widely used conceptual tools by which to map and analyse these contexts. More recently, social capital has emerged as another theoretical concept that can be used to explore issues of social exclusion and inclusion, which can be relevant to people with mental health difficulties.

Systems theory

Social systems are sets of interactive relationships that may be organized around a collective identity, function or process and may vary in formality and permanence.

Having roots in ecology and functionalist social theory, some versions of systems theory have tended to overemphasize order and harmony: an expectation that the various components of people's social worlds should somehow fit together to mutual benefit, with in-built regulatory mechanisms that ensure ongoing harmonious interaction. Nevertheless, ecological approaches, such as that of Bronfenbrenner (1979), may be helpful in mapping out the various overlapping micro-social systems of which a person may be part and which collectively form their meso-system, and also the wider exo- and macro-systems that may more indirectly influence interactions within this. More recent developments of this have started to recognize the importance of relations of power and structural oppression in shaping system dynamics and patterns of interaction (Germain and Gitterman, 1996). Within mental health, Polak (1971) suggests a more pragmatic approach in which social systems are seen to be more inherently unstable – sensitive to external stresses and liable to develop internal conflicts and tensions.

On the one hand, social systems such as families, workplaces or faith groups may constitute our most effective sources of social support and social opportunity – defining the settings in which we may access protective and cooperative forms of power: they can be vital to maintaining our wellbeing and can also act as gateways to wider networks of social resources. However, these same social systems may potentially constitute some of the most potent locations for oppression, abuse and collusion. Particularly when compounded by such power issues or inequalities, relationship difficulties and conflicts within an immediate social system may trigger a mental health difficulty for someone if they are already vulnerable – often because they may be too powerless within the system organization to take action to resolve what is going on. Thus, for many people with mental distress, their involvement within certain social systems may have been part of their problems; but, with the right sorts of support, these (or the development of alternative relationship systems) systems may often also be part of the solution to their current distress and disablement.

The organization of social systems depends on the operation of certain 'rules' – often implicit rather than explicit – which govern how people are supposed to interact with one another. Thus, membership of any social system inevitably involves a degree of constraint – one has, to a certain extent, to abide by these 'rules' if one is to participate within the system. In some instances, these 'rules' may operate to one's advantage, for example in ensuring a degree of stability that can underpin supportive relationships. In other instances, these 'rules' can be oppressive and damaging to (some) system members, perhaps by reinforcing hierarchies of power and status within the system. System 'rules' may determine (Tew, 2011, p. 82):

- *permitted and prescribed identities:* the various identities that system members may (have to) take on, both in relation to each other and to the outside world
- *norms/expectations:* how people believe they (and others) ought to act and present themselves
- *patterns of communication and interaction:* what can be expressed, how it can be expressed and by whom; how is closeness and distance regulated?

Theory

■ *boundary processes:* who is in and who is out, and how open is the system to inter-acting with the wider world?
■ *the organization of power and authority:* how are decisions made or contested; who has power over whom; in what ways are power relations limiting or productive?

Such 'rules' are closely linked with the dominant narratives by which the system upholds its collective identity and functions, and by the wider social and cultural context in which it is situated – but may also emerge through internal processes of interaction and 'jostling' for position, and may sometimes appear at odds with wider social attitudes and expectations.

System 'rules' may be more or less flexible and open to renegotiation in the face of either changing external circumstances or internal discontent. Systems that are based around relations of cooperative and protective power are more likely to be comfortable with challenge and ongoing negotiation of how people are in rela-tion to each other. (Dialogue is central to the operation of cooperative power and the aim of protective power is always to nurture people towards taking power back for themselves.) However, systems that are organized, at least in part, around rela-tions of collusive and oppressive power may be most potentially damaging to certain system members and also most resistant to change. It is these systems that are most likely to be injurious to the mental health of particular system members. Although it may not be straightforward, it may nevertheless be crucial for social workers to engage with such systems in order to negotiate potential changes in the 'rules' that would enable the system to be more flexible and supportive, perhaps using narrative or solution-focused approaches (de Shazer, 1982, 2005; White and Epston, 1990).

Social capital

Another approach to examining connectedness is that of social capital. Building on the concept of economic capital, social capital looks at social networks and relationships as a resource that people can draw upon, both in order to access opportunities and achieve the sort of lifestyle to which they may aspire, and also to provide a sense of belonging and an availability of support in times of need. It comprises the 'features of social life – networks, norms and trust – that enable participants to act together more effectively to pursue shared objectives' (Puttnam, 1996, p. 56). More specifically, this involves:

■ *structural social capital:* available infrastructures of organizations, informal networks, meeting places and so on
■ *discursive social capital:* shared norms of trust, belonging and reciprocity that can underpin social connections within particular sections of the community
■ *cognitive social capital:* individually held social skills and dispositions, including internalized knowledge of the social codes that may determine whether or not one is seen as 'acceptable' within particular networks or places.

It can also be helpful to distinguish between:

- *bonding social capital:* our relationships with others where we may have a shared identity and context ('people like us'), which may be particularly important for belonging and support
- *bridging social capital:* which reaches out across identities and social divisions and may be particularly helpful in opening up wider social opportunities.

Both bonding and bridging social capital involve relations of power together – often cooperative, but, particularly in the case of bonding social capital, also potentially collusive, including some but excluding others (see Bourdieu, 1977). Being kept on the outside of otherwise cohesive and connected communities can be particularly bad for people's mental health, as in the case for black people living in predominantly white areas (Boydell et al., 2001). Once one becomes labelled as 'mentally ill', such exclusionary processes can become particularly extreme.

In a more general sense, lack of social capital may be a contributory factor in reducing people's options and supports when dealing with stresses or adverse circumstances – and hence increasing their likelihood of developing mental distress. Whether or not this has already started to occur, a mental health crisis may often result in a sudden and catastrophic loss of social capital, particularly if service responses such as hospitalization serve to cut people off from their normal family and social networks, and if prevailing social or cultural attitudes foster fear and prejudice towards those deemed strange or 'mad'. If positive action is not taken immediately to help to maintain links and deal with fears and concerns, then such losses can quickly become permanent. As people move beyond crisis, recovery may depend at least as much on mobilizing effective forms of social capital around a person as it does on any more individually focused treatment strategy.

Psychodynamic, attachment and cognitive theories

There are a number of theoretical perspectives that can help to illuminate various mechanisms whereby particular patterns of relating to the world may be developed and embedded in response to particular life experiences – often (but not exclusively) those that may occur in childhood. At the time, these response patterns may have served as survival strategies if we had been exposed to systematic patterns of abuse or discrimination, or they may simply represent our idiosyncratic ways of making sense of (and getting by in) the world as we saw it. In adult life, some of these familiar and often unconscious patterns and adaptations may not work so well for us. Some may start to interfere with our perception or understanding of what is going on around us; some may lead us to avoid personal relationships, or leave us open to exploitation or abuse; some may involve repeated self-harm or violence to others; some may cut us off from, or lock us into, particular emotions or feelings.

Such patterns and adaptations may operate at different levels of intensity, usually in response to current social and personal circumstances. At lower levels of intensity, they may simply constitute a bit of a nuisance or an eccentricity – one which does not interfere greatly with everyday life but which nevertheless may increase our vulnerability and our ability to deal with certain forms of stress. At higher levels of intensity, they may not just make us more vulnerable to mental distress, but actually come to be seen as a 'complaint' or distress experience in their own right. A tendency towards suspiciousness in the cognitive evaluation of our environment may escalate into a paranoid delusionary framework. A pattern of impulsiveness, self-harming and a difficulty in negotiating the give and take of close relationships may escalate into an ensemble of distress experiences that may attract the label of 'borderline personality disorder'.

From psychodynamic theory, the concepts of repression, defence mechanism and the 'return of the repressed' offer some understanding as to how issues from the past may exert an influence over the present. Recent research is indicating the high proportion of people with all forms of mental distress, including psychosis, who are survivors of trauma or childhood abuse (Read et al., 2005; Larkin and Morrison, 2006), and we may see how particular manifestations of mental distress may be consequences of living through such experiences (Plumb, 2005). Psychodynamic theory suggests that when we do not have the external support or internal resources to deal with painful or extreme experiences – often due to being situated in positions of isolation or powerlessness – we may find ways of (just about) repressing unresolved feelings and traumatic memories from our everyday awareness. Our ability to contain such emotional 'hot potatoes' may depend on utilizing certain defence mechanisms, including:

■ denial: of feelings, memories and so on
■ discounting the emotional significance of events
■ splitting off our 'good' from our 'bad' feelings about self or others and only being able to be in touch with one aspect or the other at any one time
■ projecting onto others what we cannot accept within ourselves
■ self-harming: substituting pain that is under our control for pain that threatens to overwhelm us
■ using drugs, alcohol or other substances.

Defence mechanisms operate as last-ditch coping mechanisms – and should be respected as such – but they may also seriously impair aspects of our functioning or put us at other forms of risk.

At some point in the future, repressed feelings and traumatic memories may start to return to our conscious awareness, and this 'return of the repressed' may be triggered by current stressful life situations, particularly those that may touch on or remind us of past issues. However, this may not necessarily happen in a way where it is easy to recognize what is going on. People who hear voices may feel persecuted by abusive or derogatory voices but cannot immediately make sense of what this may be about. However, perhaps with support, they may be able to relate the source of such voices to actual people who may have abused them in the past, or find within the content of what is spoken echoes of past traumatic experiences (Coleman and

Smith, 1997). Acts of self-harm may also sometimes be understood as an 'intermediary language', whereby experiences of pain and terror may be re-enacted and articulated (Lefevre, 1996). Linking to our earlier discussion of crisis theory, such expressions of mental distress may be seen both as desperate escalations of defence mechanisms, trying to contain an experience that still seems too terrifying to confront, and also as elements of repressed experiences (partially) spilling out and breaking through these defences.

As well as past experiences coming to influence the internal dynamics of our personalities, they may also affect how we relate to others. Attachment theory focuses on our history of making 'strong affectional bonds to particular others' and how this may influence our current propensities to make (or avoid) particular forms of relationships, and hence explain 'many forms of emotional distress and personality disturbance' (Bowlby, 1982, p. 39). Depending on the responses we may receive from significant others, particularly in early childhood, we may develop a familiar 'style' of attachment behaviour (Ainsworth et al., 1978).

Where significant others have been there for one in a meaningful way and proved themselves reasonably trustworthy, in the sense of offering *consistent* love and recognition, one may generalize this into a more general assumption that close relationships can be worthwhile and secure. However, where relationships with significant others may have been more problematic or even abusive, one may develop a more desperate or inconsistent approach to relationships – perhaps swinging between a fantasy of imagined closeness and anger at possible rejection, or going to extreme lengths to cling on to relationships that may be far from satisfactory and even abusive. Alternatively, one may conclude (not necessarily at a conscious level) that it may be safer to avoid close relationships altogether and develop alternative strategies for self-nurture.

In general, those with less secure attachment styles may find themselves without the sorts of personally supportive relationships that may help them deal with stressful circumstances – or their very relationships may become a serious source of stress in themselves – and this may increase their vulnerability to mental health difficulties. However, mental health crises may also be points at which people may be open to re-examining their usual relationship style and, with support and encouragement over a longer period of time, learning how to go about making closer and more stable relationships. What can be particularly helpful in this is having a stable and longer term working relationship with a key worker or care coordinator, which can provide the safety net to underpin experiments at getting closer and also surviving the inevitable setbacks when things may go wrong.

Although often seen as opposed to psychodynamic or relational perspectives, cognitive (and cognitive behavioural) theory can actually lend a complementary perspective that can flesh these out and offer useful practice strategies. Our current patterns of emotional and behavioural response may be seen to be mediated by cognitive appraisals that are informed by an underlying and entrenched 'schema' of basic attitudes and beliefs about self, others and the world – some of which may play a crucial role in trapping us within feeling states such as depression or in maintaining

Theory

Making connexions

In what way is theory a 'contested area' in mental health social work? What are the consequences of this in practice?

damaging or distressing psychotic experiences (Beck et al., 1979; Ellis, 2001). However 'irrational' they may seem now, such schemas may make more sense if they are viewed as understandable responses to childhood events, circumstances and relationships. We may take on board messages about our competence, 'lovability' and personal efficacy that may shape our view of ourselves and how we can become involved in our social world. Our attachment styles may be underpinned to particular generalized beliefs about others and how to relate to them. Our beliefs and attitudes towards the world in general will come to influence how we come to interpret subsequent situations, for example whether we approach these with an underlying optimism or pessimism, or with a tendency towards trust or suspicion.

Although many defence mechanisms and attachment styles may be laid down on the basis of preverbal forms of cognition, they may nevertheless become operationalized on the basis of subsequent rationalizations, and so become embedded within (and reinforced by) systems of belief. Bringing these beliefs up to the surface, and re-examining them in terms of how they may influence a person's current emotional and behavioural responses, may provide a practical and focused way in enabling people to make changes in how they deal with their world – and indirectly promote their ability to form more effective attachments to others, and to find coping strategies that may be less risky or damaging than holding on to familiar defence mechanisms.

Integrating theories

Using theories can illuminate what may otherwise seem confusing and apparently meaningless sets of experiences and outward behaviours – enabling us to move beyond just seeing them as symptoms of underlying medical illnesses, but as closely interconnected with people's life experiences and their social and family contexts. External experiences may adversely affect mental and emotional functioning and, in turn, mental health difficulties may have a major effect on lifestyle, social capital and personal relationships, particularly where there are wider contexts of stigma and discrimination. Such interactions between inner and outer worlds are ongoing. These may either take the form of downward spirals, in which inner turmoil leads to social exclusion which leads to further exacerbations of mental distress, or they may signal the start of recovery processes, in which acceptance, support and opportunities provide people with safe spaces in which to renegotiate their place in the world, often finding new forms of value and purpose in the process.

Particular theoretical perspectives on their own may be of limited value in unpicking the complexity of this, hence the importance of integrating social and psychological perspectives and identifying overarching themes such as power relations that permeate both the personal and the social. The theoretical perspectives discussed in this chapter can provide a useful conceptual core (see Figure 8.3), but these may usefully be augmented by other perspectives from social and psychological theory.

The process of integrating theories may not be entirely straightforward: they may rest on different assumptions as to the nature of mental health difficulties and how social relations may be structured. Any engagement with theory must include a critical examination of such issues, but it is often by putting theoretical perspectives together that each perspective can be made more relevant and useful for exploring the 'bigger picture' of a person's current situation. For example, earlier versions of labelling theory failed to interrogate the power relations of the social mainstream whereby some groups were in the position to impose labels on others. More recent developments of such perspectives have started to take this into account, and this can start to give a more comprehensive analysis of why it may be so hard for people identified as 'mentally ill' to achieve social inclusion.

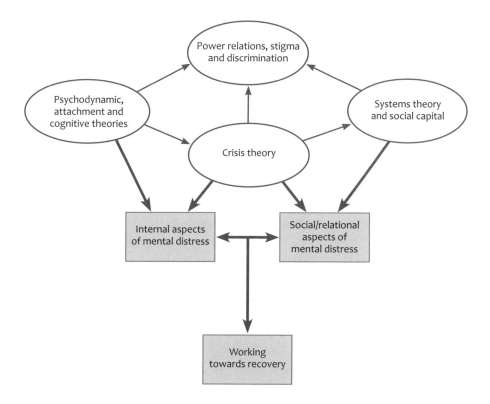

Figure 8.3 Integrating core theoretical perspectives in order to understand mental distress and promote recovery

It has not been possible to do justice to the depth and potential of different bodies of theory in opening up our understanding of mental distress. Nevertheless, this chapter provides a 'taster' of how theories can enable social workers to develop 'whole person' and 'person-in-social-context' approaches that go beyond the inherent reductionism of 'illness' or 'risk' models, with their overreliance on medication and their inability to engage with many of the issues that may make a crucial difference in enabling (or disabling) people's prospects of recovery.

Further reading

■ Read, J., Mosher, L. and Bentnall, R. (eds) (2004) *Models of Madness*. Hove: Brunner Routledge.

Provides a review of psychological, social and biological approaches to psychosis and a comprehensive critique of the 'medical model' of madness.

■ Tew, J. (2011) *Social Approaches to Mental Distress*. Basingstoke: Palgrave Macmillan.

Sets out an alternative paradigm for mental health practice, which explores how people's social experiences may lead to mental health difficulties and may be crucial in enabling recovery.

■ Webber, M. and Nathan, J. (eds) (2010) *Reflective Practice in Mental Health*. London: Jessica Kingsley.

Applies a range of psychosocial perspectives to mental health practice, linking them to the latest research evidence.

References

Ainsworth, M., Biehar, M., Waters, E. and Wall, S. (1978) *Patterns of Attachment*. Hillsdale, NJ: Erlbaum.

Baker Miller, J. (1991) 'Women and power', in J. Jordan, A. Kaplan, J. Baker Miller et al. (eds) *Women's Growth in Connection*. New York: Guilford Press.

Barnes, M. and Bowl, R. (2001) *Taking Over the Asylum: Empowerment and Mental Health*. Basingstoke: Palgrave – now Palgrave Macmillan.

Barnes, M., Davis, A. and Tew, J. (2000) 'Valuing experience: users' experience of compulsion under the Mental Health Act 1983', *Mental Health Review*, **5**(3): 11–14.

Beck, A., Rush, A., Shaw, B. and Emery, G. (1979) *Cognitive Therapy for Depression*. New York: Guilford Press.

Birchwood, M., Meaden, A., Trower, P. et al. (2000) 'The power and omnipotence of voices: subordination and entrapment by voices and significant others', *Psychological Medicine*, 30, 337–44.

Bourdieu, P. (1977) 'Cultural reproduction and social reproduction', in J. Karabel and A.H. Halsey (eds) *Power and Ideology in Education*. New York: Oxford University Press.

Bowlby, J. (1982) *Attachment and Loss*, vol. 1. London: Hogarth Press.

Boydell, J., van Os, J., McKenzie, K. et al. (2001) 'Incidence of schizophrenia in ethnic minorities in London: ecological study into interactions with environment', *British Medical Journal*, **323**(7325): 1336–8.

Bridgett, C. and Polak, P. (2003) 'Social systems intervention and crisis resolution: Pt 1, assessment', *Advances in Psychiatric Treatment*, **9**(6): 424–31.

Bronfenbrenner, U. (1979) *The Ecology of Human Development: Experiments by Nature and Design*. Cambridge, MA: Harvard University Press.

Burns, T., Catty, J., White, S. et al. (2009) 'The impact of supported employment and working on clinical and social functioning', *Schizophrenia Bulletin,* **35**(5): 949–58.

Caplan, G. (1965) *Principles of Preventive Psychiatry*. London: Tavistock.

Chamberlin, J. (1997) 'A working definition of empowerment', *Psychiatric Rehabilitation Journal,* **20**(4): 43–6.

Coleman, R. and Smith, M. (1997) *Working with Voices: From Victim to Victor.* Gloucester: Handsell.

De Shazer, S. (1982) *Patterns of Brief Family Therapy: An Ecosystemic Approach*. New York: Guilford Press.

De Shazer, S. (2005) *More than Miracles: The State of the Art of Solution-focused Therapy*. Binghamton, NY: Haworth Press.

Ellis, A. (2001) *Overcoming Destructive Beliefs, Feelings, and Behaviors: New Directions for Rational Emotive Behavior Therapy.* New York: Prometheus Books.

Fearon, P., Kirkbride, J., Dazzan, P. et al. (2006) 'Incidence of schizophrenia and other psychoses in ethnic minority groups: results from the MRC AESOP study', *Psychological Medicine*, 26, 1–10.

Foucault, M. (1982) 'The subject and power', in H. Dreyfuss and P. Rabinow (eds) *Michel Foucault: Beyond Structuralism and Hermeneutics*. Chicago: University of Chicago Press.

Germain, C. and Gitterman, A. (1996) *The Life Model of Social Work Practice* (2nd edn). New York: Columbia University Press.

Golan, N. (1986) 'Crisis theory', in F. Turner (ed.) *Social Work Treatment: Interlocking Theoretical Approaches.* New York: Free Press.

Healy, K. (2005) *Social Work Theories in Context : Creating Frameworks for Practice*. Basingstoke: Palgrave Macmillan.

Herman, J. (1997) *Trauma and Recovery: The Aftermath of Violence from Domestic Abuse to Political Terror*. New York: Basic Books.

Hiday, V.A. (2006) 'Putting community risk in perspective: a look at correlations, causes and controls', *International Journal of Law and Psychiatry*, **29**(4): 316–31.

Hughes, R., Haywood, M. and Finlay, W. (2009) 'Patients' perceptions of the impact of involuntary inpatient care on self, relationships and recovery', *Journal of Mental Health,* **18**(2): 152–60.

Janssen, I., Hanssen, M., Bak, M. et al. (2003) 'Discrimination and delusional ideation', *British Journal of Psychiatry*, **182**(1): 71–6.

Johnson, S. and Needle, J. (2008) 'Introduction and concepts', in S. Johnson, J. Needle, J. Bindman and G. Thornicroft (eds) *Crisis Resolution and Home Treatment in Mental Health*. Cambridge: Cambridge University Press.

Jorm, A., Korten, A., Rodgers, B. et al. (2002) 'Sexual orientation and mental health: results from a community survey of young and middle-aged adults', *British Journal of Psychiatry*, **180**(5): 423–7.

Kanel, K. (2003) *A Guide to Crisis Intervention*. Pacific Grove, CA: Brooks/Cole.

Larkin, W. and Morrison, A. (2006) *Trauma and Psychosis: New Directions for Theory and Therapy.* Hove: Routledge.

Theory

Lefevre, S. (1996) *Killing Me Softly. Self-harm: Survival not Suicide*. Gloucester: Handsell.

Loughran, H. (2011) *Understanding Crisis Therapies*. London: Jessica Kingsley.

Mancini, M. (2007) 'The role of self-efficacy in recovery from serious psychiatric disabilities', *Qualitative Social Work*, **6**(1): 49–74.

Masterson, S. and Owen, S. (2006) 'Mental health service users' social and individual empowerment', *Journal of Mental Health*, **15**(1): 19–34.

Mezzich, J., Salloum, I., Cloninger, C. et al. (2010) 'Person-centred integrative diagnosis: conceptual bases and structural model', *Canadian Journal of Psychiatry*, **55**(11): 701–8.

Nelson, G., Lord, J. and Ochocka, J. (2001) 'Empowerment and mental health in community', *Journal of Community and Applied Social Psychology*, 11, 125–42.

O'Hagan, K. (1994) 'Crisis intervention: changing perspectives', in C. Hanvey and T. Philpot (eds) *Practising Social Work*. London: Routledge.

Perry, B., Pollard, R., Blakely, T. et al. (1995) 'Childhood trauma, the neurobiology of adaptation, and 'use-dependent' development of the brain: how states become traits', *Infant Mental Health Journal*, **16**(4): 271–91.

Plumb, S. (2005) 'The social/trauma model', in J. Tew (ed.) *Social Perspectives in Mental Health*. London: Jessica Kingsley.

Polak, P. (1971) 'Social systems intervention', *Archives of General Psychiatry*, **25**(2): 110–17.

Puttnam, R. (1996) 'The strange disappearance of civic America', *The American Prospect*, 7(24): 34–48.

Ramon, S. (2009) 'Adult mental health in a changing international context: the relevance to social work', *British Journal of Social Work*, **39**(8): 1615–22.

Read, J., van Os, J., Morrison, A. and Ross, C. (2005) 'Childhood trauma, psychosis and schizophrenia: a literature review with theoretical and clinical implications', *Acta Psychiatrica Scandinavica*, **112**(5): 330–50.

Roffman, J., Marci, C., Glick, D. et al. (2005) 'Neuroimaging and the functional neuroanatomy of psychotherapy', *Psychological Medicine*, **35**(10): 1385–98.

Szasz, T. (1961) *The Myth of Mental Illness: Foundations of a Theory of Personal Conduct*. New York: Harper & Row.

Tew, J. (2002) *Social Theory, Power and Practice*. Basingstoke: Palgrave Macmillan.

Tew, J. (2011) *Social Approaches to Mental Distress*. Basingstoke: Palgrave Macmillan.

Topor, A., Borg, M., Mezzina, R. et al. (2006) 'Others: the role of family, friends and professionals in the recovery process', *American Journal of Psychiatric Rehabilitation*, **9**(1): 17–37.

Tsang, H., Lam, P., Ng, B. and Leung, O. (2000) 'Predictors of employment outcome for people with psychiatric disabilities: a review of the literature since the mid 80s', *Journal of Rehabilitation*, **66**(2): 19–31.

Warner, R. (2004) *Recovery from Schizophrenia: Psychiatry and Political Economy* (3rd edn). New York: Routledge.

White, M. and Epston, D. (1990) *Narrative Means to Therapeutic Ends*. New York: WW Norton.

Williams, J. (2005) 'Women's mental health: taking inequality into account', in J. Tew (ed.) *Social Perspectives in Mental Health*. London: Jessica Kingsley.

9
What research findings tell social workers about their work in mental health

SHERRILL EVANS AND PETER HUXLEY

Mental health research and practice cover a wide spectrum of disorders and a wide range of social influences affecting the causation, course and outcome of episodes of illness. It is impossible in a single chapter to do justice to this wealth of information and practice wisdom, and we have chosen to focus on adults of working age. A major reason for concentrating on adults of working age is that the incidence and prevalence of common mental disorders (depression/anxiety and so on) is considerable and the economic costs to society are huge. Also, as demonstrated some years ago (Huxley et al., 1989a, 1989b), in the average social workers caseload, whether made up of childcare cases or older people or a mixture of all types, one can confidently expect about two-thirds of the people being helped to have some form of common mental disorder. Similarly, Isaac et al. (1986) showed that a huge proportion of the parents of the children being helped have a psychiatric history themselves.

Another reason is that, although the life course issues in these illnesses have received greater attention in the past decade, it is in the adult years that disorders most commonly manifest themselves and have the most impact economically on the sufferer and society. For example, a diagnosis of the most common childhood mental health problem, conduct disorder, is strongly predictive of adult mental health problems, substance misuse, smoking, teenage pregnancy, poor performance at school and, in the workplace, poor quality relationships and criminal behaviour (Scott et al., 2001; Fergusson et al., 2005; Stewart-Brown, 2005).

Many of the research findings referred to in this chapter are uncontroversial. In other areas, considerable debate continues. For instance, the research base for functional teams (early intervention, crisis resolution and assertive outreach) is contested, as is the use of certain interventions such as ECT, self-management, peer support and employment. For some other interventions, the evidence base is not yet well established, for example community treatment orders. Where there is conflicting evidence, we have tried to take a balanced approach and have reported the most robust and recent research. The following topics will be explored:

- the social work contribution to the evidence base
- research into the costs of mental illness
- depression research
- schizophrenia research
- recovery research
- interventions to support recovery and inclusion
- measuring outcomes
- stress research in social work.

The social work contribution to the evidence base

Before we embark on a description of the useful research that can inform practice, it is worth remembering that many contemporary developments in practice are a legacy from research undertaken by social workers (Trinder and Reynolds, 2000). This legacy should be valued: many of the fundamental findings remain influential in modern social work practice as well as in the delivery of contemporary mental health service. For example, Peter Huxley was involved in the production of the model of the pathway to psychiatric care (Goldberg and Huxley, 1980), which had a considerable impact on shifting the emphasis from hospital treatment to community, primary and social care in the UK. Sir David Goldberg and Peter Huxley then went on to describe the common mental disorder model of vulnerability, destabilization and restitution (Goldberg and Huxley, 1992), since updated by Goldberg and Goodyer (2005).

Case management was developed in the USA by social workers among others (Bachrach and Harris, 1988; Rapp, 1992, 1998) and adopted in the UK as 'care management' (SSI, 1990). In the brokerage model, the assessment and care planning aspects of the work were separated from the direct delivery of care by the worker concerned. This resulted in the removal of many social workers from the front line of care delivery and into an assessment and brokerage role. The US research found this to be unpopular with service users, but its adoption went ahead in the UK despite this evidence. It has continued to prove unpopular with social workers in the UK up to the present day. This quote illustrates the point very well:

> It is difficult to believe that so many more senior managers were once, hopefully, enthusiastic and person-centred social workers – too many have now become budget-obsessed/target-driven 'clones' of the State … We have largely forgotten the origins of social work and it is now seen as bureaucratic and an 'arm' of the State. Where is the 'soul' of our profession? Who really cares any more? Much as he became out of favour, are social workers aware of, for instance, 'The Casework Relationship' by Biestek? – he saw social work as having the most positive effect

through our caring relationships with those we sought to help. That religious/ pseudo-religious approach lost favour but was it not a case of 'throwing the baby out with the bathwater'? We now seem to be far more Case Managers and increasingly distant from our 'Service Users.' (Measures, 2008)

The strengths model advocated by Charles Rapp and colleagues (Rapp, 1992, 1998; Saleebey, 1996, 2005) is an outstanding example of the change of emphasis from an approach based on the assessment of need and deficits, to one that takes a much more positive view of people's skills, abilities, aptitudes and preferences, and the contexts in which these can be maximized. The development of this model by mental health social workers has underpinned the shift of emphasis from deficit models.

Modern multidisciplinary research in mental health now includes service users as co-researchers or as researchers in their own right, as advocated almost two decades ago by Rapp et al. (1993), and leans towards an interest in recovery and the use of participatory and emancipatory research methods – as represented by the contributions of people like Marian Farkas in the USA and Peter Beresford in the UK.

Research into the costs of mental illness

We now recognize that the personal and societal costs of mental illness are considerable and more costly than well-known disorders such as diabetes and heart disease. For example:

- 1 in 4 people will suffer from a mental illness at some point in their lives
- 30% of visits to GPs relate to mental ill health
- 3 out of 10 people take mental health-related sick leave every year
- over 90 million working days a year are lost through mental health problems.

Mental health problems in England were estimated to have had economic and social costs of £105 billion in 2009/10, including £30 billion in lost economic output (Centre for Mental Health, 2010). Community mental health teams (CMHTs) account for some of the highest spending. The annual cost for working age adults in contact with CMHTs is £696 million.

Depression has been associated with a fourfold increase in the risk of heart disease, even when other risk factors such as smoking are controlled for (Hippisley-Cox et al., 1998; Osborn et al., 2007). There is a strong association between mental ill health and physical health problems, such as diabetes, arthritis and cardiovascular disease (Chapman et al., 2005; Evans, D.L. et al., 2005; Roy-Byrne et al., 2005; McVeigh et al., 2006). Co-morbid mental health problems can lead to poorer quality care for the physical illness, reduced adherence to treatment, and increased costs and poorer outcomes (Chapman et al., 2005; Evans, D.L. et al., 2005; McVeigh et al., 2006; Kisely et al., 2007; Nuyen et al., 2008; Unützer et al., 2009). The financial impact of co-morbidity can be significant; for example, for diabetes, the costs to the health service of each person with diabetes and co-morbid depression is up to 4.5

Research

times greater than for a person with diabetes alone (Egede et al., 2002). More recently in the USA, Unützer et al. (2009) found that the healthcare costs for medically ill older adults with depression are higher than for those without depression. This research suggests that improving a person's mental health can improve the prognosis of physical disease and reduce associated costs.

A great deal of the costs associated with mental ill health occur outside the health service. For example, 43% of those on incapacity benefit in the UK receive it mainly on mental health grounds (DWP, 2009).

Depression research

Depression has been described as a social and economic time bomb (Dawson and Tylee, 2001). Depression in adults costs more than £9 billion a year, but only a fraction of these costs, £370 million, are direct treatment costs. There were 109.7 million working days lost and 2,615 deaths due to depression in 2000 (Thomas and Morris, 2003).

Three other studies – two in the USA, one in the UK – provide further intelligence on the links between depression and employment. Almond and Healey (2003) show that (self-reported) depression/anxiety is the single most important cause of workplace absenteeism in the UK. Kessler et al. (2001) described the hidden impact of depression on reduced productivity at work – an impact that will not be adequately measured by absenteeism rates. There is also evidence that remission of depressive symptoms more rapidly affects employment status than health service utilization (Simon et al., 2000). Although usually discussed in terms of lost national productivity, the employment effects of depression are most immediately felt by people with the illness. For most people, employment is not only their major source of income and pension entitlements (and perhaps various fringe benefits), but also generates self-esteem, gives social identity and expands social networks (Knapp, 2003).

Campaigns to improve the recognition of depression have been conducted in the UK and Australia. Self-help books proliferate, as well as clear and thought-provoking accounts of personal illness. Celebrities, sportspeople, media and political heavyweights have increasingly been reporting their own episodes of illness, In 2006, *The Independent* newspaper printed the comments of 40 celebrities who had suffered from the illness. Also in 2006, Dr Geoff Gallop, the Western Australian premier, resigned his post, to receive treatment for depression. Dr Gallop said the 'debilitating' illness forced him to seek expert help. In a media statement, he said:

> It is my difficult duty to inform you today that I am currently being treated for depression. Living with depression is a very debilitating experience, which affects different people in different ways. It has certainly affected many aspects of my life. So much so, that I sought expert help last week. My doctors advised me that with treatment, time and rest this illness is very curable. However, I cannot be certain how long I will need. So in the interests of my health and my family I have decided to rethink my career. (ABC News Online, 2006)

The symptoms of depression are sleep problems, including early morning wakening; feeling worse in the morning due to the failure of the normal cortisol peak at that time; loss of appetite, energy, enthusiasm, drive, concentration, memory, confidence, self-esteem, sex drive, enjoyment, patience, feelings and hope. As Gallop indicated, not everyone experiences all the symptoms and the illness affects people in different ways – the common perception of despair and unhappiness can be less debilitating than the physical symptoms of loss of drive and energy and disturbed sleep. Dr Paul Skerrit, the president of the Western Australian branch of the Australian Medical Association, was shocked to hear of Dr Gallop's resignation, saying that it shows that depression can strike people in all kinds of jobs: 'Depression is a thing that smites people when they're in their prime and doing very well. People think that you've got to have something wrong with you to get this illness but it's not the case at all' (ABC News Online, 2006).

Nevertheless, even before symptoms emerge, it is possible to identify people who may be at risk. The seminal work of Brown and Harris (1978) into risk factors for women showed that life events, such as marriage, divorce, bereavement, losing one's job, are likely to prompt episodes of depression. They also found that for women who had lost their own mother before the age of 11, who had three or more children under 15 and who did not have the support of a confiding partner, the risk of depression was increased. They called these factors 'vulnerability factors'. They went on to show that parental indifference and sexual and physical abuse during childhood raise the risk of anxiety and depression in later life. Parental neglect or abuse can produce a state of helplessness and low self-esteem, with feelings of insecure attachment. This may make teenage pregnancy more probable, which in turn can lead to poor adult support, poor material conditions and a higher expectancy of life events. Although the rates of these factors is similar in boys and girls, the ensuing disorders are different, leading to anxiety and depression for the daughters and conduct disorders for the sons (Goldberg and Goodyer, 2005).

It is important for social workers to realize that not all depressive episodes have their origins in vulnerability and life events. In the Brown and Harris cases, while 65% of those with both life events and vulnerability factors became depressed, 35% of those with neither life events nor vulnerability factors also became depressed. This is a well-known and repeated finding (Goldberg and Goodyer, 2005).

Cantopher (2003) has pointed out that people with certain personal characteristics are more likely to become depressed. These characteristics include moral strength, reliability, diligence, strong conscience, strong sense of responsibility, a tendency to focus on the needs of others before one's own, sensitivity, vulnerability to criticism, and self-esteem dependent on the evaluation of others. It is worth noting that many of these characteristics are valued by the profession of social work, suggesting that selection factors may make social work one of the professional groups most likely to succumb to depression.

It is most important, therefore, that social workers become skilled in the recognition of depression and anxiety and are able to point the sufferer to the most appropriate intervention for them. In addition, monitoring their own wellbeing, taking steps to promote it and reduce their own stresses and to obtain support from peers and managers are all supported by research findings (Cantopher, 2003; Evans et al., 2006; Williams et al., 2007).

Schizophrenia research

Warner (2004) summarizes the available evidence on the cause and course of schizophrenia, and reports an essentially similar model (as in depression) for the illness, predisposing factors, and vulnerability factors including life events. The lifetime risk for developing the illness is about 1% but this increases in groups of people who are related, so children of parents who have a diagnosis of schizophrenia have a 13% lifetime risk and monozygotic twins (from the same egg) of a parent with schizophrenia have a 48% lifetime risk. As Warner notes, even an identical genetic make-up only produces a 50% risk, so environmental factors play a significant role in the development, course and outcome of the illness. He also shows that recovery rates were similar before and after the introduction of antipsychotic medicines, and rates were considerably lower during economic recessions. Leaving aside the economic environmental factor, complete recovery occurs in 20–25% of people with schizophrenia, and social recovery in 40–45%. These arguments are encouraging for those providing social interventions as part of the care plan for people with this disorder and supports the optimism for work based on ideas of recovery and hope. The overriding conclusion of all this research is that all psychiatric disorders, including psychotic disorders, are best treated by a combination of medication and other forms of social support and psychological help, especially those likely to reduce the chances of relapse. A great deal of research is currently being undertaken into the value of different forms of additional assistance, and one that is supported by the Mental Health Foundation in the UK is 'mindfulness' (Williams et al., 2007), a combination of psychological and meditation methods.

It is important for social workers working in the mental health team to understand that a combined medical and social approach will produce the best outcomes. Many people will recover fully from an acute episode of schizophrenia, and two in five will benefit from social interventions that promote social recovery.

Recovery research

Warner's initial work on the recovery of schizophrenia predated the development of the so-called 'recovery movement' but both provide us with a generally optimistic view of the outcome of major and common disorders; only a minority of people suffering from schizophrenia or depression go on to have a chronic or lifelong episodic outcome. We will consider outcome in more detail in the next section, but now we consider what the 'recovery movement' will mean for social workers.

Anthony (1993, p. 15) gave an early definition of recovery that is still widely used:

> a deeply personal, unique process of changing one's attitudes, values, feelings, goals, skills, and/or roles. It is a way of living a satisfying, hopeful and contributing life even with the limitations caused by illness. Recovery involves the development of new meaning and purpose in one's life as one grows beyond the catastrophic effects of mental illness.

Unlike the 'medical model' of diagnosis based on symptoms, then treatment and cure, recovery is a more dynamic concept with three core components – hope, agency and opportunity (Repper and Perkins, 2003; South London and Maudsley/South West London and St George's trusts (SLAM/SWLSTG), 2010). How each person reaches their personal goals is a matter for them, and in recovery (rather than feeling themselves recovered), each person has an individual approach, which means that recovery lends itself to current ideas about personalization and inclusive practice (Repper and Perkins, 2003).

The SLAM/SWLSTG report (2010) explains the core concepts:

- *Hope:* a central aspect of recovery, as recovery is probably impossible without hope. It is essential to sustaining motivation and supporting expectations of an individually fulfilled life.
- *Agency:* refers to people gaining a sense of control. Recovery means service users taking control over their own problems, the services they receive and their lives. It is concerned with self-management, self-determination, choice and responsibility.
- *Opportunity:* links recovery with social inclusion and thus people's participation in a wider society. People with mental health problems wish to be part of communities, to be a valued member of and contribute to those communities, and to have access to the opportunities that exist within those communities.

Recovery is now a core component of the Department of Health's policy *New Horizons* (DH, 2009) and the coalition government's White Paper *Equity and Excellence: Liberating the NHS* (DH, 2010a), with its clear focus on service user experience and shared decision-making – 'no decision about me without me'. In addition, the profession of medicine is changing. It is becoming more collaborative, with a greater emphasis on shared decision-making, self-care and patient choice, and greater recognition of the contribution of service users as experts in their own conditions (SLAM/SWLSTG, 2010).

Among the lessons from this research for social workers is that recovery is not a single specified model, but that a key component of all approaches to recovery is to provide help for service users, which is person centred and will help to prevent a recurrence of the illness. Repper and Perkins (2003) give examples of the coping mechanisms used by Leete (1989) to cope with stressful situations likely to lead to relapse. The importance of adaptation to the stresses of daily living was first proposed by Selye in *The Stress of Life* in 1956. Selye's term for some of the mechanisms

Research

described by Leete three decades later is 'tuning down' (p. 265), and he anticipated ideas of work–life balance, which are not only of significance to service users but to social workers as well. So research on stress teaches us all that we need to reach a healthy balance between rest and work and to develop and use coping strategies that suit us personally. It is also clear that, for most of us, employment and empowerment are good for our mental health (Crowther et al., 2001; Warner, 2009; Kinoshita et al., 2011).

Interventions to promote recovery and inclusion

Employment research

Work represents an important goal for many people with severe mental illnesses (Warner, 2009). Gainful employment addresses practical needs as well as therapeutic needs, improves economic independence, and enhances self-esteem and overall functioning. Although vocational rehabilitation has been offered in various forms to people with severe mental illnesses for over a century, its role has weakened because of discouraging results from earlier vocational rehabilitation efforts, financial disincentives to work, and a general pessimism about outcomes. The traditional model uses a 'train and place' approach, offering training in sheltered workshops and then placing individuals in real-life work settings. The individual placement and support (IPS) programme is a specific approach to vocational rehabilitation that reverses this as 'place and train', in which service users are placed in real jobs and then offered variable amounts of direct personal support to be able to retain their work positions.

Service user and carer advocacy groups have made work and occupation one of their highest priorities to enhance both functional status and quality of life. Governments in different countries have adopted a variety of welfare-to-work programmes and, in many cases, people with severe mental health problems have benefited from these schemes. This is partly in response to some evidence that there are substantial economic impacts of employment difficulties, such as unemployment, absenteeism, low productivity, among people with, for example, schizophrenia and depression. Rates of unemployment among samples of people with schizophrenia often exceed 90% (Warner, 2009).

More recently, employment specialists have been integrated within many CMHTs to deliver an IPS service that offers both employment support and welfare benefits advice. A 12-month study found that the IPS service helped 37% of service users to gain or maintain paid work, compared with just 17% in a comparable nonintegrated service, at one-sixth of the cost of the traditional approach (Rinaldi and Perkins, 2007).

Randomized controlled trials undertaken in several different countries provide strong evidence for the effectiveness of IPS. IPS has been shown to achieve employment rates two/three times better than traditional alternatives such as interview training and sheltered workshops. More than half of those receiving IPS achieved successful placements in paid employment, compared with only 20–25% of controls. Those supported by IPS worked significantly more hours, had higher earnings and better job tenure. The higher rates of employment resulting from IPS also have positive long-term benefits in terms of improved confidence and wellbeing and reduced reliance on mental health services (Sainsbury Centre for Mental Health, 2009).

The most recent meta-analysis of 17 studies comparing IPS with other approaches (altogether these included 2,565 people) confirmed that people receiving IPS spent more days in competitive and paid employment and had longer job tenure. There were no significant differences in quality of life outcome (Kinoshita et al., 2011).

Among the lessons for social workers are that supported employment schemes are more successful than any other type, and evidence suggests that it is useful to have employment specialists within the CMHT.

Empowerment research

One means of empowerment is through the involvement of service users in key decisions regarding their treatment and management. There is extensive evidence that a reduced sense of empowerment is associated with lower self-esteem, a higher sense of stigma, poorer quality of life and a range of negative outcomes (Warner, 2009). Evidence in this area comes from three approaches:

1 The *shared decision-making model* for medication management developed by Deegan and Drake (2006). Research shows us that shared decision-making in mental health has the potential to improve mental health care as it impacts on quality of life, autonomy, choice and health outcomes (Simon et al., 2009).
2 The use of *joint crisis plans*, sometimes known as advance directives, to cover arrangements for admission to hospital, which can reduce involuntary admissions and improve service users' sense of control of their mental health problems (Henderson et al., 2004, 2008).
3 The use of an *educational approach*, rather than a therapeutic approach, to illness management and recovery is designed to provide people with severe mental illness with the information and skills necessary to manage their illness effectively and work towards achieving personal recovery goals (Mueser et al., 2002). The benefits for service users include an increased knowledge of their illness, coping skills, personal goal identification and attainment.

Self-management research

Through an educational approach, service users can learn more about their conditions and make supported decisions based on this learning. Self-management aims to enable people to develop practical tools of everyday living in order for them to make daily decisions that will maintain or improve their health. Self-management has developed from supporting people who have long-term health conditions and has begun to be applied to people who experience mental health conditions. Two streams of mental health self-management have developed: condition-specific self-management (Rinaldi, 2002) and generic self-management (Lawn et al., 2007; Cook et al., 2009). Evaluation of this work is still in its infancy and there is a need for more systematic research in this area (Onyett, 2003).

Peer support research

Peer support concerns people with lived experience of mental health problems acting as workers who directly help others experiencing similar problems. There are now a number of trials and studies of peer support interventions (Chinman et al., 2008), which show that appropriately trained and supported peers can increase service users' satisfaction, their sense of control (self-efficacy), empowerment and progress towards recovery (Rinaldi, 2009). They can also help the person expand their social networks, gain hope and become more involved in their own care. Evidence shows that peer support specialists working within mental health services and alongside professionals can reduce the length of hospital admissions and support earlier discharge (Slade, 2009).

There is a growing evidence base, mainly from outside the UK, that various forms of peer support can reduce the likelihood of psychiatric hospitalization and demand for other services (Solomon, 2004; Min et al., 2007; Lawn et al., 2007, 2008; Landers and Zhou, 2009). Satisfaction rates among people using peer support services are often high, and an expansion in peer support is something that many user groups have advocated for a number of years. Further research is needed on cost-effectiveness, but some evidence suggests that net savings can be made while increasing the quality of care (Lawn et al., 2008).

Further research to identify which models of peer support are the most effective is also needed. Existing research (SLAM/SWLSTG, 2010) suggests that the following factors could be important:

- combining emotional support with information-sharing, for example, on how to manage your condition (Dale et al., 2008)
- peer support might be particularly helpful at times of transition, for example during and after discharge from hospital (Forchuk et al., 2007)
- there could also be a particularly strong case for using peer support to deliver care to specific populations, such as homeless people or minority groups (Solomon, 2004).

Peer support is an important component of efforts to make services more focused on recovery (Shepherd et al., 2008). In the longer term, peer support could play a central role in striking a new balance in the mental health system between professional intervention and other forms of support (Perkins, 2010).

Service user research

The growing influence of the mental health service user movement has stimulated increased synergy between mental health social work research and user-led research. To some degree, this is because both have an interest in the wider quality of life domains such as work, education, support and safety rather than addressing the health domain only. The synergy is typified by participative methodologies (Tew et al., 2006), and early partnerships have achieved some local success. For example, Castillo and Ramon influenced the development of user-led services for people with a diagnosis of personality disorder in one locality in the UK following a participative study (Ramon et al., 2001; Castillo, 2003). The growth of academic mental health service user/consumer research units in the UK, Australia and the USA in recent years – encouraged by government policy for consumer involvement in research and stimulated by the growing influence of the service user movement – will undoubtedly influence the future of mental health social work research (Simpson and House, 2002; Doughty and Tse, 2005). Mental health social worker research and user-led research will continue to share a broad focus on demonstrating real improvements in people's lives (outcomes) in terms of quality of life, social inclusion and social capital. We briefly examine research in these outcome-related areas in the following sections.

One of the longest established user research groups in the UK is the Service User Research Enterprise (SURE) at the Institute of Psychiatry in London. In 2002, SURE published *Review of Consumers' Perspectives on Electro Convulsive Therapy*, a Department of Health-commissioned systematic review of what patients thought about electroconvulsive therapy (ECT). The results influenced 2003 guidelines from the National Institute for Health and Clinical Excellence (NICE) about obtaining consent to ECT and giving information about the treatment. An analysis of research papers, reports by user organizations and first-hand testimonies from patients showed that about half the people receiving the treatment felt they had not received enough information about the procedure and its common side effect of memory loss. About a third felt they had not freely consented – as they must do by law – even when they had signed a consent form (SURE, 2002). Two of the researchers involved in this project had themselves received ECT, but the study has been the subject of serious criticism and controversy, as reported in the *British Medical Journal* (Andre, 2003; Pearlman, 2003a, 2003b; Plummer, 2003; Seymour, 2003).

Measuring outcomes in mental health

The coalition government has emphasized that 'The NHS will be held to account against clinically credible and evidence-based outcome measures, not process targets' (DH, 2010a, p. 1).

It is important that mental health features prominently in the planned NHS outcomes framework (DH, 2010b), which proposes that the use of standardized outcome measures will allow providers and commissioners to measure and compare performance effectively. The choice of outcome measures is critical. If measures are chosen that capture aspects of performance that are of highest priority to people who use mental health services, the increased emphasis currently being placed on measuring outcomes could refocus services on what matters most to those who use them.

Transparency in Outcomes: A Framework for the NHS (DH, 2010b) suggests measuring the performance of mental health services by:

■ *effectiveness:* measured in terms of:
  – the gap in mortality rates between people with and without mental health problems
  – employment rates for people with mental health problems
■ *patient experience:* measured using standardized instruments
■ *safety:* measured in terms of suicide rates on inpatient units.

Clearly, these measures are focused largely on serious mental illness in adults and, as such, are somewhat limited. Any outcomes framework would also need to include appropriate measures for children and adolescents and for people with common mental health problems such as depression and anxiety. The following outcomes might be considered.

Quality of life outcomes

Quality of life (QoL) is measured as disease specific, health related or generic. For mental health social work research, the emphasis tends to be on the latter, and research focuses on how mental ill health affects QoL in several major life domains, as well as in respect of overall wellbeing (Evans et al., 2007). Research focuses on how treatments and social interventions can improve QoL outcomes. Ventegodt et al. (2011) examined the treatments of over 2,000 chronically ill patients and more than 20 different types of health problems. QoL improving interventions helped 30–90% of the patients, typically within one year, independent of the type of health problem, and this included mental illnesses.

Oliver (1996) originally intended that the Lancashire Quality of Life Profile (LQoLP) should be used by social workers as part of their routine social assessment work, when assessing long-stay hospital patients. It quickly became clear, however, that it had potential use as an outcome indicator, as many clinical and social services were adopting 'improved quality of life' as a service objective. The original profile was used in several sites as a practice tool for assessment and outcome, and individual case studies showing change over time were published. It has been used in major research studies (Huxley et al., 2001) and translated into several languages (for example van Nieuwenhuizen et al., 2001). The LQoLP was rather lengthy for the measurement of outcomes and a briefer tool was developed – again by a multidisciplinary team in which social workers and social scientists were predominant. The Manchester Short Assessment of Quality of Life (MANSA) (Priebe et al., 1999) has also been used as a research and clinical tool. Evans, S. et al. (2005) went on to develop the QuiLL (Quality of Life in Later Life) for older people, which is also being used in service and research settings. They also made a significant contribution to the debate about the use of QoL measures in mental health by showing that change over time can be measured using these instruments (Huxley et al., 2001). In a comparison of people with severe and common mental health problems with the general population, they found that common mental disorders can have an equally devastating effect on QoL as more severe disorders – and in some domains even more devastating (Evans et al., 2007).

Evans and Huxley (2005) also investigated the phenomenon of 'response shift' in people with severe disorders. This is said to occur in health-related QoL studies when the patient 'shifts' their subjective rating thresholds to take account of their altered circumstances. Evans and colleagues showed that contrary to popular opinion at the time, response shift is not common in people with severe mental health problems, and when it does occur, it is not mainly in the direction of 'resignation' (adapting to worsened circumstances by raising current subjective ratings) but mainly in the direction of 'aspiration' (aspiring to better circumstances by lowering current subjective ratings).

As well as providing evidence about the effectiveness of interventions, QoL assessment can be helpful to individual service users by providing them with graphic feedback on the QoL scores in domains relevant to their problems. One example, given to us by a team leader in Macclesfield in Cheshire, found that while the social workers and others were concerned about the service user's accommodation, it turned out that his QoL assessment showed that he was having much more difficulty adapting to his medication regime. The team was able to help him by refocusing their efforts.

Social workers can make use of structured (and published) QoL tools, and this can help the service user to articulate the areas that are currently problematic for them as well as identifying strengths and skills. Graphic feedback can easily be created from measures such as the MANSA (Priebe et al., 1999).

It is important for social workers and others to bear in mind that structured and published instruments are more valid and reliable than untested measures that have been designed for use in a particular service, or have never been subject to peer review and publication. Marshall et al. (2000) were able to show that the latter type of measure exaggerated the favourable impact of interventions compared to published standardized measures.

Social inclusion outcomes

For some people, the concepts of social exclusion and inclusion (SEU, 2004) are still too narrow as a basis for the development of effective local and national social policies and practices (Berman and Phillips, 2000). Earlier, Beck et al. (1997) proposed an alternative overarching conceptual framework of social quality, defined as: 'the extent to which citizens are able to participate in the social and economic life of their communities, under conditions which enhance their wellbeing and individual potential' (Beck et al., 1997, p. 3). This concept of social quality is similar to the conception of QoL assessment used by mental health social work researchers (see above and Oliver et al., 1996), in that it encompasses objective and subjective interpretations. Social quality has at least four overlapping elements that bear a close resemblance to the life domains of QoL assessments. They are:

- *socioeconomic security:* protection against unemployment, poverty, ill health and other material deprivations
- *social inclusion/exclusion:* equal access to supportive infrastructures, labour conditions and collective goods
- *social cohesion/anomie:* the availability of social networks, equal access to services
- *empowerment/disempowerment:* being able to develop their full potential in social, economic, political and cultural processes.

Vogel's (1994) taxonomy of social quality is virtually the same as the life domains covered by QoL measures: health, education, work, income, housing, safety, social attachment and leisure.

Huxley et al. (2011) used a comprehensive literature review and concept mapping exercise (capturing the views of people with mental health problems, their carers, professionals in the field and the general population) to develop the conceptual framework to be used in the SCOPE (Social and Community Opportunities Profile). SCOPE was developed for use in general population settings and mental health service research, and in routine outcome measurement in mental health services. SCOPE:

- is multidimensional and captures multiple life domains
- incorporates objective and subjective indicators of inclusion
- has sound psychometric properties including responsiveness
- facilitates benchmark comparisons with normative general population and mental health samples, including common mental disorder and severe mental illness groups
- can be used appropriately with people with mental health problems receiving and not receiving support from mental health services
- can be used across a range of community service settings.

The ratings of perceived opportunities were significantly lower in people with common mental disorders than the general population or mental health service users with more severe illnesses. The three mental health status groups also differed significantly in their average ratings on the single item 'overall satisfaction with inclusion'. The healthy general population scores were significantly higher than those for the unwell groups.

The three mental health status groups differed significantly on 11 of the 14 objective opportunity items, and on 9 of the 13 participation items. The groups were similar in terms of frequency of family contact or social activity, accommodation type, and debt and qualification levels. In most respects, a higher proportion of the healthy general population sample had opportunities to be socially included compared to the mentally unwell groups.

Among the lessons for social workers from this work is that social inclusion can be measured and that social exclusion seems to be worst for people with common mental disorders (Huxley et al., 2010).

Social capital outcomes

Social capital refers to the social context of people's lives. It is a multidimensional concept that variously encompasses other concepts such as trust (Coleman, 1988), civic engagement, social norms and reciprocity (Putnam, 1993), features of social structures and networks (Lin, 2001) and the resources embedded within them (Bourdieu, 1986). Although the concept has attracted multiple definitions, mental health social work researchers have made the case for two distinct social capitals rather than one unified concept (Webber and Huxley, 2004), an idea that is now receiving wider currency (Kawachi, 2006; Kawachi et al., 2007). The communitarian conceptual approach to social capital, derived from the work of political scientist Robert Putnam (1993), has been highly influential in psychiatric epidemiology. This sees social capital as a 'public good' arising from participation in civic activities, mutually beneficial norms of reciprocity and the trust people place in other members of the community. It is often measured at the ecological level to explore associations with prevalence rates of mental disorders (for example Rosenheck et al., 2001; Boydell et al., 2002). However, the neo-capital approach derived from sociologists such as Pierre Bourdieu (1986) and Nan Lin (2001) arguably offers more promise to mental health social work research.

Predominantly derived from social network analysis, the neo-capital conception maintains a focus on social structure while mostly using the individual as the unit of analysis. Lin's (1999, p. 39) definition of social capital as 'investment in social relations by individuals through which they gain access to embedded resources to enhance expected returns of instrumental or expressive actions' emphasizes the dynamic qualities of the concept and its potential utility for mental health.

Social workers have worked with social scientists to derive and validate appropriate measurement strategies. Applied in general population and clinical samples, these have demonstrated inequalities in access to social capital for people with a common mental disorders (Webber and Huxley, 2007; van der Gaag and Webber, 2008). They are also being used in intervention research as outcome measures.

The concept of social capital has renewed the focus on the social context of people's lives in mental health research. Its connections with traditional social work concerns of social support and social networks may see the concept as becoming influential in the future practice and research of mental health social workers.

Making connexions

What outcome measures might be expected to 'capture aspects of performance that are of highest priority to people who use mental health services'?

Research

Stress research in social work

The numbers and proportion of social workers in the new functional teams in England are low, which brings an attendant risk of personal or professional isolation. Huxley et al. (2010) found that social care workers make up only 19% of new teams' staffing compared to an average of 32% in CMHTs. Almost one-third of new teams have no social care presence at all compared to just 7% of CMHTs. The intention to leave was more common among social workers than among nursing staff, and more likely where they worked in teams with a lower proportion of social care staffing. Higher (better) 'teamwork' scores were associated with having more social support from colleagues and higher (better) quality of care ratings by workers were associated with the social care composition of the team being greater than 60%.

Where managers or the agency value social work staff, they are more likely to feel satisfied and less likely to want to leave (Evans et al., 2006). Prendergast (2011) expresses the concern that a health-dominated integrated service risks the marginalization of social work and social care. She found that this was the case in the case study area she looked at. The merging of the health and social care cultures produces what has been termed 'acculturative stress' (Burke and Cooper, 2000), and this has been observed after services have been merged or integrated, leading to stress and anxiety among the workforce (Gulliver et al., 2002) and service users (Barr and Huxley, 1999; Prendergast, 2011). Evans et al. (2006) found job dissatisfaction and poor mental health among social workers in mental health teams, many feeling over-stressed, emotionally exhausted and undervalued. Social workers in teams with a greater staff mix suffered more emotional exhaustion and more days off sick. Prendergast suggests that other factors leading to stress could be:

- the removal of structural supports for social work/care staff
- the small number of social care/work staff in the teams
- social work practice being overshadowed by healthcare practices
- health professionals having difficulty adopting the whole systems model of care embraced by social work/care staff.

A chief nursing officer's review of mental health nursing argued that for it to be fit for the future, it would have to change from the biomedical perspective to the whole systems approach (DH, 2006).

Onyett has written extensively about mental health teams, and in *Teamworking in Mental Health* (2003), he provides advice and guidance on looking after team members because, as he says, if effective long-term relationships with staff are important to the user's experience of mental health services, then clearly they will need to be working with people who are likely to stay, who have high morale and low absenteeism. Among the factors he cites as important for keeping staff mentally healthy are:

- role clarity
- manageable workloads
- keeping paperwork to a minimum

- good practice in relation to the safety of staff
- promoting supportive contact between team members
- having decision latitude (freedom to control work and exercise discretion)
- access to good supervision
- effective team meetings
- continued integrated education and training.

Having greater decision latitude, co-worker support, good management and feeling valued by managers and the organization all counted towards better mental health, better quality care, greater job satisfaction and less likelihood of leaving the job (Huxley et al., 2010). These are significant factors for all team members, but given the potential marginalization of social work/care in these teams (Prendergast, 2011), social workers in particular need to be aware of this research evidence.

Further reading

- Cantopher, T. (2006) *Depressive Illness: Curse of the Strong*. London: Sheldon Press.

Highly practical text with sound advice for both sufferers and helpers.

- Goldberg, S.D. and Goodyer, I. (2005) *The Origins and Course of Common Mental Disorders*. Hove: Routledge.

Best summary of research into common disorders, taking a life course perspective and integrating biological and social research.

- Warner, R. (2010) *Recovery from Schizophrenia: Psychiatry and Political Economy* (4th edn). Hove: Routledge.

Best summary of what is known about schizophrenia and social influences on the causes, courses and outcomes.

References

ABC News Online (2006) 'Gallop quits citing depression', press statement, 16 January, available at http://www.abc.net.au/news/newsitems/200601/s1548426.htm, accessed 24 February 2011.

Almond, S. and Healey, A. (2003) 'Mental health and absence from work: new evidence from the UK Quarterly Labour Force Survey', *Work, Employment and Society*, 17(4): 731–42.

Andre, L. (2003) 'Does underlying depression or ECT itself cause amnesia after ECT?', *British Medial Journal*, **326**(7403): 1363–7.

Anthony, W.A. (1993) 'Recovery from mental illness: the guiding vision of the mental health system in the 1990s', *Psychosocial Rehabilitation Journal*, **16**(4): 11–23.

Bachrach, L. and Harris, M. (1988) *Clinical Case Management*. New York: Jossey Bass.

Barr, W. and Huxley, P.J. (1999) 'The impact of community mental health reform on service users: a cohort study', *Health and Social Care in the Community*, 7(2): 129–39.

Research

Beck, W., van der Maesen, L. and Walker, A. (eds) (1997) *The Social Quality of Europe*. The Hague: Kluwer Law International.

Berman, Y. and Phillips, D. (2000) 'Indicators of social quality and social exclusion at national and community level', *Social Indicators Research*, 50, 329–50.

Bourdieu, P. (1986) 'The forms of capital', in J. Richardson (ed.) *Handbook of Theory and Research for the Sociology of Education*. New York: Greenwood Press.

Boydell, J., McKenzie, K., van Os, J. and Murray, R. (2002) 'The social causes of schizophrenia: an investigation into the influence of social cohesion and social hostility. Report of a pilot study', *Schizophrenia Research*, 53, 264.

Brown, G.W. and Harris, T. (1978) *The Depressed Woman*. London: Tavistock.

Burke, R. and Cooper, C. (eds) (2000) *The Organisation in Crisis: Downsizing, Restructuring and Privatisation*. Oxford: Blackwell.

Cantopher, T. (2003) *Depressive Illness: The Curse of the Strong* (2nd edn). London: Sheldon Press.

Castillo, H. (2003) *Personality Disorder: Temperament or Trauma? An Account of an Emancipatory Research Study Carried Out by Service Users Diagnosed with Personality Disorder*. London: Jessica Kingsley.

Centre for Mental Health (2010) *The Economic and Social Costs of Mental Health Problems in 2009/10*. London: Centre for Mental Health.

Chapman, D.P., Perry, G.S. and Strine, T.W. (2005) 'The vital link between chronic disease and depressive disorders', *Preventing Chronic Disease*, 2(1): A14.

Chinman, M., Lucksted, A., Gresen, R. et al. (2008) 'Early experiences of employing consumer-providers in the VA', *Psychiatric Services*, 59, 1315–21.

Coleman, J. (1988) 'Social capital in the creation of human capital', *American Journal of Sociology*, 94, S95–120.

Cook, J.A., Copeland, M.E., Hamilton, M.M. et al. (2009). 'Initial outcomes of a mental illness self-management program based on wellness recovery action planning', *Psychiatric Services*, 60(2): 246–9.

Crowther, R.E., Marshall, M., Bond, G.R. and Huxley, P. (2001) 'Helping people with severe mental illness to return to work: a systematic review', *British Medical Journal*, 322(7280): 204–8.

Dale, J., Caramlau, I.O., Lindenmeyer, A. and Williams, S.M. (2008) 'Peer support telephone calls for improving health', *Cochrane Database of Systematic Reviews*, issue 4, article CD006903.

Dawson, A. and Tylee, A. (2001) *Depression: Social and Economic Time Bomb*. London: BMJ Books.

Deegan, P.E. and Drake, R.E. (2006) 'Shared decision making and medication management in the recovery process', *Psychiatric Services*, 57, 1636–9.

DH (Department of Health) (2006) *From Values to Action: The Chief Nursing Officer's Review of Mental Health Nursing*. London: DH.

DH (2009) *New Horizons*. London: DH.

DH (2010a) *Equity and Excellence: Liberating the NHS*, White Paper. London: DH.

DH (2010b) *Transparency in Outcomes: A Framework for the NHS*, available at http://www.dh.gov.uk/en/Consultations/Liveconsultations/DH_117583, accessed 24 February 2011.

Doughty, C. and Tse, S. (2005) *The Effectiveness of Service User-Run or Service User-Led Mental Health Services for People with Mental Illness: A Systematic Literature Review*. Wellington, NZ: Mental Health Commission.

DWP (Department for Work and Pensions) (2009) 'November 2009 claimant data', available at http://statistics.dwp.gov.uk/asd/index.php?page=tabtool, accessed 24 February 2011.

Egede, L.E., Zheng, D. and Simpson, K. (2002) 'Comorbid depression is associated with increased health care use and expenditures in individuals with diabetes', *Diabetes Care*, **25**(3): 464–70.

Evans, D.L., Charney, D.S., Lewis, L. et al. (2005) 'Mood disorders in the medically ill: scientific review and recommendations', *Biological Psychiatry*, **58**(3): 175–89.

Evans, S. and Huxley, P. (2005) 'Adaptation, response shift and quality of life ratings in mentally well and unwell groups', *Quality of Life Research*, **14**(7): 1719–32.

Evans, S., Banerjee, S., Leese, M. and Huxley, P. (2007) 'The impact of mental illness on quality of life: a comparison of severe mental illness, common mental disorder and healthy population samples', *Quality of Life Research*, **16**(1): 17–29.

Evans, S., Gately, C., Huxley, P. et al. (2005) 'Assessment of quality of life in later life: development and validation of the QuiLL', *Quality of Life Research*, **14**(5): 1291–300.

Evans, S., Huxley, P., Gately, C. et al. (2006) 'Job satisfaction and burnout in mental health social workers: results from a UK national survey', *British Journal of Psychiatry*, **188**(1): 75–80.

Fergusson, D.M., Horwood, L.J. and Ridder, E.M. (2005) 'Show me the child at seven: the consequences of conduct problems for psychosocial functioning in adulthood', *Journal of Child Psychology and Psychiatry*, **46**(8): 837–49.

Forchuk, C., Reynolds, W., Sharkey, S. et al. (2007) 'The transitional discharge model: comparing implementation in Canada and Scotland', *Journal of Psychosocial Nursing and Mental Health Services*, **45**(11): 31–8.

Goldberg, D.P. and Goodyer, I. (2005) *The Origins and Course of Common Mental Disorders*. London: Routledge.

Goldberg, D.P. and Huxley, P.J. (1980) *Mental Illness in the Community: The Pathway to Psychiatric Care*. London: Tavistock.

Goldberg, D.P. and Huxley, P.J. (1992) *Common Mental Disorders: A Biosocial Model*. London: Routledge.

Gulliver, P., Peck, E. and Towell, D. (2002) 'Evaluation of the integration of health and social services in Somerset: Part 2: lessons for other localities', *Managing Community Care*, **10**(3): 33–7.

Henderson, C., Flood, C., Leese, M. et al. (2004) 'Effect of joint crisis plans on use of compulsory treatment in psychiatry: a single blind randomised controlled trial', *British Medical Journal*, 329, 136–8.

Henderson, C., Flood, C., Leese, M. et al. (2008) 'Views of service users and providers on joint crisis plans', *Social Psychiatry and Psychiatric Epidemiology*, 44, 369–76.

Hippisley-Cox, J., Fielding, K. and Pringle, M. (1998) 'Depression as a risk factor for ischaemic heart disease in men: population based case-control study', *British Medical Journal*, **316**(7146): 1714–19.

Hogarty, G.E. (1991) 'Social work practice research on severe mental illness: charting a future', *Research on Social Work Practice*, **1**(1): 5–31.

Huxley, P., Evans, S., Baker, C. et al. (2010) *Integration of Social Care Staff within Community Mental Health Teams*, Final Report to the NIHR SDO Programme. London: HMSO.

Huxley, P., Evans, S., Burns, T. et al. (2001) 'Quality of life outcome in a randomized controlled trial of case management', *Social Psychiatry and Psychiatric Epidemiology*, **36**(5): 249–55.

Huxley, P., Evans, S., Madge, S. et al. (2011) *The Development of a Measure of Social Inclusion*, Final Report. National Institute for Health Research, Health Technology Assessment Programme. London: HMSO.

Huxley, P., Raval, H., Korer, J. et al. (1989a) 'Psychiatric morbidity in social workers' clients: clinical outcome', *Psychological Medicine*, 19, 189–97.

Huxley, P., Raval, H., Korer, J. et al. (1989b) 'Psychiatric morbidity in social workers' clients: social outcome', *Social Psychiatry and Psychiatric Epidemiology*, 24, 258–65.

Isaac, B.C., Minty, E.B. and Morrison, R.M. (1986) 'Children in care: the association with mental disorder in the parents', *British Journal of Social Work*, **16**(3): 325–39.

Kawachi, I. (2006) 'Commentary: social capital and health: making the connections one step at a time', *International Journal of Epidemiology*, **35**(4): 989–93.

Kawachi, I., Subramanian, S.V. and Kim, D. (eds) (2007) *Social Capital and Health*. New York: Springer-Verlag.

Kessler, R.C., Greenberg, P.E., Mickelson, K.D. et al. (2001) 'The effects of chronic mental health conditions on work loss and work cut back', *Journal of Occupational and Environmental Medicine*, 43, 218–25.

Kinoshita, Y., Furukawa, T.A., Omori, I.M. et al. (2011) 'Supported employment for adults with severe mental illness', *Cochrane Database of Systematic Reviews*.

Kisely, S., Smith, M., Lawrence, D. et al. (2007) 'Inequitable access for mentally ill patients to some medically necessary procedures', *Canadian Medical Association Journal*, **176**(6): 779–84.

Knapp, M. (2003) 'Hidden costs of mental illness', *British Journal of Psychiatry*, **183**(6): 477–8.

Landers, G.M. and Zhou, M. (2009) 'An analysis of relationships among peer support, psychiatric hospitalization and crisis stabilization', *Community Mental Health Journal*, 24 June (e-pub ahead of print).

Lawn, S., Smith, A. and Hunter, K. (2008) 'Mental health peer support for hospital avoidance and early discharge: an Australian example of consumer driven and operated service', *Journal of Mental Health*, **17**(5): 498–508.

Lawn, S., Battersby, M.W., Pols, R.G. et al. (2007) 'The mental health expert patient: findings from a pilot study of a generic chronic condition self-management programme for people with mental illness', *International Journal of Social Psychiatry*, **53**(1): 63–74.

Leete, E. (1989) 'How I perceive and manage my illness', *Schizophrenia Bulletin*, 15, 197–200.

Lin, N. (1999) 'Building a network theory of social capital', *Connections*, 22, 28–51.

Lin, N. (2001) *Social Capital: A Theory of Social Structure and Action*. Cambridge: Cambridge University Press.

McVeigh, K.H., Sederer, L.I., Silver, L. and Levy, J. (2006) 'Integrating care for medical and mental illnesses', *Preventing Chronic Disease*, **3**(2): A33.

Marshall, M., Lockwood, L., Bradley, C. et al. (2000) 'Unpublished rating scales: a major source of bias in randomised controlled trials of treatments for schizophrenia?', *British Journal of Psychiatry*, 176, 249–53.

Measures, P. (2008) Comment on 'Service users and social care practitioners: making ourselves felt', The Social Care Experts Blog, 6 March, http://www.communitycare.co.uk/blogs/social-care-experts-blog/2008/03/service-users-and-social-care.html, accessed 24 February 2011.

Min, S.Y., Whitecraft, J., Rothbard, A.B. and Salzer, M.S. (2007) 'Peer support for persons with co-occuring disorders and community tenure: a survival analysis', *Psychiatric Rehabilitation Journal*, **30**(3): 207–13.

Mueser, K.T., Corrigan, P.W., Hilton, D.W. et al. (2002) 'Illness, management and recovery: a review of the research', *Psychiatric Services*, 53, 1272–84.

Nuyen, J., Spreeuwenberg, P.M., van Dijk, L. et al. (2008) 'The influence of specific chronic somatic conditions on the care for co-morbid depression in general practice', *Psychological Medicine*, **38**(2): 265–77.

Oliver, J., Huxley, P. and Mohamad, H. (1996) *Quality of Life and Mental Health Services.* London: Routledge.

Onyett, S. (2003) *Teamworking in Mental Health.* Basingstoke: Palgrave Macmillan.

Osborn, D.P., Levy, G., Nazareth, I. et al. (2007) 'Relative risk of cardiovascular and cancer mortality in people with severe mental illness from the United Kingdom's General Practice Research Database', *Archives of General Psychiatry*, **64**(2): 242–9.

Pearlman, C.A. (2003a) 'Valuing memory loss', *British Medical Journal*, accessible at http://www.bmj.com/content/326/7403/1363/reply, accessed 27 February 2011.

Pearlman, C.A. (2003b) 'Problems with this review', *British Medical Journal*, accessible at http://www.bmj.com/content/326/7403/1363/reply, accessed 27 February 2011.

Perkins, R. (2010) 'Professionals: from centre stage to the wings', in R. Grove and S. Duggan (eds) *Looking Ahead: The Next 25 Years in Mental Health*. London: Sainsbury Centre for Mental Health.

Plummer, W. (2003) 'Allowances for clustering', *British Medical Journal*, accessible at http://www.bmj.com/content/326/7403/1363/reply, accessed 27 February 2011.

Prendergast, L. (2011) Organisational Culture, Secondment and Social Care: An Exploration of a Partnership Organisation in the East of England. Unpublished PhD thesis, University of Essex.

Priebe, S., Huxley, P.J., Knight, S. and Evans, S. (1999) 'Application and results of the Manchester Short Assessment of Quality of Life (MANSA)', *International Journal of Social Psychiatry*, **45**(1): 7–12.

Putnam, R. (1993) *Making Democracy Work: Civic Traditions in Modern Italy*. Princeton, NJ: Princeton University Press.

Ramon, S., Castillo, H. and Morant, N. (2001) 'Experiencing personality disorder: a participative research', *International Journal of Social Psychiatry*, **47**(4): 1–15.

Rapp, C.A. (1992) 'The strengths perspective of case management with persons suffering from severe mental illness', in D. Saleeby (ed.) *The Strengths Approach in Social Work*. New York: Longman.

Rapp, C.A. (1998) *The Strengths Model: Case Management with People Suffering from Severe and Persistent Mental Illness*. New York: Oxford University Press.

Rapp, C.A., Shera, W. and Kishardt, W. (1993) 'Research strategies for consumer empowerment of people with severe mental illness', *Social Work,* **38**(6): 727–35.

Repper, J. and Perkins, R. (2003) *Social Inclusion and Recovery: A Model for Mental Health Practice*. London: Baillière Tindall.

Research

Rinaldi, M. (2002) 'Manic depression and self management', in R. Ramsey, A. Page, T. Goodman and D. Hart (eds) *Changing Minds: Our Lives and Mental Illness*. London: Gaskell.

Rinaldi, M. (2009) *Peer Support Specialists Within Mental Health Services: A Brief Review*. London: South West London and St George's Mental Health NHS Trust.

Rinaldi, M. and Perkins, R. (2007) 'Comparing employment outcomes for two vocational services: individual placement and support and non-integrated pre-vocational services in the UK', *Journal of Vocational Rehabilitation*, **27**(1): 21–7.

Rosenheck, R., Morrissey, J., Lam, J. et al. (2001) 'Service delivery and community: social capital, service systems integration, and outcomes among homeless persons with severe mental illness', *Health Services Research*, 36, 691–710.

Roy-Byrne, P.P., Stein, M.B., Russo, J.E. et al. (2005) 'Medical illness and response to treatment in primary care panic disorder', *General Hospital Psychiatry*, **27**(4): 237–43.

Sainsbury Centre for Mental Health (2009) *Commissioning What Works: The Economic and Financial Case for Supported Employment*. London: Sainsbury Centre for Mental Health.

Saleebey, D. (1996) 'The strengths perspective in social work practice: extensions and cautions', *Social Work*, **41**(3): 296–305.

Saleebey, D. (2005) *The Strengths Perspective in Social Work Practice*. Boston: Pearson/Allyn & Bacon.

Scott, S., Spender, Q., Doolan, M. et al. (2001) 'Multicentre controlled trial of parenting groups for child anti-social behaviour in clinical practice', *British Medical Journal*, **323**(7306): 194–7.

Selye, H. (1956) *The Stress of Life*. London: McGraw-Hill.

SEU (Social Exclusion Unit) (2004) *Social Exclusion and Mental Health*. London: Office of Deputy Prime Minister.

Seymour, J. (2003) 'Does underlying depression or ECT itself cause amnesia after ECT?', *British Medical Journal*, accessible at http://www.bmj.com/content/326/7403/1363/reply, accessed 27 February 2011.

Shepherd, G., Boardman, J. and Slade, M. (2008) *Making Recovery a Reality*. London: Sainsbury Centre for Mental Health.

Simon, D., Willis, C.E. and Harter, M. (2009) 'Shared decision-making in mental health', in A. Edwards and G. Elwyn (eds) *Shared Decision-making in Health Care: Achieving Evidence-based Patient Choice* (2nd edn). Oxford: Oxford University Press.

Simon, G., Revicki, D., Heiligenstein, J. et al. (2000) 'Recovery from depression, work productivity, and health care costs among primary care patients', *General Hospital Psychiatry*, 22, 153–62.

Simpson, E.L. and House, A.O. (2002) 'Involving users in the delivery and evaluation of mental health services: systematic review', *British Medical Journal*, **325**(7375): 1265.

Slade, M. (2009) *Personal Recovery and Mental Illness: A Guide for Mental Health Professionals*. Cambridge: Cambridge University Press.

SLAM/SWLSTG (South London and Maudsley NHS Foundation Trust/South West London and St George's Mental Health NHS Trust) (2010) *Recovery is for All: Hope, Agency and Opportunity in Psychiatry. A Position Statement by Consultant Psychiatrists*. London: SLAM/SWLSTG.

Solomon, P. (2004) 'Peer support/peer provided services underlying processes, benefits and critical ingredients', *Psychiatric Rehabilitation Journal*, **27**(4): 392–401.

SSI (Social Services Inspectorate) (1990) *Community Care: Draft Guidance on Assessment and Case Management*. London: SSI/DH.

Stewart-Brown, S. (2005) 'Interpersonal relationships and the origins of mental health', *Journal of Public Mental Health*, **4**(1): 24–8.

SURE (Service User Research Enterprise) (2002) *Review of Consumers' Perspectives on Electro Convulsive Therapy*. London: DH.

Tew, J., Gould, N., Abankwa, D. et al. (2006) *Values and Methodologies for Social Research in Mental Health*. Bristol: Policy Press.

Thomas, C. M. and Morrris, S. (2003) 'Cost of depression among adults in England in 2000', *British Journal of Psychiatry*, 183, 514–19.

Trinder, L. and Reynolds, S. (2000) *Evidence-based Practice: A Critical Appraisal*. Oxford: Blackwell Science.

Unützer, J., Schoenbaum, M., Katon, W. J. et al. (2009) 'Healthcare costs associated with depression in medically ill fee-for-service medicare participants', *Journal of the American Geriatrics Society*, **57**(3): 506–10.

Van der Gaag, M.P. and Webber, M. (2008) 'Measurement of individual social capital: questions, instruments, and measures', contribution to I. Kawachi, S.V. Subramanian and D. Kim (eds) *Social Capital and Health*. New York: Springer-Verlag.

Van Nieuwenhuizen, C., Schene, A.H., Koeter, M.W. and Huxley, P. (2001) 'The Lancashire quality of life profile: modification and psychometric evaluation', *Social Psychiatry and Psychiatric Epidemiology*, 36, 36–44.

Ventegodt, S., Omar, H.A. and Merrick, J. (2011) 'Quality of life as medicine: interventions that induce salutogenesis. A review of the literature', *Social Indicators Research*, **100**(3): 415–33.

Vogel, J. (1994) 'Social indicators and social reporting', *Statistical Journal of the United Nations*, 11, 241–60.

Warner, R. (2004) *Recovery from Schizophrenia: Psychiatry and Political Economy* (3rd edn). New York: Brunner-Routledge.

Warner, R. (2009) 'Recovery from schizophrenia and the recovery model', *Current Opinion in Psychiatry*, 22, 374–80.

Webber, M. and Huxley, P. (2004) 'Social exclusion and risk of emergency compulsory admission', *Social Psychiatry and Psychiatric Epidemiology*, **39**(12): 1000–9.

Webber, M. and Huxley, P. (2007) 'Measuring access to social capital: the validity and reliability of the Resource Generator-UK and its association with common mental disorder', *Social Science and Medicine*, 65, 481–92.

Williams, M., Teasdale, J., Segal, Z. and Kabat-Zinn, J. (2007) *The Mindful Way Through Depression: Freeing Yourself from Chronic Unhappiness*. London: Guilford Press.

Research

10

Social work practice in mental health

CAROLINE LEAH

Contemporary mental health practice in a field of changing policy and legal requirements presents many challenges to the inexperienced and experienced social worker.
In recent years, the rapid rate of changes to policy and practice has served to exacerbate the complexity of social work practice in an increasingly uncertain world. What
then for the morale of the social worker and the service user? How can the competing ideological concepts of recovery and risk be reconciled in a world of dwindling
resources? These are some of the challenges that frontline practitioners face.

It is worth remembering that in these times of uncertainty, the social work role
is needed more than ever. You are a resource, and your knowledge, skills and values,
the interventions you are trained to implement and the therapeutic relationships you
build with service users and carers are an invaluable asset.

The four case interventions outlined in this chapter illustrate the complexity of
service users' lives and their needs, along with the important role of the social worker.
The strength of multidisciplinary working is highlighted. However, it is in the conclusion to these case illustrations that the tensions of competing paradigms of belief held
among mental health professionals are addressed.

The task of the social worker requires stamina and resilience, the ability to advocate for change and to make change happen. It also requires hope. Long before the
recovery movement, Harvey Milk, US gay rights activist and the first openly gay man
to be elected to public office, advocated for change in the American political system.
In a speech in 1978, known as the hope speech, he proclaimed:

> There is hope for a better world; there is hope for a better tomorrow. Without
> hope, not only gays, but those blacks, and the Asians, the disabled, the seniors,
> the us's: without hope the us's give up. I know that you cannot live on hope alone,
> but without it, life is not worth living. And you, and you, and you have got to
> give them hope.

The service users whose story is told in this chapter all had a common goal – hope for a better future. It is part of a social worker's role and responsibility to enable service users to believe in a better future and to assist them to identify and make the changes they want to happen.

Practice example 1   Lauren

Lauren had a difficult childhood. Her mother, Florence, was often in and out of psychiatric hospital and would disengage on a regular basis from community mental health services. Lauren was neglected as a child and did not experience models of good parenting.

On three occasions she was placed on the child protection register. The first time was when she was born because of concerns about her mother's mental health and her ability to parent a new baby. Professionals observed difficulties in Florence forming attachments with Lauren. It was thought that although Florence met Lauren's basic care needs, there was a lack of maternal warmth and nurturing behaviour.

The second time was at age four when Florence experienced a psychotic episode and was passively neglecting Lauren's care needs. She also held a fixed delusional belief that Lauren was a special child who was 'chosen by God to cure the world of evil'. Florence was detained under section 2 of the Mental Health Act 1983 (MHA) and Lauren was placed in temporary foster care for five weeks. Florence was much better on discharge and engaged well with the support offered by the community mental health team (CMHT) and workers from the children and families team.

The third occasion was when Lauren was aged nine. Florence again held a delusional belief that Lauren was 'special' and sent Lauren out canvassing door to door 'to cure the world of evil'. She was again detained under section 2, later converted to a section 3 (MHA 1983), and Lauren was placed in temporary foster care for three months.

Lauren spent most of her teenage years acting as a young carer to her mother. This was difficult for her and she struggled to manage school attendance, maintain friendships or have a social life outside school. When Lauren was aged 16, she became pregnant after a one-night stand. She has never disclosed who is the father of her son, Daryl.

Lauren's first mental health referral

Lauren was first referred to the CMHT by her GP following her attendance at the practice for an antenatal check-up. The GP assessed her mental and physical health and believed that Lauren was experiencing a psychotic episode. She reported that

Lauren was hearing voices and appeared guarded in her manner. The GP had discussed Lauren's pregnancy with her and had explained that she believed she was having a psychotic episode. Lauren did not agree with her GP. She said she was 'just stressed out at the idea of having a baby'. Lauren said she had told her mum about it, and she had said for her to go and see the GP. The GP expressed grave concern at Lauren's inability or unwillingness to accept that she was mentally unwell. She believed that Lauren required an urgent assessment by a social worker and a psychiatrist.

A joint assessment was conducted the following day at Lauren's home by the CMHT social worker and the team psychiatrist. The background information obtained from the GP, the school and Lauren's mother revealed a picture of Lauren's behaviour becoming increasingly bizarre in the previous two months. Teachers reported that she had been withdrawn and isolated and appeared vague in her responses to teachers. Her personal appearance had deteriorated: normally, she was well dressed and had well-groomed hair, but of late she appeared dishevelled and unwashed. It was clear from the joint assessment that Lauren was experiencing a psychotic episode marked by fixed delusions concerning her unborn child, auditory hallucinations, and neglect of her personal appearance. She had become socially withdrawn and was guarded in her manner.

She appeared willing to engage with a care and crisis plan, which comprised daily visits from a social worker to monitor her mental health, the prescription of antipsychotic medication that was safe for use during pregnancy, and the involvement of a support worker to help with the practicalities of preparing for the birth of her child and to support her with appointments, including an outpatient appointment to see a psychiatrist the following week. A copy of the plan was given to her.

Lauren's admission to hospital

In the following few days, however, Lauren's mental health deteriorated further. She became increasingly distracted and guarded in her manner and disengaged from CMHT involvement. Her mother contacted the care coordinator expressing concern about Lauren: she was mumbling to herself, shouting out incoherently and not eating adequately. She had been refusing all help and today had refused to allow the midwife to examine her.

Due to the risks to Lauren and her unborn child, it was decided by the psychiatrist and the approved mental health professional (AMHP; a role created by the MHA 2007) to conduct a MHA assessment. The assessment was coordinated by an AMHP who was also her care coordinator. The GP, a section 12 approved doctor, made a recommendation under section 2 of the Mental Health Act 1983. The consultant psychiatrist and the AMHP then conducted a joint assessment in Lauren's own home. Lauren's mother was also present (under the 'participation principle'; MHA 2007).

The assessment concluded that Lauren was experiencing an acute psychotic episode, characterized by hearing voices, a fixed delusional belief that she was special and had the ability to heal people of their ailments. She had paranoid ideas about cameras spying on her and watching her every move, and ideas of reference, where she believed that a famous TV personality was talking to her through the TV, telling her to 'go forth and heal'. She had lost weight from constant walking and had not been eating adequately. Her appearance was one of self-neglect. The assessment included a full risk assessment, identifying hazards, obstacles and risks, and used positive and negative risk factors to form an overall picture of Lauren's current situation.

Lauren had been asked if she would consider an informal admission to hospital due to the risk of further self-neglect, risk to her mental and physical health, and the risk of harm to her unborn child. At the same time, however, she was assessed under the Mental Capacity Act 2005 (ss. 2(1), 2(2), 3(1)), and it was determined that she did not have the capacity to make a decision about an informal admission to hospital for care and treatment. The AMHP considered the alternatives to admission in conjunction with the guiding principles of the MHA 1983, but concluded that Lauren could not engage with community alternatives due to a lack of insight into her situation, the risk to self and the risk to her unborn child. In the interests of her own mental health, which required a full assessment and treatment plan, a recommendation was made for a hospital admission under section 2 of the MHA.

Lauren was initially admitted to a local psychiatric unit before being transferred to a mother and baby psychiatric ward when she was six months pregnant.

Daryl's birth

When Daryl was born, Lauren had great difficulty in bonding with him. The birth had been traumatic and involved an emergency Caesarean. Following Daryl's birth, the ward team and psychiatrist had started Lauren on olanzapine, an antipsychotic medication, because of a further psychotic episode.

Under the local perinatal policy, all the professionals met and involved Lauren in a perinatal care plan. A plan was drawn up in conjunction with a child protection care plan and a 'children in need' assessment. It focused on Daryl's and Lauren's needs. Present at the meeting was the consultant psychiatrist, the ward manager, the CMHT social worker, the children's social worker, the GP, Lauren and an independent advocate.

Lauren's needs on discharge were shared with her and the rest of the multidisciplinary team. The CMHT social worker expressed concern about her ability to care for Daryl. Lauren was also concerned but felt that she could be a good mother to Daryl with the right kind of support.

A care package at home was agreed. It consisted of support twice a day from a childcare support worker, including support to attend weekly parenting skills classes, support with play therapy from children's services, and mental health visits from her social worker and community psychiatric nurse. Lauren would attend monthly outpatient appointments with her psychiatrist and receive support from

Practice

her health visitor, including weekly weight checks for Daryl, all with her full consent. A crisis and contingency plan was agreed, consisting of the emergency contact number of the crisis team and the telephone number of the emergency out-of-hour's team.

Daryl's placement in foster care

Shortly after she was discharged home, professionals became concerned at Lauren's care for Daryl as he was not meeting the developmental milestones. Lauren appeared to be suffering from the negative effects of schizophrenia, leaving her feeling unmotivated and lethargic. Lauren would leave Daryl in soiled nappies and he was underweight. She was not meeting his emotional needs and workers felt that Lauren was having difficulty forming an attachment with Daryl.

It was important that this was assessed, as there was a concern that what may have been construed as the negative symptoms of schizophrenia could be depression. The psychiatrist reviewed Lauren's mental health and undertook a medication review; he concluded that she was indeed experiencing the negative symptoms of schizophrenia triggered by the stressful and life-changing experience of being a new mother and her limited coping strategies in dealing with this.

An emergency 'children in need' meeting was called where a decision was reached to place Daryl in foster care, subject to a care order (Children Act 1989, ss. 31, 38). It was important that Lauren was consulted and that her wishes and feelings were taken into account. Lauren had mixed emotions. She felt upset and guilty that she had not bonded with Daryl, but also reluctantly resigned to the decision. She was aware that Daryl's needs came before her own (Children Act 1989, s. 17), but was encouraged that she would still have ongoing contact with Daryl. Lauren had regular contact with Daryl for the first two years of his life but, after this, she felt that he was doing well with his foster carers and she ceased having contact with him, despite the best efforts of the multidisciplinary team to encourage her.

After this, Lauren lived with her mother until she was again admitted to a psychiatric hospital two and a half years ago. She and Florence lived in a two-bedroom council flat in a deprived inner city area with a high degree of crime and drug and alcohol misuse. The flat was in a building where there were often used needles and rubbish in the communal areas. This made Florence upset and angry as nothing was ever done to remedy this situation despite numerous telephone calls to the local council.

Some time after her readmission to hospital, Lauren moved to the rehabilitation unit where she has been for two years. Now aged 25, she has expressed a desire to regain contact with her son Daryl, to do some cooking and join a weight management group. Her medication, olanzapine, has caused a significant weight gain of three stone in the time she has been at the unit. She still needs motivation and encouragement to look after her daily self-care needs, but is a pleasant although vulnerable lady who relates well to female staff. At this stage, she was referred to a community-based social worker.

The social work response

Daryl, now aged 9, still lives with his foster parents. Lauren's mother, Florence, aged 50, is still known to the same CMHT.

When the social worker began working with Lauren, she felt that because Lauren had experienced many losses in her life, it would be important to build a trusting and therapeutic relationship. With the recovery approach in mind, the social worker completed a wellness recovery action plan, where Lauren was encouraged to identify her hopes, aspirations and plans for the future. The social worker used a strengths-based model to enable Lauren to recognize her personal strengths and thereby improve her low self-esteem (Rapp, 1998). It was important to the social worker and to Lauren that Lauren was enabled to take an active role in her recovery, was listened to and her views acknowledged and respected.

The social worker began visiting Lauren once a week at the rehabilitation unit and noted her sense of sadness and isolation. Lauren didn't readily mix with other people at the unit and isolated herself. However, she did have two close friends, Maria, an old neighbour, and Janet, a fellow service user.

The social worker explored activities and social occupations with Lauren, who expressed a desire to go clothes shopping in town and to a café. She also wished to lose weight and was supported to visit the local weight management group run by occupational therapists from the CMHT. Lauren began attending and was supported by staff and other service users. Although it wasn't easy, Lauren made progress and was able to lose one stone. Lauren wanted to learn how to cook, particularly the Jamaican dishes her mother had once cooked. A support worker from the black and ethnic minority support worker service was arranged who enabled Lauren to learn to cook Jamaican and other dishes once a fortnight. She proved to be a good cook.

Lauren wished to regain contact with her son Daryl. This piece of work would require sensitive and careful planning, as Daryl had lived with the same foster carers from birth. He had some behavioural issues and had not seen his mum for seven years, although she had always sent him birthday and Christmas cards and presents.

A number of meetings were held, where discussions, assessments and plans were agreed for Lauren and Daryl to regain contact. Daryl was receiving therapy from a child psychologist once a fortnight and it was decided that Lauren would meet Daryl following these sessions, where the psychologist and Lauren's social worker would be present. Following tentative engagement initially, both Daryl and Lauren began to look forward to these visits. This was built up to include a visit to Daryl at home with his foster parents, which went well.

Currently, Lauren remains in the rehabilitation unit and plans are in progress for her to move into a woman's supported accommodation one-bedroom flat. She continues to enjoy cooking and has gained daily living skills in terms of shopping, budgeting and self-care. She sees Daryl on a fortnightly basis with her social worker and his psychologist. The psychologist thinks they both still need the support struc-

Practice

ture that has been put in place during these visits. Lauren is always ready to see Daryl and this is a highlight in her life.

Discussion

Lauren's engagement with social work was a pivotal component of her recovery journey. Lauren had been dismissed as a 'hopeless case' by her workers in the rehabilitation unit. Such pessimism is insidious and can form a culture of negativity in workers, which then permeates their attitudes towards service users.

Part of the challenge of working with Lauren was encouraging her to believe that she could have a better future. This was achieved by making small but meaningful steps that led to Lauren's sense of self-worth and confidence increasing. Small steps such as going out locally, learning to cook, and valuing friendships were reinforced as positive achievements. From the small steps, Lauren was then able to approach with more confidence steps that she would have previously found daunting. This led to her believing that she was worth something and that her son Daryl would benefit from having contact with her.

The wellness recovery action plan that was undertaken jointly between Lauren and her social worker set out key aims and aspirations for the future. It was essential that this should be shared with others and that it formed part of Lauren's comprehensive care plan. This meant that her psychiatrist, support workers and childcare workers were all involved in Lauren's recovery journey and provided her with support along the way.

> **Making connexions**
>
> Lauren had been dismissed as 'a hopeless case'. What elements in the social work response do you think contributed to the emergence of more hopeful signs?

Practice example 2 | Leo

Leo is a 35-year-old black British male who lives in a one-bedroom housing association high-rise flat in a deprived inner city area. He has a twin brother, a younger sister and a younger brother, but he is estranged from all his family including his mother Janet. The estrangement followed his involvement in theft and stealing cars between the ages of 15 and 25. He stole his mother's car and, since then, his family have refused to see him.

Leo's diagnosis, symptoms and treatment

Leo has been given a number of different mental health diagnoses. His initial diagnosis was psychosis, followed by a dual diagnosis of psychosis and substance misuse. He has recently been given a diagnosis of schizophrenia. He is on a methadone programme and experiences acute psychotic episodes. During these episodes, he hears voices. The dominant voice is that of an army sergeant major who provides a running commentary on his daily activities. The voice is derogatory and critical in nature and erodes Leo's self-esteem and self-confidence. The other two voices belong to the same 'army': one voice is repetitive and repeats the statement 'we can hear you' in a loop; the other is a female voice that is instructive, but not critical.

Leo has been observed covering his ears when responding to voices and looks visibly distressed. He finds it hard to concentrate on conversations with others and has become isolated and vulnerable. He hears voices on a daily basis and the psychiatrist and social worker have explored with him the option of clozapine (an antipsychotic, often a drug of last resort), as Leo is considered treatment resistant, and clozapine is very effective with this patient group. But Leo used to inject heroin and the use of needles now has worrying associations for him.

Leo's care coordinator is a social worker from the CMHT, whom he sees once a fortnight at the local resource centre. Leo is dyslexic and brings his correspondence to his social worker. They go through it together. He has quarterly appointments with his consultant psychiatrist at the same centre. His treatment plan consists of 10 mg oral olanzapine daily. He is referred to the community drug service for drug rehabilitation and a daily methadone prescription.

Missed appointments

Following three weeks of no contact, a missed outpatient appointment with his psychiatrist and two days of not collecting his methadone prescription, which is out of character, the psychiatrist and social worker decide to visit Leo at his flat.

On arrival at the flat, Leo answers the door. He is unkempt and dishevelled in appearance. He seems to be under the influence of a substance. The psychiatrist and social worker go in and see that the flat is in an extreme state of neglect. The floorboards are bare, there are used needles littered around the flat and dog faeces on the floor. The only bed is a soiled mattress and there is no other furniture. There are three other men in the flat in a state of stupor and a thin-looking dog.

When Leo is asked how he is, he asks the social worker and psychiatrist to leave, saying 'You shouldn't have come'. However, he does agree to come and see the social worker the next day.

The social work response

The social worker sees Leo without the psychiatrist. He informs her that he met the men four days ago outside the benefit office. They said they were homeless and asked him if he knew of anywhere they could stay. The weather was cold and icy and Leo felt sorry for them and offered to let them stay in his flat. They had persuaded Leo to buy heroin and had spent the last few days in his flat injecting heroin. Leo himself had injected heroin with them and is now worried about the possibility of infection.

Leo asks for help. He does not want the men in his flat and says the dog belongs to them. Leo appears distracted and covers his ears. He has not been taking his olan-

Practice

zapine for over one week, saying he forgot to collect his prescription. An urgent outpatient appointment is arranged for Leo later that day where he agrees to have home treatment – including twice-daily visits. He asks to restart resperidone, a drug he knows, which reduces but doesn't ameliorate his symptoms, but he can tolerate the side effects. A worker from the crisis team goes with Leo to his GP so that he can be tested for infections. He is worried about contracting HIV and hepatitis. The housing association is contacted. It is agreed that it will help to remove the men from the flat. It says the flat has been due for refurbishment for some time but that Leo has ignored its letters. He has significant rent arrears.

A care plan review is coordinated by the social worker. In attendance are the psychiatrist, the community psychiatric nurse, the social worker and Leo. Leo is relieved to know that he has not contracted any infection. Positive plans are made by Leo and the team. Leo wishes to receive more support and is in a state of mind to make some changes in his life, although he says that this will not be easy. He agrees to watch a educational DVD about clozapine with his social worker and to spend time visiting supported accommodation flats. His long-term hope is that he will regain contact with his family.

After three months, Leo moves into a refurbished supported accommodation flat. He has decided not to start clozapine. He joins the hearing voices network group and a local walking group. He finds walking therapeutic and is enjoying the support from the friends he is making at the group. He is being helped to regain contact with his twin brother through a family finding scheme. Leo receives support with managing his finances, shopping and daily budgeting from the support workers at the scheme. Leo's views of his situation are that he is making small but meaningful steps forward.

Discussion

It was apparent that Leo had experienced the onset of psychosis at the age of 15 when he was involved in stealing cars. He found that the use of heroin gave him respite from distressing psychotic experiences. Within his peer group, these experiences were normalized and he did not come to the attention of mental health services until he had experienced a number of psychotic episodes. This was due in part to Leo's reluctance to be referred by his drug worker and his fear of being labelled as mentally ill. However, following referral to mental health social work, Leo built a secure and trusting relationship with his social worker and he was able to seek help during a crisis.

The occurrence of a crisis in Leo's life was a major catalyst for change, although it should be remembered that this is not the case for all. Leo had the motivation to make changes in his life and this was recognized by his social worker who had experience of motivational interviewing. Research has demonstrated the effectiveness of motivational interviewing in situations such as Leo's (Miller and Rollnick, 1991; Miller and Heather, 1998). The cycle of contemplation was pivotal to the social worker seeing an opportunity to help Leo make positive changes in his life.

On reflection with Leo, the social worker was able to establish that he was vulnerable to influence from strong personalities and, having been homeless, Leo was sensitive to their plight. Leo reflected on his vulnerability, and was able to move forward to make important changes in his life. It was Leo's hope that the changes he made with social work support would form firm foundations on which he would build a better quality of life.

Practice example 3   Amy

Amy was referred to the CMHT for social work assessment by her GP, Dr Adams. Dr Adams has known Amy since childhood and described her as a friendly, outgoing lady who worked on the airlines as cabin crew. Amy had attended the GP practice with a request for sleeping pills. She said she had worked on several long-haul flights and had been doing some extra shifts recently, which had disrupted her sleep pattern.

Dr Adams found Amy's presentation to be completely out of character, however, stating that she was giggling uncontrollably one minute and irritable the next. There was concern that Amy might be under the influence of illegal substances, but she adamantly denied this. Dr Adams therefore requested an urgent assessment of Amy's mental health needs.

Amy's arrest and detention

Shortly after the request from Dr Adams, Amy was arrested under section 136 of the MHA 1983 and taken to the local place of safety, a section 136 suite situated at the psychiatric hospital. She had been stopped by the police for dangerous driving after she'd been reported by passers-by to be driving the wrong way up a main road. The police report indicated that she had been verbally abusive towards them and had refused to cooperate with their requests. She had attempted to run across a busy road when the car was stopped and they had to restrain her for her own safety.

Amy was interviewed by the specialist registrar and AMHP in the section 136 suite with two police officers present. A full mental health and risk assessment was undertaken by the AMHP and specialist registrar, and the GP was contacted by telephone for her views. During the interview, Amy was pacing about and her mood was elated and grandiose. She believed that she was just having fun and could not appreciate the risk that her actions had presented to herself or to other people. She shouted that she felt 'on top of the world' and 'invincible' and, in response to questions posed about her dangerous driving, she said 'I did it for kicks' and began laughing. At this point, it was unclear if Amy had been using illegal substances. A decision was made to contact Amy's mother Irene for further information, while Amy continued to be held under section 136 of the MHA 1983. This gave the power to hold Amy against her will for up to 72 hours for the purpose of interviewing her and then making any necessary arrangements for her care and treatment.

Practice

When the AMHP contacted her, Irene said that she had not seen Amy for a week following a row at home and initially she thought that she had gone to work. However, Amy's workplace had phoned two days ago to say that Amy had not been in as expected. She had noticed her car was missing and had contacted the police that morning to report it stolen. The AMHP advised Irene that a section 2 assessment was being considered, having identified her as the nearest relative. Under section 2, there is a duty to inform the nearest relative that an application is to be made or has been made (MHA 1983, s. 11(13)) and to have regard to any wishes expressed by Irene (MHA 1983, s. 13(1)).

Dr Adams also believed that a medical recommendation was required for more detailed and lengthy assessment within an inpatient setting. Alternatives to admission were explored by the AMHP but thought to be too risky to manage in a community setting.

The grounds for detention under section 2 of the MHA 1983 were met, in that Amy was:

(a) suffering from mental disorder of a nature or degree which warrants the detention of the patient in a hospital for assessment (or for assessment followed by medical treatment) for at least a limited period; and

(b) ought to be so detained in the interests of his own health or safety or with a view to the protection of other persons.

Amy in hospital

In hospital, Amy responded well to the care and treatment plan and made good progress. She was started on a mood stabilizer, which gradually helped to stabilize her mood and level of arousal. As her mental health improved, there was a consequent improvement in her relationship with her boyfriend and her mother.

During her inpatient stay, she was able to form a trusting and therapeutic relationship with her social worker who had been the AMHP involved in her detention. She learned that Amy had lived in California five years ago with her boyfriend Thomas, and had been admitted to a private psychiatric facility where she was diagnosed with bipolar disorder. Her mother had not been informed. During this time, her stepfather, to whom she was very close, had died of cancer and Amy could not fly back home for his funeral. She said she felt embarrassed and ashamed of her diagnosis, and guilty that she had not gone to her stepfather's funeral or confided in her mother. Amy had been successfully treated for the bipolar episode and had gone back to work.

Prior to this episode of mania, Thomas had noticed some early warning signs of Amy becoming unwell. She had not been sleeping well, had appeared irritable and disinhibited. He asked her to see her GP, but Amy had refused. They had a terrible row, after he said he couldn't cope with her behaviour, and they had split up.

The provision of social work support

Following a full multidisciplinary assessment in hospital, a holistic plan of support was identified with Amy to meet her needs under the care programme approach (CPA) (DH, 2008). Education began with her social worker concerning the psycho-social factors that had triggered her episodes of mania. This was undertaken in conjunction with the identification of her early warning signs. A pivotal aspect of this work was Amy's ability to articulate the key triggers involved in her mental health relapse and her motivation to work on these with her social worker. A key trigger was a disruption in her daily rhythms as a result of flying through several time zones in the course of her work. Amy had attempted to manage this, albeit unsuccessfully, through self-prescribed sleeping tables.

Through liaison with her occupational health department, and her social worker acting as an advocate, Amy agreed to have a phased return to work. This involved resuming her duties as ground crew initially. Amy believed it was important to regulate her daily rhythms and establish regular routines for waking and sleeping.

A personalization package was implemented, which consisted of weekly exercise classes and 20 counselling sessions. It was felt that counselling was needed to help Amy deal with some unresolved issues about her stepfather's death. Her social worker undertook work with Amy on her daily rhythms, together identifying key triggers that disrupted them. Education about the signs and symptoms of bipolar disorder was also undertaken with her mother at Amy's request.

Discussion

Research indicates that bipolar disorder is a debilitating illness with a high rate of reoccurrence. It carries significant implications for service users' quality of life and their support networks. Judd et al. (2003) have reported that the median reoccurrence of changes in symptoms is as high as six per year and most people with the disorder experience frequent and severe episodes.

Stressful life events can have a direct impact on daily rhythms, increasing arousal leading to reductions in sleep and appetite, resulting in dramatic changes in daily routine, levels of occupation and social stimulation. It was essential that Amy should be supported to maintain equilibrium.

Issues of stigma, whether perceived externally or subjectively, can affect social relationships. Amy did not confide in her mother because of the shame a mental health diagnosis had for her. This brings to the fore the wider role of the social worker to promote social inclusion and ameliorate inequalities at a societal level. Tackling stigma and exclusion is one of the key tasks of Time to Change (www.time-to-change-org.uk), the anti-stigma programme run by Mind and Rethink Mental Illness. Social workers can join the campaign, many are aware of it and it is on most trust websites; it aims to promote inclusion and educate the wider public on mental

Practice

health inequalities and the effects of societal prejudice. It helps service users like Amy to know that the stigma they feel is real.

For many, a label of mental illness leads to negative attitudes and damaging perceptions of dangerousness (Goffman, 1961; Becker, 1963). The promotion of social inclusion through support to get Amy back to work, participation in exercise classes and education around Amy's early warning signs with Amy and her mother were therefore essential stepping stones within her recovery. With this was the optimism that was shared by the social worker, which was a crucial element for effective care planning; this led to the cultivation of a positive therapeutic relationship and a meaningful recovery for Amy.

Practice example 4 James

A referral was received from the local psychiatric hospital for James, aged 18, a young black British man who was allocated to children's services. He had been admitted to the hospital following an incident where he had walked into a local shop and stabbed himself in the chest, sustaining severe lacerations and stab wounds. He was taken to A&E where he was treated and, from there, transferred to the psychiatric ward and placed under a section 2 for an assessment of his mental health. This was later converted to a section 3 – involving admission for treatment (MHA 1983).

James in hospital

James was diagnosed with severe psychotic depression. He was actively suicidal and was under one-to-one observations by nursing staff on the psychiatric intensive care unit for the first two weeks of his admission. During the admission, he had made a further suicide attempt when he tried to strangle himself with an item of clothing while visiting the bathroom. He was prevented from coming to harm by nursing staff intervention.

James said that he had heard voices commanding him to harm himself and saying things such as 'You are worthless' and 'You're better off dead'. He also saw images of the devil, which were terrifying for him. The image of the devil often coincided with a voice saying 'You're going to hell'. James had insight into his illness and knew that the auditory and visual hallucinations were manifestations of a mental illness, but this did not ease his distress.

He spent six months on the ward where he made satisfactory progress. A number of antipsychotics and antidepressants were tried before finding the one that best suited his treatment needs. This was because he experienced some unpleasant side effects. After six months in hospital, James had made sufficient recovery to be considered for discharge. At this point, further information was gathered from childcare and GP records.

James's childhood and transition to adulthood

James had been in foster care from the age of nine. He had no contact from this time with either his mother or father. His mother had mental health problems and his father, who misused alcohol and was a drug dealer, was sent to prison for manslaughter, with a string of other serious crimes being taken into account. Although social services had worked hard to keep James together with his mother, she was thought to have had a relapse in her mental health and her whereabouts was unknown.

James lived with foster parents until the end of his foster placement, when he went to live in a one-bedroom council flat. He had found this transition extremely difficult and had shown signs and symptoms of developing a depressive illness. His transition workers reported that around this time James had become very withdrawn and would not let social workers into his flat. When they attempted to engage with him during visits to his flat, he would either not open the door, although they could see he was in, or shout at them to go away. This behaviour was not usual for James. The workers also noticed that he appeared low and sad; they could hear him crying by himself in his flat.

James's school records were viewed: he was described as a sensitive but quiet young man with a keen interest in music and sports. He had a number of friends and enjoyed playing football locally. He did not drink alcohol or take illicit substances, but had a number of close friends who did. He always said that he would not touch them because he didn't want to end up like his dad.

Social work intervention

A section 117 (MHA 1983) meeting was held, where a discussion took place with James concerning issues of engagement with services and the risk of disengagement. James was informed that the multidisciplinary team was considering placing him on a community treatment order, but was keen to hear his view of the proposal. James stated that he disliked the medication he was on and did not want to take it due to the unpleasant side effects. He had read the information leaflets and was concerned about gaining weight and losing his libido. However, he agreed to take the medication as prescribed and said he would discuss any side effects that arose with his consultant psychiatrist at his outpatient appointment.

James had been to visit a flat in supported accommodation for young black men, and had really liked it. He liked being close to the city centre and to local shops and they ran a music course at the nearby college. Funding was agreed for James to move there from the hospital. His social worker from the early intervention team supported James to claim the relevant benefits, including obtaining social funds to purchase necessary items for his new flat. He was further supported to end his previous tenancy.

James expressed reluctance to engage with workers initially. However, by working with James on this issue, he was able to confide that, in the past, he had felt let down and abandoned by social workers and social services. He held a great deal of hostility towards his transition workers, in particular, as he associated them with loss,

Practice

having been moved from his foster home. It transpired that James did not want to leave his foster home where he said he felt safe and happy. He reported that since he had left, he felt that when he had gone back to visit, he had been a nuisance and was in the way. These issues were deep-rooted and it was thought that James would benefit from psychotherapy.

Although it took over six months on a waiting list, James received psychotherapy to help him to manage his feelings of anger, loss and abandonment. He attended the session on a fortnightly basis, and made good progress. Although he continued to experience days when his mood was low, he had a network of support on which to draw and take strength from.

He was encouraged to visit his foster family who were upset that James had not confided in them. They had no idea that he had felt that way, but described being busy with a new foster child during the time of his relapse. James was encouraged to go whenever he wished to and, from then, usually visited twice a week.

In recognition of his support needs, the support workers at the supported accommodation project helped James develop independent living skills; in particular, he was enabled to manage his own finances, including budgeting skills, and he was given encouragement with shopping and cleaning. He enrolled on a short college course for music, which he enjoyed attending and where he made some new friends who shared his love of music.

Despite the initial concerns about James's difficulty engaging with services, he made good progress and attended all his psychiatric outpatient appointments.

Discussion

It was important that James was allowed the freedom to express his discontent with his previous social work experience, given the issues he faced: he was a vulnerable young man who had not yet developed the life skills that would enable him to cope with living alone at the age of 18.

The stress of leaving a safe and secure environment where he had formed loving bonds and close attachments had a severe impact on James's mental health. His involvement with new workers from a transition service with whom he had not built a relationship served to exacerbate his sense of loss and isolation, as he could not utilize the support being offered due to a lack of trust. The stress vulnerability model takes such major changes into account and advocates the need for social workers to enable people like James to build effective coping strategies and develop support networks (Zubin and Spring, 1977). It was essential that James's social worker should understand the links cited in research studies that have shown associations between neglectful childhood experiences, inadequate parental care and the later occurrence of depression – often triggered by stressful life events.

By working in partnership with other mental health professionals and support services, James was enabled to develop social and life skills that will assist him to seek support in a crisis. This will ultimately provide some future protection in the event of a further major stressful life event leading to the reoccurrence of a mental illness. By effectively communicating with all key parties under the CPA, the social worker worked collaboratively with James and others. This led to an improvement in James's sense of self-worth, his confidence, his coping strategies and, essentially, his recovery.

Conclusion

The four case studies demonstrate good social work practice. However, it is easy, perhaps even convenient, to assume that the practicalities of care planning and working together involve a shared understanding of the origins of mental health presentations and the belief structures underlying this. Professional power and responsibility are often negotiated and contested and the paradigms of belief are often hidden unconsciously by professionals in the care planning process.

The recovery model, with its aspirational and hopeful philosophy of improving the quality of life satisfaction as defined by service users themselves, is at odds with a CPA model, which is needs led and dictated by government political agendas and resource limitations.

The concern reflected in recent government policy on health and social care emphasizes the need for greater independence, choice and control for service users. In order to avoid stagnant responses and fragmented interventions by mental health professionals, work with service users and carers must be deployed by utilizing effective communication. This means that the underlying assumptions on the causes and the nature of mental health presentations should be critically scrutinized and reflectively evaluated by such professionals.

Through a process of critical reflection, social work and clinical practice's understanding of mental health will facilitate an understanding of the thought processes behind our underlying assumptions. By articulating our understandings of mental health, it will enable the implicit to become explicit and assist social workers to become evidence-based and research-minded practitioners, accountable for their practice and proud of their achievements.

Appendix 10.1 Key sections of Mental Health Act 1983 referred to in the chapter

Section 2: admission for assessment

Concerned with detaining a person for the primary purpose of assessment in an inpatient unit, for a period of up to 28 days. The person must satisfy legal criteria in order to be detained under this part of the Act. The criteria states that the patient is suffering from a mental disorder of a nature (the nature of the mental health diagnosis) or degree (the severity of the symptoms) which necessitates detention, and that they must also be detained in the interest of their own health and safety or with a view to

Practice

protecting others. The AMHP makes the application. This is founded on the recommendations of two registered medical practitioners, usually a GP and a psychiatrist.

Section 3: admission for treatment

Concerned with the detention of a person for treatment for up to six months. The criteria for treatment are that the person is suffering from a mental disorder of a nature or degree which makes it appropriate for them to be admitted and to receive medical treatment in hospital. Further, that it is necessary that they are detained for their own health and safety and for the protection of others. Importantly, medical treatment *must* be available.

In sections 2 and 3, it is the AMHP's role to identify if there are any safe alternatives to hospital. The principles of least restriction and the adherence of AMHP practice to the Human Rights Act 1998 are important facets of the AMHP role.

Section 11: general provisions to applications

Relates to the general provision of applications and concerns a number of important safeguards for patients and nearest relatives, one of which is the duty of the AMHP to inform a person who has been identified as a patient's nearest relative (this is a legal definition and should not be confused with the next of kin) of the detention of a person under the Mental Health Act.

Section 13: duty of an AMHP to make applications for admission or guardianship

Gives the AMHP the duty to make an application for detention that takes into account all the relevant circumstances of the person and involves interviewing the person in a manner that is consistent with their human rights.

Section 117: aftercare

An important provision for those who have been detained under section 3 of the Act. The local health board and local authority have a duty to ensure that aftercare, consisting of health and social care needs, is delivered, in conjunction with any voluntary or charitable agencies. Gives a comprehensive entitlement to a coordinated plan of care and treatment following the end of the detention period.

Section 136: mentally disordered persons found in public places

Concerns the arrest, by a police officer, of a person who is found in a public place who they think may be suffering from a mental disorder and appears to them to be in 'immediate need of care or control'. The person is then removed to a place of safety, in either a hospital setting or police station. Good practice guidance advocates the need for designated section 136 suites in local psychiatric hospitals. The person may be detained for up to 72 hours, so that they can be interviewed by an AMHP and doctor and provisions made for their care and treatment.

Further reading

■ Brown, R. (2007) *The Approved Mental Health Professional's Guide to Mental Health Law*. Exeter: Learning Matters.

Accessible, good introduction to the Mental Health Act 2007 and the role of the AMHP. Highly recommended for professionals interested in becoming AMHPs.

■ Rogers, A. and Pilgrim, D. (2010) *A Sociology of Mental Health and Illness*. Maidenhead: Open University Press.

Fascinating journey through the mental health landscape. Deconstructs professional concepts of illness and wellbeing with a compelling argument that mental illness is constructed through the discourse of those in power; critically questions and offers insight into a range of mental health perspectives, inviting the reader to develop their own critical understanding of mental illness.

■ Webber, M. (2008) *Evidence-based Policy and Practice in Mental Health Social Work*. Exeter: Learning Matters.

Highlights skills, knowledge and values-based social work practice within an evidence-based practice framework; essential reading for the modern mental health practitioner.

References

Becker, H. (1963) *Outsiders: Studies in the Sociology of Deviance*. New York: Free Press.

DH (Department of Health) (2008) *Refocusing the Care Programme Approach*. London: DH.

Goffman, E. (1961) *Asylums: Essays on the Social Situation of Mental Patients and Other Inmates*. Harmondsworth: Penguin.

Judd, L., Scheffler, P.J., Arkiskal, S. et al. (2003) 'Long term symptomatic status of bipolar 1 vs bipolar II disorders', *International Journal of Neuropsychopharmacology*, **6**(2): 127–37.

Miller, W.R. and Heather, N. (ed.) (1998) *Treating Addictive Behaviours*. New York: Plenum Press.

Miller, W.R and Rollnick, S. (1991) *Motivational Interviewing*. London: Guilford Press.

Rapp, C. (1998) *The Strengths Model: Case Management with People Suffering from Severe and Persistent Mental Illness*. New York: Oxford Press.

Zubin, J. and Spring, B. (1977) 'Vulnerability: a new view of schizophrenia', *Journal of Abnormal Psychology*, **86**(2): 103–24.

Practice

Part III
Social Work and Substance Use

Substance use problems are common in the UK and social workers work with substance users on a daily basis. Research has persistently identified the fact that social workers need to be better trained if they are to respond appropriately to drug and alcohol issues.

The move to a recovery-focused agenda reflected in the most recent national drug strategy for England provides a timely opportunity for social work; it has signalled a greater recognition that people need support in their recovery journey and as they become reintegrated into their families and communities. The Munro (2011) review of childcare social work has identified parental alcohol and drug use among the potentially harmful factors to children.

Part III of this book outlines for the reader the range of current knowledge and research on social work practice with adults, children and families experiencing substance use problems.

In Chapter 11, Sarah Galvani and Angela Thurnham place drug and alcohol use in a policy context, historically dominated either by criminal sanctions or the healthcare framework. This served to marginalize people with substance use problems by overlooking their social care needs, and, to a large extent, excluded social workers from substance use training and practice. A commentary is provided on how the UK policy process is rapidly changing and the key drivers for this change, where there is now recognition of the role social workers can play in safeguarding and supporting individuals with substance use problems. The chapter concludes with a view to how such policy and practice might better serve people with alcohol and drug problems in the future.

In Chapter 12, Michael Preston-Shoot's examination of the legislative framework brings into sharp relief several tensions that surround or pervade social work and substance use legislation generally. He reflects on how legislation in the field of drug and alcohol use is contentious and the tension between balancing duties of care and human rights and choices. A core tenet in this examination is how the attitudes and values of social workers empowered to act on behalf of the state may shape how law is implemented in practice.

In Chapter 13, Donald Forrester and Aisha Hutchinson outline the strong theoretical and developing empirical evidence for the contribution that social work can make for people with drug or alcohol problems. There is an examination of key theoretical constructs in understanding substance use and misuse, including ambivalence and behaviour change. Interventions with a strong evidence base of effectiveness, such as motivational interviewing, are evaluated from a social work perspective. The theoretical approach proposed is to achieve a marriage between the best elements of psychological methods with the social model that lies at the heart of social work. The authors explore social work's fit with the emerging recovery approach and how the time is ripe for a wide-ranging reappraisal of substance use interventions.

In Chapter 14, Donald Forrester, Georgia Glynn and Michelle McCann present a recent literature review of rigorously evaluated social work interventions for drug and alcohol problems. A summary of the key features of effective social work interventions across the literature is provided. In particular, factors associated with positive outcomes centre on engagement and building trusting relationships when working with individuals who have substance use problems.

In their review of social work practice in Chapter 15, Sarah Galvani and Sarah Wadd present a framework for social work assessment of substance use issues. Case scenarios are presented, and the topics discussed include the need to identify an individual's stage of change, to work with ambivalence, to assess and to communicate in a manner that elicits change. This chapter is extremely useful for social work students and practitioners, as it highlights the importance of skilled assessment and uses case scenarios ranging from parental substance use to older adults' substance use, providing a toolkit of suggested responses and questions the social worker could use in practice.

Working with substance use is not just about better subject knowledge and awareness of effective interventions; it also requires reflection on professionals' attitudes, skill development and informed supervision. This theme runs throughout Part III. Because substance use issues will have an impact on up to half of social workers' clients, it is essential that they learn better how to understand and engage with substance use and misuse.

Michelle McCann

Reference

Munro, E. (2011) *The Munro Review of Child Protection. Interim Report: The Child's Journey*, available at http://www.education.gov.uk/munroreview/ downloads/ Munrointerimreport.pdf, accessed 3 February 2011.

11

Social policy and substance use

SARAH GALVANI AND ANGELA THURNHAM

Box 11.1

A note on terminology

What we call people, the labels we assign them or their behaviours, give powerful messages about our value base. In the alcohol and drug field, there are a plethora of terms, many of which are stigmatizing and negatively labelling. People with alcohol and other drug problems should not be defined by their problem. Social work principles have always rejected pejorative terms and the homogenization of individuals. Where alcohol and drugs are concerned, these include terms such as 'alcoholics', 'winos', 'addicts' and 'junkies'. Such terms do little to help motivate or support someone to change, nor do they accurately reflect the fact that people with alcohol and drug problems have a range of identities, including being professionals, partners, parents, family members or members of a local community. They are, first and foremost, people.

The UK government has moved from using the long-established and somewhat nebulous policy term 'substance misuse' to the medical model language of 'drug or alcohol dependence'. There is always a reason for such changes, and the politics behind this choice of language appears to support the government's emphasis on abstinence-oriented goals and 'freeing' people from their dependence (HM Government, 2010a).

The use of substances, be they alcohol or other drugs, is not a new phenomenon. From the Bible through Shakespeare to the present day there is evidence that people have used substances to excess. Yet our attitude to substance use can be fickle and deeply contradictory. Substance use is embedded in many cultural rituals and can be a popular and enjoyable social behaviour, but it can also attract judgement and condemnation. The use of substances can be a criminal act, can present a potential risk to people's health, and can harm the social wellbeing of the individual and the people close to them.

It is not surprising therefore that we have an ambivalent attitude towards substance use. On the one hand, alcohol is a legal drug and, for many of us, a staple part of our cultural diet and upbringing. For centuries, drinking alcohol has been an aid to socializing, a perceived 'rite of passage' into adulthood, and a core component of celebrations and commiserations. On the other hand, the use of illicit drugs is socially abhorrent. Such drugs are given classifications according to their potential for harm. Penalties for possession and supply are severe and there is a rebellious and deviant image attached to their use. Users are criminalized and vilified, regardless of the amount they use or the impact on their behaviour. As a result of this dichotomous attitude to alcohol and other drugs, policy has been developed separately, led by different government departments. Health, criminal justice and social policy are all relevant homes for alcohol and drug policy, yet politicians have struggled to develop cross-cutting policy and it is social policy in particular that has been left out in the cold.

This chapter argues that this policy gap has resulted in minimal attention being paid to alcohol and drugs in social work training and practice – a profession that is ideally placed to identify and respond to the difficulties their use can sometimes pose among a range of service user groups. We provide a summary of the development of alcohol and drug policy, defining key current policies and their relationship with and relevance to social work policy and social work practice. The chapter concludes with a view to how such policy and practice might better serve people with alcohol and drug problems in the future.

National drugs strategy: an overview

The development of policy frameworks emerged from government concerns about the use of alcohol and other drugs. As with any policy, its purpose is to outline the government's plan of action, identify its primary concerns and outline its priorities and focus. For drugs, the priorities have primarily been health responses and crime and disorder, and funding has been allocated accordingly. Until the 1980s, there had been no UK national strategy on drugs. Health-oriented guidance on how to 'treat' drug users was available, with a clear focus on the health of the individual user, albeit with an element of social control enshrined in law. Treatment was dispensed by the medical profession, usually a GP or consultant psychiatrist, who chose the length and type of treatment available (Lart, 2006).

The 1980s brought with it the emergence of the HIV (human immunodeficiency virus) epidemic and an acceptance that harm reduction measures were needed. Following research showing high rates of HIV among injecting drug users, needle exchanges and safer injecting practices were introduced (Stimson et al., 1988). This put harm reduction firmly on the agenda for those who continued to use or found it difficult to abstain. At the same time, Margaret Thatcher's government published the first national strategy, *Tackling Drug Misuse* (Home Office, 1985). It identified five key priorities:

1 reducing supply
2 enhancing the effectiveness of enforcement
3 tightening domestic controls and deterrence
4 developing prevention
5 improving treatment and rehabilitation.

These priorities clearly laid out a move towards social control and criminal justice responses to illicit drug use, with only one of the five focusing on drug treatment. Since then, successive governments around the UK have published drug strategies with key priorities that have always included criminal justice and treatment priorities.

What emerged for the first time in the Conservative strategy 10 years later, *Tackling Drugs Together* (Home Office, 1995), was a new focus on young people's use and an acknowledgement of the broader harms resulting from drug use:

> By creating a broader definition of 'harm', to include harms to the community as well as harms to the individual, it created a policy umbrella under which the law-and-order and medical approaches could combine, even if the resources were still going primarily into the criminal justice system and into efforts at supply reduction. (RSA, 2007, p. 111)

This focus on young people continued with the publication of *The Substance of Young Needs* (NHS Health Advisory Service, 1996) and the Labour government's drug strategy *Tackling Drugs to Build a Better Britain* (Cabinet Office, 1998). The former provided guidance to service commissioners and providers on the delivery of services for young people with substance problems. Importantly for social work, it also introduced the concept of four tiers of specialist substance use service delivery. Social workers were included in tier 1, alongside a range of professionals not specializing in substance use but who were expected to be able to offer basic advice and information on substance use. In addition to the inclusion of young people's service needs, the 1998 drug strategy also emphasized drug-related crime and called on the Home Office and the Department of Health to work together rather than in separate policy silos (RSA, 2007). The strategy's spotlight on criminal justice was reinforced by the transfer of drugs policy responsibilities from the Cabinet Office to the Home Office (RSA, 2007).

However, the introduction of concerns over young people's use brought with it the need to consider issues such as safeguarding and the social context in which young people's use occurred. For the first time in a national strategy, the social and environmental context was acknowledged. In 2008, this was made even more explicit with the introduction of the new drug strategy entitled *Drugs: Protecting Families and Communities* (Home Office, 2008, p. 5), which stated: 'The difference that the new strategy brings is that we will:

■ focus more on families, addressing the needs of parents and children as individuals, as well as working with whole families to prevent drug use, reduce risk, and get people into treatment;

■ give a stronger role to communities, protecting them from the damage that drugs cause through strong enforcement action, using all available powers, sanctions and levers, giving them a voice and listening to their concerns.

Again, the increased emphasis on families and communities in the strategy was a significant change in focus for the national strategy. It had moved, in a relatively short space of policy time, from a focus on health and criminal justice interests to a policy that at least began to recognize the role of families and communities as being affected by problematic substance use and having needs in their own right.

The change of government in the UK in 2010 resulted in a further national drug strategy from the Conservative/Liberal Democrat coalition. Again the title of the strategy firmly nailed the coalition's colours to the mast, *Drug Strategy 2010: Reducing Demand, Restricting Supply, Building Recovery: Supporting People to Live a Drug Free Life* (HM Government, 2010a). The focus on demand and supply located the government's priorities firmly in the criminal justice camp. Importantly, however, there were two crucial developments that had not previously been seen in national drug strategies:

1   It planned to move power and accountability for the implementation of the drug strategy from 'top-down state intervention' to the local level via new statutory police and public health bodies.

2   It included alcohol and drugs in the *same* national strategy, suggesting a possible merging of funding and service commissioning arrangements.

In England and Wales, the strategy introduced, at a national level, a focus on 'recovery', following the Scottish government's lead (Scottish Government, 2008). From a policy perspective, a recovery focus moves away from notions of harm reduction to an emphasis on abstinence. The government wants to ensure that people achieve long-term abstinence and start contributing again to society (HM Government, 2010a). The implications of the recovery agenda for alcohol and drug service provision and its potential for moving closer to social work services will be discussed further below.

National alcohol strategy: an overview

The UK has a very different relationship with alcohol in policy and in practice than with other drugs. In spite of clear evidence of harm related to alcohol use, successive governments have shied away from tackling it wholeheartedly. Calls for changes to taxation and pricing as a method for reducing alcohol-related harm (Chisholm et al., 2004; Meier et al., 2008; NICE, 2010; Wagenaar et al., 2010) go unheeded in spite of a great deal of money being spent on independent government inquiries into the issue (House of Commons, 2009; HM Government, 2010b).

The financial cost of alcohol problems to society is estimated at between £18–25 billion a year (HM Government, 2010a), but the revenue the alcohol industry generates and the unpopularity of any government decision to introduce greater restrictions on alcohol are thought to outweigh these costs. In its 2010 national strategy, the government demonstrated its ambivalence to addressing alcohol-related harm:

> Alcohol plays an important part in the cultural life of this country, with large numbers [of people] employed in production, retail and the hospitality industry. Pubs, bars and clubs contribute to community and family life and also generate valuable revenue to the economy. However, alcohol is a regulated product. Some individuals misuse it, contributing to crime and anti-social behaviour, preventable illness and early death. (HM Government, 2010a, p. 7)

It is this ambivalence that has led to a resistance to address alcohol-related harm in spite of clear evidence of harm to health, criminal justice problems and social harm in the UK and northern Europe (Anderson and Baumberg, 2006; WHO, 2006), and in spite of evidence that some people in particular are at greater risk from alcohol than other drugs (Nutt, 2010).

The first national alcohol strategy in England was published in 2004. The long-awaited *Alcohol Harm Reduction Strategy for England* (AHRSE) was greeted with some amusement due to its unfortunate acronym (Cabinet Office, 2004). As with its drug counterparts, the focus was primarily on crime reduction and the health consequences of heavy alcohol use. It also prioritized better education and communication about alcohol and its associated risks. Finally, it set out a commitment to work with the alcohol industry to introduce a voluntary code of good practice and social responsibility schemes in relation to manufacture and product marketing. This was met with much cynicism from the alcohol field. The alcohol strategy did, however, acknowledge the impact on families and the need to support people with particular vulnerabilities, including those experiencing mental distress, young people and homeless people.

The second national alcohol strategy in England emerged in 2007, this time a combined effort from a range of government departments – the Department of Health (DH), Home Office (HO), Department for Education and Skills (DfES) and Department for Culture, Media and Sport (DCMS). Entitled *Safe. Sensible. Social,* it listed a number of 'next steps'. These were:

- sharpened criminal justice for drunken behaviour
- a review of NHS alcohol spending
- more help for people who want to drink less
- toughened enforcement of underage sales
- trusted guidance for parents and young people
- public information campaigns to promote a new 'sensible drinking' culture
- public consultation on alcohol pricing and promotion
- local alcohol strategies (DH/HO/DfES/DCMS, 2007, p. 5).

What this strategy also did was recognize the impact of alcohol problems on 'family, children and friends' (p. 10), as well as the relationship of alcohol with domestic violence. Increasingly, the negative social impact of problematic alcohol use was beginning to be reflected at a national level.

Other key policy influences

Although not a policy document, the publication of *Hidden Harm* (Advisory Council on the Misuse of Drugs, 2003) led to a great deal of attention on parental illicit drug use and its negative impact on children and young people. This emerged alongside a major cross-departmental review of childcare policy following the death of Victoria Climbié in 2000 (Laming, 2000). The findings from that inquiry echoed those of other inquiries into child deaths – frontline services had failed to coordinate, share information and adopt a 'strong sense of accountability' (DfES, 2003). The resulting Green Paper, *Every Child Matters* (DfES, 2003), along with the Children Act 2004, set the national agenda for better interagency working and joint accountability for safeguarding children. The Children Act 2004 mandated 'cooperation to improve wellbeing' (s. 10) among all health and social care bodies and any other individual or agency they employed to deliver services (s. 11). It also introduced Local Safeguarding Children Boards (LSCBs) (s. 13) as a vehicle for bringing together all agencies on a regular basis. *Every Child Matters* highlighted the fact that substance use played a key role in affecting children's outcomes, yet much of the workforce had little or no training in this area. What this meant in practice was that safeguarding children became a uniting force among all frontline organizations who were legally obliged to work together.

Two further key policy documents from the substance use field identified social services as having a role to play in working with people with alcohol and drug problems, although in social work education and practice they had little impact. *Models of Care for Treatment of Adult Drug Misusers* (NTA, 2002, updated in 2006) and *Models of Care for Alcohol Misusers* (DH/NTA, 2006)[1] were key documents in the field. As with a predecessor, *The Substance of Young Needs* (NHS Health Advisory Service, 1996), they set out a framework for the commissioning of services into four tiers of service, as well as introducing concepts such as care planning and integrated care pathways into substance use services. Interventions at tier 1 were still expected to be delivered by non-alcohol or drug specialists or 'generic' services, including social workers (NTA, 2006a). Both documents (NTA, 2002; DH/NTA, 2006) stated that social services, among other frontline services such as primary care and housing, should be able to:

- give drug and alcohol advice and information
- undertake screening and assessment
- conduct brief interventions where appropriate
- make referrals to specialist alcohol or drug services
- carry out partnership or 'shared care' working with specialist alcohol or drug services.

However, it is clear from research among social workers that the appropriate training and education required to do this has not been forthcoming (Cleaver et al., 2007; Galvani, 2007; Galvani and Forrester, 2011; Loughran et al., 2010).

At a national level, therefore, social care's involvement in responding to alcohol and drug problems has not been reflected adequately in strategy documents. While the National Treatment Agency for Substance Misuse (NTA) has suggested that social services could deliver interventions described in the Models of Care documents, the partnership required to make this a reality has not been in place at policy level, resulting in minimal change on the ground.

At a regional and local level, the mechanisms for implementing these strategies and other related policies have seen some involvement by social care. The nine regional government offices in England were tasked with implementing the national drug and alcohol strategies by bringing together local strategic partnerships, crime and disorder reduction partnerships and drug and alcohol action teams. Between them, the teams and partnerships comprise representatives from the police, primary care trusts, the fire service, probation and local authorities (NAO, 2010). A review of progress of the implementation of the drug strategies found government office performances varied greatly between regions (NAO, 2010), as did the strength and involvement of the various partnerships within them (CHAI/NTA, 2008). Anecdotally, however, it seems that there is greater involvement in drug and alcohol partnerships from children's social care than adults' social care and that the primary mechanism for involvement is through attendance at joint commissioning groups and LSCBs. The coalition government's *Spending Review* (HM Treasury, 2010), however, announced the closure of all regional government offices in England. The impact this will have on the implementation of drug and alcohol policy is yet to be seen, as we await the transition to the coalition government's new locally led police and public health structures.

Policy drivers in social work

Prior to the national strategies, guidance for working with people with alcohol and other drug problems had emerged around the UK from the relevant health departments. In England, one of the key drivers that promoted social workers engaging with drug and alcohol issues followed the introduction of the NHS and Community Care Act 1990. A Department of Health local authority circular issued in 1993 made it clear that local authorities were responsible for the social care of alcohol and drug users by:

- assessing the needs of the local population for alcohol and drug services
- including services for alcohol and drug misusers in their community care plans
- assessing the social care needs of individual alcohol and drug misusers
- arranging appropriate packages of care, which may include a range of options (DH, 1993, p. 2).

In adult services, this requirement remains and has resulted in a range of responses from local authorities, including specialist social work teams or individual social workers focused on assessment and arranging packages of care, including referrals and funding, for residential treatment.

In children's services, the introduction of LSCBs, combined with a growing recognition in the substance use field of the impact on children of parental substance use, has led to a wider range of initiatives across substance use and social care. There are specialist services throughout the UK for children and families affected by parental substance use, although provision and capacity varies greatly from one authority to the next. These are often jointly commissioned by health and social care and provided by voluntary service sectors. There are also a number of specialist posts for children and family social workers within substance use services and vice versa.

One area where social care has been more involved is in the sphere of young people's substance use and youth offending. National strategies and other policy documents have, for some time, reflected concerns about young people's substance use and it has been one of the key foci of drug and alcohol strategies. In 2005, as part of the *Every Child Matters: Change for Children* raft of policy documents, the government published *Young People and Drugs* (DfES/HO/DH, 2005), which set out clear responsibilities for local authorities and drug and alcohol action teams in terms of the provision of services for young people. This focus has continued, with a plethora of policy documents to help local authorities and young people's strategic partnerships to plan and commission their drug services for young people (DfES, 2004; NTA, 2005; DrugScope and Alcohol Concern, 2006; Britton, 2007; Donaldson, 2009), as well as provide information on particular drug-related requirements as part of dispensations in youth rehabilitation orders (YJB, 2010; NTA, 2011).

Similarly, young people's alcohol use has been a key focus. *The Children's Plan* (DCSF, 2007, p. 17) made a commitment to publish a youth alcohol action plan as part of its efforts to 'tackle behaviour that puts young people at risk and help young people manage these risks'. The resulting *Youth Alcohol Action Plan* (DCSF/HO/DH, 2008) highlighted the concerns over increases in alcohol consumption among young people who drink, and identified five priorities, one of which included support for young people in their choices about alcohol use. In November 2010, the annual data on young people, alcohol and other drug use showed better retention in services, greater levels of successful treatment completion and a fall in the number of young people (under 18 years) accessing help for alcohol and drug treatment (NTA, 2010).

In terms of other social work service user groups, policy is lacking, although a greater degree of guidance is available for people experiencing mental distress and substance use (Banerjee et al., 2002; DH, 2002; Turning Point, 2007; NICE, 2010). Coexisting substance use and mental distress are common bedfellows and the guidance stresses the need for joint working across mental health and substance use services (DH, 2002). Unfortunately, some evidence suggests a number of barriers to joint working in practice (Galvani, 2008).

What has yet to be addressed well, in any policy frameworks, is the increasing concern about older people's alcohol and other drug use. In an ageing population, there is evidence that more people are using substances at an older age and taking with them into older age some of the excesses of their youth (Beynon et al., 2007; Gossop, 2008; Hallgren et al., 2009; Institute of Alcohol Studies, 2009). Evidence suggests that older people's drinking in particular is an area that requires greater policy and practice attention. We also know very little about substance use among people with physical disabilities or people with learning difficulties and disabilities.

From policy to practice

While policy informing social work education and practice with people with substance problems has been lacking, what policy does exist is only helpful if it is translated into practice realities. For the majority of social workers who do not specialize in substance use, there has been little education, or guidance, in working with people with alcohol and drug problems and how to identify, assess, intervene and refer on. In 2003, the first *Every Child Matters* policy document stated:

> all professionals working with children and young people should be able to identify, assess and undertake appropriate action for addressing substance misuse issues. In order to enable them to do this effectively, training on substance misuse should form part of initial and ongoing professional development. (DfES, 2003, p. 32)

Other research has persistently identified the need for all social workers to be trained in alcohol and other drug issues, not just children and families workers, and to ensure supervision and support is available to them in their workplace (Gassman et al., 2001; Boylan et al., 2006; Cleaver et al., 2007; Galvani, 2007; Bina et al., 2008; Loughran et al., 2010). More than two decades earlier, Harrison and colleagues worked with the government and the social work training body, Central Council for Education and Training in Social Work (CCETSW), to draw up guidance for the 'new' social work qualification (DipSW) on the inclusion of substance use in the social work curriculum (CCETSW, 1992; Harrison, 1992). The impact of the guidance was never monitored. Evidence from social workers suggests that little has changed in terms of input on alcohol and other drugs on qualifying social work training (Galvani and Forrester, 2011; Galvani et al., 2011). These studies found that many social workers still report receiving little or no input on alcohol and drugs in qualifying training and even experienced social workers identify significant training needs, including how to talk to people about alcohol and drugs and risk assessment (Galvani and Forrester, 2011; Galvani et al., 2011).

Social workers are working with substance use issues on a regular basis. For those working in children and family settings, this can be a daily occurrence, while for those working with some adult groups, for example people with learning disabilities, it is likely to be less frequent. However, the policy emphasis on health and criminal justice responses has resulted in the majority of social workers being excluded from the workforce development they need in order to work confidently with the alcohol and drug issues they face. Since the separation in England and Wales of probation from social work training in the mid-1990s, criminal justice issues are no longer the remit of the new social worker. The probation service continues to have national strategies for working with people with substance problems (Ministry of Justice, 2008) and guidance on how to do it (YJB, 2009) as well as specialist substance-related roles. There is no similar national strategy or guidance for social workers. The lack of fit between substance use policy foci and the priorities of social workers has created a chasm that appears to be difficult to cross.

Further, there is a lack of fit between social work and substance use policy due to its overwhelmingly medical model approach to interventions. In spite of psychosocial approaches to working with people with drug and alcohol problems dominating the substance use field, the language of 'treatment' in policy is also alienating for a social work profession that sees treatment as a health worker's role, and support and intervention as a social worker's role. The specialist treatment available for people with alcohol or other drug problems is predominantly short term and focused solely on their substance use. Social work's engagement with the often complex and diverse needs an individual has is not usually short-term work, nor does it adopt a single focus. What makes social work a unique profession is its starting point of seeing the person in their wider family, social and community environment. It assumes that there are relationships between all aspects of a person's life. Thus there are fundamental differences in the models and theoretical frameworks that underpin social work and substance use practice.

What the future holds: a glass half-full?

The move towards a recovery-focused agenda reflected in the 2010 national drug strategy in England has a number of potential implications for social work education and practice. It may provide a timely opportunity for substance use services and social work to move closer together, given the recognition of families and communities as requiring support, and acknowledgement that factors such as housing, good physical and mental health, and employment will contribute to an individual's recovery journey. In other words, it is no longer just about 'treating' their substance use or punishing their antisocial behaviour – people need to be able to see a better future and have support to aim for it. While the strategy again focuses on criminal justice responses and enforcement, there are some significant changes in emphasis.

First, at its core, is a very clear move away from harm reduction options for people with drug and alcohol problems to abstinence-focused 'treatment'. One of the ways it may enforce engagement with abstinence-based treatment is through the benefits system:

> We will offer claimants who are dependent on drugs or alcohol a choice between rigorous enforcement of the normal conditions and sanctions where they are not engaged in structured recovery activity or appropriately tailored conditionality for those that are. (HM Government, 2010a, p. 23)

For some people, 'sanctions' and 'rigorous enforcement' may enhance their motivation to seek help, but it would be naive to think that every person with a drug or alcohol problem will be ready to face their demons, however much they are financially punished. Unfortunately, the withdrawal or reduction of benefits could mean higher levels of individual poverty, higher levels of family poverty, increases in homelessness and acquisitive crime. This will clearly have an impact on the workload of social workers.

Second, the strategy places far more emphasis on reintegrating people back into their communities, ensuring that they have housing and employment and can contribute to society. The strategy suggests that this needs to happen by working in partnership with other services. What social workers do well is juggle many balls in the air – it is possible that social workers will be called on to coordinate care or to work with specialist substance use staff who are taking on care coordination roles. A recent review of social work interventions and their effectiveness when working with people with substance problems found case management approaches the most promising (Galvani et al., 2010). While these approaches vary, they generally involve care coordination, longer term support, and therapeutic input – similar to many forms of care management that currently operate around the UK. The recovery agenda should also bolster the work that has been started within specialist substance use services in relation to care planning and building integrated care pathways. While these are not new concepts within social work and some other parts of the medical professions, it was *Models of Care for Treatment of Adult Drug Misusers* (NTA, 2002) that initially introduced the concept to substance use services, followed by formal care planning guidance in 2006 (NTA, 2006b).

Third, the strategy mentions keeping children and families safe where there are parental substance problems. The detail on how it intends to do this is weak but it suggests that substance use services ensure that they have accessed child protection training and 'encourages those working with children and families affected by substance misuse to undertake appropriate training so they can intervene early to protect children from harm' (HM Government, 2010a, p. 22). There is also evidence that the substance use field is starting to work more closely with families, with joint working protocols issued by the DCSF, the DH and the NTA (2009). This should bring children and families social workers and the substance use field more closely together. Social workers will be in a good position to support this work and offer their experience and advice on the range of other issues that families can present with and may make family work unsafe, for example domestic violence.

Finally, the strategy acknowledges the need for social workers to have training on substance use. The Munro (2011) review of childcare social work has identified parental alcohol and drug use among the potentially harmful factors to children. She stressed the importance of services being developed to meet locally identified needs. Clearly, parental alcohol and drug problems are a national issue for children and families, and social care needs to respond nationally as well as locally. The Social Work Reform Board (2010) has published a framework for social work education at qualifying and post-qualifying level , and it is to be hoped that social workers' knowledge about alcohol and drugs will be included in changes to the social work curriculum and that monitoring mechanisms will be put in place to ensure it happens. Without mandating changes to the curriculum, history shows, repeatedly, that change is unlikely to happen within social work education (Galvani, 2007).

Conclusion

The policy process for substance use is rapidly changing, and it is clear that there is some recognition of the role social workers in particular groups can play in supporting people in their recovery journey and becoming reintegrated into their families and communities. What is needed is joined-up policy-making at a national and local level that includes social workers and social issues, not just those related to child protection, important though these are. There needs to be commitment to embedding substance use knowledge and skills in social work education and practice, starting with the appropriate policy frameworks.

The new era of substance use policy presents real opportunities for social work to embrace; however, policy and practice leadership must take this forward and equip frontline social workers to engage with these issues.

Acknowledgement

The authors would like to thank Trevor McCarthy for his advice and support in the development of this chapter.

Note

1   The Models of Care documents are under review at the time of writing.

Further reading

■ Galvani, S. (2012) *Supporting People with Alcohol and Drug Problems*. Bristol: Policy Press.

Discusses alcohol, drugs and social policy within the context of a text focused on social work practice.

■ Hughes, R., Lart, R. and Higate, P. (eds) (2006) *Drugs: Policy and Politics*. Maidenhead: Open University Press.

Reflects on drugs policy in relation to particular areas of interest to social care, including gender, young people and social exclusion.

■ McKeganey, N. (2010) *Controversies in Drugs Policy and Practice*. Basingstoke: Palgrave Macmillan.

Combines debates about drug treatment, enforcement and legalization with reflection on the needs of drug-using children and cannabis classification.

References

Advisory Council on the Misuse of Drugs (2003) *Hidden Harm: Responding to the Needs of Children of Problem Drug Users*. London: Home Office.

Anderson, P. and Baumberg, B. (2006) *Alcohol in Europe: A Public Health Perspective. A Report for the European Commission*. London: Institute of Alcohol Studies.

Banerjee, S., Clancy, C. and Crome, I. (2002) *Co-existing Problems of Mental Disorder and Substance Misuse (Dual Diagnosis): An Information Manual*. London: Royal College of Psychiatrists' Research and Training Unit.

Beynon, C.M., McVeigh, J. and Roe, B. (2007) 'Problematic drug use, ageing and older people: trends in the age of drug users in northwest England', *Ageing & Society*, 27, 799–810.

Bina, R., Harnek-Hall, D.M., Mollette, A. et al. (2008) 'Substance abuse training and perceived knowledge: predictors of perceived preparedness to work in substance abuse', *Journal of Social Work Education*, **44**(3): 7–20.

Boylan, J., Braye, S. and Worley, C. (2006) 'Life's a gas? The training needs of practitioners and carers working with young people misusing volatile substances', *Social Work Education*, **25**(6): 591–607.

Britton, J. (2007) *Assessing Young People for Substance Misuse*. London: NTA.

Cabinet Office (1998) *Tackling Drugs to Build a Better Britain: The Government's Ten-year Strategy for Tackling Drugs Misuse*. London: TSO.

Cabinet Office (2004) *Alcohol Harm Reduction Strategy for England*. London: TSO.

CCETSW (Central Council for Education and Training in Social Work) (1992) *Substance Misuse: Guidance Notes for the Diploma in Social Work*. London: CCETSW.

CHAI/NTA (Commission for Healthcare Audit and Inspection/National Treatment Agency for Substance Misuse) (2008) *Improving Services for Substance Misuse: Commissioning Drug Treatment and Harm Reduction Services*. London: CHAI.

Chisholm, D., Rehm, J., van Ommeren, M. and Monteiro, M. (2004) 'Reducing the global burden of hazardous alcohol use: a comparative cost-effectiveness analysis', *Journal of Studies on Alcohol*, 65, 782–93.

Cleaver, H., Nicholson, D., Tarr, S. and Cleaver, D. (2007) *Child Protection, Domestic Violence and Parental Substance Misuse: Family Experiences and Effective Practice*. London: Jessica Kingsley.

DCSF (Department for Children, Schools and Families) (2007) *The Children's Plan: Building Brighter Futures – Summary*. London: TSO.

DCSF/DH/NTA (Department for Children, Schools and Families/Department of Health/ National Treatment Agency for Substance Misuse) (2009) *Joint Guidance on Development of*

Local Protocols between Drug and Alcohol Treatment Services and Local Safeguarding and Family Services. London: DCSF.

DCSF/HO/DH (Department for Children, Schools and Families/Home Office/Department of Health) (2008) *Youth Alcohol Action Plan*. London: TSO.

DfES (Department for Education and Skills) (2003) *Every Child Matters*, Cm 5860. London: TSO.

DfES (2004) *Drugs: Guidance for Schools*. London: DfES.

DfES/HO/DH (Department for Education and Skills/Home Office/Department of Health) (2005) *Young People and Drugs*. London: DfES.

DH (Department of Health) (1993) *Alcohol and Drug Services within Community Care*, LAC (93)2. London: DH.

DH (2002) *Mental Health Policy Implementation Guide: Dual Diagnosis Good Practice Guide*. London: DH.

DH (2006) *Models of Care for the Treatment of Alcohol Misusers*. London: NTA.

DH/NTA (Department of Health/National Treatment Agency) (2006) *Models of Care for Alcohol Misusers (MoCAM)*. London: NTA.

DH/HO/DfES/DCMS (Department of Health/Home Office/Department for Education and Skills/Department for Culture, Media and Sport) (2007) *Safe. Sensible. Social: The Next Steps in the National Alcohol Strategy*. London: DH.

Donaldson, L. (2009) *Guidance on the Consumption of Alcohol by Children and Young People*. London: DH.

DrugScope and Alcohol Concern (2006) *Drugs: Guidance for the Youth Service*, available at http://www.drugscope.org.uk/Resources/Drugscope/Documents/PDF/Education%20and%20 Prevention/Drugsguideservice.pdf, accessed 7 February 2011.

Galvani, S. (2007) 'Refusing to listen: are we failing the needs of people with alcohol and drug problems?', *Social Work Education*, **27**(7): 697–707.

Galvani, S. (2008) 'Working together: responding to people with alcohol and drug problems', in K. Morris (ed.) *Social Work and Multi-agency Working: Making a Difference*. Bristol: Policy Press.

Galvani, S. and Forrester, D. (2011) 'How well prepared are newly qualified social workers for working with substance use issues? Findings from a national survey', *Social Work Education*, **30**(4): 422–39.

Galvani, S., Dance, C. and Hutchinson, A. (2011) *Substance Use and Social Work Practice: Findings from a National Survey of Social Workers in England. Final Report*. Available at www. beds.ac.uk/goldbergcentre.

Galvani, S., Forrester, D. with Glynn, G. et al. (2010) *Social Work Services and Recovery from Substance Misuse: A Review of the Evidence*, available at http://www.scotland.gov.uk/Resource/ Doc/346164/0115212.pdf, accessed 29 November 2011.

Gassman, R.A., Demone, H.W. and Albilal, R. (2001) 'Alcohol and other drug content in core courses: encouraging substance abuse assessment', *Journal of Social Work Education*, **37**(1): 137–45.

Gossop, M. (2008) *Substance Use among Older Adults: A Neglected Problem*, Drugs in Focus, no. 18. Briefing of the European Monitoring Centre for Drugs and Drug Addiction, Lisbon.

Hallgren, M., Hogberg, P. and Andreasson, S. (2009) *Alcohol Consumption Among Elderly European Union Citizens: Health Effects, Consumption Trends and Related Issues*. Report for the Expert Conference on Alcohol and Health, 21–22 September, Stockholm, Sweden.

Harrison, L. (1992) 'Substance misuse and social work qualifying training in the British Isles: a survey of CQSW course', *British Journal of Addiction*, 87, 635–42.

HM Government (2010a) *Drug Strategy 2010. Reducing Demand, Restricting Supply, Building Recovery: Supporting People to Live a Drug Free Life*. London: TSO.

HM Government (2010b) *The Government Response to the Health Select Committee Report on Alcohol*, Cm 7832. London: TSO.

HM Treasury (2010) *Spending Review 2010*, Cm 7942. London: TSO.

Home Office (1985) *Tackling Drug Misuse*. London: HMSO.

Home Office (1995) *Tackling Drugs Together: A Strategy for England 1995–1998*. London: HMSO.

Home Office (2008) *Drugs: Protecting Families and Communities. The 2008 Drug Strategy*. London: Home Office.

House of Commons (2009) *Health Committee First Report: Alcohol*, session 2009–10, available at http://www.publications.parliament.uk/pa/cm200910/cmselect/ cmhealth/151/15102.htm, accessed 4 February 2011.

Institute of Alcohol Studies (2009) *Alcohol and the Elderly*. London: IAS.

Laming, Lord (2000) *The Protection of Children in England: A Progress Report*. London: TSO.

Lart, R. (2006) 'Drugs and health policy', in R. Hughes, R. Lart and P. Higate (eds) *Drugs: Policy and Politics*. Maidenhead: Open University Press.

Loughran, H., Hohman, M. and Finnegan, D. (2010) 'Predictors of role legitimacy and role adequacy of social workers working with substance-using clients', *British Journal of Social Work*, **40**(1): 239–56.

Meier, P., Brennan, A., Purshouse, R. et al. (2008) *Independent Review of the Effects of Alcohol Pricing and Promotion: Part B, Modelling the Potential Impact of Pricing and Promotion Policies for Alcohol in England: Results from the Sheffield Alcohol Policy Model*, version 2008(1-1), available at http://www.dh.gov.uk/ prod_consum_dh/groups/dh_digitalassets/documents/digitalasset/dh_091364.pdf, accessed 4 February 2011.

Ministry of Justice (2008) *The National Offender Management Service Drug Strategy 2008–2011*, available at http://www.justice.gov.uk/publications/docs/noms-drug-strategy-2008-11.pdf, accessed 7th February 2011.

Munro, E. (2011) *The Munro Review of Child Protection. Interim Report: The Child's Journey*, available at http://www.education.gov.uk/munroreview/ downloads/Munrointerimreport.pdf, accessed 3 February 2011.

NAO (National Audit Office) (2010) *Tackling Problem Drug Use*. London: NAO.

NHS Health Advisory Service (1996) *Children and Young People Substance Misuse Services: the Substance of Young Needs: Commissioning and Providing Services for Young People Who Use and Misuse Substances*. London: HMSO.

NICE (National Institute for Health and Clinical Excellence) (2010) *Alcohol-use Disorders: Preventing the Development of Hazardous and Harmful Drinking*, NICE public health guidance 24, available at www.nice.org.uk/guidance/PH24, accessed 4 February 2011.

NICE (2011) *Psychosis with Substance Misuse*, available at http://guidance.nice.org.uk/CG/Wave15/8, accessed 4 February 2011.

Policy

NTA (National Treatment Agency for Substance Misuse) (2002) *Models of Care for the Treatment of Adult Drug Misusers*. London: NTA.

NTA (2005) *Young People's Substance Misuse Treatment Services: Essential Elements*. London: NTA.

NTA (2006a) *Models of Care for the Treatment of Adult Drug Misusers: Update 2006*. London: NTA.

NTA (2006b) *Care Planning Practice Guide*. London: NTA.

NTA (2010) *Substance Misuse Among Young People: The Data for 2009–2010*, available at http://www.nta.nhs.uk/uploads/nta_substance_misuse_among_yp_0910.pdf, accessed 31 January 2011.

NTA (2011) *Frequently Asked Questions: Youth Rehabilitation Order*, available at http://www.nta.nhs.uk/young-people.aspx, accessed 28 January 2011.

Nutt, D.J., King, L.A. and Phillips, L.D. (2010) 'Drug harms in the UK: a multicriteria decision analysis', *Lancet*, 376, 1558–65.

RSA (Royal Society for the Encouragement of Arts, Manufactures and Commerce) (2007) *Drugs: Facing the Facts*, Report of the RSA Commission on Illegal Drugs, Communities and Public Policy. London: RSA.

Scottish Government (2008) *The Road to Recovery. A New Approach to Tackling Scotland's Drug Problem*. Edinburgh: Scottish Government.

Social Work Reform Board (2010) *Building a Safe and Confident Future: One Year On: Detailed Proposals from the Social Work Reform Board*, available at http://www.education.gov.uk/swrb/downloads/Building%20a%20safe%20and%20confident%20future%20-%20One%20year%20on,%20detailed%20proposals.pdf, accessed 4 February 2011.

Stimson, G.V., Dolan, K., Alldritt, L. and Donoghoe, M. (1988) 'Syringe exchange schemes for drug users in England and Scotland', *British Medical Journal*, 296, 1717–19.

Turning Point (2007) *Dual Diagnosis: Good Practice Handbook*. London: Turning Point.

Wagenaar, A.C., Tobler, A.L. and Komro, K.A. (2010) 'Effects of alcohol tax and price policies on morbidity and mortality: a systematic review', *American Journal of Public Health*, **100**(11): 2270–8.

WHO (World Health Organization) (2006) *Framework for Alcohol Policy in the WHO European Region*. Copenhagen: WHO Europe.

YJB (Youth Justice Board) (2009) *National Specification for Substance Misuse*, available at www.yjb.gov.uk, accessed 4 February 2011.

YJB (2010) *The Youth Rehabilitation Order and other Youth Justice Provisions of the Criminal Justice and Immigration Act 2008: Practice Guidance for Youth Offending Teams*, available at www.yjb.gov.uk, accessed 7 February 2011.

12

The legal foundations of social work in the field of drug and alcohol abuse

Michael Preston-Shoot

Working with children and adults who misuse drugs and/or alcohol, or who are affected by their use by those around them, although challenging in itself, brings into sharp relief several tensions that surround or pervade social work more generally. To begin with, there is nothing inevitable about the shape or content of the legal rules that are enacted.[1] Rather, they reflect the nature of society and its social divisions, which is demonstrated in how diverse European countries have legislated differently with respect to misuse of drugs (EMCDDA, 2005). Consequently, debate and contestation are characteristic of law-making, and the outcome is frequently one that exhibits elements of compromise, moral judgement, lack of clarity and/or political ideology. It can be instructive, therefore, to discern the push-pull dynamics surrounding legislative developments.

The aftermath of the enactment of primary legislation, in the form of policy and practice guidance issued by central government departments, or indeed in the run-up to parliamentary debates on proposed laws, may be characterized by the use of research. However, the pursuit of research-informed or evidence-based policy and practice can become corrupted by the uses to which research can be put. Weiss (1979) captured this well by noting, for example, that research can be commissioned as part of a knowledge-driven or problem-solving approach to policy-making. However, its use can also be tactical, namely to delay decision-making, or selective and political. Here, research is used selectively, chosen for its support for a particular ideological or interest position on an issue. The heated arguments surrounding how to classify cannabis included the selective use of research to serve the constellations comprising those who favoured particular assessments on the dangers or otherwise of the drug and positions on decriminalization and depenalization. The sacking by government ministers of Professor Nutt, an adviser on UK drugs policy, in October 2009, illustrates what may happen when the interpretation of research findings contradicts the principles on which official policy rests. It can also be instructive, therefore, to analyse what and how research has been used to inform policy and practice proposals.

Drawing closer to social work, the fragmentation of social services into children's services and adult services, and the integration variously with education, housing and healthcare practitioners, has created a new set of boundary challenges in the name of overcoming familiar barriers to interprofessional working. Working with people who use and misuse drugs and/or alcohol, who may be children as well as adults, is one area that demands skills of working at boundary edges. It will often require practitioners to be knowledgeable of different legal mandates. To illustrate, drug and alcohol misuse, sometimes coexisting alongside mental health problems, is a feature in adoption and a risk factor underlying children's entry into the care system (Forrester and Harwin, 2006; Cossar and Neil, 2010; Wigley et al., 2011). Loss of a child in this way can exacerbate drug and alcohol misuse, and be associated with a low take-up of services (Cossar and Neil, 2010). Young people may also abuse drugs or alcohol as a manifestation of emotional difficulties (Wigley et al., 2011).

Practitioners will need to be skilled in directly implementing or bringing together practitioners and managers who control the resources located respectively within childcare law and community care law. Particular cases may also require knowledge of youth justice and/or adult criminal justice legislation, and an ability to work alongside colleagues in youth offending teams and probation. The same may apply to healthcare legislation and work with staff in the NHS, particularly mental health services. Practitioners' and managers' knowledge of the law, and their legal literacy in its implementation, has been found to be highly variable, often characterized by ignorance and uncertainty, and by reliance on agency procedures and personal sense-making (Braye and Preston-Shoot, 2009).

This particular practice arena also demonstrates the distinction between social work law and social welfare law (Preston-Shoot et al., 1998). Social workers must appreciate where they themselves, acting on behalf of their employing authority, have a power or a duty to act – social work law. Equally, they must be fully cognizant of social welfare law, that variety of legal rules surrounding, for example, housing, antisocial behaviour or domestic violence, where their role is less to exercise statutory authority but rather to offer advice concerning people's rights, entitlements and responsibilities.

The social work code of practice (GSCC, 2002) requires licensed practitioners to practise lawfully but also to uphold social work ethics and knowledge base. Healthcare practitioners are also bound by their respective ethical codes. When what is lawful is also ethical, and when what is unlawful is also regarded as unethical by professional practitioners, problems are unlikely to arise. However, there are times when what is lawful may appear to practitioners or managers as professionally unethical. Equally, there will be cases that raise the spectre that what is unlawful may appear to the same practitioners and managers as professionally ethical. The GSCC code is not alone in being silent on how practitioners and managers are meant to resolve such dilemmas. It is conceivable, for some at least, that working with people who misuse alcohol and/or drugs might present moments when the ethical thing to do (doing right things) contrasts with what is lawful (doing things right).

Some people who abuse drugs or alcohol will spend time in residential institutions. Accordingly, practitioners must be mindful of the incidence of institutional abuse, where children and adults in hospital or nursing care, residential care, custodial settings, or reliant on domiciliary services have been neglected or abused. Equally, there is evidence that councils with social services responsibilities have sought to evade their statutory duties, or misapplied their legislative powers, or, in the exercise of legal mandates, have displayed attitudes and values that have been considered on judicial review or scrutiny by the ombudsman to be unprofessional (Preston-Shoot, 2010). Social workers have not always felt able or required to speak out against such phenomena, while service users and their carers may have neither the knowledge nor the perceived power to challenge organizational procedures and practices. It is instructive, then, to reflect on how organizations are translating into practice the law in theory and values in theory.

One purpose of this chapter is to survey the range of legal rules that practitioners might have to draw on when working with people who misuse drugs and alcohol, and their families. Another is to comment on the nature and content of the legal rules themselves, and the ongoing debates that surround them, in order that social work can contribute authoritatively to policy-making as well as ensure sound practice.

The international context

The UK is signatory to three United Nations conventions relating to drugs. They are the Single Convention on Narcotic Drugs (1961), the Convention on Psychotropic Substances (1971) and the Convention against Illicit Traffic in Narcotic Drugs and Psychotropic Substances (1988). They seek to prohibit trade and trafficking, and to criminalize the possession, acquisition, distribution and selling of drugs. Signatory countries may also determine that personal use is a criminal offence and must transpose convention provisions into domestic law. Implementation by signatory countries of convention provisions is overseen by the International Narcotics Control Board. Created by the 1961 convention, it advises on the meaning of convention provisions and may recommend that national jurisdictions modify their legislative enactments in order to remain faithful to them. The board was critical of the UK government's decision to amend the classification of cannabis in 2004 (EMCDDA, 2005).

Within the EU, a range of legislative approaches exist, for example concerning whether the use of illicit drugs is a criminal offence, a civil offence or not directly prohibited. Taking cannabis as the example, since it is the drug most often involved in drug law offences (EMCDDA, 2005), possession and use is unlawful in some European countries, such as Sweden and France, while in others, it is illegal but personal use may not result in prosecution, the UK and Switzerland being examples.

In other countries, for instance Portugal and Italy, use has been decriminalized. Two social policy approaches may therefore be discerned, one focusing on criminal sanctions and the other on harm reduction and health and social welfare interventions. However, research on decriminalization and depenalization may not remove the controversy that surrounds how to legislate on drug use.

UK drug legislation

The Misuse of Drugs Act 1971 is the foundation stone of UK drug legislation. It created three classes of controlled drugs. Class A includes cocaine, crack, heroin and ecstasy, Class B contains barbiturates and, once again from 2008, cannabis, and Class C includes minor tranquillisers. The 1971 Act was used in 2009 to ban new 'legal highs' (Davies et al., 2010). In line with the UN conventions, the 1971 Act creates offences of unlawful supply, intent to supply, trafficking, unlawful production and unlawful possession. Police officers may stop and search if they have reasonable suspicion that an individual may possess controlled drugs. The maximum penalties for possession and for supply vary according to a drug's classification. In practice, however, a range of disposals other than a custodial sentence may be used by the courts, especially for possession rather than supply. These alternatives include fines, suspended prison sentences, probation orders, community service or cautions.

The Customs and Excise Management Act 1979 prohibits the import and export of controlled drugs except for approved scientific and medical uses. The Drug Trafficking Act 1994 creates an offence of selling goods to assist with the preparation and/or administration of controlled drugs. It allows the seizure of an individual's assets and income if they have been found guilty of drug trafficking. The growing criminalization of UK legislation may be seen in the Proceeds of Crime Act 2002 and the Drugs Act 2005. The former enables courts to make confiscation orders and removes the need to distinguish between types of crime when seeking to identify and confiscate money made from offences relating to drugs. The latter contains three significant provisions. It reverses the burden of proof concerning possession when the amount found is greater than required for personal use. This means that the onus is on the defendant to prove that they did not intend to supply. In another context, namely the Mental Health Act 1983, such a reversal of the burden of proof has been judged by the courts to breach Article 5 of the European Convention on Human Rights and Fundamental Freedoms (*R (H)* v *MHRT North and East London and Another* [2001]).

The Drugs Act 2005 also makes drug testing compulsory where the police have reasonable grounds for believing that a Class A drug has been involved in an offence committed by an arrested individual. Failing to comply with the test is itself an offence. A positive test will result in a compulsory drug treatment[2] assessment. Finally, the Act also requires that any individual made subject to an antisocial behaviour order should undergo compulsory drug testing and, where appropriate, treatment. There are also provisions in the Anti-Social Behaviour Act 2003 that allow the police and courts to close houses used for the production, supply and use of Class A drugs.

The Medicines Act 1968 governs the manufacture and supply of three groups of drugs: those available for general sale, those that may only be sold by pharmacists, and those that require prescription prior to acquisition. The possession of a prescription-only drug without a prescription is a criminal offence if the drug is controlled within the meaning of the Misuse of Drugs Act 1971.

The Licensing Act 2003 imposes restrictions on the sale to young people, or acquisition by young people, of alcohol, including in premises which are and are not designed primarily for its consumption.

Youth justice, substance misuse and social work

Social workers may be involved in several settings when young people are arrested and prosecuted for offences relating to drug and alcohol misuse. In the role of an appropriate adult, they must be present at the police station when detainees over the age of 14 are tested for Class A drugs because the police believe that they may be implicated in specified offences, including burglary, theft and taking vehicles without consent. The appropriate adult must ensure that young people are aware that they are entitled to access legal advice and that refusal to provide samples is a criminal offence (Police and Criminal Evidence Act 1984; Criminal Justice Act 2003). The test results may be used to inform decisions about bail and sentencing, and the provision of advice on treatment.

As managers or practitioners in youth offending teams, they must ensure that arrangements are secured for young people's substance misuse to be tested and assessed in order to determine their treatment needs. When considering, as part of a request for a pre-sentence report, a drug treatment requirement, a drug testing requirement or an intoxicating substance treatment requirement (Criminal Justice and Immigration Act 2008), they must refer the young person to a substance misuse worker for assessment. The outcome of that assessment must be made available to the court for consideration as part of sentencing (YJB, 2010). If the practitioner considers recommending that the court makes a youth rehabilitation order under the 2008 Act, with a drug treatment requirement, a drug testing requirement or an intoxicating substance treatment requirement, then they must establish that the young person is willing to comply, fully understands what is proposed and required, and is aware of possible consequences of breaching the order.

The drug treatment requirement imposes an obligation on the young person to accept treatment for dependency on, and misuse of, controlled drugs (Misuse of Drugs Act 1971). The treatment may be residential or nonresidential. The drug testing requirement may be made alongside a drug treatment requirement and requires the young person to provide specified samples on specified occasions in order to establish the presence or otherwise of controlled drugs in their body during the treatment period (Ward and Bettinson, 2008).

Courts may order samples to be taken from young people aged at least 14 if they are considering a community sentence or a suspended sentence. The outcome of such tests may be used to determine sentence. If a young person is sentenced to a secure establishment, they must be seen by a qualified nurse or doctor where substance misuse is suspected or known to be a factor. If withdrawal treatment is required, the young person must be referred to specialists and, in preparation for release, referral to community services should be made (YJB, 2010). If a youth rehabilitation order with a drug treatment requirement, a drug testing requirement or an intoxicating substance treatment requirement is made, youth offending team staff must ensure that an intervention plan is completed within 15 working days and that support services and training programmes are available on alcohol awareness and drug misuse. Staff must maintain contact with the young person throughout the duration of the order (YJB, 2010).

Adult criminal justice provisions

Probation officers in respect of adults may also recommend a community sentence with an alcohol or drug treatment requirement (Criminal Justice Act 2003). This requirement may also be imposed by a court as part of a suspended sentence and replaces the drug treatment and testing order originally contained in the Crime and Disorder Act 1998. Research evidence on the effectiveness of the drug treatment and testing order is equivocal at best. Although offenders have reported reductions in drug use and associated offending, reconviction and order revocation rates have been high, and completion rates low, although some fall in conviction rates appears to accompany completed orders. Improved retention and completion rates require the provision of timely and responsive treatment programmes, as well as individual decisions to address drug use and offending behaviour (Hough et al., 2003).

Prior to the court appearance, the police may decline bail if they believe that the offence was connected with Class A drugs (Criminal Justice Act 2003). They may also use an arrest referral scheme, established to disrupt the well-researched link between substance misuse and offending by seeking to improve people's uptake of alcohol and drug services (Birch et al., 2006). There are three models (Edmunds et al., 1998):

1   an *information model*, where advice on available services is provided but subsequent take-up appears low
2   an *incentive model*, where decisions about bail and caution may be linked with an individual's response to the availability of services
3   a *proactive model*, where close cooperation is established between police officers and alcohol and drug workers, including assessment in police stations and courts.

Edmunds et al. (1998) found that offenders reported declining drug use and engagement in acquisitive crime as a result of participation in proactive arrest referral schemes. However, the findings may have been affected by response bias. Nonetheless, the researchers concluded that the availability and adequate resourcing of treatment services, coupled with ongoing support and a working style that established trust between offenders and staff, were helpful in combating crime and drug

Law

abuse. Birch et al. (2006) also concluded that arrest referral schemes were effective in reaching offenders with substance misuse problems, many of whom were not known to service providers, and engaging and retaining them in support and treatment. The provision of harm reduction information appeared helpful to offenders alongside assessment, liaison with community addiction services and referral on. Co-locating arrest referral workers with police officers was helpful in reducing delay and building effective working relationships.

Each local authority area is required to have a crime and disorder reduction partnership (Crime and Disorder Act 1998, s. 17). Comprising, as a minimum, senior representatives from the primary care trust, local authority, fire authority, probation service and the police, this multi-agency partnership must establish the type and level of crime locally and then devise and keep under review a strategy for preventing and reducing offending.

For completeness, the Road Traffic Act 1972 makes it a criminal offence to drive a vehicle while unfit through drugs and/or alcohol. Included here are both prescribed and illicit drugs.

Community care law

Adults with problems associated with drugs and alcohol may also have physical, social and psychological needs and so come within the ambit of community care legislation. This suite of legal rules has been reviewed by the Law Commission (2011), with recommendations for how community care law might be consolidated and updated. Government may now legislate to bring diverse provisions relating to assessment, adult safeguarding, vulnerability, residential care and domiciliary provision into one statutory framework.

Councils with social services responsibilities have a duty to assess individuals who appear to have a need for community care services (NHS and Community Care Act 1990). Deciding who falls within this discretionary duty is determined by eligibility criteria, the setting and review of which is governed by *Fair Access to Care Services* (DH, 2002) policy guidance. Policy guidance, issued under section 7, Local Authority Social Services Act 1970, must be followed by local authorities. There are four levels at which risks to independence and wellbeing arise if needs are not addressed: low, moderate, substantial and critical. Annually, or more frequently, mindful of the resources available, local authorities will decide which levels will determine eligibility for assessment. Ineligible individuals will be signposted to other organizations that offer advice and service provision.

A government circular, issued to local authorities, advises that eligibility criteria should be sensitive to the needs and characteristics of people with alcohol and drug problems (DH, 1993a). It also advises that councils with social services responsibilities should form close working relationships with probation services and avoid delay in assisting people with alcohol and drug problems, otherwise more serious legal, social and care issues might arise. It recognizes that care plans will be needed to address both drug and/or alcohol issues, together with other problems that may be associated with transient lifestyles, childcare, and a reluctance to engage with statutory services. Close working relationships should also be established between adult social care and housing departments (DH, 1992) in order to ensure the availability of residential care, supported living, floating support services, and eventual transfer into independent living.

For those in need of care and attention that would not otherwise be available, councils must provide residential accommodation for people with alcohol and drug problems (National Assistance Act 1948, s. 21; DH, 1993b). Alternatively or additionally, community care services may be provided (National Assistance Act 1948, s. 29; DH, 1993b; NHS Act 2006, schedule 20) to people who misuse drugs and/or alcohol. Alongside daycare, counselling and welfare benefit advice, this may include programmes geared towards prevention, harm reduction, specialist assessment and treatment. When adults are approaching discharge from custodial institutions, their future community care needs must be assessed by the local authority (*R* v *Mid Glamorgan CC, ex parte Miles* [1994]). Perhaps reflecting moral judgement, or distrust about the use of public funds, those recovering from alcohol or drug misuse are currently ineligible for direct payments in lieu of service provision (Health and Social Care Act 2001; Leece, 2007).

Residential provision and other services are often provided by voluntary organizations, which receive funding from local authorities through a process begun by the Voluntary Organisations (Alcohol or Drug Misusers) Directions 1990. In a climate of financial constraint, such funding may be severely curtailed. However, when reducing or withdrawing funding from voluntary agencies, and also when tightening eligibility criteria, as a rationing by directive and rationing by diversion device, local authorities must conduct, and pay due regard to the findings of, equality impact assessments (Equality Act 2010). Such changes may be more likely to impact on disabled people, for example, and thus local authorities must remember the duty on all public bodies to counteract discrimination and promote equality of opportunity. Recent case law, however, has cast doubt over local authority performance of this duty (*R (Kaur)* v *Ealing LBC* [2008]; *R (Chavda)* v *Harrow LBC* [2008]; *R (Meany & Others)* v *Harlow DC* [2009]).

Close cooperation will also be required between local authority social workers, responsible for community care assessment and service provision, and/or children in need or child protection inquiries, and drug action teams.[3] Locally, these spearhead the healthcare contribution to prevention, treatment and support. In relation to drugs and alcohol, they should work within the guidance in the various Models of Care (DH/NTA, 2006; NTA 2006),[4] which essentially recommend four service tiers and three levels of assessment for a planned and integrated treatment system. The four service tiers comprise:

1 information and advice, initial screening and referral to specialist services
2 assessment and brief interventions, harm reduction, including needle exchange, and aftercare

3 community-based specialist assessment, care planning and treatment
4 residential specialist treatment and aftercare.

The three assessment levels revolve around:

1 *screening* to establish the nature of present drug/alcohol and other problems, immediate risk and possible onward referral
2 *triage* to evaluate the seriousness and urgency of problems, appropriate treatment and support, risk factors, the individual's level of motivation, culminating in a care plan
3 *comprehensive assessment*, when structured and intensive interventions appear indicated, possibly involving significant psychiatric and/or physical issues, significant risk of harm to self or others, a history of disengagement, children at risk, and multiple service providers.

A care plan will be produced by drug and alcohol workers, with an emphasis on keeping individuals within treatment and support provision, and a focus on health problems, physical needs and offending. Ideally, this should connect with the care plans produced by adult social care and children's social work colleagues, as a result of their assessments, and, where appropriate, with probation officers supervising community penalties and licence provisions.

Guidance (DH, 2002) also clarifies that disabled parents, who may include people who have misused drugs and/or alcohol, should be assessed for community care provision in order to support them with their parenting roles. Their children are not automatically to be regarded as children in need or children requiring protection (Children Act 1989), although if the parents' needs are not fully met with the support of community care law service provision, then a further assessment of the needs of young people in the family will be necessary. This is one example of where close cooperation between children's and adult social care departments will be fundamental.

Another area demanding close collaboration relates to carers. Partners and/or children who provide regular and substantial amounts of care[5] (Carers (Recognition and Services) Act 1995) might be living with individuals who abuse drugs and/or alcohol. They are entitled to an assessment, followed by service provision to meet their needs, irrespective of whether the individual they are caring for has accepted an assessment or service provision (Carers and Disabled Children Act 2000). They are also entitled to the provision of information about their entitlement to assessment, and to support in meeting their work, education, training and leisure needs (Carers (Equal Opportunities) Act 2004). This Act also requires interagency collaboration when planning services for carers.

Childcare law

Young people may themselves abuse drugs and/or alcohol, or be living with adults who misuse. The Children Act 1989 (CA) is the key statute in these circumstances,

supported by policy guidance on assessment (DH, 2000) and interagency cooperation to safeguard children (HM Government, 2010a). Drug action teams, adult
social care departments and voluntary organizations must have in place agreed
arrangements for referring young people and their families to childcare social workers
where there is evidence of significant harm, or it is likely, due to parental substance
misuse or a child's own misuse (HM Government, 2010a). Local Safeguarding Children Boards, established by the Children Act 2004, will be responsible for ensuring
that such arrangements are in place and auditing their effectiveness.

The key here will be assessment, which should be ongoing and interagency. Adult
mental health services, for example, will have an important assessment contribution
to make in determining the degree to which mental distress may impact on an individual's capacity to parent appropriately (DH, 2000). Not all parents who misuse
drugs and/or alcohol, and who may or may not have additional mental health needs,
neglect or abuse their children. Although poverty, criminal activity and poor housing
may accompany drug use, not all children exhibit behavioural or emotional disturbance as a result (HM Government, 2010a). Indeed, some young people demonstrate
considerable resilience and adaptation (Bancroft et al., 2004). Equally, it may be
possible to support parents in their parenting role using provisions derived from
community care law and the services offered through drug action teams.

However, drug and/or alcohol misuse, which may sometimes be coupled with severe
mental distress, may affect a parent's capacity to look after their children. Violence, physical abuse and neglect may feature in some cases. A child's vulnerability may be heightened
if a parent disengages from treatment and support, experiences withdrawal symptoms,
or leaves them unattended while acquiring and using their supply. Noteworthy here is
section 2, Licensing Act 1902, which makes it an offence to be drunk in charge of a child
under seven, and section 5, the Children and Young Persons Act 1933, which creates an
offence of giving or causing to be given intoxicating liquor to a child under five. Along
with section 4, Misuse of Drugs Act 1971, which prohibits offering or supplying Class
A drugs to children, convicted adults may pose a risk to children that should be addressed
locally through multi-agency risk assessment conferences (MARAC) and/or multi-
agency public protection arrangements (MAPPA) meetings.

Social workers, midwives and health visitors should be aware of the dangers to
unborn and newborn babies as a result of drug and/or alcohol use. They should assess
the degree to which parents are able to engage with their babies. The impact of drug
and alcohol misuse on a child's development may be offset by the presence of a non-
abusing parent or other family members who can meet the child's developmental
needs (Bancroft et al., 2004; HM Government, 2010a).

All agencies involved with children and young people should be mindful of the
outcomes now embedded in law (Children Act 2004) (CA). Section 10 of the CA
2004 requires that a focus is maintained on:

- improving young people's physical and mental health and emotional wellbeing
- protecting them from harm and neglect

■ promoting their education and recreation
■ enhancing their social and economic wellbeing and contribution to society.

Assessment should focus on child development, parenting capacity and family and environmental factors (DH, 2000). This may conclude that children are in need and that they can, with their family, be appropriately supported using the services available in section 17 and schedule 2 (CA 1989), in conjunction with those that may be provided by adult social care and drug and alcohol workers. Section 17 services include advice and counselling. After assessment, however, social workers may conclude that the welfare of children who use drugs or alcohol, or who witness parents doing so, cannot be safeguarded and promoted if they remain at home. Following negotiation with those with parental responsibility, children may be accommodated by the local authority (CA 1989, s. 20), where appropriate with extended family members but otherwise preferably with foster parents. Where greater levels of protection are thought necessary, social workers may initiate care proceedings (CA 1989, s. 31) or apply for an emergency protection order (s. 44). Where a family proceedings court is not certain what may ultimately be in the best interests of a child, it may direct that examinations and assessments are completed, including residential assessments of the family (CA 1989, s. 38(6)). However, it may not order treatment or therapy, even if that would facilitate an individual's rehabilitation and, therefore, ongoing family life (*Re C (a minor) (interim care order: residential assessment)* [1996]; *Re G (a child) (interim care order: residential accommodation)* [2005]). Once the child has been protected, the focus should switch to longer term planning. A parent's continuing misuse of drugs or alcohol may suggest a poor outcome to efforts to return their child safely (DH, 2000).

Where young people have been looked after by the local authority, either accommodated (CA 1989, s. 20) or with a care order (CA 1989, s. 31), they will probably be eligible for enhanced leaving care support (Children (Leaving Care) Act 2000). Young people who have lived with parents who misuse drugs or alcohol are vulnerable themselves to misusing substances (HM Government, 2010a). Their academic performance may have been adversely affected. These factors give an added importance and dimension to the pathway planning that should characterize the transition to adulthood. Prior to leaving care, the young person's needs should be assessed, which include accommodation, health and development. The support available from the family should be considered. The assessment should result in a pathway plan, and provision of a young person's adviser. The plan, which should be reviewed every six months, should itemize how financial, education, training, employment, health, support and accommodation needs will be met, the supports that will be provided, and how 'what if' situations will be tackled (Braye and Preston-Shoot, 2009). However, these assessment and pathway plan directives have not always been completed adequately by local authorities (*R (P) v Newham LBC* [2004]; *R (J by his litigation friend MW) v Caerphilly CBC* [2005]). While transition services are important to young people, research has found that they could be improved (Bancroft et al., 2004).

Children of parents who misuse drugs and alcohol may be young carers. They have the same entitlement to assessment as adult carers under the Carers and Disabled Children Act 2000. However, they are also children in need (CA 1989, s. 17) and eligible after assessment for the services listed in schedule 2 of the CA 1989. Once again, the key will be assessment, to ensure that the young person's voice and experience is heard, and that they are involved in decision-making. Research again suggests that support for young carers could be improved (Bancroft et al., 2004).

Mental health and domestic violence legislation

Commonly associated with cases of drug and/or alcohol misuse is the presence of severe forms of mental distress and domestic violence (Bancroft et al., 2004; HM Government, 2010a). Dependence on drugs or alcohol is not itself a mental disorder but it may prove necessary to invoke the provisions of the Mental Health Act 1983 (as amended by the Mental Health Act 2007) for the assessment and treatment of mental disorder, including where drug and/or alcohol abuse triggers psychotic illness.

Provisions that seek to protect the victims of domestic violence, through restraining, occupation, exclusion and non-molestation orders, are available in the Family Law Act 1996 and the Domestic Violence, Crime and Victims Act 2004. The Crime and Security Act 2010[6] enables a senior police officer to issue a domestic violence protection notice to an adult behaving or threatening to behave violently, having considered the views of the victim and the welfare of any child or young person affected. The notice may exclude the adult from their home and surrounding area. It will trigger a police application to a magistrates' court for a domestic violence protection order. Courts may make such orders if satisfied on a balance of probability that an individual has behaved or is likely to behave violently, and that it is necessary to make such an order to protect the victim. The court must consider the views of any victim (although their consent is not required) and the welfare of any child. The order can exclude the adult from their home and surrounding area, and prohibit molestation. If granted, this lasts between 14 and 28 days.

Children who witness or are the victims of domestic violence should be considered children in need within the meaning of section 17, CA 1989. Where children require protection in situations of domestic violence, social workers may apply for an emergency protection order or an interim care order (CA 1989) but, with the agreement of the non-abusing parent, may ask the court to impose an exclusion order (Family Law Act 1996). If the perpetrator is then successfully excluded from the home, the child may be left in the care of the other parent rather than themselves being removed. Such cases should be referred to the local authority's MARAC arrangements (Braye and Preston-Shoot, 2009).

Making connexions

'Working with people who misuse alcohol and/or drugs might present moments when the ethical thing to do contrasts with what is lawful.'

Can you conceive of any such situations occurring in the course of social work practice? If so, how would you resolve the dilemma?

Law

Concluding discussion

Legislating in the field of drug and alcohol abuse is contentious, particularly when some argue that various controlled drugs are no more or less harmful than substances that it is legal to purchase and consume, for instance alcohol and tobacco. In terms of effectiveness, some argue that less money should be spent on law enforcement and more on education, prevention, treatment and rehabilitation (Joseph Rowntree Foundation, 2000). The provision of advice and information appears to be more effective as a preventive measure when combined with programmes that promote reasoning and social skills, and help people to resist the pressure to misuse drugs and alcohol. This reflects a multi-component approach, where some programmes are focused specifically on alcohol and drugs, while in others substance misuse is embedded alongside other aspects of community living (Joseph Rowntree Foundation, 2000; Thom and Bailey, 2007).

Children and adults who misuse drugs and/or alcohol may be hard to reach and hard to engage. They may be especially resistant towards engaging with statutory provision, preferring assistance from voluntary organizations and specialist services (DH, 2000). Particularly important may be the social work skills of building trust through relationships, although such provision may be vulnerable during times of financial constraint. Statutory and voluntary agencies may both have insufficient capacity to meet demand. Moreover, close interagency collaboration will be necessary. Service users value integrated service provision (Bancroft et al., 2004), which demands of agency staff the willingness to negotiate working practices (Thom and Bailey, 2007). However, the track record here is not promising (Sinclair and Bullock, 2002; Braye and Preston-Shoot, 2009). For example, adult and children's social care departments may operate different thresholds of eligibility and understanding of significant harm and risk. Communication may be poor, with insufficient attention to what young people say and to case chronology.

The challenge of multiprofessional and interagency collaboration is heightened by the different emphases to be found on needs and welfare or criminalization and justice. Agreement will have to be reached locally on how the needs of individual offenders are balanced with the rights of victims and their communities, and the needs of families, and on how the values and orientations of different professional groups can facilitate rather than undermine integrated working. The challenge is also greater when services have to be sustained with short-term financial resources and in a climate of resource shortage, as a result of which agencies may seek to limit or avoid their legal duties (Preston-Shoot, 2010).

This chapter has captured the range of social work law and social welfare law with which practitioners and their managers must be cognizant. However, research has found that within and between agencies, different understandings may exist of the legal rules surrounding information-sharing (Data Protection Act 1998) and the right to private and family life (Human Rights Act 1998) (Braye and Preston-Shoot,

2009). Moreover, in the background will be the attitudes and values of individual practitioners, which may shape how the law is implemented in practice.

Strategies for tacking the supply and consequences of misuse of drugs and alcohol demonstrate that this is a volatile and contested policy arena where competing imperatives collide. A focus on reducing harm and supporting people who choose recovery (Welsh Assembly Government, 2008; HM Government, 2010b) sits alongside a more coercive, sanction-oriented approach involving requirements for assessment, testing, treatment and rehabilitation. Equally, while these same strategies recognize the importance of housing, intensive individual and family support, and cooperation between adult, mental health, offender and children's services, it is questionable whether the legal rules, as currently framed, can deliver the vision of such a whole person, individual-centred journey. The construction of the legal rules, which impose duties on services to cooperate and share information, and the reality of different thresholds and eligibilities for receipt of separate services, aggravated by financial cutbacks, all combine to undermine the policy intention of delivering outcomes for people who wish to engage in order to improve their health and wellbeing.

Notes

1   To varying degrees, the legal rules described in this chapter relating to community care, childcare and criminal justice are differently configured in Wales, Scotland and Northern Ireland. The law relating to drugs is UK wide but there are separate substance misuse strategies for Wales, Scotland and Northern Ireland.
2   Healthcare terminology, such as treatment or triage, and social care terminology, such as intervention, is used according to the policy and practice context being considered.
3   In some local authority areas, they are now drug and alcohol action teams.
4   The Models of Care may be replaced or updated as policies and strategies that inform practice on substance misuse evolve.
5   The Law Commission has recommended that the requirement to be providing regular and substantial amounts of care be removed from eligibility for a carer's assessment in any reform of community care law.
6   At the time of writing (October 2011), this provision has yet to be implemented.

Appendix 12.1 Table of cases

R (Chavda) v Harrow LBC [2008] 11 CCLR 187
R (H) v MHRT North and East London and Another [2001] EWCA Civ 415
R (J by his litigation friend MW) v Caerphilly CBC [2005] 8 CCLR 255
R (Kaur) v Ealing LBC [2008] EWHC 2062 (Admin)
R (Meany & Others) v Harlow DC [2009] EWHC 559 (Admin)
R v Mid Glamorgan CC, ex parte Miles [1994] Legal Action, January
R (P) v Newham LBC [2004] 7 CCLR 553
Re C (a minor) (interim care order: residential assessment) [1996] 4 All ER 871
Re G (a child) (interim care order: residential accommodation) [2005] UKHL 68

Law

Further reading

■ Banks, S. and Nøhr, K. (2012) *Practising Social Work Ethics Around the World: Cases and Commentaries*. Basingstoke: Palgrave Macmillan.

Useful text to assist practitioners engage with and navigate through practice dilemmas.

■ Braye, S. and Preston-Shoot, M. (2009) *Practising Social Work Law* (3rd edn). Basingstoke: Palgrave Macmillan.

Exploration of the values and dilemmas surrounding legally literate social work practice, coupled with identification of the skills that will assist with decision-making and application of relevant legal rules to case scenarios.

■ Clements, L. and Thompson, P. (2011) *Community Care and the Law* (5th edn). London: Legal Action Group.

Comprehensive exploration of adult services law.

References

Bancroft, A., Wilson, S., Cunningham-Burley, S. et al. (2004) *Parental Drug and Alcohol Misuse: Resilience and Transition among Young People*. York: Joseph Rowntree Foundation.

Birch, A., Dobbie, F., Chalmers, T. et al. (2006) *Evaluation of Six Scottish Arrest Referral Pilot Schemes*. Edinburgh: Scottish Government.

Braye, S. and Preston-Shoot, M. (2009) *Practising Social Work Law* (3rd edn). Basingstoke: Palgrave Macmillan.

Cossar, J. and Neil, E. (2010) 'Supporting the birth relatives of adopted children: how accessible are services?', *British Journal of Social Work*, **40**(5): 1368–86.

Davies, C., English, L., Lodwick, A. et al. (eds) (2010) *United Kingdom Drug Situation: Annual Report to the European Monitoring Centre for Drugs and Drug Addiction (EMCDDA) 2010*. London: DH.

DH (Department of Health) (1992) *Housing and Community Care*, LAC(92)12. London: DH.

DH (1993a) *Alcohol and Drug Services within Community Care*, LAC (93)2. London: DH.

DH (1993b) *Approvals and Directions for Arrangements from 1 April 1993 made under schedule 8 to the National Health Service Act 1977 and Sections 21 and 29 of the National Assistance Act 1948*, LAC (93)10. London: DH.

DH (2000) *Framework for the Assessment of Children in Need and their Families*. London: TSO.

DH (2002) *Fair Access to Care Services: Guidance on Eligibility Criteria for Adult Social Care*. London: DH.

DH/NTA (Department of Health/National Treatment Agency for Substance Misuse) (2006) *Models of Care for Alcohol Misusers*. London: DH.

Edmunds, M., May, T., Hearnden, I and Hough, M. (1998) *Arrest Referral: Emerging Lessons from Research*. London: South Bank University/Home Office.

EMCDDA (European Monitoring Centre for Drugs and Drug Addiction) (2005) *Illicit Drug Use in the EU: Legislative Approaches*. Lisbon: EMCDDA.

Forrester, D. and Harwin, J. (2006) 'Parental substance misuse and childcare social work: findings from the first stage of a study of 100 families', *Child and Family Social Work*, **11**(4): 325–35.

GSCC (General Social Care Council) (2002) *Codes of Practice for Social Care Workers and Employers*. London: GSCC.

HM Government (2010a) *Working Together to Safeguard Children: A Guide to Inter-Agency Working to Safeguard and Promote the Welfare of Children*. London: TSO.

HM Government (2010b) *Drug Strategy 2010. Reducing Demand, Restricting Supply, Building Recovery: Supporting People to Live a Drug Free Life*. London: TSO.

Hough, M., Clancy, A., McSweeney, T. and Turnbull, P. (2003) *The Impact of Drug Treatment and Testing Orders on Offending: Two Year Reconviction Rates*. Findings, 183. London: Home Office.

Joseph Rowntree Foundation (2000) *Drugs: Dilemmas, Choices and the Law*. York: Joseph Rowntree Foundation.

Law Commission (2011) *Adult Social Care*. London: TSO.

Leece, J. (2007) 'Direct payments and user-controlled support: the challenges for social care commissioning', *Practice*, **19**(3): 185–98.

NTA (National Treatment Agency for Substance Misuse) (2006) *Models of Care for Treatment of Adult Drug Misusers: Update 2006*. London: DH/Home Office.

Preston-Shoot, M. (2010) 'On the evidence for viruses in social work systems: law, ethics and practice', *European Journal of Social Work*, **13**(4): 465–82.

Preston-Shoot, M., Roberts, G. and Vernon, S. (1998) 'Social work law: from interaction to integration', *Journal of Social Welfare and Family Law*, **20**(1): 65–80.

Sinclair, R. and Bullock, R. (2002) *Learning from Past Experience: A Review of Serious Case Reviews*. London: DH.

Thom, B. and Bailey, M. (2007) *Multi Component Programmes: An Approach to Prevent and Reduce Alcohol-related Harm*. York: Joseph Rowntree Foundation.

Ward, R. and Bettinson, V. (2008) *Criminal Justice and Immigration Act 2008: A Practitioner's Guide*. Bristol: Jordan.

Weiss, C. (1979) 'The many meanings of research utilization', *Public Administration Review*, 39, 426–31.

Welsh Assembly Government (2008) *Working Together to Reduce Harm: The Substance Misuse Strategy for Wales 2008–2018*. Cardiff: Welsh Assembly Government.

Wigley, V., Preston-Shoot, M., McMurray, I. and Connolly, H. (2011) 'Researching young people's outcomes in children's services: findings from a longitudinal study', *Journal of Social Work*, doi: 10.1177/1468017310394036.

YJB (Youth Justice Board) (2010) *National Standards for Youth Justice Services*. London: Youth Justice Board.

Law

13

A theoretical perspective on social work and substance use

DONALD FORRESTER AND AISHA HUTCHINSON

At the heart of this chapter are two beliefs. The first is that social work and social workers need to know how to work with substance misuse issues. The second is that the substance misuse field would benefit from social work involvement because social work brings a distinctively critical and characteristically psychosocial approach to alcohol and other drug problems. As a result, a strong engagement by practitioners and researchers from social work with theories in relation to substance use and misuse is likely to be beneficial for social work and the substance misuse field. It is worth exploring these beliefs further before outlining the content of the chapter.

Why do social workers need to know about key theories in relation to drug and alcohol issues? The most obvious issue is that so many of the people who we work with have drug or alcohol problems, and working effectively with these clients requires an understanding of what substance use and misuse are. The use and misuse of drugs and alcohol are common in society in general and even more common in the groups of people who social workers tend to deal with (see Galvani and Forrester, 2010). It is therefore not possible to consider drugs and alcohol to be 'somebody else's problem', such as that of a specialist worker. If social workers cannot understand and work with an issue that has an impact on up to half of their clients, then they are not ready to do social work. Furthermore, many individuals are not at a stage where they will accept the help of a specialist substance use worker. So it is simply not an option to believe that they can be referred on for this issue. In practice, social workers need to be able to understand and engage with substance use and misuse.

This alone makes a compelling case for every social worker to be equipped to work with drug and alcohol issues, but we believe that there are more profound reasons why social workers should be ready to work with drug and alcohol problems.

At heart, responding to drug and alcohol issues is about understanding and working to help people change their behaviour. This process is at the core of good social work. As a result, we believe that *good practice with drug or alcohol problems is good practice, full stop*. This is true both in the sense that we can learn many lessons from the substance use field and apply them in other areas of social work; it also implies that if we apply the principles of what works from other areas of social work, we will tend to find that they are effective ways of working with drug or alcohol issues.

If this argument is accepted, then there are potentially enormous advantages in social work engaging with the substance misuse field. The most important of these is that social work could learn much from the substantial literature exploring what works in helping people with drug or alcohol issues and developing theories underpinning these approaches. Introducing some of the theoretical concepts underlying this body of work is at the heart of this chapter. In social work, we have few rigorous studies examining what works, and as a result our theories remain largely untested.

Yet our argument goes beyond claiming that social work as a discipline might benefit from engaging with the more established substance misuse field. As noted above, we believe that the benefit is potentially mutual – that the substance misuse field would benefit from engaging with social work. This is true on a practical level: for many people with drug or alcohol problems, and particularly those with the most challenging and complex problems associated with their difficulties, there is strong theoretical and developing empirical evidence for the contribution that social work can make. However, there are also reasons to believe that social work could and should be able to make a distinctive contribution to our understanding and theory development in relation to substance misuse.

To explore these issues, this chapter starts by considering key theoretical understandings of 'addiction' and misuse from a predominantly psychological perspective. This focuses on a brief introduction to theories of ambivalence, inner conflict and change. This is followed by an outline of two particular approaches based on working with inner conflict to promote recovery from alcohol or drug problems – motivational interviewing and social behaviour network therapy. These are then critically evaluated from a social work perspective and it is concluded that a distinctively social work approach requires a more critical and social model of 'addiction'. Some elements of this are outlined and linked to developing concepts within the 'recovery' approach. It is concluded that social work needs to learn from the best elements of the 'medical model', but retain its critical and psychosocial focus, in order to develop effective theories and practices in relation to drug and alcohol problems.

Understanding substance use, misuse and addiction

The challenges in defining substance use, misuse and 'addiction' were touched upon in Chapter 11 and are discussed in depth elsewhere (see, for example, Forrester and Harwin, 2011). In this chapter, we use the term 'addiction' to refer to a strong and often overwhelming subjective feeling that one's use of a substance is hard or impossible to control (see Orford, 2001). Developing an addiction is a complex process that is affected by many factors. It is useful to consider it in relation to a variety of stages, such as the process of trying a substance, using it regularly, developing problems with use, developing feelings of addiction or dependence and finally the process of ceasing or moderating use (see Orford, 2001). Each of these stages has multiple determinants. There is little doubt that there is some element of genetically increased risk, although no gene(s) for an 'addictive personality' has been identified (for reviews of recent evidence in these areas, see Hasin et al., 2006; Hesselbrock and Hesselbrock, 2006). Rather, it seems likely that certain predispositions and preferences – from being outgoing and taking risks to enjoying the flavour of alcoholic drinks – may, in part, be transmitted genetically. It is certainly true that genetic predispositions interact with environmental factors and life events in complex ways. For instance, one's chance of trying alcohol and starting to use it regularly is very much affected by culture, gender and a host of other factors. In addition, an individual's experiences in their family, including modelling of patterns of drinking or experiencing abuse or neglect, can influence the development of patterns of substance use. These factors also interact with the broader social context: the legality, availability and acceptability of use of substances influences whether people are likely to use or develop problems in using a substance at every stage (see Orford, 2001).

All this presents an incredibly complex picture. While researchers can draw out general patterns, for each individual, their journey will be unique. However, as Forrester and Harwin (2011, pp. 27–8) comment:

> a sense of the sheer complexity of substance misuse may not be a bad thing. Understanding the difficult and interrelated nature of the issues when people misuse substances is a good first step towards being able to assess and intervene effectively. It provides a solid grounding in humility from which the professional can engage with the person who is most expert in their particular circumstances: the individual with the drug or alcohol problem.

A particular feature for most individuals with an addiction is a sense of inner turmoil. Orford (2001) proposes this as a central element of an alcohol or drug problem.

We will now explore the concepts of 'ambivalence' and 'conflict', as these are key concepts to equip social work practitioners for working with people who misuse alcohol and other drugs. The term 'ambivalence' is often associated with indecisiveness or an 'on the fence' attitude, with no strong feelings either way. In fact, the term 'ambivalence' in relation to substance misuse refers to a state where people have strong yet conflicting, sometimes opposite, feelings about the same thing. Someone who is defined as alcohol dependent or addicted to heroin, for example, can both passionately love and hate their substance use at the same time, genuinely planning to reduce consumption one day while increasing it the next. Ambivalence is usually experienced as psychologically distressing, resulting in internal conflict because both states, to refrain from consumption and engage in consumption, are powerful influences with significant consequences (Orford, 2001).

What the term 'ambivalence' does is draw attention to the important positive reinforcers for alcohol and drug use, as well as the negative factors associated with giving up, alongside the many reasons for reducing or abstaining from substance use. In his classic work *The Heroin Users* (1987), Pearson likens the effort put into raising money and accessing a good supply of heroin to employment, this activity structuring the day for a user as a job does for a non-user. Because of a complex (affective-behavioural-cognitive) attachment to the behaviour, an individual becomes committed to it, building a whole set of personal and social associations around it (Janis and Mann, 1977). Routines of daily living, circles of friends, elements of identity and levels of self-esteem become built around patterns of alcohol or drug use. Reducing consumption could therefore mean the loss of the social and personal benefits associated with it. Problematic alcohol or drug use may also be linked to the avoidance of difficult life events, such as the death of a spouse or an unfulfilling job, or ongoing difficulties, such as low self-esteem or depression. Reducing consumption would eliminate this escape route and require people to face things they are trying to avoid, thereby creating a negative association with giving up. Essentially, while it can appear to outsiders, such as health professionals and social workers, that the most obvious course of action to reduce the harm caused by substance misuse is to reduce or abstain from consumption, this completely disregards the huge conflict, both internal and external, caused by such a course of action. As Forrester and Harwin (2011, p. 24) write:

> The addicted person is likely to be acutely aware of all the negative effects that substance misuse is having for them and those they care about. However, they also have powerful reasons for continuing with the problem behaviour. This may be in the form of the rewards for their addiction, or the challenges and difficulties of changing.

The paradox at the heart of addiction is that often the quickest and easiest way to forget or reduce the internal and external conflict caused is to engage in further consumption. Orford (2001) frequently refers to models based on the approach-avoidance conflict put forward by Miller (1944) and Janis and Mann's (1977) model of affective-behavioural-cognitive attachment to understand this 'vicious circle' that seemingly takes place for those who try and reduce their alcohol or other drug use. The state of ambivalence is one of quite distressing conflict, with mixed messages of pleasure and restraint, avoidance, motivation and desire for change, alongside the guilt and hopelessness brought on by relapse. Dissonance between what we think we should do, what we want to do and what we actually do is unsettling, often highlighting the moral elements of addiction and the pressure from others for behavioural change. The distress is such that people will develop different strategies to manage or remove this conflict, which often results in the sometimes chaotic and changeable behaviour observed in people who are considered as 'addicts' (Orford, 2001).

Reducing conflict by disassociating one's self from consumption cues, changing patterns of daily living, working through the physical effects of withdrawal, or finding other strategies for dealing with stress are some ways of reducing distress. Other means include conflict avoidance strategies, such as denial, developing persuasive internal and external arguments for maintaining consumption or the temporary relief through continued substance use. Immediate gratification and intoxication can end up having more sway in the moment than the negative consequences that will come later. Easier and more immediate ways of reducing the conflict are also associated with the 'abstinence violation effect', when broken abstinence, for example a single drink, often leads to a massive binge (Wardle and Beinart, 1981). A loss of control or the breaking of promises regarding consumption can lead to feelings of hopelessness, guilt or lack of self-esteem and can increase conflict (both internal and external), which, in turn, makes people even more susceptible to continued substance use. Factors such as the strength of social and physical cues associated with addiction, the presence of different audiences, the nearness of the substance, the rewards associated with restraint and levels of cognitive functioning can all sway the balance sheet, leading to either restraint or consumption, sometimes on a moment-to-moment basis.

It is important to remember that similar internal and external conflicts occur during any kind of behavioural change activity, such as a commitment to eating more healthily, a plan to exercise more often, to stop smoking or nail biting, even watching less TV. We all know reasons why we should change in these situations, yet often use powerful excuses to convince ourselves it is OK not to change – 'I'm not really that much overweight', 'the gym costs too much money', or 'I am too stressed at work right now to give up smoking'. However, it is unlikely that the internal and external conflict caused in these situations will result in the same levels of distress experienced by those seeking to change behaviours they have built their life around, as can be the case with alcohol and drug use.

Having considered the concept of inner conflict and ambivalence at some length, we now consider two approaches to working with alcohol or drug addiction that place these issues at their heart: motivational interviewing and social behaviour network therapy.

Motivational interviewing

Ambivalence is a central concept within motivational interviewing (MI). It is conceptualized as a continuum: at one extreme are individuals who do not feel they have a problem and at the other are those who have determined to make a change. For the first group, no intervention is likely to work because people need to want to change; for the second, many make changes without professional help, and where a professional is involved, it is likely that the work will progress well. MI is concerned with the majority who lie somewhere in between: those who are ambivalent.

A key insight of MI is that the coercive, authoritarian and argumentative techniques practised by some professionals tend to prompt the receiver to engage in counterargument (Miller and Rollnick, 2002). In effect, by making the arguments for change, one tends to elicit from the client the other side of their ambivalence: the arguments for *not* changing. In effect, the client's ambivalence is acted out in the interaction between worker and client, with the client taking the position of arguing against change. In fact, this is a deeply counterproductive thing for a worker to do. Not only is it an argument that the worker cannot win – because the client is the expert on their individual situation – but there is increasing evidence that doing so makes change *less* likely (see Miller and Rollnick, 2002). The more our behaviour as helpers elicits arguments for not changing, the less likely change is.

Conversely, MI aims to work with people to elicit the arguments for change – called 'change talk'. This is done using a wide variety of methods, but at the heart of it is client-centred, empathic listening combined with a directive approach aimed at eliciting change talk. MI draws heavily on Rogerian techniques of reflective listening as a foundation for building a trusting relationship, and its empathic form of communication is perhaps the most important element of the approach. However, it marries this to a directive attempt at eliciting and reinforcing 'change talk' from clients. This can range from simple questions, such as: 'what problems does this cause for you?', through to more complex formulations, such as using the 'miracle question', often used in solution-focused approaches, and combines questions to elicit reflections to reinforce the client's own arguments for change. Professionals using MI place emphasis on personal choice and on a person's responsibility for deciding future behaviour (Miller and Rollnick, 2002). Negative labels are to be avoided, as well as commanding individuals to change. The aim is to create an openness to change by harnessing motivation through specific interactions with an MI therapist. Knowledge of how practitioners can positively influence people through an exchange in social interaction is incredibly useful for social workers who engage with those who are resistant to change. It may be for some that MI is a prelude to treatment, as it aims to create an openness to change, which could then lead on to other therapeutic interventions (Miller and Rollnick, 2002).

MI is a powerful way of working with people with a strong evidence base. Yet it is essentially an individualistic way of understanding and working with substance use issues. It has little to say about the contribution of broader social factors or how they may influence effective intervention. This leaves out some important elements in understanding and working with substance misuse. In this respect, social behaviour and network therapy may be more akin to social work theories and ways of working.

Social behaviour and network therapy

Social behaviour and network therapy (SBNT) is based on the central belief that a person's supportive network, for example family and friends, and social environment play a significant role in substance-using behaviours. SBNT takes into account the impact of problematic alcohol and drug use on others, and the role others play in reinforcing or challenging these behaviours. While friends and family, even work colleagues, may be concerned about a person's alcohol or drug use, they often lack sufficient knowledge to determine whether it is problematic and don't know how to approach the subject or what to do about it. Unwittingly, some actions and responses may further compound a drinking problem rather than facilitate behaviour change. SBNT helps to reduce this confusion and ambiguity for both the focal client (the person with an alcohol or drug problem) and their network by bringing them together to make joint decisions about the treatment process. The therapist seeks to utilize the network's concern and desire to help by unifying a supportive message to the focal person and creating new positions for everyone concerned (Copello et al., 2009). As Copello et al. (2009, p. xvi), the developers of the approach, describe it:

> Focal clients, rather than being viewed as the ones who must take responsibility for change, are now seen as people who need to draw on the support from family members and friends that is available to them in their social network. Family and friends (network members), rather than being kept on the margins, or even contributing to the problem, are now cast in the role of supporters of change.

The main tenet of this approach is to gather together as much support as possible in the formal treatment setting to facilitate attempts to change behaviour and maintain that change over time (Copello et al., 2009). The therapist works alongside the person's positive social network to develop a coherent set of coping strategies for both the person with the problem and their network members (Copello et al., 2009). Therefore network members are integrated into the treatment alongside the focal person, and network members have the same access to the therapist. Therapists attempt to enhance and increase the benefits of the network's support for the chosen goal as well as decrease any reinforcement for continuation of the problem substance use. This is in contrast to MI, which is primarily concerned with the relationship between the therapist and the individual, although it does also take into account the social networks that may or may not surround a person.

Yet it would be wrong to portray too crude a contrast. Key studies into SBNT, such as the United Kingdom Alcohol Treatment Trial (Russell et al., 2005) expect all the therapists delivering SBNT to have high levels of MI skills. MI may therefore provide a foundational set of communication skills for working with alcohol/drug problems, while SBNT, in addition, stresses the role the social environment plays in initiating and maintaining problematic substance use. Research has shown that social networks can be highly influential in terms of helping people with alcohol/drug problems to initiate treatment, in affecting the course and outcome of interventions, and influencing the likelihood of relapse and long-term maintenance of change (Copello et al., 2009). SBNT draws together a number of different social and family approaches to develop this unique approach within the context of substance misuse.

The focus on social networks and the impact of substance use on others makes SBNT attractive from a social work perspective. Yet it is still a distinctively psychological approach. SBNT has little to say about the broader social determinants of substance misuse such as poverty and deprivation. There is also little critique of the family as a site for abuse or neglect, including domestic violence. It is noted that SBNT is not appropriate when there is the abuse of power relationships, but given the ubiquity of violence in families affected by substance misuse, this creates a serious limitation in SBNT as an approach (Galvani, 2007).

MI and SBNT provide powerful theories and practical approaches to working with drug or alcohol problems, but each has significant limitations. The strengths and the limitations that MI and SBNT share are in large part because they are part of a shared tradition of relatively individualized, short-term interventions, based on rigorous evaluative research, which has emerged in the substance misuse field. Inspired by psychiatry and psychology, these approaches are characterized within social work as part of the 'medical model'. Given that MI arose in contrast to concepts of addiction as an illness, and SBNT took this further to emphasize broader social networks, it is likely that proponents of each approach would object to being characterized as part of a medical model. Nonetheless, from a social work perspective, both share key elements of a medical model approach.

The next section considers critiques of the medical model before the chapter concludes by arguing that the way forward for both substance misuse and social work is to marry the best elements of the medical model with a broader social critique, and that this can be done through a focus on the concept of 'recovery'.

The medical and social models

The medical model is something of a 'boo' word in social work and the social sciences. It is rare for anyone to use the term in a positive sense. Indeed, when it is used, it is almost like a pantomime villain entering the stage. Heifer (1982) captures this well when he tells of asking a class of students what the medical model is. After a long pause, one of them tentatively puts up their hand and says: 'I'm not sure what it is, but I know that it's bad.' So what is the medical model and is it 'bad'?

At the core of the medical model is the process of individual diagnosis and treatment. Thus, the doctor uses skill to understand the nature of the presenting issue and to diagnose the appropriate treatment based on evidence. This has proved an incredibly powerful way of helping people with a variety of illnesses – and its success in this has led to the medical model having credibility for working with issues such as drug and alcohol problems, where it may not be the most appropriate approach.

The social model is at the heart of social work. It was developed in explicit opposition to, and as a critique of, the medical model, and is characterized by three elements:

1 It is critical of the definition of the issue or problem, for example who defines child abuse or mental illness?
2 It emphasizes social contributions and causes. Often issues that are characterized as individual problems or deviance are seen as having multiple causes.
3 It emphasizes the importance of social elements in effective interventions.

How, then, might a social model be applied in relation to substance misuse and addiction?

Theory

The medical model works well for illnesses, but the definition of social 'problems' is much more complicated. Thus, what society considers to be a drink or drug problem is, in large part, defined by social norms and opinions. Some drugs are illegal, others are controlled, while others, such as caffeine, have virtually no legal controls. Furthermore, our understanding of what constitutes a problem with a substance and what are unacceptable levels of use have varied enormously over time. Indeed, the terms at the heart of drug and alcohol use are contested. When does use become misuse? Who makes this definition? What is dependency? It may appear to be a medical condition, but if one studies the symptoms, they are predominantly behavioural or social in nature, for example the pattern of drinking or the prioritization of alcohol over other things. There are also terms – such as 'addict' or 'alcoholic' – that are highly politically contested. Some commentators suggest that these terms imply that there is an illness called 'addiction', when there is little evidence for this pattern of behaviour being an illness. Indeed, it has been argued that the term 'alcoholic' is, in fact, a hypothesis that a wide variety of problem behaviours relating to alcohol are in fact linked.

It is beyond the remit of this chapter to attempt to resolve these issues. Indeed, such a resolution is probably unachievable. However, juxtaposing the social critique with medicalized views of substance use, misuse and addiction highlights that the terms often used in this field are contestable. Indeed, it does more than that, for these terms are in large part political – at least with a small 'p'. By this we mean that the terms used reflect and shape our understanding and are produced and reproduced through power relationships that work themselves out in the real lives of clients and professionals on a day-to-day basis. For instance, take the following quote from a real social worker interviewing an actor playing a client:

> It's your job, you're the grown up. I've offered you support services, right, it's up to you to use them. I can't make you go to them, you're his mum, you're grown up, you do it, you have, and the way I look at it, I consider you have an addiction, an illness, your job is to get it treated, if you don't, what could happen, what could happen down the line, is you won't be looking after your boy. (Forrester, 2010)

An interesting aspect of this comment by the worker is that, despite there being no mention of 'addiction' in the case study they were presented with, the worker imposed the term upon the client. This was not uncommon in the research that this was part of, which highlights that these processes of definition and the value bases underlying them are matters of practice on a day-to-day basis as well as theory. The social model provides a critical view of such definitional processes, highlighting the potential for words to stereotype and control clients.

The second element of the social model is to emphasize the importance of social factors in causing difficulties. Social factors are important at every stage of the development and maintenance of a drug or alcohol problem. Peer groups and neighbourhoods influence individuals' exposure to drugs and their likelihood of trying them. Histories of abuse or current unemployment may affect whether use becomes regular or problematic. The availability of social support, housing and money can have a major impact on whether individuals seek out and use treatment and whether they maintain the positive changes they make. So at every stage of the journey, social factors are crucial. It would be wrong to argue that social factors explain substance misuse. They interact with individual characteristics and values in complex ways. But any account of substance misuse that does not take these social factors into account is lacking.

The third characteristic of the social model is an emphasis on social aspects in solutions. This is in part because if social factors cause problems, then interventions probably need to have a social element in the solution. More importantly, there is evidence that adding social work elements to individual interventions can make a difference. Thus, for instance, case management approaches based on developing a positive relationship with the client and coordinating a variety of services to meet their needs have been shown to improve outcomes for people receiving or leaving substance misuse services. There is a relatively commonsense reason for this, and it goes back to core social work values. If an individual with a drink problem is experiencing violence at home, then simply listening to them may not be enough – they may need an alternative place to live. If someone is isolated and living in extreme poverty, then drug use may be a way of coping with the problems they have – however temporarily and self-destructively in the long term. Helping the client to a better social situation may be more important and pressing than talking to them about how confident they are that they can address their drug use. As social workers, we have a long history of conceptualizing individuals as nested within families, within communities and within society, and our ways of working are – at least ideally – aimed at intervening on all these levels.

Social work and the recovery approach

The social model that is characteristic of social work is likely to lead to a rather different approach to working with individuals with drug or alcohol problems. It is not that it rejects theories and approaches such as MI and SBNT; rather, it looks to complement them by a more critical

> **Making connexions**
>
> How might the theoretical techniques of 'service user involvement' and 'self-led change' be employed in any case you are aware of that contains elements of problematic substance use? What difficulties might have to be overcome if the techniques are to be effective?

and holistic approach. Interestingly, there is widespread recognition within the substance misuse field that the time is ripe for a wide-ranging reappraisal, and the key features of this reappraisal seem consistent with social work ideas and principles.

In particular, many are interested in moving away from conceptualizations of brief treatment provided for people towards an approach that has much in common with social work and the social model. This contrasting approach to helping those with drug or alcohol problems is called the 'recovery approach' (Jacobsen and Greenley,

2001; Scottish Government, 2008). It is relatively new in the alcohol and drug field, but it is rapidly becoming influential. Key elements of the recovery approach include:

- a more ambitious focus on supporting human flourishing, rather than simply reducing drug or alcohol problems
- a recognition that each individual's journey to recovery will be different, and that recovery will mean different things for different people
- a focus on service users identifying their needs and goals, and provision that is tailored around this rather than what suits the service
- the provision of longer term support where this is considered helpful
- an understanding of the individual within their social context, which places an emphasis on helping individuals to address their broader social problems.

This approach can be contrasted with the type of medical model approach that has concentrated on tightly specifying interventions to test their effects. There are certainly differences, but in fact the recovery approach also places an emphasis on using evidence-based approaches to help people. The key issue here is that approaches such as MI or SBNT are seen as only part of a broader focus on providing user-focused and, where possible, user-led services.

At present, the recovery approach is stronger on vision than it is on evidence. Nonetheless, it does indicate a growing belief within the substance misuse field that a narrow focus on medical model-style evidence has produced disappointing results. There is now an open engagement with wider considerations, such as service user involvement, the place of self-led change, the importance of social factors and a recognition that our approach to substance use needs to be inspired as much by values, such as dignity, respect and social justice, as by evidence. These developments provide a perfect illustration of the potential contribution that social work can and should make to the substance misuse field, as these factors are so characteristic of social work. Indeed, they do more than that, for marrying the two offers the prospect of improving theory, research and practice in both social work and work with people who have drug or alcohol problems.

Further reading

- Barber, J.G. (2002) *Social Work with Addiction* (2nd edn). Basingstoke: Palgrave Macmillan.

Great short introduction on why the substance misuse field needs social work, and why social work needs to understand drug and alcohol issues.

- Orford, J. (2001) *Excessive Appetites: A Psychological View of Addictions* (2nd edn). Chichester: Wiley.

Comprehensive review of the literature brought together in a coherent and thought-provoking theory.

■ Petersen, T. and McBride, A. (eds) (2002) *Working with Substance Misusers: A Guide to Theory and Practice*. London: Routledge.

Easy-to-read, straightforward and comprehensive introduction to working with substance use across the disciplines, written for students and new staff members.

References

Copello, A., Orford, J., Hodgson, R. and Tober, G. (2009) *Social Behavioural Network Therapy for Alcohol Problems*. New York: Routledge.

Forrester, D. (2010) 'How do Social Workers Talk to Parents about Alcohol and Drug Issues?', presentation at Social Work and Policy conference, 4 April, Higher Education Academy, Birmingham.

Forrester, D. and Harwin, J. (2011) *Parents Who Misuse Drugs or Alcohol: Effective Interventions in Social Work and Child Protection*. Chichester: Wiley.

Galvani, S. (2007) 'Safety in numbers? Tackling domestic abuse in couples and network therapies', *Drug and Alcohol Review*, 26, 175–81.

Galvani, S. and Forrester, D. (2010) 'How well prepared are newly qualified social workers for working with substance use issues? Findings from a national survey', *Social Work Education*, **30**(4): 422–39.

Hasin, D., Hatzenbuehler, M. and Waxman, R. (2006) 'Genetics of substance abuse disorders', in W.R. Miller and K.M. Carroll (eds) *Rethinking Substance Abuse: What the Science Shows, and What We Should Do About It*. New York: Guilford Press.

Heifer, R.E. (1982) 'Editorial comment', *Child Abuse and Neglect*, **6**(3): 247.

Hesselbrock, V.M. and Hesselbrock, M.N. (2006) 'Developmental perspectives on the risk for developing substance abuse problems', in W.R. Miller and K.M. Carroll (eds) *Rethinking Substance Abuse: What the Science Shows, and What We Should Do About It*. New York: Guilford Press.

Jacobsen, N. and Greenley, D. (2001) 'What is recovery? A conceptual model and explication', *Psychiatric Services*, 52, 482–5.

Janis, I. and Mann, L. (1977) *Decision-making: A Psychological Analysis of Conflict, Choice and Commitment*. New York: Free Press.

Miller, N.E. (1944) 'Experimental studies of conflict', in J. McV. Hunt (ed.) *Personality and the Behaviour Disorders*, vol. I. Ronald Press: New York.

Miller, W.R. and Rollnick, S. (2002) *Motivational Interviewing: Preparing People for Change* (2nd edn). New York: Guilford Press.

Orford, J. (2001) *Excessive Appetites: A Psychological View of Addictions* (2nd edn). Chichester: Wiley.

Pearson, G. (1987) *The New Heroin Users*. Blackwell: Oxford.

Russell, I., Orford, J., Alwyn, T. et al. (2005) 'Effectiveness of treatment for alcohol problems: findings of the randomised United Kingdom Alcohol Treatment Trial (UKATT)', *British Medical Journal*, **331**(7516): 541–4.

Scottish Government (2008) *The Road to Recovery: A New Approach to Tackling Scotland's Drug Problem*. Edinburgh: Scottish Government.

Wardle, J. and Beinart, H. (1981) 'Binge eating: a theoretical review', *British Journal of Clinical Psychology*, 20, 97–109.

Theory

14
Social work research and substance misuse

DONALD FORRESTER, GEORGIA GLYNN AND MICHELLE MCCANN

Chapter 13 argued that social work would benefit from better knowledge of what works with drug and alcohol problems. It also suggested that the substance misuse field could learn from the theoretical insights and practice approaches typical of social work. These arguments were outlined by illustrating the contribution that key approaches in the substance misuse field (specifically motivational interviewing and social behaviour and network therapy) might make to improving social work practice and the ways in which social work's critical and sociopsychological approach might strengthen these interventions. It was also suggested that this might be a good fit with a general move towards a focus on 'recovery' in substance misuse work. This chapter develops these ideas further by considering some research studies that look at social work contributions to substance use and misuse intervention; in essence, it illustrates the arguments outlined in the theory chapter.

An overview of the relevant research

This chapter considers three pieces of social work research in some detail as 'case studies' of the potential social work contribution to helping people with drug or alcohol problems. The studies were chosen because they provide key lessons for social work in working with drug or alcohol problems. In particular, they provide examples of distinctively social work contributions in this field. The studies were identified as part of a review of the evidence on the social work/social care contribution to the substance use field (see Galvani and Forrester et al., 2010). Before looking at the specific studies, it is worth outlining the general picture in relation to social work research and drug and alcohol issues uncovered by the review.

The overall outlook is somewhat depressing, as there is little research exploring social work's contribution to helping those with drug or alcohol issues, and the limited research that does exist is predominantly from the USA. This inadequate state of affairs is all the more unfortunate when some of the studies that have been published suggest that social work can make an important contribution to helping people with drug or alcohol problems. Indeed, social work approaches seem particularly likely to be helpful for those with more serious drug or alcohol problems or those for whom substance misuse is linked to other difficulties, such as homelessness, mental illness or child abuse – groups for whom normal interventions tend to have particularly disappointing outcomes.

Across the literature that does exist, there are some key features that stand out about effective social work interventions for those with drug or alcohol problems:

1   Social work interventions tend to be characterized by an attempt to meet the person who misuses in their home or natural environment. These are not services provided to people seeking treatment; they reach out to those with drug or alcohol problems. Of course, this is a common feature of social work in general, but it is one that we perhaps do not emphasize enough and it is certainly one that is likely to make our interventions particularly helpful to those with the most serious drug or alcohol issues.

2   The best services make repeated attempts to engage individuals. These are not services that are simply offered to people on a 'take it or leave it' basis; they tend to involve multiple visits and numerous attempts at engagement.

3   At the heart of this effective engagement strategy is a focus on the relationship between worker and client. Many studies looked at case management, that is, arrangements for professionals to coordinate services for those with substance misuse issues. There was a strong tendency for forms of case management that emphasized the central importance of the relationship between worker and client to be more effective than those that solely emphasized the coordination of services. This was particularly true for clients with complex or interrelated problems.

4   While social work interventions tended to be multifaceted, at their core were some of the key evidence-based ways of working. In particular, motivational interviewing and cognitive behavioural therapy seemed to be particularly common foundational sets of theories and skills.

5   However, social work interventions tended to go beyond these, and were characterized by an attempt to provide complex interventions that combined multiple elements. In particular, they provided greater attention to the social context and the support needed to help individuals on the road to recovery.

Three relevant studies

The next sections discuss in turn three studies that effectively illustrate these general points. The conclusion then considers lessons to be learned and in particular their implications for the recovery approach to substance misuse.

Research

Case management in addition to therapeutic treatment

Case management in addition to therapeutic treatment was undertaken in the USA by McLennan et al. (1998), who were interested in whether clients who were offered 'case management' in addition to standard group counselling benefited. They studied a large number of clients (more than 1,200) over three periods (before, 12 and 26 months after case management was introduced) and used a 'quasi-experimental' design, in which case management in eight areas was compared to four areas not using case management. In many ways, this is a test of social work's contribution to substance misuse treatment at the simplest level, as case management – with its individually tailored coordination of services – is similar to forms of care management that characterize much of current social work in the UK. From this perspective, McLennan et al.'s findings were encouraging. They found that patients receiving case management had significantly less substance use, fewer physical and mental health problems and better social functioning when followed up 6 months after intervention. An interesting finding was that the size of the effect increased markedly over time, that is, the impact was greater once the case management system had been in place for 26 months than it was at 12 months.

On the face of it, these findings suggest that case management produces positive outcomes for clients. Unfortunately, this is not necessarily so. In various reviews of the evidence, both in relation to substance misuse and more generally in relation to mental health services, it would be more true to say that the evidence is mixed. There are undoubtedly studies that indicate that case management can produce better outcomes for clients, but there are also many studies indicating that it has little or no impact. In fact, 'case management' is a wide term – almost as wide as 'social work' – so it is not surprising to discover that the effectiveness of case management varies enormously.

It is perhaps most helpful to examine what elements of case management seem to be most closely linked to positive outcomes. Key elements identified in our review were noted above. Yet care needs to be taken in drawing conclusions in relation to even these elements of case management. In particular, the preponderance of studies from the USA makes drawing conclusions difficult. Not only is it not possible to be sure that the service would have the same impact in a UK context, but there are also grounds for believing that the 'control' group might fare somewhat better within a society in which there is free access to healthcare and a generally stronger welfare state (that is, the UK) when compared to the residual welfare state of the USA.

In light of this, it is worth considering the intervention described by McLennan et al. (1998) in some depth – indeed, this is true for any intervention reported in research. There are several features of the McLennan et al. (1998) intervention that are consistent with the features of successful case management outlined above:

1   The caseload of case managers (who were all social workers) was restricted to 15–20 clients at a time, allowing them the time to build meaningful helping relationships as well as dealing efficiently with the needs of their allocated clients.

2   The range and quality of services they had access to increased over time. For example, by the end of the study, they were able to refer clients to drug-free housing, a service not available earlier in the intervention phase. It is likely that this contributed to the increasing impact of case management over time.

3   The case managers were not simply coordinating existing services, they had access to specific services themselves. For instance, each case manager had control of a budget of up to $60,000 (£38,252) worth of services per client to meet their client's needs. Furthermore, the in-depth analysis found much higher levels of engagement in a range of other services, such as housing, healthcare or involvement with other professionals; and the greater this engagement, the increased likelihood of reduced substance misuse.

In these respects, McLennan et al. (1998) provide a good example of the nature and impact of a successful case management service for clients receiving therapeutic support for drug problems.

It seems clear that case management can make a positive difference for clients with drug or alcohol problems and the characteristics of successful interventions highlight the importance of skilled social work interventions. In general, case management seems most likely to be helpful when delivered with a high level of proficiency to particularly difficult to engage groups. In this respect, the intervention reported on by Whetten et al. (2006) and Bouis et al. (2007) is an excellent case study of effective social work intervention.

Intensive social work intervention for traditionally 'hard to engage' groups

Whetten et al. (2006) and Bouis et al. (2007) report on an integrated drug and alcohol treatment package for individuals with a 'triple diagnosis' of HIV, mental health needs and substance misuse in the USA. This is a group for whom few interventions have been proved to work effectively. The intervention is strongly focused on social workers' skilled communication and the development of effective relationships with problematic substance users. The model of treatment is based on motivational interviewing (MI) (see Miller and Rollnick, 2002) and combined individual counselling, group therapy, psychiatric medication management, assertive case management, and collaboration between social workers, medical and behavioural healthcare professionals. The intervention took an approach consistent with the roles and functions of social work, that is, working with individuals within their wider social context or community, such as coordinating services or assisting with housing. It also focused on developing individuals' social networks and peer support.

Participation in this intervention led, 12 months after referral, to statistically significant reductions in illicit drug use, alcohol use and psychiatric symptoms, as well as statistically significant increases in antiretroviral use and appropriate psychotropic medication usage. Participants' A&E visits and hospital stays also

Research

decreased, resulting in considerable cost savings. In reflecting on the apparent success of the service, Bouis et al. (2008) felt that the development of an effective relationship between the social worker and the individual is critical to working with a marginalized group of individuals who have frequently experienced stigma and treatment failure.

At the initial stage of this service, most of the individuals were described as being at the 'pre-contemplation' stage, where people will have little or no awareness that their substance use is problematic and they do not want to change it, or at the 'contemplation' stage, where there is general awareness of the problem but not of the action needed (Prochaska et al., 1992). Often individuals stopped or restarted treatment several times before fully engaging. At this initial stage, it was essential to engage and establish a connection with individuals. Social workers provided assertive and persistent engagement, which involved outreach and allowed for significant time to build a trusting relationship. MI techniques were used to enable change in problematic substance use, as well as addressing other medical and behavioural health risk factors. Goal development and action plans provided opportunities to enhance individual motivation for treatment.

Individuals rarely began treatment with the aim of abstaining from substance use or improving medication adherence; instead, they were much more concerned with other needs, such as their housing or finances. Rather than dismissing these concerns, the social workers linked individual identified needs with programme goals, for example an individual wanting help with claiming disability benefits was told that treatment participation would help the social worker assess physical capacity for the disability benefit decision. Furthermore, social workers reframed reoccurring expressions of stress as a result of depression or substance misuse: focusing on ways to reduce stress was an opportunity to make more difficult changes. Contingency management of incentives was introduced to reinforce achievement of treatment goals; for example, consistent group attendance was rewarded with highly valued individual appointment slots with social workers.

Although individual counselling with the social worker developed a therapeutic connection, group treatment for triply diagnosed individuals was often pivotal to enhancing motivation in treatment. A primary goal of the group was to offer individuals a place to gain peer support, find a sense of hope and belonging, and reduce the isolation that could be common among this group of individuals. Groups also functioned to provide information and education on relapse prevention, planning, medication adherence and psychiatric symptom management.

There were specific programme tasks for each stage of this intervention. During the assessment, the social worker addressed acute stabilization such as physiological withdrawal from substances, immediate medical care, mental health needs, and the risk of suicide. Throughout the intervention, important information was provided for triply diagnosed individuals such as information regarding HIV risk behaviours and the potentially harmful interactions between substance use and antiretroviral medications. At the intermediate stage, tasks included building coping skills, extending social support, attending self-help meetings, group therapy and participating in meaningful activities. Involvement in group therapy or meaningful activities helped build social support, self-worth and the belief that individuals could make changes. It was also identified that participation in meaningful activities could compete with substance use. Stress management, tolerating difficult emotions and developing effective social skills were among the most important skills addressed at the intermediate stage, as ineffective skills were common triggers to substance use and psychiatric deterioration. During this stage, as individuals made progress, their personal narratives changed and they began to define themselves as being 'in recovery'.

The final stage of treatment focused on maintaining change, relapse prevention, individual strengths, extending social supports and planning for setbacks. Individuals frequently experienced setbacks during this stage. Unresolved psychiatric issues, particularly trauma, emerged during this stage and so individuals began to address trauma. Most individuals (81%) had been victims or witnesses to trauma, and one-third of those disclosing trauma had experienced sexual trauma. Many individuals used substances to avoid emotionally distressing memories. From the onset of this intervention, social workers assumed post-traumatic experiences but delayed addressing these until individuals had developed coping skills. At this final stage, giving back was considered critical to the individual's recovery and wellbeing; as such, most individuals were actively promoting HIV and substance use prevention within their communities.

The social workers' skilled communication and sensitivity are apparent at each stage of the intervention, from the initial to the intermediate and the final stages, during the therapeutic relationship development, the assessment and goal planning. Exceptional communication skills and positive attitudes to working with substance-using individuals are crucial features, allowing workers to engage with individuals who have often experienced stigma and multiple disadvantages over many years. These foundational relationship-based skills need to be complemented by an ability to keep working with people through patterns of behaviour change that may involve lapse and relapse, and by a focus on creating broader social changes for the individuals concerned.

The final research study develops many of these themes, but it does so by considering a UK study focusing on children living in families affected by parental substance misuse.

Option 2: crisis intervention for families affected by parental substance misuse

Option 2 is an intensive family preservation service based in Cardiff and the Vale of Glamorgan, which began in 2000. It is an adapted version of an American model called 'homebuilders'. Option 2 was identified by the Welsh Assembly Government as a promising method of working with families affected by serious issues relating to parental use of drugs or alcohol.

Forrester et al. (2008) provide an evaluation of Option 2. Key elements of Option 2 include (see Forrester and Harwin, 2011):

- *intervention at the crisis point:* The response is informed by crisis intervention theory and focuses on immediate, intensive and short-lived intervention. Services are concentrated in a brief period (four to six weeks), are intensive, and are provided in the client's home.
- *low caseloads:* Therapists carry only one active family on their caseload, although they provide follow-up support for previously active families.
- *flexibility:* Therapists provide a wide range of services, from helping clients meet their basic needs of food, clothing and shelter, to therapeutic techniques.

Particular or unusual features of the Option 2 model include the fact that:

- all the families have substance misuse problems
- the intervention is based on MI and solution-focused approaches – homebuilders does not specify the therapeutic approach to be used, only the crisis intervention framework
- the UK context is different from that in the USA. For instance, the UK has a stronger welfare state and significantly fewer children per head of population are taken into public care.

Hamer (2005) sets out in some detail the ways in which Option 2 works. MI provides the basic set of communication skills, augmented by elements of a solution-focused approach. Some structured sessions are used, and these use cards as a prompt for discussion of values. Option 2 is run by a manager experienced in MI with knowledge of substance misuse and child welfare issues. Workers receive extensive training and supervision devoted to the development of skills needed to deliver the Option 2 intervention. The service has been unusually successful in retaining staff, with comparatively low turnover and a strong commitment to the values and worth of Option 2.

The evaluation of Option 2 used mixed methods (Forrester et al., 2008). A quasi-experimental element compared data solely relating to care entry, for example how long children spent in care and its cost, collected from local authority records for 279 children whose family had received the Option 2 service and a comparison group of 89 children who were referred but not provided with the service because it was full. Option 2 does not run a waiting list because of its crisis intervention framework. The follow-up period was on average 3.5 years after referral. The study found that about 40% of children in both groups entered care; however, Option 2 children took longer to enter, spent less time in care and were more likely to be at home at follow-up. As a result, Option 2 produced significant cost savings.

A small-scale qualitative element of the study involved interviews with 11 parents and 7 children in eight families. Parents reported that they very much appreciated Option 2 and thought it was a professional service. For some families, it achieved what appeared to be long-lasting or perhaps permanent positive change. For others, particularly those with complex and longstanding problems, significant positive changes were often not sustained. An interesting feature of the evaluation was that Option 2 succeeded in meeting every family referred to the service, and a high proportion of these were engaged with the work of Option 2. This seems related to the ability of workers from the service to visit families repeatedly, often outside normal working hours, in an attempt to engage them.

The evaluation of Option 2 suggests that the service has had some success in reducing the use of public care and this may generate cost savings, and the qualitative interviews suggest a professional service that is much appreciated. However, there are important limitations in this evaluation. The most important is that it reports solely on outcomes related to care entry. Child welfare and parental drinking issues were not measured directly; these are the subject of a further ongoing evaluation by Forrester and others. This is an important limitation, because children's welfare often improves after coming into care (Forrester et al., 2009). A service that delays or reduces the use of care may therefore not always have a positive impact on children in the long term. On the other hand, it perhaps points to the importance of longer term support and intervention for some families. A strange feature of the UK system of children's services is that we are prepared to make permanent interventions in children's lives by removing them from home, but it is rare for us to be prepared to provide permanent family support services (Forrester, 2008; Forrester et al., 2009).

Despite the potential limitations of the study, it has some important strengths:

1   This is a long follow-up period – far longer than is generally available in the research literature. Finding lasting effects over such a long time period is rare, and is particularly noteworthy with such a brief intervention.
2   The comparison group would have received some services. The referring social workers were highly likely to have made referrals to a wide variety of other supportive services. The comparison is therefore not of Option 2 compared to receiving no service, but of Option 2 compared to 'normal' support services. Again, this means that a finding of statistically significant difference is worthy of note.
3   As noted above, this appears to be the only UK study using a comparative design in relation to serious parental substance misuse issues (see Galvani and Forrester et al., 2010). Option 2 therefore provides a promising place to start developing evaluations of what might work for this group.

It is interesting and important to note the similarities between Option 2 and the two studies discussed above. All the studies involved interventions in which social workers had limited caseloads and were encouraged to develop high levels of skill in order to engage groups of service users often found 'hard to engage'. All the interventions paid considerable attention to developing a good working relationship and provided a variety of services to meet the needs of the clients being worked with. The studies found that this approach to delivering excellent services for challenging client groups led to real and measurable improvements. Quality social work services produced findings that not only helped people but also seemed to be cost-effective.

Research

Concluding discussion

The studies discussed in this chapter illustrate the potential contribution that social work can make to helping those who have alcohol and/or drug issues to improve their lives. In particular, the key elements of effective social work with substance use and misuse that were illustrated included:

- A focus on engaging and retaining individuals who often have serious challenges in their behaviour with services, by providing services at times and places likely to be of help to them. Equally, services that worked tended to be persistent in offering help: they never gave up on clients.
- At the heart of the effective services was a helping relationship.
- The relationship skills for working with substance misuse were often related to MI. MI might be seen as providing core or foundational skills for those working with drug-/alcohol-using clients.
- Yet social work interventions provided more than MI. MI might provide a basis for helpful communication, but typically social workers coordinated services, assisted with practical issues and might provide group or network-related interventions.

These key features of social work with substance use issues are consistent with the theoretical approaches discussed in Chapter 13, in that they combine the best of evidence-based interventions for alcohol or drug problems with a more holistic attempt to address the multiple factors that may contribute to such difficulties.

In this respect, social work approaches appear particularly consistent with recent developments in the substance misuse field that have seen arguments for moves towards a 'recovery' focus. The nature of recovery as an approach was briefly outlined in Chapter 13. In broad terms, there has been increasing interest in recovery as a response to perceived limitations in the current dominant models. The substance misuse field has to date had three main approaches to helping people with drug or alcohol problems. The most long-established is that associated with the disease model of addiction, which focuses on helping people achieve abstinence. Such an approach has also been characteristic of Alcoholics Anonymous and related organizations. In contrast to this, harm minimization developed as an approach, which became influential from the 1980s onwards, around the time that concern was growing for HIV/AIDS. Harm minimization emphasizes working with drug or alcohol users to minimize the harm they may cause themselves or others. It is nonjudgemental and simply attempts to work with those who have drug or alcohol problems to reduce harm. A classic example of harm minimization is offering drug users free needles in order to reduce the spread of illnesses such as HIV and hepatitis.

A third approach to working with drug or alcohol problems has been the development of evidence-based approaches. The nature of evaluative research and the realities of limited resources for attempts to find out what works have tended to result in evaluations of relatively brief and certainly time-limited interventions. This has produced a strong body of evidence showing that even relatively short interventions can make a positive difference, but there has been increasing concern that they do not fully capture the fact that for many individuals, substance misuse problems may be a long-term relapsing condition that requires lengthy support and intervention.

> **Making connexions**
>
> According to this chapter, what are the three main approaches to helping people with drug or alcohol problems? How does the recovery approach relate to them?

The recovery approach combines key elements of each of the second and third approaches. An emphasis is placed on the users of services defining not only their own goals but also the types of support they need in order to achieve them. Evidence-based approaches have a place but they may need to be adapted for the longer term support needs that many who have experienced drug and/or alcohol problems feel they need. At the heart of the recovery approach is a more flexible, more service user-focused and more holistic attempt to provide help for people with drug or alcohol problems.

Such an approach appears particularly appropriate for social work. Social work values and practices have long put the views of the service user at the heart of good practice, and the social work role often involves coordinating services or accessing resources. Social work has a lengthy history of longer term work, and is often focused less on creating therapeutic change than on providing support for people to maintain themselves in the community (Davies, 1994). The research discussed in this chapter illustrates what more holistic approaches might look like and provides evidence that they can make a significant difference in the lives of some of the groups with the worst drug or alcohol problems in society. As such, they provide excellent examples of the good fit between social work approaches to substance misuse and the general philosophy associated with the move towards 'recovery' as a central concept within the substance misuse field. Indeed, they suggest that the move towards an interest in 'recovery' may indicate a move in the substance misuse field towards an approach that is more akin to that of social work, and as such provide potent examples of the contribution that social work can and should make to helping those with drug or alcohol problems.

Further reading

■ Forrester, D. and Harwin, J. (2011) *Parents who Misuse Drugs and Alcohol: Effective Interventions in Social Work and Child Protection.* Chichester: Wiley.

Useful book on interventions for those social workers and students working in child protection who encounter parents with drug and alcohol problems.

■ Galvani, S. and Forrester, D. with Glynn, G. et al. (2011) *Social Work Services and Recovery from Substance Misuse: A Review of the Evidence,* available at http://www.scotland.gov.uk/Publications/2011/03/18085806/0.

Research

In-depth review that outlines social work and social care's contribution to supporting people with drug and alcohol issues and places the research in a UK context.

■ Miller, W. and Rollnick, S. (2002) *Motivational Interviewing: Preparing People for Change* (2nd edn). New York: Guilford Press.

Important read for any student working with clients who face challenging problems, such as substance misuse. MI is a well-evidenced approach for communicating with clients who are ambivalent about change.

References

Bouis, S., Reif, S., Whetten, K. et al. (2007) 'An integrated, multidimensional treatment model for individuals living with HIV, mental illness, and substance misuse', *Health and Social Work,* **32**(4): 268–78.

Davies, M. (1994) *The Essential Social Worker* (2nd edn). Aldershot: Arena.

Forrester, D. (2008) 'Is the care system failing children?', *Political Quarterly*, **79**(2): 206–11.

Forrester, D. and Harwin, J. (2011) *Parents who Misuse Drugs or Alcohol: Effective Interventions in Social Work and Child Protection*. Chichester: Wiley.

Forrester, D., Copello, A., Waissbein, C. and Pokhrel, S. (2008) 'Evaluation of an intensive family preservation service for families affected by parental substance misuse', *Child Abuse Review*, **17**(6): 410–26.

Forrester, D., Cocker, C., Goodman, K. et al. (2009) 'What is the impact of public care on children's welfare? A review of research findings and their policy implications', *Journal of Social Policy*, **38**(3): 439–56.

Galvani, S. and Forrester, D. with Glynn, G. et al. (2010) *Social Work Services and Recovery from Substance Misuse: A Review of the Evidence*, available at http://www.scotland.gov.uk/Resource/Doc/346164/0115212.pdf, accessed 29 November 2011.

Hamer, M. (2005) *Preventing Breakdown: A Manual for Those Working with Families and the Individuals within Them*. Plymouth: Random House.

McLennan, A.T., Hagan, T.A., Levine, M. et al. (1998) 'Supplemental social services improve outcomes in public addiction treatment', *Addiction*, **93**(10): 1489–99.

Miller, W.R. and Rollnick, S. (2002) *Motivational Interviewing: Preparing People for Change* (2nd edn). New York: Guilford Press.

Prochaska, J.O., DiClemente C.C. and Norcross J.C. (1992) 'In search of how people change: applications to addictive behaviors', *American Psychologist*, **47**(9): 1102–14.

Whetten, K., Reif, S., Ostermann, J. et al. (2006) 'Improving health outcomes among individuals with HIV, mental illness, and substance use disorders in the southeast', *AIDS Care*, **18**(1): 18–26.

15
Working with people who use substances

SARAH GALVANI AND SARAH WADD

Social workers from all areas of practice work with people affected by their own or someone else's alcohol or other drug problems. Problematic substance use (alcohol and other drugs) is common within child and family social work practice, adolescent work and in mental health settings. Social workers working with older adults and people with learning difficulties also report increased substance use among their service user groups. It is important therefore that whichever group of people you are working with, you are prepared to identify and assess their substance use. Set within the wider context of a range of social work assessment processes, this requires few additional skills but it does require an understanding of what to ask, how to ask it and what to do with the responses you receive.

We know from asking social workers about their experiences that service users rarely disclose their alcohol or other drug problems at their first social work meeting. Information on a person's substance use is far more likely to come from referral sources or to emerge in the course of work with the individual or family (Galvani et al., 2011) – work that is often focused on completely different issues.

Social workers have told us that they feel unprepared for talking to their service users about substance use and the risk it can sometimes pose (Galvani and Forrester, 2011; Galvani et al., 2011). This chapter focuses on presenting a general framework for social work assessment of substance use and concludes by describing a model for brief interventions.

A framework for social work assessment

In substance use services, a widely used theoretical framework that explains the process of changing substance use behaviours is called the 'stages of change' (Prochaska et al., 1992). What the model does is help staff and service users to understand the process of behaviour change. It acknowledges the fact that people will often make many attempts to change their substance-using behaviour before successfully doing so. This is not only an issue for people who use alcohol or illicit drugs but also for anyone who has tried to give up an entrenched, habitual behaviour, such as smoking, overeating, gambling, or excessive use of computer games.

The stages of change model (Figure 15.1) illustrates the phases people will go through when they attempt behaviour change, from not even thinking they have a problem (pre-contemplation), to thinking about making a change (contemplation), then doing something about it (action). Importantly, however, the change process does not stop there. Service users often report that the hardest part of the process is maintaining the change (maintenance) as they try to fill the void previously filled by substance use activities. Because this can be a difficult time, relapse – when someone reverts back to problematic levels of substance use – is common.

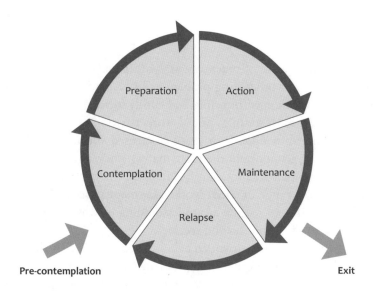

Figure 15.1 The stages of change

The amount of time an individual remains within each stage varies considerably. For example, some people will move from contemplation through preparation to action very quickly. Others will spend longer in contemplation before making any decision or preparation for change. The model includes relapse as a distinct stage but does not assume that everyone will relapse; many people will exit at the maintenance stage and maintain their behaviour change long term.

For the purposes of social work assessment, the stages of change model allows us to understand behaviour change in relation to substance-using behaviours. It also provides a framework for thinking about what questions we need to ask and when. Consider the following practice scenarios and then answer two questions:

1 Which of the five stages of change do you think they have reached?
2 What will your questions focus on?

Practice example 1 | Norman

Norman is a 68-year-old man who has been hospitalized for leg and wrist injuries following a fall at home. He lives with his wife who is shy and appears quite withdrawn. He has one son who has very little contact with him and does not live nearby. Norman has a number of physical health problems, some of which are consistent with problematic alcohol use, and some memory problems. The referral information shows a long history of alcohol use and he was intoxicated on admission to hospital. During the admission process, he had become verbally aggressive and resistant to going to hospital but the paramedics were able to placate him and he became quite passive and apologetic. You have visited him on the ward to conduct an assessment to determine whether he has support needs at home. When you ask him about alcohol and drug use, he gets cross and says he has a drink occasionally but that's all and he just wants to get his leg sorted and go home so people will stop bothering him.

Practice example 2 | James

James is 16 and lives with his mum and dad and two younger siblings. He spent a short period of time in a young offenders institution after getting involved in a gang on a nearby estate where he was arrested for a number of offences from shop theft to assault and criminal damage. He was a heavy user of cannabis for two years until his arrest, and used other drugs, including ecstasy and methamfetamine, when he could afford it. He and his family moved away from the area and he has not been using any drugs for the last 12 months. He has been attending your child and adolescent mental health service for support. You have a good relationship with him and are winding down your work with him. He recently disclosed that he is finding it hard to stay off the cannabis as a few of his new friends use it quite regularly.

Practice example 3 | Tracey

Tracey, 33, is a single mum with a three-year-old son. She has been separated from her partner for three and a half years after a six-year relationship with him. She has come into contact with your service due to ongoing mental health problems including a history of depression and self-harm. She has had a stable period of good mental health but her GP has referred her as she has admitted to having suicidal thoughts and to cutting herself. The GP also discloses that she has a history of heroin use but, to his knowledge, she has not used it in almost three years. Children's social care had previous involvement during her pregnancy but closed her case when she stopped using heroin and separated from her partner who they suspect was violent towards her and prostituting her. On a visit to Tracey at home, you notice a sharps bin in the bathroom and foil wraps in the ashtray. The house is in a poor state of cleanliness. When you ask whether she has begun using again, she says she has but only once, she's not sure whether she needs help but doesn't know what to do as her ex-partner has returned to the area and has been threatening her.

Practice example 4   Susie

Susie is seven and lives with her mum Pat and stepdad Tom. The school has referred her to your team following concerns about her increasingly withdrawn behaviour and deteriorating appearance. It has made contact with Pat and Tom and invited them to the school on a number of occasions but only Pat has attended, saying she has been ill lately and that now she's better things will improve. Staff at the school have smelt alcohol on both Tom and Pat when they have picked Susie up from school. On visiting them at home, the house is sparsely furnished, with the smell of stale alcohol throughout. It is clear that Pat and Tom have few material resources and are nervous about you being there. In discussion with them, they say they know things are not good but love Susie dearly and don't want to lose her and that they'll do what it takes. They say they need help with their drinking and have already tried cutting down.

Pre-contemplation

At this stage, people will often be unaware that their substance use is problematic. If they are aware of it, they simply do not want to do anything about it. Pre-contemplation in the context of behaviour change refers to the stage before someone considers any change in their substance use. In the scenarios above, Norman could be said to be 'pre-contemplative'. An assessment of his alcohol use therefore needs to be nested in a holistic assessment and normalized as part of that assessment. Assessments can be seen as interventions in themselves and raising the issue of substance use may start someone thinking about it differently. For someone who is pre-contemplative, you may be the first to have raised the issue, or the first in a long time to do so. You may be the first person to use an empathic tone, rather than a judgemental one. Expecting 'action' at this stage would be overly optimistic but highlighting concerns and offering support in case the person changes their mind is important, whatever their initial reaction.

Importantly, you must consider the context within which you're asking the questions; if you are conducting an assessment on other matters, you can add in the following:

> We also ask everyone about their alcohol and drug use. Can you tell me how much you drink each day (week)? How does your drinking help you? Has your drinking ever caused problems for you? Would you like to change your drinking? How confident are you that you could change your drinking if you wanted to change? How can I support you to make that change? (where appropriate)

The questions can be repeated about drug use (including prescription drugs).

Of course, if the person denies any use of alcohol or other drugs but you have concerns about its impact on them or those around them, your approach is going to be different, but, again, be careful of your tone so as not to sound confrontational:

> So if I understand you correctly, you're saying you have no problems with/do not use alcohol or drugs. I'm a bit confused now, as the information I have from (referrer/school/GP and so on) tells me otherwise and I need your help to make sense of that. Do you have any idea why they may have provided this information?

For someone with caring responsibilities, where there are serious concerns over the welfare of the dependent, a more directive approach will be necessary. You may not have the time to wait for the person to disclose at a later date because of the harm the parent or carer's problematic substance use is having on their ability to keep their dependent(s) safe. Faced with ongoing denial of substance use combined with a child or adult at potential risk, you will need to be open about your next steps:

> It seems we are likely to disagree on this but I want to be honest with you and tell you that I do have some concerns relating to your drug/alcohol use and the impact it is/may be having on (dependent). It seems to me you care very much about (dependent), but I suspect your drug or alcohol use may be getting in the way of that. Part of my job is to make sure (dependent) is alright, so I just want to be honest about my concerns. I'm not here to judge your substance use and I'm willing to offer what support I can, but I cannot leave things as they are at present. I'm hoping you'll choose to talk to me about it and tell me your view. I really don't want to have to start making decisions about (dependent)'s care without you.

Raising concerns is a legitimate role for a social worker in relation to a person's substance use, but how it is done and the tone that is used will often determine the reaction you get. Avoiding a paternalistic or judgemental tone is crucial and may make the difference between the person discussing the issues at a later date or, alternately, doing their best to hide them from you.

Contemplation

In Practice example 3, Tracey is thinking about her substance use, is ambivalent about seeking help but clearly her social environment and her safety are a real cause

Practice

for concern. The fact that she is thinking about getting help gives you a clue about how to approach the assessment. Questions need to support her decision processes and emphasize the positives of change, while acknowledging there might be disadvantages for her.

In a technique called motivational interviewing (MI) (Miller and Rollnick, 2002), ambivalence is considered a natural thought process when contemplating change. When making changes, people will often weigh up the pros and cons of doing so. This decisional balance is where you can begin to help using appropriate assessment questions. Through skilled questioning, you will be seeking to highlight the positives of change as well as reflecting back the negatives the person discloses. This is not through directly telling the person what you think are the positives and negatives but by asking questions in such a way that they start talking about possible changes and the advantages of making them.

Examples of questions to help motivation and develop what MI refers to as 'change talk' include:

- How has your substance use changed over time?
- What are the good things about your alcohol/drug use?
- What are the downsides to it?
- What would be the advantages and disadvantages of changing your alcohol or drug use?
- What support might you want if you were to cut down/stop this time?

When the person responds to these questions, it is important to reflect back their answers to them. This demonstrates that you've been listening, either by summarizing what they've been saying or simple reflection. Listening to service users rather than trying to fix things immediately is vital and takes practice.

For Tracey or anyone else who is fearful for their safety, safety has to be the priority. Anecdotal evidence suggests that social workers often focus on substance use without identifying or addressing domestic abuse. Given the high prevalence of coexisting domestic abuse and substance use, this must not be overlooked. Clearly, the safety of Tracey's son is paramount, be it from domestic violence and/or Tracey's substance use, but helping Tracey to feel safe and deal with the return of her abusive partner will, in turn, keep Tracey's son safe from the violence and abuse too. It does not address the potential risk from her substance use but she will be in a far better position to address her drug use if she feels safe. If the choice is focusing on safety or drug use, safety must always take precedence. It is not about ignoring the concerns that problematic substance use brings; it is about understanding that, when someone lives in fear of violence and abuse, substance use can be a coping mechanism.

Preparation/action

The stages of preparation and action can be distinct or can merge into one. In Practice example 4, Pat and Tom fall into this group. They have been open about their use and the fact that they need help (preparation). They have said that they have been trying to cut down their drinking (action). Not only have they recognized the problems it is causing them but they are trying to do something about it. Other people in the preparation stage may have thought about where they might go for support or what they do and don't want from specialist services. People in the action stage will be actively engaged in changing their substance use, perhaps by cutting down themselves or by attending specialist services.

To support people fully at this stage, you need to be aware of what services are available locally and what approaches they use. People can be fearful of attending services when they don't know what to expect and this can be a barrier to seeking help. You need to be able to dilute these fears and also provide factual information on the options available. If you don't know what services there are, make sure you ask what type of support they would prefer, for example group, individual or couple work; then go away and do your homework, quickly. Even in the preparation and action stage, people will still experience ambivalence so make sure you capitalize on their current motivation. A week can be a long time when people are trying to change substance-using behaviours. In the preparation and action stages, assessment questions will include:

- It sounds like you've given this a lot of thought and have chosen to make some changes to your alcohol/drug use. What got you to this point of choosing to make some changes?
- Have you tried cutting down or stopping before?
- If so, why? How did you do that? What happened?
- What do you see as the advantages and disadvantages to changing your substance use?
- Have you thought about the kind of service you'd like to attend?
- What support can I offer you at this time?
- In Practice example 4 with Tom and Pat: How do you think Susie will benefit from your decision to make these changes?
- How do you think it might affect Susie if you carry on drinking as you are?
- What does Susie think about your drinking? And your commitment to making some changes?

At the action stage, the role of the social worker is to support the change. This may mean facilitating practical arrangements, for example the care of Susie while Tom and Pat attend alcohol services. It might include making referrals to a range of specialist services or conducting joint home visits with local substance use services. It might include providing information on the impact of substance problems on children or making telephone contact to see how appointments have gone.

Maintenance

Some service users who have changed their substance-using behaviour report that the hardest thing to do is maintain the change. In some cases, maintaining abstinence or

Practice

reduced levels of use can actually be harder than giving up or cutting down in the first place. This is primarily because the change in substance use can leave a void in people's lives on practical and emotional levels. For some people with substance problems, their routine is set by their substance use; their waking hours are spent thinking about the substance, how to afford it and physically get hold of it. Their drinking and drug-using friends may be the only friends they have and the only social contact they have. The cessation or reduction of substance use can eliminate these routines, behaviours and friendships. In addition, the emotional reawakening that can occur following abstinence may bring with it difficult emotions and painful memories, which can be hard to bear when substance free. For the people whose use of substances has been a coping mechanism, abstinence means having to find a different way to cope. In sum, the cessation of substance use in a person's life can leave people socially isolated and wondering how to structure their time as well as deal with physical and emotional changes.

However, not everyone who changes their substance use behaviours will experience these challenges. The goal of assessment at the maintenance stage is to ask questions that elicit self-motivating statements and support the person's self-efficacy to maintain the changes they've already made. James, in Practice example 2, has some ongoing support through a child and adolescent mental health service, which is positive, but he is clearly struggling to maintain his abstinence from cannabis in light of the temptation he faces when he is with his new friends. Questions that could be helpful include:

- Thanks for telling me about the pressures you're feeling. It must be hard for you at the moment. Remind me why you decided to stop using last time?
- Do those same reasons for stopping still exist?
- What do you think would happen if you started using again?
- James, you've been stopped for 12 months now – that's a great achievement. What have been the pros and cons of not using during those 12 months?
- Tell me when you feel most at risk of using again? When else?
- How do you think you can overcome those risky situations? NB: talk through each one to ensure that it is realistic and achievable.
- What support do you have at home and work/college?
- What else can I do to support you at the moment?
- What is it about yourself that helped you to come off and stay off for the last 12 months?

Writing down the risk factors in one column and the solution/s in another can provide a helpful *aide-mémoire* to James and one he can keep with him and share with his family and friends if appropriate. It might also be worth discussing with James how close these friends are, to what extent he can confide in one or more of them about his own cannabis use, and how hard it is for him trying to stay off it when they use around him. Alternately, does he have friends who don't use who he could hang out with more? Essentially, your questions need to be phrased to help James identify one or more solutions rather than you telling him what to do.

Relapse

Relapse is when someone returns to problematic patterns of alcohol or drug use. This is different to a 'lapse' or 'slip', which is the use of substances on a one-off basis. Relapse tends to refer to ongoing problematic use. People who relapse often feel doubly ashamed because they know how

> **Making connexions**
>
> 'Asking the right questions in the right way' is at the heart of good social work practice in work with people who use substances. What are 'the right questions'? And what is 'the right way'?

well they were doing and subsequently feel a huge sense of failure. Being able to support someone at this stage is vital and can make the difference between the person re-engaging with services (returning to 'action') or returning to ongoing problematic substance use (pre-contemplation). For people in these situations, the questions shouldn't reinforce those negative feelings or convey a sense of disappointment. The questions and responses at this stage should be focused on rebuilding the person's self-determination and self-esteem, as well as reminding them what they can achieve, the choices available to them, and helping them to think about why they changed their behaviour in the first place.

Some of the questions in the maintenance stage above will work well here too. Although the context of assessment is different, questions relating to the pros and cons of change and what worked previously can all build confidence and move someone towards making changes again. Questions that may help include:

- You were successful in giving up/cutting down before. You clearly have the strength and determination to do this. I wonder if we can think about what we can learn from this. Tell me what was going on before you relapsed?
- How had you dealt with those situations previously?
- What would it take to make you want to try again?
- What are the things you would find hardest to deal with?
- What support would you have if you were to choose to try again?
- What other support would you want in place?
- What are some of the alternatives to drinking/using that you found useful previously?

In Practice example 3, Tracey might also be considered to have relapsed, although further questioning would determine if she had really relapsed or had experienced a lapse or slip. Talking to someone about relapse should provide you and them with an opportunity to learn more about what led to the relapse and how to avoid a similar situation in future.

Additional assessment information

Where people have dependent children or adults living with them, additional information needs to be sought about the impact of their substance use on their dependents. The wider home environment needs to be assessed to ensure that it is a safe environment for the child or vulnerable adult. Additional inquiries will be made in the course of your

Practice

assessment, including information from external agencies. As always, safeguarding the child or adult will be paramount and the substance use assessment will be conducted in that context. An effective assessment of the parent's or carer's substance use is part of supporting a change in the dependent's environment and care. Encouraging people to be open about the impact of their substance use on their dependent(s) and how they think their substance use might affect their ability to care are appropriate questions to pose. Seeking the view of the dependent adult or child where appropriate is also important.

Assessment is a skilled and complex task, often with time limits for completion attached. Nevertheless, other issues commonly overlap with parental substance use and need to be explored during the assessment process. For example, the relationship between domestic violence and substance problems is particularly strong. Assessment of these overlapping issues requires sensitive but direct exploration. The following is an example of some of the questions that could be asked:

- As well as asking about alcohol and drug use, we are also asking everyone about violence or abuse in the home because this is very common. How often do arguments ever result in you feeling put down or bad about yourself?
- How often do you become frightened by what your partner says or does?
- Do arguments ever result in hitting, kicking or pushing? If so, how often?
- Does your partner control who you can and cannot see?
- Do you think there is a link between any of these problems and your/their substance use? If yes, how so?
- To what extent does your substance use help you to cope with the violence and abuse you've experienced (where disclosed)?
- Have you got, or thought about getting, help for your experiences of violence and abuse? (If appropriate, then point out contact details on an information sheet, and so on.)
- Has your partner forced you to use drugs or alcohol? Or withheld drugs or alcohol from you on purpose?
- Has your partner stopped you from attending a drug or alcohol service?

You will need to be comfortable asking these questions, otherwise the service user will also feel uncomfortable and is less likely to discuss the issue with you. Because of safety concerns, these questions must only be asked if someone is on their own. It could be unsafe to ask them if both partners, or other family members, are present. Further advice is available from the AVA (Against Violence & Abuse) website, where the Stella Project's toolkit is full of questions to ask and issues to consider (AVA/Stella Project Toolkit, 2007).

Brief interventions

The evidence around case management approaches and, in particular, MI is outlined in Chapter 14; the evidence for the success of these approaches is strong, particularly within healthcare settings. What the case management evidence suggests is that longer term involvement and greater resources appear to have better outcomes for service users. However, there is also evidence that brief interventions are effective, although largely for people whose substance use is not so entrenched. Social workers are well placed to conduct brief interventions where specialist support is not already involved.

Brief interventions do exactly what their name suggests. They are brief, taking anything from minutes to hours, and are usually administered in a single meeting. Brief interventions are often based on MI techniques. Miller and Sanchez (1994, cited in Rollnick and Miller, 1995) identified six key aspects of brief interventions and summarized these using the acronym FRAMES (Figure 15.2).

	Feedback
F	Once people have disclosed their substance use, you need to provide some feedback. Giving people feedback on their alcohol and drug use, for example whether it is excessive or not compared to benchmarks, the potential it has for health and social harms and so on, must be accurate and positive. Wherever possible, it must be based on fact, not your view, as the latter will allow it to be dismissed more easily. It must also be positive. Even when the use appears to be problematic and harmful, there is a need to give some positive feedback as this will enhance motivation. This may be reflecting on the fact they have been open about their substance use, allowing a better discussion about it or it may reflect the person's contemplation about their use or their willingness to do something about it.
	Responsibility for change
R	Encouraging a sense of responsibility is about ensuring that the person feels some ownership of the decision to make changes. What it is not is telling someone to act responsibly or admonishing the person for not taking adequate responsibility. This is not motivational. In an empathic and confidence-building way, be clear that they have the power to choose whether or not to change – nobody else. Others can offer support but they are in control about what they do and don't do.
	Advice-giving
A	FRAMES adopts a more directive approach than MI, including giving advice to change. Again this has to be done in a factual way based on the information the person has given you about their use. The advice to cut down or stop has to be clear, backed up with some choices they may consider if they choose to accept the advice given. Don't assume that someone else has given the advice – you may be the first. Even if someone else has offered advice, it might not have been heard that time or delivered in a way that encouraged consideration. Further, your approach and your role is likely to be different from other professionals they have encountered and may have more impact.
	Menu of choices
M	If someone is considering your advice to change, it is likely they will want to know what their choices are. You need to be able to offer a menu of change options from trying to make changes themselves, to attending a local specialist service to trying a mutual aid support group. Knowing what is available locally and having some idea of what they entail is important. You must be prepared for this stage in order to capitalize on the person's interest.
	Empathy
E	As previous chapters have highlighted, an empathic approach is essential. In more direct and advice-giving interventions, this can be harder to do. Remember, tone of voice and how your questions and responses are phrased demonstrate empathy. If the service user feels that you have some understanding of their situation and are listening to them, they are more likely to reciprocate and take what you say seriously. Empathy is vital in building good therapeutic relationships.
	Self-efficacy
S	Whatever the change people are looking to make, self-belief that they can do it is essential. Part of the assessment and intervention process is to help the person achieve a sense of self-efficacy, which in turn promotes responsibility and independence. Ambivalence about the change itself and their ability to make that change will lie side by side. Your role is to support the person to see that they are capable of making that change.

Figure 15.2 The FRAMES model

Practice

What FRAMES offers social workers is a model for intervention that does not require a heavy investment of time and is akin to the principles of empowerment that underpin social work practice. Where longer term involvement is not possible or appropriate, brief interventions offer you a way to intervene while other support or referrals are put in place as needed.

Summary

Good assessment practice for substance problems requires excellent communication skills and an awareness of the ambivalence and challenges people face when contemplating change. Understanding the process of change can help you to choose your questions appropriately and help you to lay the foundations for building a good therapeutic relationship. People with alcohol and other drug problems often feel ashamed, stigmatized, marginalized and excluded. Your job is to help them to see things differently, to promote self-efficacy and support their efforts to change, both for their own sake and for the sake of the people who are dependent on them. Asking the right questions, in the right way, is at the core of this task.

Appendix 15.1 Alcohol and drug information

Alcohol Concern – www.alcoholconcern.org.uk

National charity (England and Wales) that provides information on policy and practice relating to alcohol. Also offers training and consultancy services.

DrugScope – www.drugscope.org.uk

UK-wide drugs charity that provides information on all aspects of drug use and offers an online service directory for all regions of the UK. Also provides helpful summaries of research evidence to support practice development.

Talk to Frank – www.talktofrank.com

Online resource from the English government providing information on drugs including videos and case studies. Originally targeting young people, is now accessible for all ages.

Adfam – www.adfam.org.uk

A charity supporting the family members and friends of people who have alcohol and other drug problems. Provides information on what to do if a friend or relative has substance problems as well as providing a directory of support services.

Good Practice Guidance for Working with Children and Families Affected by Substance Misuse – http://www.scotland.gov.uk/Resource/Doc/47032/0023960.pdf

Provides a checklist of information on parental substance use (pp. 72–4).

Further reading

■ Barber, J.G. (2002) *Social Work with Addictions* (2nd edn). Basingstoke: Palgrave Macmillan.

Highlights how the stages of change can support good social work practice with people with alcohol and drug problems.

■ Galvani, S. (2012) *Supporting People with Alcohol and Drug Problems: Making a Difference.* Bristol: Policy Press.

Offers practical tips for working with people with substance problems, based on the research evidence and illustrated with case studies.

■ Miller, W.R. and Rollnick, S. (2012) *Motivational Interviewing* (3rd edn). London: Guilford Press.

MI is an evidence-based collaborative approach for supporting people to change behaviours, particularly problematic substance use. Is highly relevant for social work practice in terms of its values and skills base.

References

AVA/Stella Project Toolkit (2007) *Domestic Violence, Drugs and Alcohol: Good Practice Guidelines* (2nd edn), http://www.avaproject.org.uk/our-resources/good-practice-guidance--toolkits/stella-project-toolkit-(2007).aspx, accessed 1 December 2011.

Galvani, S. and Forrester, D. (2011) 'How well prepared are newly qualified social workers for working with substance use issues? Findings from a national survey', *Social Work Education,* **30**(4): 422–39.

Galvani, S., Dance, C. and Hutchinson, A. (2011) *Substance Use and Social Work Practice: Findings from a National Survey of Social Workers in England.* Available at www.beds.ac.uk/goldbergcentre.

Miller, W.R. and Rollnick, S. (eds) (2002) *Motivational Interviewing: Preparing People to Change Addictive Behaviour* (2nd edn). London: Guilford Press.

Prochaska, J.O., DiClemente, C.C. and Norcross, J.C. (1992) 'In search of how people change: applications to addictive behaviors', *American Psychologist,* **47**(9): 1102–14.

Rollnick, S. and Miller, W.R. (1995) 'What is motivational interviewing?', *Behavioural and Cognitive Psychotherapy,* **23**(4): 325–34.

Practice

Part IV
Social Work and Old Age

The changing global demographic profile focuses our attention on the importance of understanding and responding to the needs of people across the life span. The ageing of populations, spurred by increased longevity and decreasing birth rates in developing and developed countries, creates economic and fiscal challenges, while demanding social and healthcare approaches that address these shifts. There are also demands for re-examining our views of old age and doing battle with some of the stereotypical or homogenizing images of older people, such as dependence and decline. The Department of Health's promotion of personalization and person-led services grows apace, unsettling the social work response and its understanding of its fit within contemporary social services. This is extended within the Department of Health's three-month consultation *Caring for our Future: Shared Ambitions for Care and Support,* launched in September 2011, which will inform debates including funding, family and informal caring, and end of life care. Part IV will enable readers to locate themselves and professional social work within that debate.

In Chapter 16, Tony Gilbert and Jason Powell consider some of the implications that social policies may have on older people, recognizing that those policies may, in themselves, construct particular understandings of and approaches to older people. These policies may be helpful in providing services to meet specific needs, but they may also generate views of older people, and old age in general, that lead to unhelpful practices. Gilbert and Powell invite readers to explore the social policy context within the UK through the 'lens of governmentality' – an approach that identifies the subtle, underlying ways in which policies mould and direct individual behaviours and beliefs. In the current social context, this policy direction concerns self-management, a political/economic approach championed within neoliberal governmental systems.

In Chapter 17, Ann McDonald examines the disparate legal corpus relating to old age, and highlights the differences with law relating to children. Readers are engaged in a tour of legislation detailing the responsibilities social workers have within a changing policy environment. She identifies some of the ways in which older people are constructed as vulnerable and as passive recipients of welfare services. She points out the multiple ways in which legislation can be used by older people, and assists readers in negotiating the different social functions of legislation, including the promotion of a rights-based approach, much in concert with social work practice.

Chapter 18 addresses the problematic and contested area inhabited by theories of old age and how they might impact on social work. Jonathan Parker explores a range of social gerontological theories that aid readers in understanding old age in society, the social welfare and social work systems that have evolved, and the ways in which social workers might practise with individuals. In a common theme throughout Part IV, Parker recognizes that theories construct and are constructed by the various understandings we have of old age. He argues that readers should avoid partisan allegiances when reading and adopting theoretical positions but should use these pragmatically to inform and assist practice as the situation dictates.

Research evidence is central to developing appropriate, ethical social work practice. In Chapter 19, Paul Clarkson examines two broad themes, which, again, permeate Part IV. First, the changing demographics and the potential ramifications of this, and, second, increasing health and social care needs among older people. His review of the research is optimistic and tempers some of the worst prognostications made of these shifts. Clarkson's masterly sweep of the research allows readers to see how social work decisions can be made and what these might be.

The book ends with Rhiannon Jones's practice-focused Chapter 20. Using four case scenarios, she exemplifies how social workers may assess, intervene and follow up on what has happened in terms of future social work or other support needed. Her focus is optimistic and she uses legislation, social policy and theoretical understandings to describe social work practice with older people.

The global challenges arising from changing demographic profiles, increased longevity, fiscal constraints and continued neoliberal government act as a lens through which we approach old age. Social work constitutes a central response to resulting social needs. However, the way in which social workers respond to and construct old age is crucial, if we are to develop appropriate practices. The chapters in Part IV provide a rich diet to feed the thoughts and actions underlying these possibilities.

Jonathan Parker

16

The place that social policy plays in shaping the social context of older people

TONY GILBERT AND JASON L. POWELL

Old age is not, of itself, a 'problem', a pathology or a statement of need. 'Older people' are not a homogeneous group and categorization as a distinct service user group is, arguably, contentious (Phillipson, 1998). Furthermore, since the advent of personalization, conceptualizing support by user groups is considered by many as obsolete (Poll and Duffy, 2008). People do not receive social services by virtue of being 'older'; rather, they are in need of a service because of, for example, ill health, physical impairment, mental health difficulties, addiction or offending.

This chapter looks in more detail at the incidence and consequence of social policies for older people through the distinctly poststructuralist lens of governmentality (Foucault, 1977). This will enable us to consider the implications of the refiguring of the relationship between the state, older people and social work. This refiguring constructs an ambiguous place for older people: they feature either as a resource – captured in the idea of the 'active citizen', as affluent consumers, volunteers or providers of childcare – or as a problem in the context of poverty, vulnerability and risk. In many ways, policy provides three trajectories for older people:

1   as independent self-managing consumers with private means and resources
2   as people in need of some support to enable them to continue to self-manage
3   as dependent and unable to commit to self-management.

Governmentality provides the theoretical framework through which to view policy and practice that is largely governed by the discourses of personalization, safeguarding, capability and risk.

Demographics, poverty and ageism

Before moving on, it is useful to explore and problematize the notion of old age through consideration of demographics, poverty and ageism, because these issues are intertwined with the way social policy targets both older people and those who work with them.

Demographics

First we consider demographics and some of the contradictions that lie within the figures. Much of the anxiety that surrounds the debate about old age concerns the proportion of the population that is older, non-economically productive and in some way dependent. In addition, changes in intergenerational family relations provoke concerns and anxiety over who has responsibility for supporting older people – the family or the state. Media hype fuels such concerns with suggestions that the costs of supporting an 'explosion' of older dependent people will overwhelm the ability of the reducing proportion of the population that is economically active and paying taxes to fund the provision of care (Kemshall, 2002). In addition, a parallel argument suggests that the state is committing future generations to an unaffordable financial burden via pension payments and state-funded support. Such beliefs work to construct an image of older people as dependent and a burden on their children and the taxpayer and do much to fuel discrimination and ageism (Gilleard and Higgs, 2005).

It is true that demographic changes are occurring, with a reduction in the birth rate and an extension of life expectancy. Projections suggest that there will be over 10 million people aged 65 and over by 2021 or, alternatively, that the over-65s will make up 17.2% of the population (Phillipson, 2008). It is also the case that, in percentage terms, the over-65s are the highest users of health and social care services (Kemshall, 2002). Nevertheless, it is a cause for celebration that the past 25 years or so have seen progressive increases in life expectancy. In 2008, approximately 8.3% of the population were aged 65–74, 5.8% were aged 75–84 and 2.2% were 85 or older, while 410,000 people were over 90 and 10,000 over 100 (Bayliss and Sly, 2010). But despite the headline costs, only a small proportion of people in the older age bands require personal social services (Johnson, 1999). Many of us can look forward to an active and relatively healthy old age.

It is clear that predicting the future needs for support for specific individuals is more difficult in old age than in other periods of life. Nevertheless, the influence of major social variables, such as class, 'race' and gender, continue to show a differential impact on morbidity and acquired limiting conditions, as well as on overall life expectancy. In particular, class-based differences show the influence of external factors from earlier parts of the life course, particularly prenatal and postnatal periods and childhood (Kuh and Shlomo, 2004) – a feature that Philp (2008) refers to as 'extrinsic ageing'. This contrasts with intrinsic ageing, which relates to the limitations of

> **Making connexions**
>
> To what extent and in what way will the anticipated expansion in the numbers of old and very old people have an impact on social work practice?

cells and other biological factors. At the same time, gender imbalances increase with age: there are 50% more women than men aged 65 and over (Phillipson, 2008).

Race and ethnicity are factors in the differential impact of ageing on particular individuals. Again, the links here are with earlier life experiences and extrinsic or environmental factors, such as manual labour in risky settings, poverty, poor housing and racism (Phillipson, 2008).

In contrast, for some individuals and groups, the limitations associated with ageing come about at an earlier age, highlighting the problem of taking chronological age as the key determining factor. People with a lifelong disability tend to experience the 'effects' of ageing at an earlier part of the life course. It is also well documented that some individuals – such as people with Down syndrome – have a higher risk of early onset Alzheimer-type conditions (Bigby, 2004). There is also a growing recognition of early onset dementia and other organic cognitive impairments, such as those linked to Creutzfeldt-Jakob disease or, in certain cases, HIV/AIDS. Estimates suggest that there are some 16,000 people below the age of 65 with early onset dementia, with approximately 33% having Alzheimer's disease (Alzheimer's Society, 2011).

In addition to an awareness of these demographics, Kerr et al. (2005) suggest three contextual elements essential to effective social work with older people – poverty, ageism and the integration of services. We will consider the first two elements here and return to the issue of services later.

Poverty

Carroll Estes (1979) claims that poverty in old age is best understood in the relationship between ageing and the economic structure, that is, how the state decides and dictates who is allocated resources and who is not. This impinges on social policy in relation to retirement and subsequent pension schemes. As Phillipson (1982) points out, the retirement experience is linked to the reduction of wages and enforced withdrawal from work, which together place many older people in the UK in a financially insecure position.

Looking at the contemporary issue of poverty and older people, we have something of a mixed picture. Hoff (2008) notes the preference of policy-makers from the late 1980s onwards to refer to the effects of poverty and social exclusion rather than just poverty. Walker and Walker (1997) highlighted the need to take account of the multidimensional effects of low income and the impact of barriers to social integration experienced by older people. Nevertheless, there are contradictory patterns in income levels. These demonstrate that despite a steep decline in pensioner poverty in the 1990s, at the turn of the twenty-first century, nearly 25% of British pensioners remained in poverty (DWP, 2005). In addition, early life experiences such as engagement in the labour market and decisions about investments and pensions impact on material resources in older age (Burholt and Windle, 2006). Burholt and Windle (2006) emphasize the vulnerability of particular groups in older age – women, the socially disadvantaged, those from deprived neighbourhoods, people with ill health or disability, and people living alone, divorced or widowed. They also note that while individuals in younger generations may move in and out poverty, in later life there is little people can do about their position. Goldfield (2005) notes that deprived areas have a higher proportion of children and older people than wealthier areas.

Ageism

Hughes and Mtejuka (1992) identify personal, structural and cultural dimensions to ageism, which they describe as the negative images and attitudes towards older people that are based solely on the characteristics of old age. In social work with older people, Dominelli (2004, p. 137) notes the complexity of the impact of social dimensions, such as gender, race, disability, mental health and sexual orientation, claiming that:

> the negative image of the older person as dependant and in need of care portrays an ageist construction that treats every older person the same by ignoring the specific needs of older individuals and the contribution that older people as a group have made and continue to make to society.

Thompson (2001) suggests that one manifestation of institutional ageism is the tendency for work with older people to be seen as routine and uninteresting, more suited to unqualified workers and social work assistants than to qualified social workers or nurses.

MacDonald (2004) describes a four-year research programme about the priorities that older people themselves defined as important for 'living well in later life'. The older people involved in the projects did not commonly refer specifically to 'ageism', but the projects reported 'strong' evidence of its existence 'in a number of spheres'. These included poverty and the lack of opportunities that arise because much policy and practice identifies older people as a problem to be solved. MacDonald argues that while older people continue to be viewed as a burden, the denial of rights and opportunities to the ordinary things in life will continue.

Governmentality

Exploring the role that social policy plays in shaping the social context of older people through the lens of governmentality is to adopt a specific approach to the analysis of this phenomenon. The use of such an analysis reflects the way that neoliberal forms of government – such as those that have existed in the UK and most of the Western world since the late twentieth century – manage populations. Our interest is in the subtle mechanisms through which the behaviour of individuals is shaped, guided and directed without recourse to coercion (Foucault, 1991; Rose, 1999). Central to this process is the concept of the self-managing citizen-consumer engaged in an endless process of decision-making in consumer-based markets. The process is supported by an array of discourses of self-management and associated social practices that are disseminated through social institutions, such as factories and workplaces, the media, banks and retail outlets, health and welfare services, schools and universities, churches, and leisure and community organizations. These discourses penetrate deep into family life and personal relationships, regulating behaviour by locating individuals in a network of obligations towards themselves and others. Simultaneously, a 'felt' responsibility for a particular locality or an imagined community is produced (Rose, 1996), whereby identity is affirmed. Examples of this process can be identified in the commitments to promoting social capital of the Blair/Brown Labour administrations or the Big Society idea of the Cameron/Clegg coalition government. Citizenship is avowed by participating in consumer-based activities and the maintenance of an accredited lifestyle (Miller, 1993). The process has been described as an 'ethic of the self' (Davidson, 1994) and is supported by an ever increasing array of experts embedded in a range of social systems, such as physicians, health professionals, social workers, beauticians, personal trainers and financial advisers (Rose, 1999).

Parallel to this process, the state is concerned with gathering statistics that help define the population and maintain a level of surveillance that affords the management of risk. Affluent older persons are identified, measured and then grouped with similar persons. Once described, the characteristics of this group are disseminated via a range of media that suggest personality, aspirations and life chances. Similarly, older people requiring support – the physically infirm, cognitively impaired, widowed and so on – are identified, measured, grouped and their characteristics disseminated. For most individuals, the level of surveillance is best described as a light touch sufficient to maintain the disciplinary focus of the state in a way that is both fleeting and total (Rose and Miller, 1992; Rose, 1996, 1999; Turner, 1997; Knowles, 2001). However, for those whose behaviour is thought to be high risk or for those who fail to conform to the notion of the self-managing consumer-citizen, this surveillance is more oppressive, leaving them vulnerable to victim-blaming (Osborne, 1997). This produces the three trajectories referred to earlier, where those individuals who are willing and able to commit to the market and to self-manage experience a particular combination of options and opportunities, while those who fail to meet this commitment, for whatever reason, experience a different and more limited set of options that are often oppressive and impersonal (Rose, 1996, 1999; Petersen, 1997; Gilleard and Higgs, 2005). The consequence of this for the 'government of government' (cf. Foucault, 1977) is that its role is clearly circumscribed. It must set out to ensure that basic freedoms are respected, but acknowledge the importance of the family and the market for the management of the care of older people.

Social policy: constructing the context

We can now explore how policy constructs what might be described as the social context of older people: how older people are identified and separated first from each other ('affluent' versus 'frail and dependent') and then from the rest of the population. Consequentially, they are then targeted by specific policies, which, in turn, construct practices and services for this section of the population. For older people, the policy initiative that had the greatest impact was the introduction of state pensions by the Old Age Pensions Act 1908 (Phillipson, 1998), which provided £31.50 a year for those over 70. Although it was means-tested, it did prevent people aged 70 or older having to seek refuge in the workhouse, and paved the way for a pension system based on the insurance principle, following on from the passing of the National Insurance Act 1911. In a sense, the limitations of the scheme were not so important as the beginnings of the break with liberalism and the symbolic move towards the provision of more state support for older people, which supplanted punitive measures. This was further reinforced by the introduction of the welfare state in 1945 and the idea of citizenship based on a set of social as well as political and legal rights (Marshall, 1950), which meant that people no longer had to rely on a myriad of local charitable organizations, the churches and the Poor Law. In the process, this led to an expansion of state-provided services, many of which were managed by local authority departments.

Analysing the impact of neoliberalism from different perspectives, both Giddens (1998) and Beck (2005) have claimed that citizens and the state are faced with the task of navigating themselves through a changing world in which globalization has transformed personal relations and the relationship between state and the individual. Since 1979, both Conservative and Labour governments have adopted a neoliberal stance characterized by an increasing distancing of the state from the direct provision of services. Instead, government operates through a set of relationships where the state sets standards and budgets for particular services but then contracts delivery to private, voluntary or third sector organizations. The underpinning rationale is that this reconfiguration of the state retains a strong core to formulate public policy alongside the dissemination of responsibility for policy implementation to a wide range of often localized modes such as social work and social workers. Neoliberal governance emphasizes enterprise as an individual and corporate strategy, supported by its concomitant discourse of marketization and the role of consumers. The strategy increasingly relies on individuals to make their own arrangements with respect to welfare and support, accompanied by the rhetoric of choice, self-management, responsibility and obligation (Jordan, 2005) – even where public money is used to pay for services.

Neoliberalism in the twenty-first century is perhaps the dominant contemporary means through which boundary adjustments are being made and rationalized, with far-reaching consequences for both states and markets. The project of neoliberalism is evolving and changing, while the task of mapping out the moving terrain of boundaries for social work and older people's experiences, although long overdue, is only just beginning. In this context, the territorial state defined by geographical space is not so much withering away as being increasingly enmeshed in webs of economic interdependencies, social connections and political power. This, in turn, leads to the development of a denser and more complex set of virtual, economic, cultural and political spaces that cut across traditional distinctions between inside and outside, public and private, left and right (Beck, 2005). In this sense, possibly the most influential piece of contemporary neoliberal social policy came with the implementation of the National Health Service and Community Care Act 1990. This brought with it the purchaser/provider split and case management, and laid the foundations for subsequent policy initiatives, such as the cash for care schemes (direct payments and individual budgets) that provide the core of the 'personalization agenda'. Much of this is inspired by global developments in the way care is funded (Powell and Gilbert, 2011).

In the second decade of the twenty-first century, we have entered an accelerated phase of retraction by the UK state in relation to its role in the provision of welfare, with actual levels of support being reduced. Rhetorically, the Conservative/Liberal Democrat coalition is committed to the idea of the Big Society, which translates into a vision of individuals and communities coming together to work to resolve common concerns, as this Cabinet Office (2010) statement confirms:

> We want to give citizens, communities and local government the power and information they need to come together, solve the problems they face and build the Britain they want. We want society – the families, networks, neighbourhoods and communities that form the fabric of so much of our everyday lives – to be bigger and stronger than ever before. Only when people and communities are given more power and take more responsibility can we achieve fairness and opportunity for all.

This 'felt responsibility' for a particular locality or 'imagined community' is core to the neoliberal project, which, alongside active citizenship, provides the discursive structure for volunteering and the promotion of a network of voluntary activity. In the process, the disciplinary effect of the self-managing individual is reproduced at neighbourhood and community levels. The third sector is crucial in such a scenario, playing a key role by interconnecting a new partnership between government and civil society. Promoting this relationship is core to the functions of the new Office of Civil Society established by the coalition government in 2010, whose role is to enable people to develop social enterprises, voluntary and charitable organizations while promoting the independence and resilience of the sector.

Evidence of public intervention to support the renewal of community through local initiatives not only advances the status of professional social work organizations but fetishizes the day-to-day operations of social work. Equality, mutual respect, autonomy and decision-making through communication with socially disadvantaged and/or dependent older people come to be seen as integral to the sector and provide an opportunity to encourage socially excluded groups and communities to participate as active citizens in, rather than be seen as a potential burden to, community engagement (Gilleard and Higgs, 2005). Neoliberalism is especially concerned with inculcating a new set of values and objectives oriented towards incorporating citizens as both players and partners in a marketized system. As such, social workers are exhorted to become entrepreneurs in all spheres and to accept responsibility for the management of civic life (Beck, 2005). There is also an apparent dispersal of power (Foucault, 1977) achieved through establishing structures in which social workers and older people are coopted into or co-produce governance through their own accountable choices (Gilbert and Powell, 2010).

As Burchell (1993) has observed, this is directly connected with the political rationality that assigns primacy to the 'autonomization' of society, in which the paradigm of the enterprise culture comes to dominate forms of conduct including that of social work with older people. The very significance of autonomization is that there is a strategic aim to diffuse the public sector's monolithic power to encourage diversity and fragmentation of provision of care to private and voluntary sectors. Such a strategy constitutes a fundamental transformation in the mechanisms for governing social life. It has combined two interlinked developments: a stress on the necessity for enterprising subjects and the resolution of central state control with older people articulates with a desire to promote organizational social work autonomy through service provision. Each of these has redefined previous patterns of social relationships within and between those agencies and their clients.

The important point to note is that there is great contingence and variation in such relationships, with unevenness across time and space. These relationships involve the development of new forms of statecraft – some concerned with extensions of the neoliberal market-building project itself, for example trade policy and financial regulation, and some concerned with managing the consequences and contradictions of marketization, for example social policy. It also implies that the boundaries of the state and the market are blurred and constantly being renegotiated (Kendall, 2003). Theoretically, we identify the need to engage with key social debates about the future of welfare and individual relationships to and expectations of the state. One of the central debates has been on neoliberalism and its impingement on the repositioning of older people and the collective organization of modern society.

Integrating services: social policy and older people

Previous sections have sought to identify the changing relationship between the state and older people by exploring the notion of governmentality. The discussion now moves on to consider more specifically how social policy shapes the social context for older people. Here we need to take account of the social and economic backdrop that frames older people's experiences of support and care. In the process, we identify key developments in social policy such as personalization, risk and safeguarding, and their congruence with the neoliberal project. The neoliberal project constructs as its core subject the self-managing citizen-consumer who is actively making choices within markets. In the context of welfare, this involves individuals making choices about the type of support they want and who will provide that support as the range of providers is expanded in two broad ways. First, new providers enter the market providing new services or providing services in new ways. Second, and of key importance, people seeking support move outside the segregated confines of welfare services to obtain services from mainstream providers (Dickinson and Glasby, 2010). Such innovative moves may include, for example, a physical exercise programme from a sports centre instead of physiotherapy, an art course instead of time at a day centre, a holiday abroad instead of respite care.

In many ways, the 'personalization agenda', as it is set out in *Putting People First* (DH, 2007), represents the high point of the neoliberal project with respect to welfare. This approach is largely constructed through a framework of earlier policy, which includes the Community Care (Direct Payments) Act 1996, *Independence, Wellbeing and Choice* (DH, 2005) and *Our Health, Our Care, Our Say* (DH, 2006). This was then supplemented by the coalition government with the publication of *Capable Communities and Active Citizens* (DH, 2010) and *Think Local, Act Personal* (DH, 2011), which aim to tie the shift to self-directed support outlined by the personalization agenda more closely to the notion of the Big Society. The discourses articulated within this policy framework are those familiar to neoliberalism: independence, choice, freedom, responsibility, quality, empowerment, active citizenship, partnership, the enabling state, co-production and community action.

Alongside this policy framework are constructed a number of specific techniques that target individuals, families and communities. These include an alternative method of allocating cash to individuals in the form of individual budgets, online self-assessment to augment local authority assessment processes, and community-based advocacy to support lifestyle choices. In addition, commissioning models and approaches are being developed that aim to promote opportunities by responding proactively to the aspirations of people receiving services. Self-directed support is significant as it breaks with the tradition where state support is mediated by professionals who undertake assessments and organizations that are funded to provide places. Even in more recent times, when individuals might be afforded a choice between two or more places or opportunities, the organizations received funding from the state. Under personalization, assessment takes place to identify the overall budget a person is entitled to receive, but the money is allocated to the individual either through a direct payment or by establishing an individual budget. In terms of governmentality, the personalization agenda effectively shifts the responsibility for organizing support from the state to the individual needing support via a form of cash transfer – described by Ferguson (2007) as the 'privatization of risk'.

The advance of the personalization agenda has drawn support from a number of sources including specific groups of service users (Glendinning et al., 2008), politicians from across the spectrum (Ferguson, 2007), and social care managers and social workers (Samuel, 2009). One possible reason for this is that personalization is conceptually ambiguous, making it difficult to disagree with its basic premise while it retains a number of contradictory ideas (Ferguson, 2007). However, it has also drawn criticisms particularly from older people who have reported lower psychological wellbeing due, possibly, to added anxiety and stress brought on by the burden of organizing their own care (Glendinning et al., 2008). There are also concerns expressed regarding the impact of personalization on the integration and stability of adult social care; this includes unease with the emphasis on individualistic solutions that may undermine democratic and collective approaches to transforming existing services or developing new services (Newman et al., 2008). Doubts have also been expressed over the readiness of the third sector to take on the demands of providing support. At the same time, while the disaggregation of budgets might suit some small, innovative niche organizations, the disruption of funding streams may be perceived as a threat and bring instability to larger, more mainstream third sector organizations (Dickinson and Glasby, 2010). Other issues arise due to the somewhat fragmented process of implementation and the differences that occur in service provision between urban and rural areas (Manthorpe and Stevens, 2010). Ferguson (2007), drawing on the Canadian experience, suggests that personalization favours the better educated, may provide a cover for cost-cutting and further privatization and marketization of services, while the employment conditions of personal assistants may give rise to concern.

Governmentality enables the identification of the parallel concerns of neoliberalism – the promotion of the self-managing individual and the management of risk. So far we have explored self-management in social care through the promotion of self-directed care as part of the personalization agenda. We now turn to the management of risk. This can be seen to take two forms, each dealt with by different elements of social policy. Protection from the risks posed by others are managed through safeguarding and policy, such as *No Secrets* (DH/HO, 2000) in England and Northern Ireland and *In Safe Hands* in Wales (National Assembly for Wales/Home Office, 2000). In *Capable Communities and Active Citizens* (DH, 2010), the government clearly states that safeguarding is central to personalization. Risks posed by the individual to their own person are contained by the Mental Capacity Act 2005 and its powers to override individual choice or replace autonomy by measures such as enduring or lasting powers of attorney or the Court of Protection.

No Secrets has provided the basis of policy towards safeguarding for over a decade. It defined abuse in the context of an abuse of trust and the Human Rights Act 1998, and set out a model for interagency working that has been adopted by local authorities in England and Northern Ireland. In Wales, the corresponding policy is *In Safe Hands*. *No Secrets* drew from experience in relation to safeguarding children and described a number of categories of abuse, including physical, sexual, neglect and financial abuse. However, it lacked the legal imperative to share information that is included in safeguarding children. Furthermore, the environment within which *No Secrets* operates has seen considerable change since implementation. One key change was the discursive shift from vulnerable adult to safeguarding that took account of the dangers of victim-blaming implied in the notion of vulnerable adults, while the concept of safeguarding suggests the focus should be on the environment within which people find themselves. However, this rhetorical shift has not removed abuse. A recent prevalence survey suggests levels of abuse of between 2.6% and 4%, depending on how the estimates are constructed (O'Keeffe et al., 2007). Action on Elder

Abuse, one of the organizations that sponsored the study, uses evidence of underreporting to reinterpret this estimate as 9% (Gary Fitzgerald, personal communication).

In 2008, the Department of Health set up a consultation over the review of *No Secrets*, where a number of organizations, including the Association of Directors of Adult Social Care and Action on Elder Abuse, campaigned for a legislative framework to put adult protection on the same footing as child protection (Samuel, 2008). However, no significant changes in guidance or legal status occurred, as the coalition government maintained that safeguarding was an issue for local communities, thus maintaining the distance between the state and individuals. Discourses of safeguarding operate and produce their effects via the multiple interactions of institutions embedded in local communities. Furthermore, the advent of personalization has seen an increasing focus on financial abuse as direct payments and rules about eligibility for state support for care costs increase the opportunities for financial exploitation, fraud and theft. *No Secrets* treats financial abuse as an artefact of other, apparently more serious forms of abuse. However, in 2004, the House of Commons Select Committee identified financial abuse as possibly the second most commonly occurring form of abuse experienced by older people. Estimates in the USA suggest that financial abuse is the most common form of abuse, with up to 40% of older people victims (Gorbien, 2011).

In conclusion

This chapter has explored the place that social policy plays in shaping the social context of older people. To achieve this, we have drawn on the concept of governmentality to identify how neoliberal forms of government construct older people as active consumers within welfare markets, shifting the responsibility for organizing support from the state to the individual. The contemporary context for working with older people who need some form of support is formed by the relationship between personalization and safeguarding. These set out the twin pillars of neoliberal governance, namely self-management through self-directed support and the management of risk through safeguarding. Individuals are constructed as citizen-consumers actively making choices about what their needs are and identifying appropriate services, sometimes with the support of advocates or workers, such as social workers, in a process of co-production. In circumstances where risks are considered too high, the power to make choices can be temporarily or permanently restricted.

Further reading

■ Gardner, A. (2011) *Personalization in Social Work*. London: Sage.

Gives a clear understanding of competent practice within a personalization context and aims to encourage students to explore the major tensions, dilemmas and themes emerging within the personalization agenda.

■ Hunter, S. and Ritchie, S. (eds) (2007) *Co-production and Personalization in Social Care: Changing Relationships in the Provision of Social Care.* London: Jessica Kingsley.

Explores co-production as a model of practice in which service providers work with service users in the provision of social care services; examples are given, including housing initiatives where the users provide support to each other.

■ Sanderson, H. and Lewis, J. (2011) *A Practical Guide to Delivering Personalization: Person-centred Practice in Health and Social Care.* London: Jessica Kingsley.

Covers why person-centred practice is relevant to the personalization agenda and what person-centred thinking and person-centred reviews are, introducing the tools that can help the worker carry them out.

References

Alzheimer's Society (2011) *What is Dementia*, Factsheet 400, http://alzheimers.org.uk/site/scripts/documents_info.php?documentID=106.

Bayliss, J. and Sly, F. (2010) *Ageing Across the UK.* Newport: ONS.

Beck, U. (2005) *Power in the Global Age.* Cambridge: Polity Press.

Bigby, C. (2004) *Ageing with a Lifelong Disability.* London: Jessica Kingsley.

Burchell, G. (1993) 'Liberal government and techniques of the self', *Economy and Society*, **22**(3): 268–82.

Burholt, V. and Windle, G. (2006) *The Material Resources and Well-being of Older People.* York: Joseph Rowntree Foundation.

Cabinet Office (2010) *Building the Big Society*, www.cabinetoffice.gov.uk/news/building-big-society.

Davidson, A.I. (1994) 'Ethics as ascetics: Foucault, the history of ethics, and ancient thought', in G. Gutting (ed.) *The Cambridge Companion to Foucault.* Cambridge: Cambridge University Press.

DH (Department of Health) (2005) *Independence, Wellbeing and Choice: Our Vision for the Future of Social Care for Adults in England.* London: TSO.

DH (2006) *Our Health, Our Care, Our Say: A New Direction for Community Services.* London: TSO.

DH (2007) *Putting People First: Shared Vision and Commitment to the Transformation of Adult Social Care.* London: TSO.

DH (2010) *A Vision for Adult Social Care: Capable Communities and Active Citizens.* London: TSO.

DH (2011) *Think Local, Act Personal: A Sector Wide Commitment to Moving Forward with Personalization and Community Based Support.* London: TSO.

DH/Home Office (2000) *No Secrets: Guidance on Developing and Implementing Multi-agency Policies and Procedures to Protect Vulnerable Adults from Abuse.* London: TSO.

Dickinson, H. and Glasby, J. (2010) *The Personalization Agenda: Implications for the Third Sector*, working paper 30. Birmingham: Third Sector Research Centre.

Dominelli, L. (2004) *Theory and Practice for a Changing Profession.* Cambridge: Polity Press.

Policy

DWP (Department of Work and Pensions) (2005) *Older People in Low-income Households*. London: TSO.

Estes, C. (1979) *The Aging Enterprise*. San Francisco: Jossey Bass.

Ferguson, I. (2007) 'Increasing user choice or privatizing risk? The antinomies of personalization', *British Journal of Social Work,* **37**(3): 387–403.

Foucault, M. (1977) *Discipline and Punish*. London: Allen Lane.

Foucault, M. (1991) 'Governmentality', in G. Burchell, C. Gordon and P. Miller (eds) *The Foucault Effect: Studies in Governmentality*. Hemel Hampstead: Harvester Wheatsheaf.

Giddens, A. (1998) *The Third Way: The Renewal of Social Democracy*. Cambridge: Polity Press.

Gilbert, T. and Powell, J.L. (2010) 'Power and social work in the United Kingdom: a Foucauldian excursion', *Journal of Social Work,* **10**(1): 3–22.

Gilleard, C. and Higgs, P. (2005) *Contexts of Ageing: Class, Cohort and Community*. Cambridge: Polity Press.

Glendinning, C., Challis, D., Fernandez, J. et al. (2008) *The National Evaluation of the Individual Budgets Pilot Programme: Experiences and Implications for Care Coordinators and Managers. Research Findings*. York: Social Policy Research Unit.

Goldfield, T. (2005) *Wealth of the Nation 2005*. Brighton: CACI.

Gorbien, M. (2011) *Protecting Against Fraud and Financial Abuse*. Chicago, IL: Rush University Medical Center.

Hoff, A. (2008) *Tackling Social Exclusion of Older People: Lessons from Europe*, working paper 308. Oxford: Oxford Institute of Ageing/University of Oxford.

House of Commons Health Select Committee (2004) *Elder Abuse*, Second Report of Session 2003–4, vol. 1. London: TSO.

Hughes, B. and Mtejuka, E.M. (1992) 'Social work and older women', in M. Langan and L. Day (eds) *Women, Oppression and Social Work: Issues in Anti-discriminatory Practice*. London: Routledge.

Johnson, N. (1999) 'The personal social services and community care', in M. Powell (ed.) *New Labour, New Welfare? The 'Third Way' in British Social Policy*. Bristol: Policy Press.

Jordan, B. (2005) 'New Labour: choice and values', *Critical Social Policy,* **25**(4): 427–46 .

Kemshall, H. (2002) *Risk, Social Policy and Welfare*. Buckingham: Open University Press.

Kendall, J. (2003) *The Voluntary Sector: Comparative Perspectives in the UK*. London: Routledge.

Kerr, B., Gordon, J., MacDonald, C. and Stalker, K. (2005) *Effective Social Work with Older People*, paper prepared for the Scottish Executive. Stirling: Social Work Research Unit, University of Stirling.

Knowles, C. (2001) 'Cultural perspectives and welfare regimes: the contributions of Foucault and Lefebve', in P. Chamberlayne, A. Cooper and M. Rustin (eds) *Welfare and Culture in Europe: Towards a New Paradigm in Social Policy*. London: Jessica Kingsley.

Kuh, D. and Shlomo, B.Y. (2004) *A Life Course Approach to Chronic Disease Epidemiology*. Oxford: Oxford University Press.

MacDonald, C. (2004) *Older People and Community Care in Scotland: A Review of Recent Research*. Edinburgh: TSO.

Manthorpe, J. and Stevens, M. (2010) 'Understanding the potential impact of personalization for social work with rural older people', *British Journal of Social Work,* **40**(5): 1452–69.

Marshall, T.H. (1950) *Citizenship and Social Class and Other Essays*. Cambridge: Cambridge University Press.

Miller, T. (1993) *The Well-tempered Self: Citizenship, Culture and the Postmodern Subject*. Baltimore: Johns Hopkins University Press.

National Assembly for Wales/Home Office (2000) *In Safe Hands: Implementing Adult Protection Procedures in Wales*. Cardiff: National Assembly for Wales.

Newman, J., Glendinning, C. and Hughes, M. (2008) 'Beyond modernisation? Social care and the transformation of welfare governance', *Journal of Social Policy*, **37**(4): 531–57.

O'Keeffe, M., Hills, A., Doyle, M. et al. (2007) *UK Study of Abuse and Neglect of Older People: Prevalence Survey Report*, for Comic Relief/DH. London: National Centre for Social Research/King's College London.

Osborne, T. (1997) 'Of health and statecraft', in A. Petersen and R. Bunton (eds) *Foucault: Health and Medicine*. London: Routledge.

Petersen, A. (1997) 'Risk, governance and the new public health', in A. Petersen and R. Bunton (eds) *Foucault: Health and Medicine*. London: Routledge.

Phillipson, C. (1982) *Capitalism and the Construction of Old Age*. Basingstoke: Macmillan.

Phillipson, C. (1998) *Reconstructing Old Age: New Agendas in Social Theory and Practice*. London: Sage.

Phillipson, C. (2008) 'The frailty of old age', in M. Davies (ed.) *The Blackwell Companion to Social Work* (3rd edn). Oxford: Blackwell Publishing.

Philp, I. (2008) 'Late life ageing', in M. Davies (ed.) *The Blackwell Companion to Social Work* (3rd edn). Oxford: Blackwell Publishing.

Poll, C. and Duffy, S. (eds) (2008) *Report of In Control's Second Phase 2005–2007*. London: In Control Publications.

Powell, J.L. and Gilbert, T. (2011) 'Personalization and sustainable care', *Journal of Care Services Management*, **5**(2): 79–86.

Rose, N. (1996) 'The death of the social? Re-figuring the territory of government', *Economy and Society*, **25**(3): 327–56.

Rose, N. (1999) *Powers of Freedom: Reframing Political Thought*. Cambridge: Cambridge University Press.

Rose, N. and Miller, P. (1992) 'Political power beyond the state: problematics of government', *British Journal of Sociology*, **43**(2): 173–205.

Samuel, M. (2008) '*No Secrets* review: the key issues', *Community Care*, 20 February.

Samuel, M. (2009) 'Practitioners back personalization but call for more support', *Community Care*, 18 March.

Thompson, N. (2001) *Anti-oppressive Social Work Practice*. Basingstoke: Palgrave – now Palgrave Macmillan.

Turner, B.S. (1997) 'From governmentality to risk: some reflections on Foucault's contribution to medical sociology', in A. Petersen and R. Bunton (eds) *Foucault: Health and Medicine*. London: Routledge.

Walker, A. and Walker, C. (eds) (1997) *Britain Divided*. London: CPAG.

Policy

17

The legal foundations and requirements for social work with older people

Ann McDonald

Within the legal system of England and Wales, there is no body of law separately identifiable as relating exclusively to older people. Old age, unlike childhood, has no separate legal status; although age thresholds may act as a gateway to welfare benefits, or as a barrier to remaining in employment, older people generally have no greater call on public services or public protection than other adults. This has both an advantage and a disadvantage. The advantage is that older people have the freedom to reject paternalistic involvement from concerned others, relying on their status as capacitated adults. The disadvantage is that legal powers and duties in relation to older people are often ill-defined, and securing rights for older people may be a contentious issue.

This chapter explores the ways in which aspects of the law influence or affect what social workers do or should do. For social workers in statutory services, the law prescribes the responsibilities of agencies; for example, the boundaries between health and social care, the process by which eligibility is determined, and the financial contributions that individuals have to make for the services they receive. The context within which service provision has been developed has changed since 1945 from a postwar universalist welfare state model, through the era of community care and care management in the 1990s, to a recent retraction of direct provision, and the development of the personalization agenda. Throughout this period, the core legal framework for working with older people has remained intact, although the roles and tasks of social work may have changed according to new policy initiatives. This has meant that social workers have been working within a sometimes anachronistic legal framework where the value base is poorly articulated; as a consequence, dissonances are experienced between the legal categories that are available to conceptualize issues for older people and the aspirations of older people themselves for a framework that supports choice and dignity across the life course.

The persistence of stereotypes, by which the law constructs the needs of older people who use services as passive and vulnerable, is at odds with an alternative construction of the legal status of older citizens as active citizens and bearers of rights. Social work practice with older people must acknowledge both the diversity of older people in terms of their individual and cultural needs, and the power of older people collectively to influence service development to meet the changing aspirations of a demographically significant group. The piecemeal development of the law relating to older people has meant that the legal framework has lacked coherence, has not responded consistently to the concerns of older people, and has not provided a principled body of law to guide ethical practice. Because the law defines the roles and tasks of social work, and because the law provides an authoritative means of resolving professional dilemmas, it is important that the legal framework for working with older people is clear, progressive and not unduly complex to apply in practice.

Older people have a range of legal needs

One difficulty in applying the law to older people is that older people themselves may not recognize that the concerns they may have are subject to legal definition or legal solutions. Genn (1999) and Pleasence et al. (2004) have conducted research into the public identification of 'justiciable issues'. They found that problems with employment, family relationships, housing and financial matters were often seen as 'personal problems' rather than issues that could also be resolved through legal intervention. A combination of two or more of these problems was often encountered, and served to make difficulties more entrenched. Social workers' integrated knowledge of personal and relationship issues, and their awareness of available services, means that they are particularly well placed to offer a range of solutions, including legal solutions, to problems of ill health, inadequate accommodation and financial difficulties. Pleasence et al. (2004) also found that referring people on for further advice from other sources was not effective unless support was given to assist individuals in accessing that advice. Again, social workers are strategically well placed within professional networks to assist older people in accessing further specialist advice that will see the resolution of problems through to a satisfactory conclusion. The internal structuring of agencies and the methods of intervention that social workers enjoy are, however, critical in facilitating this process of informing and progressing legal issues. Frontline staff need to be able to do more than signpost inquirers to further sources of assistance, and task-centred methods of intervention need to be sufficiently long term to enable outcomes to be monitored and evaluated. Service design is thus important to the realization of legal rights of citizenship by older people. Process issues, for example how approaches for assistance are recorded, allocated for assessment or redirected, and how decisions are communicated, are also critical for the meeting of 'due process' requirements, which involve people determining and refining how their concerns are to be met, while protecting the agency from challenges of maladministration.

Within social care, in-house provision of key services, such as domiciliary care and residential accommodation, is now a rarity, except for highly specialist, often short-term provision. The purchaser/provider split, whereby services are commissioned from private, voluntary and independent sector providers, is well established. This process in itself raises issues that are, in essence, legal issues: the terms on which contracts for service are established; whether third parties, including the end user of such services, are parties to the contract with legal standing; how breaches of contract are to be adjudicated; and how price and quality are to be fixed. Access to statutory social services is regulated by guidance that prioritizes eligibility for services in terms of critical, substantial, moderate and low levels of loss of function and subsequent risks to independence (DH, 2010a). Although case law (*R* v *Gloucestershire CC ex parte Barry* [1997]) emphasizes that resource constraints have to be balanced against the needs and benefits within an individual assessment, and the *Fair Access to Care Services* guidance (DH, 2003) emphasizes the value of prevention and the importance of choice, the majority of local authorities locate eligibility for services at critical and substantial levels of need. This means that significant numbers of people are outside the eligibility criteria, and are at risk of making ill-informed choices of private provision when they do not receive support for their decision-making. Increased affluence among older people also means that many are self-funding, and may give this reason for rejecting means-tested services for which they are otherwise eligible. Difficulties in meeting both health and social care needs are also problematic for older people (Care Quality Commission, 2009).

Alternatives to direct service provision through the use of direct payments and individual or personal budgets have been legal responses to changes in social policy, which have limited the role of the state to assessment and quality control functions. Direct payments, introduced by the Community Care (Direct Payments) Act 1996, enabled eligible individuals directly to purchase their own community care services (apart from residential care), subject to certain restrictions. Research has shown that older people were cautious about taking on the responsibilities of an employer, and were less enthusiastic about direct payments than younger people (Clark et al., 2004). Continuing restrictions on employing close family members to provide personal support (DH, 2009a) emphasize the false dichotomy that social policy has created between personal autonomy and support for carers. Individual budgets, which bring together different funding streams from social care, health, housing support and adaptations, are still at an early stage of development, but research by Manthorpe et al. (2009a) found that older people found the concept of an individual budget hard to understand, while concerns were also raised about safeguarding vulnerable individuals from exploitation (Manthorpe et al., 2009b). So, although older people are the largest group who use social care services, recent legal developments have extrapolated successful outcomes for younger disabled people to produce a general model of service provision, which, in its current form, does not necessarily match older people's wants and needs.

Access to healthcare

Contemporary developments within the NHS have reinforced the shift towards a primary care-led service, with a focus on public health and on action to reduce health inequalities (DH, 2010b). The core principles of the NHS are confirmed – it should be free at the point of use and available to everyone based on need. The strategic and symbolic importance of the NHS is located with 'the social solidarity of shared access to collective healthcare, and a shared responsibility to use resources effectively to deliver better health' (DH, 2010b, p. 7). Older people will have a particular interest in access to healthcare and in the equitable distribution of resources, both in relation to younger people's access to services and to compensate for accrued inequalities across the life course. Congruence between processes and policies across health and social care is also crucial to ensure that no gaps in provision are created by system change. Care pathway design and prescribing policies will also need to focus on 'autonomy, accountability and democratic legitimacy' (DH, 2010b, p. 4). A person-alized approach emphasizes partnership, coordination and the promotion of equalities at a local level, compared to the previous centralized approach of establish-ing National Service Frameworks to prescribe service developments.

The location of care

The location of care is a central issue for many older people. Housing policy was never properly integrated with the community care developments of the 1990s, but good quality, appropriate accommodation is critical to enable older people not only to remain within the community, but to have a base from which they can be involved in the life of the community around them. The development of housing with care schemes has tended to blur the distinction between property ownership and the receipt of support services, but the legal distinction between the provision of care and its location is critical when individuals are required to relocate to receive care, or choose to do so. Consequently, social workers need to be aware of the rights and obligations involved in property ownership or the possession of a tenancy, and to differentiate these legal situations from the less secure position of the resident in a care home, who simply has a licence to occupy. A key issue is to be aware of the circumstances in which the process of relocation can be either facilitated or challenged. In some cases, this will require knowledge of housing allocation and homelessness legislation to enforce the duties of public housing authorities towards people who occupy accommodation that is no longer suitable for their needs, or which is unsustainable following relationship break-down. The responsibility of the NHS to provide accommodation as well as treatment or care for those with a primary health need has been subject to interpretation both by the courts and in guidance (*R* v *North and East Devon Health Authority, ex parte Cough-lan* [2000]; DH, 2009b) and can shift the whole cost of the care from the individual to the state. Negotiating on the boundaries between health and social care and general housing provision will thus be a key social work task.

Law

Money matters

Sustaining what is seen as an adequate standard of living, as well as paying for specialist care services, is an issue of concern for older people. Pensions policy emphasizes a primary individual responsibility alongside a limited state responsibility for financial support in older age. The opportunity to work beyond an (increasing) pensionable age may become a matter of necessity rather than choice. Maximizing income, through knowledge of welfare benefits, is a task that the social worker may undertake within a service assessment framework. In terms of disclosing income and capital for paying for services, a financial assessment is a task that the local authority is required to take for the provision of residential accommodation (National Assistance Act 1948, s. 22) and may undertake for nonresidential services (Health and Social Services and Social Security Adjudications Act 1983, s. 17). Social workers may nevertheless be ambivalent about discussing financial matters within the context of a therapeutic or compulsory relationship, making this aspect of their work particularly challenging (Manthorpe and Bradley, 2002).

The functions that law is expected to perform in society

The history of service provision for older people has thus reflected a range of approaches to assessing and meeting need, which can be explained and understood in terms of legal theory, or in the functions that law is expected to perform in society. So, a welfarist approach to service provision for older people through direct state intervention is exemplified by statutes like the National Assistance Act 1948, which lays down a core duty on the local authority to provide residential accommodation for those 'in need of care and attention not otherwise available to them' (s. 21). The duty is owed primarily to those 'ordinarily resident' in the area of the local authority, an echo of the Poor Law provision of parish relief. The National Assistance Act, while subject to reinterpretation in the context of changed social conditions, is a good example of a piece of legislation that contains on its face a clear statement of eligibility and a prescription for formal action. It creates justiciable rights for those who pass the threshold of eligibility, and thus constrains the discretion of decision-makers who may further seek to ration services in the face of increasing demand from otherwise well-qualified applicants. This service-based approach is followed within section 2 of the Chronically Sick and Disabled Persons Act 1970, which contains a 'service list' of services, such as practical assistance in the home, aids and adaptations, the provision of recreational facilities and transport, which the local authority has a duty to provide. Although appearing to be 'service led', rather than needs led, such clarity provides an opportunity for potential service users to formulate their needs in such a way that the local authority's duty is triggered.

By comparison, section 47 of the National Health Service and Community Care Act 1990 (NHSCCA), which requires the local authority to conduct a needs assessment of any person who appears to them to be in need of community care services, is a procedural provision. Service provision is located within the terms of the pre-1990 legislation, described in the NHSCCA (s. 46(3)). When resources are scarce, procedural propriety is important to give individuals an equal opportunity to compete. Basic principles of administrative law apply, such as the right to:

- be assessed according to the criteria for assessment that the agency has published
- have all relevant matters (including medical evidence, for example) taken into account
- exclude irrelevant considerations, such as the ability to buy similar services independently of the assessing authority
- be given reasons for the decision reached.

Important though due process issues are, a rights-based approach to service provision regards them as no substitute for actual entitlement to a minimum standard of service as a right of citizenship.

Fundamental to an examination of a rights-based approach is a consideration of the impact of the Human Rights Act 1998 on the status and wellbeing of older people. Key articles of the European Convention on Human Rights are relevant to decision-making in respect of older people, for example Article 3, the right to freedom from inhuman and degrading treatment and punishment, and Article 8, respect for privacy and family life. But it is the *way* these rights are acknowledged and applied in decision-making that is critical, and this is an amalgam of practitioners' knowledge base, their agency's response to rights-based arguments, and a willingness proactively to champion the values upon which such rights are based. One impact of the personalization agenda on the conceptualization of legal issues has been to substitute an outcomes-based approach for a service-based approach when looking at ways in which the interests of older people can best be realized. For example, the desired outcome of re-establishing social links within a community could be achieved through a personal budget that enables an older person to visit their family locally and to take part in leisure pursuits, rather than a service-based approach that would assess eligibility for daycare services offered by or commissioned by the local authority.

Faced with these different ways of understanding and shaping the legal basis upon which social care services for adults (including older people) are delivered, the Law Commission has begun a review of the reform of adult care law. The Law Commission (2011) acknowledged the difficulties created by the absence of a coherent legal framework for adult social care: its proposed solution is a single statute containing an assessment duty, with focus on outcomes as the criteria for service eligibility, rather than suitability for a particular existing service. The approach taken is broadly a legal positivist stance: 'a neutral legal framework that is not wedded to any particular policy and is capable of accommodating different policies and practices in the future' (Law Commission, 2010, p. 1). The future direction and context of adult care law would thus be something for Parliament to decide. The Law Commission's (2011) proposed adult care statute would emphasize the procedural aspects of assess-

Law

ment, consultation with relevant others, the eligibility decision, and the formation of a care plan. Community care services would be defined broadly within the statute, and additional duties would be added to make inquiries and take appropriate action in relation to adults in need of safeguarding. Although the Law Commission (2010) considered that the guiding principles for decision-making should appear on the face of the statute, such principles, for example choice and control, person-centred planning and independent living, are framed in terms of guidance on the exercise of professional discretion, rather than legal rights (Law Commission, 2011). Such an approach gives a centrality to professional integrity in decision-making, but also assumes an ability to overcome organizational and structural obstacles to the promotion of such principles in practice – a balance that may be difficult to sustain in a climate of managerialism and limited resources (McDonald et al., 2008).

Assessment

How, in practice, do social workers act within the existing legal framework for working with older people, and what lessons can we learn from this when considering the preferred route that legal reform should take? Assessment is critical for ensuring that the needs and the individual circumstances of older people are identified, evaluated and responded to. Section 47 of the NHSCCA 1990 imposes a duty upon local authorities to carry out an assessment of an individual who may be in need of community care services. It is the appearance of need, rather than a request for assessment, that triggers the duty to assess. This assumes a proactive response to older people who are struggling with their current circumstances, those who are no longer able or willing to rely on family support, and those who are also undergoing some other sort of assessment relating, for example, to healthcare or housing. The Community Care Assessment Directions 2004 support good practice insofar as they require the assessor to consult with the person who is being assessed, consult with carers where this is thought to be appropriate, take all reasonable steps to reach agreement on the community care services that may be needed, and provide information on any relevant charges before services are delivered. The Department of Health's policy guidance *Prioritising Need in the Context of Putting People First: A Whole System Approach to Eligibility for Social Care* (DH, 2010a) emphasizes the centrality of the person seeking support to the process of assessment, but also clarifies that the statutory duty to assess remains with the local authority, and in particular that 'self-assessment does not negate a council's duty to carry out its own assessment' (para. 84). The extent to which resources can be taken into account when framing eligibility criteria has, however, been highly contentious in case law. In *R v Gloucestershire CC, ex parte Barry* [1997], the Court of Appeal held that resources cannot be the only factor that is taken into account; resources are part of a balancing act that also needs to take into account the benefit that an individual may derive from having a particular service. In particular, eligibility criteria cannot be set so high that a disabled person would be at severe physical risk if the service was not provided. Once it has been decided that services must be provided, they cannot be withdrawn without reassessment. The local authority was also required to comply with its disability equality duty under the Disability Discrimination Act 1995 (s. 49A; now part of the general public sector equality duty under s. 149 of the Equality Act 2010) when setting eligibility criteria. So, in *R* v *Birmingham CC, ex parte Killigrew* [2000], the decision to reduce domiciliary services from twelve hours to six hours was quashed, because reassessment had failed to show why services that had previously been delivered were no longer needed. However, in *R (McDonald)* v *Kensington and Chelsea RLBC* [2011], the Supreme Court upheld the substitution, at reassessment, of incontinence pads in lieu of assistance from a night-time carer for a disabled person, on the grounds that this was an acceptable way of meeting a physical need, although arguably not a social need. How a need is framed, whether in medical or social terms, may therefore be critical to the type of service that may lawfully be provided.

Assessment is thus a process for which social workers are legally accountable, and in working with older people, there may be advantages in looking beyond the category of older age, and stressing the disabling social consequences of an enduring functional impairment. Similarly, when dealing with mental health issues in older age, the absence of specialist provision, such as eligibility under the care programme approach, should not prevent an assessment under the NHSCCA (s. 47) for a wider range of community care services (*R (HP and KP)* v *Islington London Borough Council* [2004]). 'Older age' may not be the most relevant legal category upon which to base the assessment. Certainly, in terms of service provision, section 45 of the Health Services and Public Health Act 1968, which contains a power (but not a duty) to provide social work support, practical assistance and adaptations in the home, meals and recreation, and travel assistance for older people, is a less comprehensive piece of legislation than the Chronically Sick and Disabled Persons Act 1970, which contains all these services, and more, but expresses them in terms of a duty. In addition, the duty to provide residential accommodation under section 21 of the National Assistance Act 1948 is owed to those who are in need of care and attention by reason of illness, disability or 'any other circumstances', as well as by reason of age. The aftercare duty under section 117 of the Mental Health Act 1983 is also applied regardless of age, although it may be particularly relevant when older people detained for treatment under section 3 are discharged to residential care, as no charge for services can be imposed if the placement is made under section 117 (*R* v *Manchester City Council, ex parte Stennett* [2002]).

The legal provisions under which services can be provided

Identifying the legal provisions under which services can be provided can make a crucial difference to older people, especially in times of transition and at the end of life. Key boundaries define the respective responsibilities of health and social care at the time of hospital discharge (set out in the Community Care (Delayed Discharges) Act 2003), when intermediate care is used for 'reablement', and when continuing NHS care in hospital or in the community is being considered. Again, procedural as well as substantive aspects of care planning are important to ensure that social workers are appropriately involved in multidisciplinary assessments. Social workers may be involved for their counselling skills when dealing with bereavement and loss, but guidance through practical arrangements and advice on dealing with financial issues are equally valued (Beresford et al., 2007). Safeguarding, in its widest sense of enabling people to keep themselves safe, and being aware of the range of legal interventions to respond to abuse, is a key social work task under *No Secrets* (DH/HO, 2000). Following legal intervention, which can include the provision of services or relocation or injunctive relief, it is important that continuing support is offered to enable people to make sense of their new circumstances and to deal with feelings of anger, regret and betrayal that may be present (Pritchard, 2008). Responding to older people in transition thus engages a range of social work skills, located in a knowledge of the psychosocial impact of the changes that legal provisions have facilitated.

Having a facility in the use of legal concepts

A facility in the use of legal concepts is thus a core attribute of social work practice with older people. The law defines opportunities for older people to change their personal, social and financial position through the creation of legal categories such as 'user of community care services', 'patient', 'vulnerable adult', or 'testator'. Interprofessional work with lawyers can focus social workers' awareness of the law as an enabling mechanism. There are, however, differences between the allegiances of lawyers and social workers in working with individuals; the lawyer's professional duty is to act solely as an advocate for their client, whereas the social worker may, in many cases, have a wider responsibility to also consider the interests and wellbeing of other family members, or indeed other members of the community (McDonald and Taylor, 1995). So social workers may need to integrate the views of family carers with those of the older person, making each aware of the rights they have, or they may have to undertake risk assessments that balance the protection of the public against the interests of older people suffering from mental disorder. Being explicit about the legal powers they have, informing individuals of their rights, and stating how and when formal decisions may be challenged are important elements of good social work practice, but are dependent on the possession of adequate legal knowledge.

The use of discretion

Making legally defensible decisions is crucial, but the application of legal knowledge to decision-making is not a straightforward linear process. Other elements intervene to affect social work decision-making. An important element is the amount of discretion that the law gives to decision-makers, particularly those carrying out professional tasks. So, a social worker's decisions about who is a person 'in need', whether an older person is suffering from mental disorder of a 'nature or degree' that warrants their admission to hospital, or whether it is in their 'best interests' to pay for domestic assistance will be influenced by the social worker's own experience and value

> **Making connexions**
>
> In the absence of a coherent legal framework, what role do social workers play in the implementation of government policy in their work with older people?

base and by the pressures on the agency within which they are operating. Lipsky (1980) identified social workers, among other professionals, as 'street-level bureaucrats', who have the ability to create policy out of the individual decisions that they are required to take on a day-to-day basis. This may, however, overstate the extent to which social workers in a contemporary context are able to act autonomously. Managerialist approaches to decision-making have structured and curtailed professional discretion by prescribing processes, setting targets and limiting choice (Evans and Harris, 2004). The constraints of such a working environment have had the effect of compromising the ability of social workers to retain and refresh the range of knowledge (including legal knowledge) they have acquired through training (McDonald et al., 2008). Pressure from other organizations, with their own legal mandate, may also be difficult to resist, if policies have not been created at an organizational level to deal with potential conflicts, for example the rights of people with dementia to remain in their own home when housing authorities are instituting proceedings for eviction, or the responsibility for older people who are not ordinarily resident in the area who are facing discharge from hospital following a crisis admission. At a practitioner level, the focus on short-term, task-centred work as a method of intervention can prevent necessary long-term planning, for example with people whose mental capacity is declining; this may mean that adequate preparation cannot take place to identify potential new sources of support, to enable substitute decision-making to take place through the creation of lasting powers of attorney, and to document the expressed wishes and feelings of older people to guide decision-making in the future.

The future development of the legal agenda

When looking to the future development of social work with older people, legal agendas will continue to play a significant part in defining social work roles and tasks, although the form and content of these agendas will introduce some radical changes. As the personalization agenda develops, and money or money's worth substitutes for directly commissioned services, social work is destined to move in a more facilitative direction, which emphasizes the service brokerage role. Freedom from a preoccupation with the intricacies of care management should enable qualified staff to focus their skills on 'personal law' (Bridgeman et al., 2008), offering support to older people and their families in dealing with relationships, decision-making about the location of support to pursue lifestyle choices, and financial planning. Embedded within this role will be a concern with safeguarding, and the monitoring of mental capacity and mental health to ensure that decision-making is facilitated and supported to the greatest extent possible, before compulsory legal intervention is contemplated. This move from short-term crisis work to facilitation and support works to different legal agendas, which in turn require a radical amendment of the legal framework for working with older people.

Accordingly, in response to the development of a personalized approach to service delivery, the Law Commission (2011) has also proposed a simplification and reconfiguration of adult social care law within its proposed adult social care statute. The statute proposes a broad framework within which the tasks of assessment, determination of eligibility and care planning will take place, with a less prescriptive and more outcomes-based focus on the types of service that may be provided. This is a welcome move away from stereotyping the sorts of services from which older people may choose. Safeguarding would also be placed on a statutory basis. The statutory framework would be supported by a number of principles, including support for independent living, acknowledgement of a broad range of needs beyond conventional social care needs, and a positive approach to dignity in care. It is proposed that regulations should specify who should be consulted during the assessment process, which areas of concern should be addressed, and the form that care planning should take. The duty to meet eligible needs would be individually enforceable. There is something here of a paradigm shift towards due process and transparency in decision-making within a national, portable assessment framework. This will be a challenge to agencies and individual social workers to make decisions that are legally defensible and professionally sound.

The implementation of the Equality Act 2010 will also fundamentally affect the legal position of older people. Separate statutory protection against discrimination on the basis of gender, disability or race is being replaced by a legal regime that recognizes the interlocking nature of oppressions and also extends (from 2012) that protection to discrimination based on age. Although the Human Rights Act 1998 has not prevented discrimination by private providers and, as interpreted in the McDonald case (above), has not set a high threshold for respecting the dignity of older people, research has shown that the potential of the Act for embedding principles of respect, protection and fairness into public decision-making is congruent with the values that older people themselves support (EHRC, 2009). A legal framework that constructs older people as bearers of rights is thus being created through statutory change. This should lead to greater clarity in the responsibility of agencies to respond to older people as citizens when allocating resources or contemplating policy change. The growing consumer power of older people as a demographic group will also be a potent force, influencing service providers to design services that are responsive, flexible and inclusive of older people. Through these changes, a shift from a dependency model to a rights-based focus for social work with older people can be created, which is both ethical and professionally sound.

Appendix 17.1 Table of cases

R v Birmingham CC, ex parte Killigrew (2000) 3 CCLR 109

R v Gloucestershire CC, ex parte Barry [1997] 2 All ER 1

R (HP and KP) v Islington London Borough Council [2004] EWHC 7 (Admin)

R v North and East Devon Health Authority, ex parte Coughlan [2000] 3 All ER 850

R (McDonald) v Kensington and Chelsea RLBC [2011] UKSC 33
R v Manchester City Council, ex parte Stennett [2002] UKHL 34

Further reading

■ Clements, L. and Thompson, P. (2011) *Community Care and the Law* (5th edn). London: Legal Action Group.

Leading contemporary text on community care law and comprehensive reference book, addressing issues that concern older people as well as other user groups within adult social care.

■ Herring, J. (2009) *Older People in Law and Society*. Oxford: Oxford University Press.

Written by a lawyer, this specialist legal text explores the importance of a legal approach to older age in the context of social gerontology; particularly strong on the topics of consent and mental capacity, but also covers inheritance, grandparenthood, elder abuse and financial issues.

■ McDonald, A. and Taylor, M. (2006) *Older People and the Law*. Bristol: Policy Press.

Written from the practice base of social work and the experience of a specialist lawyer in work with older people.

References

Beresford, P., Adshead, L. and Craft, S. (2007) *Palliative Care, Social Work and Service Users: Making Life Possible*. London: Jessica Kingsley.

Bridgeman, J., Keating, H. and Lind, C. (2008) *Responsibility, Law and the Family*. Aldershot: Ashgate.

Care Quality Commission (2009) *The State of Health Care and Adult Social Care: A Look at the Quality of Care in England in 2009*. London: Care Quality Commission.

Clark, H., Gough, H. and Macfarlane, A. (2004) *'It Pays Dividends': Direct Payments and Older People*. Bristol: Policy Press.

DH (Department of Health) (2003) *Fair Access to Care Services: Guidance on Eligibility Criteria for Adult Social Care*, available at http://www.dh.gov.uk/en/Publicationsandstatistics/Publications/PublicationsPolicyAndGuidance/DH_4009653, accessed 2 December 2011.

DH (2009a) *Guidance on Direct Payments for Community Care, Services for Carers and Children's Services*. London: DH.

DH (2009b) *The National Framework for NHS Continuing Healthcare and NHS funded Nursing Care in England*. London: DH.

DH (2010a) *Prioritising Need in the Context of Putting People First: A Whole System Approach to Eligibility for Adult Social Care*. London: DH.

DH (2010b) *Equality and Excellence: Liberating the NHS*, Cm 7881. Norwich: TSO.

DH/HO (Department of Health/Home Office) (2000) *No Secrets: Guidance on Developing and Implementing Multi-agency Policies and Procedures to Protect Vulnerable Adults from Abuse*. London: DH/HO.

EHRC (Equality and Human Rights Commission) (2009) *Public Perception of Human Rights*. London: EHRC.

Evans, T. and Harris, J. (2004) 'Street-level bureaucracy, social work and the (exaggerated) death of discretion', *British Journal of Social Work*, **34**(6): 871–95.

Genn, H. (1999) *Paths to Justice: What People Do and Think About Going to Law*. Oxford: Hart.

Law Commission (2010) *Adult Social Care: A Consultation Paper*. London: Law Commission.

Law Commission (2011) *Adult Social Care: Consultation Analysis*. London: Law Commission.

Lipsky, M. (1980) *Street-level Bureaucracy: Dilemmas of the Individual in Public Services*. New York: Russell Sage Foundation.

McDonald, A. and Taylor, M. (1995) *The Law and Elderly People*. London: Sweet & Maxwell.

McDonald, A., Postle, K. and Dawson, C. (2008) 'Barriers to retaining and using professional knowledge in social work with adults in the UK', *British Journal of Social Work*, **38**(7): 1370–87.

Manthorpe, J. and Bradley, G. (2002) 'Managing finance', in R. Adams, L. Dominelli and M. Payne (eds) *Critical Practice in Social Work*. Basingstoke: Palgrave Macmillan.

Manthorpe, J., Stevens, M., Rapaport, J. et al. (2009a) 'Safeguarding and system change: early perceptions of the implications for adult protection services of the English individual budgets pilots – a qualitative study', *British Journal of Social Work*, **39**(8): 1465–80.

Manthorpe, J., Jacobs, S., Rapaport, J. et al. (2009b) 'Training for change: early days of individual budgets and the implications for social work and care management practice: a qualitative study of views of trainers', *British Journal of Social Work*, **39**(7): 1291–305.

Pleasence, P., Balmer, N.J., Buck, A. et al. (2004) 'Multiple justiciable problems: problem clusters, problem order and social and demographic indicators', *Journal of Empirical Legal Studies*, **1**(2): 301–29.

Pritchard, J. (ed.) (2008) *Good Practice in Law and Safeguarding Adults*. London: Jessica Kingsley.

18

Landscapes and portraits: using multiple lenses to inform social work theories of old age

Jonathan Parker

Theory

The application of social work theories, methods, frameworks and models often presents great challenges to practitioners in many fields of practice. Sometimes, the explicit use of theories is avoided, ostrich-like, with social workers protesting that they do not see their relevance. Some social workers espouse an anti-intellectualism, which fails to understand that all practice is based on an understanding of the world, whether that be local, at a personal level, an agency-adopted and tacit approach, or a procedural or legislatively prescribed model, rather than a more formal, recognized method of practising social work (Coulshed and Orme, 2006; Parker and Bradley, 2010). Sometimes, it may be the structure of the workforce and social policy that leads to the eschewal of theory. Social work with older people has not been the priority of policy-makers, workforce planners or academics for many years. As such, the workforce has not been able to develop its theoretical base as fully as other areas of practice.

This anti-theoretical and, concomitantly, anti-intellectual perspective may have been assisted, unwittingly, in the development of the new qualifying degree for social work (Smith, 2002). However, if social workers are to practise effectively, they must develop an understanding, grounded in knowledge and theories, of what might be happening in the situations in which they find themselves. Indeed, theories and models guide social workers' actions and provide explanatory frameworks that make effective interventions possible and, in doing so, they contribute to ethical, evidence-based and accountable practice (McDonald, 2010). The debate is not new and need not be characterized by extreme polarized views.

This chapter introduces the context of contemporary social work practice with older adults, following which the practical relevance of social gerontological theories will be explored at micro-, mezzo- and macro-levels as an example of the many ways in which theories impact on contemporary practice. The use and deployment of these theories will be presented, including a consideration of why they are important to social workers practising with individuals, their families and/or carers.

The changing context of social work with older adults

The organizational context in which social work is practised in the UK is undergoing sustained and radical change, heralded, initially, by the New Labour government when first elected in 1997, and now undergoing a period of radical retrenchment and reform following the election of the coalition government in 2010. The dominating structure of local government social services departments, which evolved in England and Wales with the adoption of many of the Seebohm Report (1968) recommendations and their inclusion within the Local Authority Social Services Act 1970 and the Local Government Act 1972, has waned following childcare restructuring (DfES, 2003), healthcare changes (Health Act 1999, 2006, 2009) and the development of the personalization, choice and consumerist agendas within adult social care (Care Standards Act 2000; DH, 2007). A more diverse, professional service, working across agencies and disciplinary boundaries, is emerging from these developments, mirrored in the (contested) increased regulation of social life (see the Safeguarding Vulnerable Groups Act 2006). These changes affect all areas of adult social welfare; however, the demands resulting from ageing are global.

The relevance of theory to social work practice lies in it providing a framework for understanding the situations of people who use services and the potential to inform and improve practice by suggesting what could be done in specific situations (Trevithick, 2005; Parker, 2007a, 2008; Parker and Bradley, 2010). The concept of theory is explanatory and predictive, and may be defined at three levels, all of which are important in working with and understanding older people (Coulshed and Orme, 2006):

1   *grand theories or macro-level theories:* seek to establish global explanations, such as Marxism
2   *mid-range or mezzo-level theories:* concern particular phenomena such as bereavement and loss, cycles of disadvantage, attachment, moral panics and so on
3   *lower level or micro-theories:* articulate specific approaches to practice; 'how to do' theories.

While the term 'ageing' is contested and its arbitrariness can itself problematize ageing, it is certain that the older we get, the more health and social care needs we have and, concomitantly, the more services we tend to use, although this may be significantly concentrated into the latter parts of our lives. In respect of social work, a range of other social divisions and categories impact on the experience – gender, ethnicity, health, geographical location, social support, living arrangements and so on. In this context, it is clear that a robust understanding of theory, at a range of levels, is important for social workers (Wilson et al., 2008).

Changing demography

The dramatic global population increase and ageing are central to social work and social policy initiatives. Powell (2010) suggests that predictions indicate an annual net gain of people over 65 years in excess of 10 million. United Nations figures posit a more rapid increase in developing rather than developed countries, 140% compared with 51%, respectively, from 2006 to 2030 (Krug, 2002). In the UK, the actual number and percentage of older people in the older age brackets are also rising (Shaw, 2006). For example, in 2011, it was estimated that there were 4.7 million people over the age of 75 years, comprising 7.7% of the general population and 41% of the population over retirement age, whereas in 2031, this is estimated to rise to 7.7 million people over 75 years old, comprising 11.9% of the general population and 50% of people of retirement age. There is great economic diversity among these people. For those people living alone and dependent on state benefits, 42% of their income is spent on housing, fuel and food costs, whereas the 56% of over-65 owner-occupiers with no mortgage own 80% of the UK's wealth.

Changes in the world's demography have important ramifications for social work with older people across the world, and demand a reinterpretation of what social work is and what it can offer, whether that is community action in developing countries, policy development across the world, or the more individualized approaches of care management in developed nations. Perhaps in the UK, the notion of the Big Society lends itself to that reinterpretation (Cabinet Office, n.d.). The economic challenges for social expenditure, pensions, the maintenance of the workforce and population replenishment come to the fore as the balance tips in favour of older rather than younger groups (Bengtson and Lowenstein, 2004); as do the health needs arising from increased longevity, and the socioemotional needs arising from increased family disruption and reconstitution and multiple losses (Wilson et al., 2008). Changes in migratory patterns also create specific needs and demands as immigrant communities age and cultures evolve.

Gerontological theories of ageing

Gerontology recognizes a diverse range of approaches to the concept of ageing, sometimes conflicting and often politicized by social and personal constructions (McDonald, 2010). As Phillips et al. (2006) state, gerontological theory concerns the study of ageing from biological, psychological and sociological perspectives. Theories from sociology, social policy and psychology predominate in social work but history, anthropology and economics are also significant. Hendricks and Powell (2009) argue that theory and theorizing are central to erecting the scaffolding on which to drape

Theory

conceptual and perceptual understandings of ageing, since theories move beyond empirical observations of the 'what' to relational understandings of the 'why'. In a similar vein, Putney et al. (2005) suggest that social gerontology may be a model for promoting sociological theory as a social and civic good, something that is central to social work practice and that indicates how theories have their place in enhancing the lives of older people.

Within the literature, social gerontological theories are often described in chronological fashion, although Putney et al. (2005) also suggest that there has been a move away from the 'grand narratives' of functionalist disengagement theories to more individuated approaches. For example, Bengtson et al. (1997) separate the linear chronology into a series of ages or shifts in thinking. However, these models can also be conceptualized in more traditional theoretical terms as macro-, mezzo- and micro-level theories (Penhale and Parker, 2008), or structural, professional and interpersonal approaches (Lymbery, 2005). This allows us to avoid the pitfalls of privileging a progressive discourse, which not only suggests that theories are improving in their explanatory power but also dismisses the value of previous theorizing. A consideration of theory by level permits viewing by explanatory breadth and, critically, makes it possible to consider theories that others may reject simply for being out of fashion or themselves 'old'. Powell and Hendricks (2009), analysing critical social gerontological theories, recognize four core themes that interweave the macro-, mezzo- and micro-explanatory levels.

Economic and political theories influence the global world and policy assumptions and developments, but theories also recognize the impact of power imbalances and how groups are theorized according to reproductive capacities, youthfulness and currently privileged aspects of productivity. This leads, for instance, to gender inequalities at all levels, including age.

Individual approaches to ageing have become atomized and subject to understanding through 'masks' reflecting the disjunctures between external appearances and internal subjectivities, as seen within cosmetic surgery, biotechnologies and lifestyle choices. Indeed, technologies of cosmeticization allow for the continual re-creation of the self within developed and economically prosperous contexts, while increased surveillance (Foucault, 1977) through assistive technologies alters the nature of the experience of social care (see Parker, 2005), in which personal identities and self-worth are diminished.

Biomedical approaches to ageing

Biological and medical approaches to ageing in developed countries have credence in the increased longevity people enjoy and advances in reducing infant and maternal mortality, leading to a reduction in the birth rate and, subsequently, monumental changes in demography, as seen earlier. In the Western world, theories of ageing from biomedical perspectives also reflect anxieties concerning individual mortality and its association with the physical and overt processes of ageing. The study of biological ageing can be further separated into specific areas, such as cellular ageing, genetic and evolutionary theories, and stochastic theories that concern the build-up of physical, environmental and lifestyle insults over time (Sauvain-Dugerdil et al., 2006).

In social work circles, there has been a rejection of a purely biomedical approach, partly because of a tendency to associate the older person solely with physical and mental decline, known as 'biological reductionism' (Biggs, 1993), and partly because of a tribal identity preference for social models. There are problems, however, in rejecting biological perspectives because of a misplaced emphasis on and uncritical acceptance of social models. The experiences and problems associated with disease, illness and physical decline in old age should not be minimized or dismissed. Also, there are clear social work needs arising from these situations. For instance, the older person who falls at night may not only be at risk of injury and broken bones but may also risk losing the ability to cook, shop or even remain in their own home, thus demanding an integrated rather than tribal response from services that is centred around the person's needs. Biological, decremental decline approaches to ageing are not necessarily the predominate ones for social workers, who would not wish to define older people simply in terms of illness and disease categories. There is a need, however, to have a sound understanding of biophysiological changes, such as age-related sensory change, and, indeed, expected psychological changes such as in cognitive processes, in order to distinguish between those aspects of ageing that one may expect and those that require further investigation and/or assistance, which might include social work.

Sociological theories of ageing

Sociological perspectives on ageing at the macro-level have also focused on decline and loss. Cumming and Henry (1961) focused on the functional tasks of disengagement from active (political and economic) social life as a preparation for the new generation and for the older person's inevitable decline and, ultimately, death. This approach failed to consider the politico-economic ramifications of the thesis, but saw the process as helping to preserve a functional social consensus and transition of social power (McDonald, 2010). A cultural critique was also missed by uncritically accepting the models developed within Western societies that were influenced by atomized, fragmented societies and the developing assumed economic hegemony and its imperatives. However, simply because these theories have fallen out of vogue does not mean they can easily be ignored. Social workers may often fall into the trap of privileging those theories and models of understanding that are assumed to be in the ascendance without engaging with them critically or searching out the many nuanced variations and contradictions found in the messier worlds of practice. For example, one may find a number of older people who actively seek to disengage from many prior roles and functions within their families and communities, but this may be a rational, individually and socially determined choice. While acknowledging some

Theory

degree of sociopolitical influence on such disengagement and withdrawal, social workers would also understand this to be wider than the simple adoption of a system of normative social belief.

Role and activity theories also derive from mid-twentieth century functionalist sociologies and focus on those roles and behaviours associated with specific ages. These theories are most closely associated with Havighurst and Albrecht (1953) and Lemon et al. (1972). The focus on roles, stages and distinct changes and a shifting of power across generations was consonant with sociological theory at the time, and reflected an understanding of society that could be associated with the eu-functionality of social systems – the maintenance of good order, the preservation of functioning and competence – and also with individualized concepts of 'successful ageing', which discount social and cultural diversity and, while assumed to be universal, tend to privilege the settings in which they develop. However, these approaches, termed by Bengtson et al. (1997) as 'first generation gerontological theories', still have relevance for social workers if they are understood as 'seeing through a glass, darkly' (1 Corinthians 13: 11); they do not show the full picture. These functionalist theories, however, underpin the operations of policy-makers throughout the Western world (Johns, 2010) and elsewhere, for example Southeast Asia (Arifin and Ananta, 2009). Ageing has been conceptualized as a time of decline and increasing need, even burden, by policy planners, health and social care professions and the general public, and negotiating the policy and legislative landscape requires engagement with these ideas, some of which may be considered antithetical to, or at least to sit in tension with, social work and its espoused values – although we must accept that these too are not absolute but are culture bound and interpreted. Although driven by concepts of 'burden' and the pathologization of older people and their experiences (see Parker, 2005; Phillips et al., 2006), there is another side to the functionalist approach, which is to understand how the component parts of society work together as a whole and how society continues to function. All social workers have a role in ensuring the good functioning of society and its maintenance (Davies, 1994). This is especially the case in the UK, since the majority of qualified practitioners work for local government and other employers who fulfil statutory obligations for the state.

Active ageing approaches represent, in part, macroeconomic theories, which underpin many of the social and health policies that drive social work and welfare across the world. However, the ways in which these are operationalized within the structures of social work organizations or in bespoke plans for individuals favour mezzo- and micro-level actions, and are often understood in terms of individual leisure or health behaviours (see Bowling, 2008). The term 'active ageing' was introduced by the World Health Organization in the 1990s (WHO, 2002), and can be defined as: 'the process of enhancing the quality of life of older persons by optimizing the opportunities for their health, participation, and self-fulfilment' (Ananta and Arifin, 2009, p. 25).

The concept of active ageing as a means of encouraging participation in social, political and economic life has global attraction (Ervik et al., 2006; Piekkola, 2006; Perek-Bialas et al., 2008; Cloos et al., 2010; Du and Yang, 2010). Contemporary theories of active ageing have been employed in Southeast Asia to address the economic imperatives associated with an increasing ageing population (Ananta and Arifin, 2009), while recognizing that making people happier and healthier through active ageing represents an end in itself. In Indonesia, Rahardjo et al. (2009) have explored the concept of active ageing positively in a context in which there are few opportunities for older people but a growing economic need as the country ages. The need for active ageing policies is also evident in rich countries. Gultiano and Agustin (2009) identify the intergenerational imperatives of active ageing in the Philippines, recognizing that focusing on the education, career choice, health and reproductive behaviour of younger women is likely to promote healthier, more active lifestyles that will continue into old age. Active ageing needs to be considered in the context in which ageing is a mediator in the ways in which resources and services are allocated or denied (Mayhew, 2005; Ney, 2005), and in relation to other social variables such as gender (Lie et al., 2009; Venn and Arber, 2011). A focus on active ageing policies is likely to have positive economic consequences and allow countries to target need and social work resources more effectively.

The ways in which these approaches are understood, with their focus on macro-economics played out in the lives of individuals, indicate a need for clarity. For social workers, these theories are important in considering future services and resource allocation, and call for an understanding of localized, nuanced approaches at the micro-level which address the individual's experiences of ageing. The confluence of these two – the macroeconomic and social imperatives of the World Health Organization and governments and the concern for the individual in this world – represent an important site for social work practice. Individual social work is possible in this context because of the global emphasis on ageing as a challenge for political, economic and social life and the needs that arise, but individual change and behaviour are also likely to influence these global structural models. There is a need to consider the interaction of the global and individual emphases and to model the mutual construction of new ways of addressing issues that impact on the local and global environments. Social workers are part of this construction.

The emphasis placed on economic as well as social productivity in active ageing (OECD, 1998) is, perhaps, indicative of the global spread of neoliberal market ideologies, although the World Health Organization also emphasizes quality of life issues (WHO, 2002). Walker (2009) is mindful that the concept allows a range of policy initiatives to be hidden within it, recognizing the difference between European emphases on health, participation and wellbeing and a more US discourse that privileges economic productivity. Moving from the dependency discourse created by older people's association with the welfare state has been important in developing the active ageing discourse. While Walker (2009) laments that this still needs reflecting in the outworkings of the EU policy process, it may also be said that the same is necessary within social work practice.

Theory

An important critique to functionalist approaches has come from critical gerontologists who challenge the existing structural frameworks, policy directions and social institutions constructed around ageing. This has led to the development of theories of the political economy of ageing and feminist gerontologies, among others. Hendricks and Powell (2009, p. 6) recognize that 'scholarly progress occurs … within the penumbra of certified professional knowledge' and that critical social gerontology provides new ways of understanding the relations between personal identity and structures.

Associated with active ageing are the more radical political economy approaches, associated predominantly in the UK with Phillipson's (1982) social constructionist approach and with Estes et al.'s (2001) 'ageing enterprise' in the USA. Putney et al. (2010) highlight that these more radical approaches hark back to functionalist roots and age stratification theories, which seek to identify the similarities and differences between age cohorts and through history, considering the interdependence of age cohorts and social structures (see Parsons, 1942). However, it is the neo-Marxist, conflict theory roots of this approach that are most commonly identified, understanding the dialectical relationship between older people and capitalism as creating the sociopolitical problems associated with ageing. Political economy theories draw attention to the ways in which politico-economic forces in society, and indeed globally, act to determine the allocation of social resources to ageing groups on the basis of that social division especially. Older people represent a drain on resources and do not contribute to them, and therefore inequalities and problem-focused social policies derive from those in power who privilege economic productivity (Phillipson and Smith, 2005). It is important for social workers approaching ageing through this lens to consider how older people fare differently according to education, employment, welfare and health policies; how these are influenced by and influence economic trends, and how social structures impact on and construct predominantly negative perceptions of ageing (Bytheway, 1995). This can provide social workers with alternative understandings of the experiences of older people and develop challenges to uncritical acceptance of (potentially) organizationally preferred functionalist gerontologies. The homogenization of older people within the political economy macro-theory is more subtly nuanced, however, with different experiences according to the levels of economic, cultural, social and individual capital that older people enjoy (Gilleard and Higgs, 2005). McDonald (2010) draws our attention to the differential experiences of older people across a range of social categories and divisions, shaped by history, demography, geography and so on.

From the 1970s, a 'second generation' of social gerontological theories evolved (Bengtson et al., 1997), which focused more on subjectivities and micro-level understandings. These included exchange theories across generations and considered individual resources and capital, building on Homans' (1961) rational choice theory, and theories deriving from symbolic interactionism (Mead, 1967). With theoretical refinement, a further generation of social gerontology has developed, much of which relates to the subjectivities that inform late modernity in Western nations (Giddens, 1991).

Sociocultural ideologies, identity theories and life course and biographical approaches represent sociological theories that often intersect with psychological approaches, although Powell and Hendricks (2009) recognize the interplay between theories of human agency, including narrative and biography, and global structural theories. These are also theories with which social workers will be familiar in other forms or applications. Indeed, Giddens' (1991) 'reflexive project of the self' is not dissimilar to much thinking in contemporary Western social work, which focuses on the life course development of the self in relation to biographies, history, experiences and contexts (Hockey and James, 2003). The self as a project can adapt to or mask the sociopolitical debilitations of ageing (Biggs, 1999; Ogg, 2003). To an increasing extent, global ageing selves are experienced and re-created in a rapidly changing set of sociopolitical and economic conditions. In the UK, this can be seen in recent White Papers and policy papers focusing on independence, choice and the individual. Phillips et al. (2006) state that biographical approaches, in fact, bring together gerontological and social work theory because they capture the sum of older people's experiences within their historically developing ecological contexts. This considers uniqueness, connectedness, continuities and discontinuities of individuals and their perceptions of the world. This has important implications for social work assessments and interventions, and should the worlds of those with whom social workers practise be inclusive of others, it demands such a recognition within that practice. This can disquiet and challenge accepted notions of confidentiality and individualized focus while respecting the central person involved. For example, the world of an older person engaged in an assessment of need with a social worker may lead them to locate themselves within a circle or group, and assume that this will be fully taken into account in the assessment, while the social worker, bound by confidentiality, may be unable to engage fully with those others so important to the individual. The tension for social work may be the emphasis on principle over and above a person's needs. As the global and local converge, social workers need to learn and adapt to diverse situations that start with the biography in context, while recognizing the influences around and on that person.

Biographical and narrative approaches have been developed in exciting ways by Gubrium and Holstein (2003), who see the ways in which history and biography converge to construct meanings, and look at ageing in the context of the lived experience of those who are classed as or consider themselves to be old(er). These theories draw on broader theoretical developments from symbolic interactionism, phenomenology and ethnomethodology, focusing on the subjectivities of individual social actors. The importance of these theories is perhaps immediately clear to social workers who come into contact on a daily basis with the lived experiences of people in diverse situations and with diverse histories (Parker, 2005, 2007b), and who assess these contexts and may intervene using life story and reminiscence-based approaches. Specifically considering people with dementia may help us to understand these approaches alongside other theoretical models for practice.

Dementia, theories and social work

Social workers make decisions that may have far-reaching consequences for people's lives and these must be made according to transparent, understandable principles that should be open to challenge (Parker, 2007a; Parker and Bradley, 2010). Since Kitwood's monumental effort to shift the care paradigm from an instrumental, pessimistic and disease-focused model to one that placed the individual centre stage, social work has become increasingly important as a service for people with dementia and their families and carers (Kitwood, 1997; Parker, 2001; Marshall and Tibbs, 2006).

The continued development of the national dementia strategy (DH, 2011) in the UK delineates a coordinated approach following research by Alzheimer's Disease International (2009) into growing needs across the world. Social work has become increasingly focused in on itself, working within bureaucracy, procedure and red tape that fails to 'see' the individuals receiving services. If social workers are to engage appropriately with people, there is a need for theoretical understandings of dementia itself.

Of course, the psychoneurobiological changes that occur in dementia, resulting from the underlying disease processes, cannot be ignored or dismissed, as some more tribal approaches may attempt. It is important that social workers have some insight into biomedical understandings and the potential for developing treatments, as well as knowledge of some of the iatrogenic side effects that may result from such, one of which, in societal terms, may include the discourses produced by acceptance of biomedical hegemony (Parker, 2001). Biomedical knowledge is common currency among many professionals with whom social workers practise – psychiatrists, geriatricians, nurses, therapists and so on – but is spurned by social workers in favour of the defensive construction of received social models. The latter models are central to social work practice because they relate to the social environment and living context of the people they work with, and offer a more optimistic engagement with their wellbeing. However, they must be seen as theories for practice that are, themselves, not only falsifiable constructs but value driven and having the potential to create a system that represents the battle cry of social workers but not the 'essential' truth.

Other theories applicable to social work and people with dementia mirror at a specific, micro-level those social gerontological aspects already covered. Marshall and Tibbs (2006) indicate that the interplay of biographical experiences and social positions is so important when understanding how the social worker, as a professional, practises with a person with dementia; multiple biographies collide to synthesize that understanding. These biographies include the structural aspects of law and policy that have shaped professional responses and the privileging of the biomedical approach, but these are mitigated by Kitwood's 'new culture' in which the inexorable decremental perspective is challenged. People are understood as such in relation to and in relationships with others. As in all relationships, emotional needs are represented – these include loss and confusion, marginalization from the day-to-day activities around them and not being engaged in meaningful occupation.

While acknowledging that there are many sociocultural as well as individual nuances within the model, Miesen and Jones (1997) have developed an advanced attachment theory for people with dementia, which takes further the emphasis on the biographies of the self. They describe the person with dementia as inhabiting a 'strange situation' (Ainsworth et al., 1978), which evokes frequent feelings of danger and initiates a search for the comfort of attachment figures. This is important for social workers working with families, carers and other professionals in seeking understanding and positive ways of working with people who are parent-searching, for example.

In summary

Theories permeate social work practice in all areas, including working with older adults. In this chapter, we have focused on social gerontological theories but recognize that these represent only one set of theories important to social workers. Integrating this emphasis with social

> **Making connexions**
>
> How can gerontological knowledge support movement from a dependency to a rights-based discourse in social work practice?

work education and research may become increasingly important as the challenges of an ageing world embed. Currently, gerontological social work is active in the USA in respect of social work curricula (Eun-Kyong et al., 2006; Curl et al., 2010; Fenster et al., 2010; Nelson-Becker, 2011; Rowan et al., 2011) and social work research (Mehrota et al., 2009). Elsewhere, this focus is less evident. In the UK, Chambers (2004) considers the importance of introducing critical gerontological theory into the curriculum as a means of understanding and responding to the challenges of ageing for women. Women are overrepresented in health and social care and in proportions overall to men. Alongside this is a recognition that ageism and sexism combine. For Chambers, critical social gerontology offers a useful model to begin to address these issues.

Theories from social gerontology range from the global macro-level to those focusing on the individual. These are central to social work practice at all levels. Social policies determine welfare provision in response to questions of ageing; mezzo-level theories help us to understand the particular situations older people find themselves in; and micro-level theories set out how social workers may practise with individuals, their families and communities.

Further reading

■ Bengstson, V.L., Gans, D., Putney, N.M. and Silverstein, M. (eds) (2009) *Handbook of Theories of Aging* (2nd edn). New York: Springer.

Comprehensive handbook covering theories from a range of disciplines from the natural and social sciences in a clear, detailed and important way for students wanting an in-depth understanding of theories relating to ageing.

■ Bond, J., Peace, S.M., Dittman-Kohli, F. and Westerhof, G. (2007) *Ageing in Society* (3rd edn). London: Sage.

Provides readers with a robust introduction to theories and perspectives on ageing within contemporary societies.

■ McDonald, A. (2010) *Social Work with Older People*. Cambridge: Polity.

For students seeking a book that pulls together the social, psychological and biological theories of ageing for contemporary social work practice, McDonald paints the landscape, while drawing the detail to catch the eye.

References

Ainsworth, M.D., Blehar, M.C., Walters, E. and Wall, S. (1978) *Patterns of Attachment: A Psychological Study of the Strange Situation.* Hillsdale, NJ: Erlbaum.

Alzheimer's Disease International (2009) *World Alzheimer Report*. London: Alzheimer's Disease International.

Ananta, A. and Arifin, E.N. (2009) 'Older persons in Southeast Asia: from liability to asset', in E.N. Arifin and A. Ananta (eds) *Older Persons in Southeast Asia: An Emerging Asset*. Singapore: ISEAS.

Arifin, E.N. and Ananta, A. (eds) (2009) *Older Persons in Southeast Asia: An Emerging Asset*. Singapore: ISEAS.

Bengtson, V. and Lowenstein, A. (eds) (2004) *Global Aging and Challenges to Families*. New York: Aldine de Gruyter.

Bengtson, V., Burgess, E. and Parrott, T. (1997) 'Theory, explanation and a third generation of theoretical development in social gerontology', *Journal of Gerontology, Series B, Psychological and Social Sciences*, **52**(2): S72–88.

Biggs, S. (1993) *Understanding Ageing*. Buckingham: Open University Press.

Biggs, S. (1999) *The Mature Imagination: Dynamics of Identity in Midlife and Beyond*. Buckingham: Open University Press.

Bowling, A. (2008) 'Enhancing later life: How do older people perceive active ageing?', *Aging and Mental Health*, **12**(3): 293–301.

Bytheway, B. (1995) *Ageism*. Buckingham: Open University Press.

Cabinet Office (n.d.) *Big Society – Overview*, http://www.cabinetoffice.gov.uk/content/big-society-overview.

Chambers, P. (2004) 'The case for critical gerontology in social work education and older women', *Social Work Education*, **23**(6): 745–58.

Cloos, P., Allen, C., Alvarado, B. et al. (2010) '"Active ageing": a qualitative study in six Caribbean countries', *Ageing and Society*, **30**(1): 79–101.

Coulshed, V. and Orme, J. (2006) *Social Work Practice: An Introduction* (4th edn). Basingstoke: Palgrave Macmillan.

Cumming, E. and Henry, W. (1961) *Growing Old: The Process of Disengagement*. New York: Basic Books.

Curl, A., Tompkins, C., Rosen, A. and Zlotnik, J. (2010) 'A case study of professional change: the impact of the National Gerontological Social Work Survey', *Gerontology and Geriatrics Education*, **31**(3): 256–73.

Davies, M. (1994) *The Essential Social Worker* (3rd edn). Aldershot: Arena.

DfES (Department for Education and Skills) (2003) *Every Child Matters*, Green Paper, Cm 5860. Norwich: HMSO.

DH (Department of Health) (2007) *Putting People First: A Shared Vision and Commitment to the Transformation of Adult Social Care*, http://www.dh.gov.uk/en/Publicationsandstatistics/Publications/PublicationsPolicyAndGuidance/DH_081118.

DH (2011) *Living Well with Dementia: A National Dementia Strategy – Good Practice Compendium*, http://www.dh.gov.uk/en/Publicationsandstatistics/Publications/PublicationsPolicyAndGuidance/DH_123476.

Du, P. and Yang, H. (2010) 'China's population ageing and active ageing', *China Journal of Social Work*, **3**(2/3): 139–52.

Ervik, R., Helgoy, I. and Christensen, D. (2006) 'Ideas and policies on active ageing in Norway and the UK', *International Social Science Journal*, 58, 571–84.

Estes, C. and associates (2001) *Social Policy and Aging: A Critical Perspective*. Thousand Oaks, CA: Sage.

Eun-Kyoung, L., Collins, P., Mahoney, K. et al. (2006) 'Enhancing social work practice with older adults: the role of infusing gerontology content into the Master of Social Work Foundation curriculum', *Education Gerontology*, **32**(9): 737–56.

Fenster, J., Zodikoff, B., Rozario, P. and Joyce, P. (2010) 'Implementing a gero-infused curriculum in advanced-level MSW course in health, mental health and substance abuse: an evaluation', *Journal of Gerontological Social Work*, **53**(7): 641–53.

Foucault, M. (1977) *Discipline and Punish: The Birth of the Prison*. London: Penguin.

Giddens, A. (1991) *Modernity and Self-identity: Self and Society in the Late Modern Age*. Cambridge: Polity.

Gilleard, C. and Higgs, P. (2005) *Contexts of Ageing: Class, Cohort and Community*. Cambridge: Polity.

Gubrium, J. and Holstein, J. A. (eds) (2003) *Ways of Aging*. London: Wiley.

Gultiano, S.A. and Agustin, S.S. (2009) 'Work, income, and expenditure: elderly and near-elderly women in Metro Cebu, Philippines', in E.N. Arifin and A. Ananta (eds) *Older Persons in Southeast Asia: An Emerging Asset*. Singapore: ISEAS.

Havighurst, R. and Albrecht, R. (1953) *Older People*. London: Longman.

Hendricks, J. and Powell, J.L. (2009) 'Theorizing in social gerontology: the *raison d'être*', *International Journal of Sociology and Social Policy*, **29**(1/2): 5–14.

Hockey, J. and James, A. (2003) *Social Identities across the Life Course*. Basingstoke: Palgrave Macmillan.

Homans, G.C. (1961) *Social Behavior: Its Elementary Forms*. New York: Harcourt Brace Jovanovich.

Johns, R. (2010) *Social Work, Social Policy and Older People*. Exeter: Learning Matters.

Kitwood, T. (1997) *Dementia Reconsidered: The Person Comes First*. Buckingham: Open University Press.

Theory

Krug, E.G. (2002) *World Report on Violence and Health*. Geneva: WHO.

Lemon, B.W., Bengtson, V.L. and Peterson, J.A. (1972) 'An exploration of the activity theory of aging', *Journal of Gerontology*, 27, 511–23.

Lie, M., Baines, S. and Wheelock, J. (2009) 'Citizenship, volunteering and active ageing', *Social Policy and Administration*, **43**(7): 702–18.

Lymbery, M. (2005) *Social Work with Older People: Context, Policy and Practice*. London: Sage.

Marshall, M. and Tibbs, M.-A. (2006) *Social Work and People with Dementia: Partnerships, Practice and Persistence*. Bristol: BASW/Policy Press.

Mayhew, L. (2005) 'Active ageing in the UK: issues, barriers, policy directions', *Innovation: European Journal of Social Sciences*, **18**(4): 455–77.

McDonald, A. (2010) *Social Work with Older People*. Cambridge: Polity.

Mead, G.H. (1967) *Mind, Self and Society from the Standpoint of a Social Behaviourist*. Chicago: University of Chicago Press.

Mehrota, C.M., Townsend, A. and Berkman, B. (2009) 'Enhancing research capacity in gerontological social work', *Educational Gerontology*, 35, 146–63.

Miesen, B. and Jones, G.M. (eds) (1997) *Care Giving in Dementia: Research and Applications*. London: Routledge.

Nelson-Becker, H. (2011) 'Advancing an aging-prepared community: models and lessons from training initiatives in gerontological social work', *Journal of Religion, Spirituality and Aging*, **23**(1/2): 92–113.

Ney, S. (2005) 'Active ageing policy in Europe: between path dependency and path departure', *Ageing International*, **30**(4): 323–42.

OECD (Organisation for Economic Co-operation and Development) (1998) *Maintaining Prosperity in and Ageing Society*. Paris: OECD.

Ogg, J. (2003) *Living Alone in Later Life*. London: Institute of Community Studies.

Parker, J. (2001) 'Interrogating person-centred dementia care in social work and social care practice', *Journal of Social Work*, **1**(3): 329–45.

Parker, J. (2005) 'Constructing dementia and dementia care: daily practices in a day care', *Journal of Social Work*, **5**(3): 261–78.

Parker, J. (2007a) 'The process of social work: assessment, planning, intervention and review', in M. Lymbery and K. Postle (eds) *Social Work: A Companion to Learning*. London: Sage.

Parker, J. (2007b) 'Constructing dementia and dementia care: disadvantage and daily practices in a care setting', in P. Burke and J. Parker (eds) *Social Work and Disadvantage*. London: Jessica Kingsley.

Parker, J. (2008) 'Assessment, planning, intervention and review', in M. Davies (ed.) *The Encyclopaedia of Social Work*. Oxford: Blackwell.

Parker, J. and Bradley, G. (2010) *Social Work Practice: Assessment, Planning, Intervention and Review* (3rd edn). Exeter: Learning Matters.

Parsons, T. (1942) 'Age and sex in the social structure of the United States', *American Sociological Review*, 7, 604–16.

Penhale, B. and Parker, J. (2008) *Working with Vulnerable Adults*. London: Routledge.

Perek-Bialas, J., Ruzik, A. and Vidovicova, L. (2008) 'Active ageing policies in the Czech Republic and Poland', *International Social Science Journal*, 60, 559–70.

Phillips, J., Ray, M. and Marshall, M. (2006) *Social Work with Older People* (4th edn). Basingstoke: Palgrave Macmillan.

Phillipson, C. (1982) *Capitalism and the Construction of Old Age*. London: Macmillan.

Phillipson, C. and Smith, A. (2005) *Extending Working Life: A Review of the Research Literature*, Research report No. 299. London: DWP.

Piekkola, H. (2006) 'Nordic policies on active ageing in the labour market and some European comparisons', *International Social Science Journal*, 58, 545–57.

Powell, J.L. (2010) 'The power of global aging', *Ageing International*, **35**(1): 1–14.

Powell, J.L. and Hendricks, J. (2009) 'The sociological construction of ageing: lessons for theorising', *International Journal of Sociology and Social Policy*, **29**(1/2): 84–94.

Putney, N.M., Alley, D.E. and Bengtson, V.L. (2005) 'Social gerontology as public sociology in action', *The American Sociologist*, **36**(4): 88–104.

Rahardjo, T.B., Hartono, T., Dewi, V.P. et al. (2009) 'Facing the geriatric wave in Indonesia: financial conditions and social support', in E.N. Arifin and A. Ananta (eds) *Older Persons in Southeast Asia: An Emerging Asset*. Singapore: ISEAS.

Rowan, N., Faul, A., Birkenmaier, J. and Damron-Rodriguez, J. (2011) 'Social work knowledge of community-based services for older adults: an educational model for social work students', *Journal of Gerontological Social Work*, **54**(2): 189–202.

Sauvain-Dugerdil, C., Leridon, H. and Mascie-Taylor, N. (eds) (2006) *Human Clocks: The Bio-cultural Meanings of Age*. Bern: Peter Lang.

Seebohm Report (1968) *Report of the Committee on Local Authority and Allied Personal Social Services*. London: HMSO.

Shaw, C. (2006) '2004-based national population projections for the UK and constituent countries', *Population Trends*, 123, 15–16.

Smith, J. (2002) 'Foreword', in DH, *Requirements for Social Work Training*. London, DH.

Trevithick, P. (2005) *Social Work Skills: A Practice Handbook* (2nd edn). Buckingham: Open University Press.

Venn, S. and Arber, S. (2011) 'Day-time sleep and active ageing in later life', *Ageing and Society*, **31**(2): 197–216.

Walker, A. (2009) 'Commentary: the emergence and application of active aging in Europe', *Journal of Aging and Social Policy*, **21**(1): 75–93.

WHO (World Health Organization) (2002) *Active Ageing: A Policy Framework*. Geneva: WHO.

Wilson, K., Ruch, G., Lymbery, M. and Cooper, A. (2008) *Social Work: An Introduction to Contemporary Practice*. London: Longman.

Theory

19
What research tells social workers about their work with older people

PAUL CLARKSON

Introductory texts often establish two broad themes in relation to older people in society. First, societies are ageing and this poses a problem for policy-makers in terms of finance and long-term care systems. Second, the growth in the numbers of older people will necessarily be accompanied by a rise in illnesses, vulnerabilities and social difficulties of old age that will put untold pressure on statutory and other services. These considerations lie largely outside the personal experiences of social workers, but they do set a context for practice. Societies are undoubtedly ageing (the first point) but research offers evidence to temper the enthusiasm with which the second point has been articulated. Research evidence also leads us to pause slightly and examine just who it is that the social worker, working with older people, might routinely offer help to.

Interpreting ageing demographics

There is no doubt that ageing societies signal a need to think clearly about the responses required if, as has been suggested, the need for formal care services will increase inexorably. Research tells us that the number of people in England aged 65 and over will rise from 7.8 million in 1996 to 12.4 million in 2031, an increase of 60%. However, numbers of the very old (aged 85 and over) will rise even more rapidly, by 88%, from 0.9 million in 1996 to 1.7 million in 2031 (Shaw, 2000). It is not these pure numbers, however, that necessarily constitute a so-called 'demographic time bomb'. It is not age per se that gives rise to the need for health and social care but levels of disability. The potential for pressure on formal services will depend, crucially, on the proportion of the population likely to suffer ill health and social difficulties that call on the resources of social workers, nurses and clinicians. Therefore, it is projections of dependency – whether one requires help with the basic tasks necessary to take part in a decent life – and ill health and its consequences that are important. In this respect, three main scenarios have been considered:

■ optimistically, population ageing could result in people living longer but healthier lives, as medical and other advances mean more people are living into a healthier old age – the so-called 'compression of morbidity' theses associated particularly with Fries (1980)
■ older people may, alternatively, tend to lead longer but more disabled lives – an 'expansion of morbidity'
■ more positively, there is the middle ground scenario, where some forms of disability rise but other, more severe forms tend to decrease in 'dynamic equilibrium' (Howse, 2006).

Current research cannot predict confidently which of these scenarios will hold sway due to limitations in the data available. However, what is clear from work on predicting long-term care finance is that, assuming constant rates of age-specific dependency, the *proportion* of older people in England likely to have problems with, say, two or more daily living activities is around 10% (Wittenberg et al., 1998). The numbers likely to be in nursing home care are even lower, around only 2% of the older population. Thus, although demands on resources may rise or fall depending on future scenarios, the fact is that the numbers of older people likely to require formal help from social work and health professionals represents a small proportion of the older population as a whole.

Therefore, the epithet 'older people' is really a misnomer; the social worker is likely to come into contact with only a minority of people designated as 'older' in society. A more precise term of reference would be those people over a prescribed age experiencing long-term illnesses and needs, who require the responses of social care, health and other agencies. Separating the relatively small proportion of older people likely to require social work intervention from the wider population who do not is an issue of 'targeting' and should be in the mind of every social worker. It should also form part of local authority referral and initial assessment systems and has been shown to be a cost-effective way of managing the workload in social services teams (Clarkson et al., 2010). As an issue, however, targeting is debated. One theme of many introductory social work texts, for example, is that assessments should not focus on the functional limitations of older people at the more severely vulnerable end but instead concentrate on investigating strengths and resources as a focus for more preventive work. However, this is a statement of intent rather than an empirical one derived from weighing up the costs and benefits of alternative courses of action. There is actually very little evidence that preventive interventions, of a more general nature, benefit users 'downstream' – one of the reasons being that such evidence is difficult to collect. There is, though, much more evidence that directing professional resources into more vulnerable cases actually benefits users in terms of enhanced satisfaction, wellbeing and quality of life (Challis et al., 2004). The quest is how to define vulnerability more precisely and here research offers some pointers.

Frailty

One helpful body of work is that by Kenneth Rockwood (Rockwood and Mitnitski, 2007), who views the idea of 'frailty' as encompassing vulnerability to several adverse outcomes, such as the likelihood of going into a care home or hospital, or further accumulation of difficulties. It is not increasing age per se that gives rise to vulnerability but the accumulation of deficits. In his original work, these deficits primarily involve the health states of older people, broadly conceived. These might include:

- ■ symptoms, for example back pain, sleeplessness
- ■ disabilities, for example not being able to get into bed or walk unaided
- ■ measurements, for example laboratory tests.

A frailty index is calculated by adding up the number of deficits an individual experiences and expressing this as a proportion of the number of deficits that are counted. This work has shown that it is the number of deficits that is important rather than the nature of them; the more things older people have wrong with them, the more vulnerable they are likely to be. This quite simple statement is relatively uncontroversial but several important insights emerge from it:

1 Frailty is related to chronological age but not in any absolute sense. As people age, there is an increased likelihood that they will accumulate deficits, but people can and do improve. However, if newly acquired deficits are not dealt with, then there is a growing likelihood of further deficits increasing exponentially.

2 Not everyone accumulates the same deficits or at the same rate; there are what are called 'cohort effects'. Those born in a particular period or people living through particular experiences – one can think, for example, of certain occupational groups – will share deficits or even the absence of them. However, on average, deficits do accumulate at a characteristic rate, about a 3% increase with every year of age, and towards the end of life, these cohort effects are less important.

3 There is a limit to frailty that is not solely dependent on age (Rockwood and Mitnitski, 2006). That is, deficits accumulate only until a certain point (a score on the frailty index of around 0.65), after which death intervenes. This finding is interesting as it means that although one would imagine the limit of frailty to be 1.0 – the point at which all measured deficits have been accumulated – it has consistently been found, for example across countries, that this limit is considerably less. After around two-thirds of possible deficits are experienced, an older person can accumulate no more. After this point, the level of frailty is dangerously high and shows little relationship to increasing age.

The relevance of this for social workers is that other elements characterizing frailty have shown similar patterns and relationships. Andrew et al. (2008), for example, developed a social vulnerability index that exhibits similar features. Their index includes information on difficulties with respect to living situation, social support, socially oriented activities of daily living (using the telephone, going to places beyond walking distance), leisure activities, feeling in control of life, family, finances, religion, transport, and socioeconomic status. This index shows a consistent relationship to mortality and frailty in health terms, although social vulnerability and frailty are distinct from each other. This study measured vulnerability in an aggregate sense: while it is helpful, and probably necessary, for an individual to know exactly which problems are present, for whole populations, it is the number of deficits and the accumulation of these that are more important. More research is required on the construction and properties of such an index in older adults but, for now, its relevance for the social worker is in recognizing its characteristic patterns and how the social factors it represents could be amenable to change from practitioners working with older people.

Based on these findings, social workers should, first, acknowledge the likelihood of vulnerability as people age. They should be aware that they and their colleagues can do something to improve the situation of older people, but that if they do not act, the likelihood is of a rapid accumulation of deficits at older ages. Social workers should be asking themselves: How many illnesses or disabilities does this particular older user have? Do my assessment systems record these so that I can monitor them? (In the author's experience, many local authorities do not collect this information sufficiently or reliably.) Are indicators of social vulnerability present in referral information? Are these sufficient to aggregate to permit the management of caseloads?

Effective assessment practice

Assessment has long been central to the social work task. However, its focus has changed, particularly from the mid-1990s community care reforms and, more recently, with the introduction of 'personalized' care. However, the principle needs reiterating: assessment, conceived as the collection of information concerning the older person, should focus on those aspects for which it is within the legitimate purview of the agency to provide help. Assessment is therefore a goal-directed activity (Kane and Kane, 2000). It is not, as some suggest, an all-encompassing process without boundaries. Assessment is a means of providing a response to an older person regarding the kind of help or assistance that might alleviate concerns or enhance aspects of life for which the agency is responsible. This definition is consistent with the activity of professional assessments as well as those, more latterly, undertaken by users themselves, such as part of resource allocation systems. With user-defined assessments, a response is still undertaken by the local authority to generate an indicative budget. Thus, that response remains constrained by the range of functions,

Research

powers, or scope of local authority influence. The particular focus of assessment in each case should be determined by what it is that the process is intended to uncover. Is it designed to collect information about difficulties and the support available to alleviate them, for example the focus of a professional assessment before hospital discharge? Or is it designed to inquire as to plans, wishes and preferences that are the means to achieve broader social goals, for example the focus of much self-directed systems? In all these cases, assessment is linked to the objectives of the agency through which assessment takes place. Some decry the use of the word 'assessment' with respect to the new world of user-centred care planning and resource allocation but the process is, by definition, the same.

Research has offered a wealth of evidence on this process. Two elements are reviewed here: the effects of following certain assessment approaches, and what domains should be included in assessments and how to operationalize them.

Approaches to assessing older people

There has been an often furious debate on the nature of assessment, how it should be conducted and what elements are important. This debate has not often appealed to research. If it had done, we would be left with a more measured and constructive body of evidence from which to learn for practice. In one corner, there are those commentators who lament the demise of free text assessments and the rise of standardized scales – many of them now electronic. To perhaps caricature slightly, they often appeal for a more qualitative and 'holistic' assessment that characterized traditional social work, arguing that the move towards standardization has robbed us of a more creative use of self in the assessment process. In the other corner are the proponents of standardized tools to structure assessments and prescribe the domains with which to work. It has been argued that these approaches offer a more comprehensive view of the person, moving us away from the dangers of idiosyncrasy. Research has shed light on the consequences of both these extreme positions.

Ellis's (1993) research was insightful, in that by studying social workers' descriptions following their assessments, she pointed to the often commonsense meanings given to circumstances. The practitioners studied did not use standardized scales but relied on their own judgements of cases gleaned from unstructured assessments. It was found that these assessments were often based on the vagaries of individual practitioners and their ideas of a user's worthiness to receive services. They were not, in keeping with the definition above, bounded by the goal of the agency; to determine the precise circumstances of each older person in order to tailor responses appropriately to the level of need experienced. Such individual variation in the way assessments are conducted can result in inequity between users and between those in different parts of the country. On the other hand, slavishly following prescribed assessment forms leaves little room for innovative solutions to problems, a core of professional judgement. The study by Challis et al. (2004) – quoted here as it represents one of the only randomized studies of assessment in social care – showed, for example, that routine community care assessments by social workers, using prescribed forms, did not pick up on many difficulties experienced by older people. However, in an experimental group where these assessments included access to health information from specialist clinicians, there was increased detection of important difficulties. For example, by following prescribed procedures, social workers had not known of cognitive impairment in 36% of their cases. What arises from these examples is that a balance must be struck between these two positions. Assessments that are free to include anything and everything fall into the danger of being biased by the variety of opinions held by individual assessors. Highly structured and prescribed approaches, however, leave little room to organize assessments differently. They need to be supplemented with a framework for decision-making that can offer innovation in the use to which information is put.

Defining and measuring assessment domains

If we accept the purpose of assessment as a means to an end, with that end being the amelioration of difficulties or the maintenance of an acceptable quality of life (Kane and Kane, 2000), then it is important to define and measure these difficulties and components of life quality. Research is rich in definitions but is also able to demonstrate how these elements can be viewed more correctly and more systematically; local authority practice in particular often not learning the lessons offered by research, with approaches to assessment tending to be formulaic.

Defining appropriate assessment domains with respect to older people has a long history. There has, however, been a tendency to ignore this. Reinvention of the wheel has therefore been inevitable. Research evidence on the most appropriate domains to consider, at least for professional assessments, has been available for some time and the social worker would do well to revisit it. Challis (1981), for example, outlined the domains by which to operationalize outcomes relating specifically to social care for older people. These included:

- *nurturance:* or basic physical care including activities of daily living
- *compensation for disability:* including activities involved in maintenance at home such as food preparation and shopping
- *maintenance of independence:* including the felt independence of the older person in retaining control over their own life
- *morale:* including personal growth, life satisfaction and the presence or absence of psychopathology, such as depression
- *social integration:* referring to boredom and loneliness and the presence of confiding relationships
- *family relationships and informal sources of help:* focusing on the stress and difficulties experienced by family and informal carers.

Overall, these domains give a view of the quality of life of the older person and point to where resources, both professional and material, may be directed.

Research

Functional assessment

Rather than merely defining appropriate domains, research can also help in viewing more systematically the domains available to assess older people. One aspect hampering this has been the unfortunate tendency for local authorities to construct their own assessment schedules. These often borrow items constructed from established research scales and add or remove items; in so doing, the validity of the tool (its measurement of the underlying construct) is compromised. An example of the neglect of research in the approach to assessment schemas has been the way in which social workers have been directed to complete information on certain domains. Often, because of the way many local schedules are constructed, this has not been informed by the way in which the original version of the tool was meant to be interpreted.

One perfect example of this is in relation to the sine qua non of assessments of older people, the activities of daily living (ADLs). Social workers are often directed merely to indicate the presence of difficulties with such activities on assessment forms. This has been viewed by many as part of a 'tick box' culture, leaving little room for understanding. However, one of the original research tools measuring the performance of ADLs by older people, the Katz scale (Katz et al., 1963), had a rationale for its use that goes against such a mechanistic interpretation. The original idea for the scale was as a measure of primary function, that is, abilities in caring for oneself, whose development follows a set pattern. Items reflecting basic functions, essential to survival – feeding, continence and transferring (moving from a bed to a chair) – are acquired first in childhood and more complex, learned activities – bathing, dressing, going to the toilet – are acquired last. In ageing, or as part of a degenerative illness, this process is reversed; more complex activities, not as essential for survival, are lost first and the more basic functions are retained longest. This progressive, cumulative pattern has been found to exist in studies of disability in older people (Williams et al., 1976).

This more precise, empirically grounded view of ADLs has important consequences for the assessment of individual cases. For example, a cumulative patterning of disability found in a large sample of those receiving pre-admission screening on entry to nursing homes (Travis and McAuley, 1990) was in the order of: bathing, dressing, toileting, transferring, feeding and continence. Such a pattern to the acquisition of ADL difficulties would mean that the social worker should be sensitized to the existence particularly of difficulties with feeding and incontinence. These are functions retained the longest and cases where difficulties with these occur should be signalled for special attention. An older person in need of help with bathing or dressing has a much better chance of remaining in the community than one who is incontinent and social workers should use this hierarchical approach to ADL assessments to investigate risk. Of course, the success of this depends on whether social workers initially identify these difficulties. One study found that although the identification of basic difficulties such as feeding and incontinence was more accurate after a policy designed to improve assessments (the single assessment process), there still remained considerable room for improvement (Clarkson et al., 2009). These studies show, however, that merely indicating which activities an older person finds difficult is not sensitive to the dynamics of disability; there needs to be sufficient interpretation of what this means for the person, in keeping with the original rationale behind the construction of the scale.

Social networks

A rich seam of research particularly relevant to assessment is that of social networks or the measurement of social support. Social supports, those networks of kith and kin that assist and provide resources (both material and emotional) to individuals, have been shown to have a protective and ameliorative effect in terms of physical and mental health (Miller and Ingham, 1976). For older people, a lack of adequate social networks may result in the person being more likely to enter a care home, or place heavy demands on domiciliary services because they are less able to call on assistance than those with adequate networks (Wenger, 1994). Social 'integration' has also been found to be associated with mortality in older people (Berkmann and Syme, 1979), particularly in the light of the relationship between depression and mortality (Jorm et al., 1991). Adequate social networks among older people have also been shown to relate to positive health features, with their influence being on a par with that of regular exercise or not smoking (Lubben, 1988).

Research on social networks is important for social workers as it highlights such relationships as a crucial aspect of the assessment of the individual older person. The importance of social networks to health and wellbeing means that this facet should be part of any assessment, whether included on local authority forms or not. It is, in fact, part of the assessment of strengths and coping resources identified above. The research of Clare Wenger (1994) is important here in operationalizing this idea to enable it to be used in practice. Wenger and Tucker (2002), for example, developed a measurement instrument to guide social worker's assessments when seeking to understand the personal situations of older people with respect to their social networks. Responses to questions such as 'How far away does your nearest child or relative live?' and 'How often do you see any of your neighbours to have a chat with?' are coded to provide a typology of 'support network type', in effect, different patterns of availability and contact with friends, family and neighbours. Network type is important, as its distribution on social workers' caseloads is very different to that in the general population. Each type also has particular relationships associated with it and can therefore be used to identify risk (Wenger, 1997). For example:

1 The *local self-contained support network*, primarily neighbours and infrequent contact with relatives, is one in which privacy is valued and contact with formal help is low. People with this type of network may not report problems and so recognition of difficulties, such as physical health problems or dementia, tends to be late.

Research

2   The *private restricted support network* is associated with an absence of relatives and few friends nearby, together with low levels of community involvement. This type is the least common in the UK population but is the dominant network on social workers' caseloads. Social isolation may be a risk here but placement in a care home, intended to ameliorate this, may trigger previously dormant psychiatric illness, as lifestyle is compromised by having to adjust to unfamiliar surroundings.

3   The *local family dependent support network*, which is focused on close family ties, with few neighbours or peripheral friends.

4   The *locally integrated support network*, including close relationships with local family, friends and neighbours.

5   The *wider community focused support network*, where there is an absence of nearby relatives but active relationships with distant relatives, usually children, and contact with friends.

Knowing an older person's network type is useful, as it not only describes important characteristics of that person's lifestyle and ways of relating but also tends to predict future risks and behaviours. The characteristics of each network type can also be used to support interventions. For example, at hospital discharge, the first two network types above may be ill prepared to support the older person at home. Domiciliary support or preparation of the home before discharge may be essential. Being aware of network type can therefore help the social worker in their decision-making.

> **Making connexions**
>
> Consider the approaches to assessment outlined in this chapter. What are their implications for social work practice?

The needs of carers

Most care provided on a day-to-day basis to frail older people is provided by informal carers, not statutory agencies. Research has shown caring to be physically and emotionally demanding (Donaldson et al., 1997). Support to carers has become a policy priority, although this is often couched in general terms through the provision of support to carers themselves, or through respite care – arranging for time away, or enabling the older person to stay away from home for a period to give the carer a break. Beyond this, at an individual level, it would help the social worker to know precisely what kind of assistance best helps the carer. In a randomized controlled study of carers' involvement with older people, viewed by care managers as at risk of entering care homes, Venables et al. (2006) found that the most effective help to carers was through helping to improve care recipients' health, behaviour and mood. Carers' wellbeing was linked directly to improvements in aspects of the behaviour of older people (Figure 19.1).

The best way of helping carers may be by helping to alleviate the difficulties of the older people for whom they care. In this study, older people were helped by pulling together social workers' assessments with those of specialist health clinicians, who often were able to recognize the presence of previously undetected health problems, arrange treatment and feed this back to social workers to arrange more appropriate care.

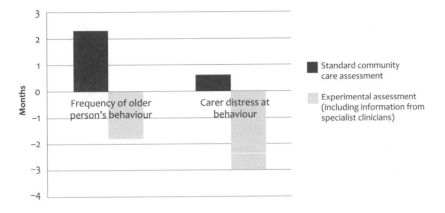

Figure 19.1 Changes over six months in frequency of older people's behaviour and degree of carer distress (average scores)

Source: Data from Venables et al., 2006

Involving older people with dementia in research and service monitoring

Dementia, and the resources needed to live with it, is likely to frame the responses of social workers well into this century (Challis et al., 2009). One issue often raised is the extent to which older people with severe levels of cognitive impairment can, or should, be involved in research and in routine evaluation of services. An older view (often erroneously equated with medicine) is that they cannot; people with severe impairments of memory or orientation are not able to answer questions concerning their lives, opinions and satisfactions. A newer, emerging view is that they should (Downs, 1997) and some research studies have suggested that they can answer such questions. In the process of investigating the potential for involving older people with quite pronounced levels of cognitive impairment in research, Mozley et al. (1999) examined their responses to a quality of life questionnaire. They inspected the reliability of older people's ratings of their quality of life and satisfaction against several 'cutoff' scores used to define a 'case' on the most widely used screening tool for dementia, the mini mental state examination. They found that more than three-quarters of people scoring at or below a threshold of 17, a commonly accepted indication of moderate to severe dementia, were able to be interviewed and reliably answer questions concerning their quality of life. Of those between a low score of 10 and 17 (out of 30), nearly half were still able to be reliably interviewed.

Research

These findings have implications not only for the extent to which older people with dementia can be involved in research but also their capabilities to reliably respond to questioning concerning their life goals and satisfaction, for example as part of assessments. Social workers should take note that, although a person with dementia may not be oriented to time or place, they may still show skills in other areas, such as attention, and may still be able to give a meaningful opinion concerning their preferences or the care they receive.

Care coordination

The care management process – case finding and screening, assessment, care planning, monitoring and review – is now applied worldwide in countries as diverse as the USA, Britain, Italy and Japan. One aspect central to the social worker's role, in addition to the assessment phase, discussed above, is care coordination. Here, recent research offers some pointers to innovative and effective practice.

Organizational networks

One theme useful to explore here is that of networks, but viewed from a slightly different perspective than that of informal networks around the older person, discussed above. There is some emerging research in care management around the idea of networks of locally delivered formal health and social care resources (Abell et al., 2010). In other words, this is the idea of social networks but applied to the resources available in constructing the care plan for an older person. For the social worker, a key characteristic of success in planning the care required is the availability of resources, and the means of accessing them, within existing networks of health and social care services. The extent to which the social worker can draw on those resources, particularly of other agencies outside their immediate contact, will depend on their knowledge of their workings and the assistance they are able to provide. By studying these networks in the same detailed manner as those informal contacts available to the older person, we may discover the ingredients of professional success in care coordination.

The idea of organizational as distinct from personal networks has its origins in the research of Provan and Milward (1995) in the USA. A network, in organizational terms, is typified by forms of cooperative alliances (agreements, integration of activities) between organizations. Their research viewed success, in terms of the wellbeing of those requiring health and social services, as dependent on the coordinated actions of many organizations. However, it went one step further by attempting to indicate which network characteristics were associated with more effective outcomes. In a study of four US cities, their research measured these characteristics in terms of density (number of linkages between providers divided by the number of agencies) and centrality (the extent to which a central agency controlled the network). They found that there was little association between density and effectiveness, but that when decisions were concentrated in a single core agency rather than dispersed among several agencies, outcomes were better. Their centrality measure was essentially about influence: it measured more formal agreements between providers sanctioned by a central agency rather than more ad hoc linkages between agencies.

Translating these insights into social and healthcare practice in this country is still at an initial stage but some indicators have emerged. By means of a survey questionnaire, Abell et al. (2010) found variable formal agreements between 10 case management services and networks of other wider health and social care resources in Greater Manchester. At this point, no effectiveness data are available but their indicators of network linkage included:

- formal agreements with other providers, for example community nursing, end of life programmes, geriatric medicine, old age psychiatry
- agreements concerning the interface between health and social care, for example whether health staff can authorize domiciliary care
- the services routinely detailed in care plans, for example adult social care, intermediate care, primary care.

In performing this core task of care management, social workers will require a broad knowledge of the entire spectrum of health and social care resources to help them in choosing the most appropriate resource for an older person at a specific time. The social worker should focus on such indicators to provide them with a detailed picture of the capacity of local networks to provide the assistance that may be needed by an older person. Such research is in its infancy and the next step will be to investigate whether different workings of networks in different areas, with differing service delivery relationships, produce differences in older people's reported wellbeing.

Conclusions

Research findings, although not consumed as avidly by practitioners in older people's services as by those in other settings, have an important role to play in systemizing practice, in setting the context for working with older people and in informing assessment in particular. Social workers can also draw on research evidence to frame their decisions concerning resources, both human and material, in involving older people in views about the impact of services and assisting carers. Social work with older people could benefit by making use of research in a more coherent way than hitherto. One practical way of doing this would be to focus on the role of assessment, using findings from research to directly influence what is looked for and what happens as a result of the delivery of services.

Further reading

- Challis, D., Sutcliffe, C., Hughes J. et al. (2009) *Supporting People with Dementia at Home: Challenges and Opportunities for the 21st Century.* Farnham: Ashgate.

Research

Presents the evidence from an experiment into case management for older people with dementia and presents a variety of research measures used for evaluation as well as exploring policy and practice issues.

■ Jones, G.M. and Miesen, B.M. (eds) (2004) *Care-giving in Dementia: Research and Applications*, vol. 3. Hove: Brunner-Routledge.

Third volume in a comprehensive series of texts bringing together evidence on dementia, including person-centred care, with commentary about 'what works'.

■ Kane, R.L. and Kane, R.A. (2000) *Assessing Older Persons: Measures, Meaning and Practical Applications*. New York: Oxford University Press.

Although written from a US perspective, it is difficult to envisage such a wide-ranging text on assessment of older people, including the marshalling of research evidence, being written in the UK.

References

Abell, J., Hughes, J., Reilly, S. et al. (2010) 'Case management for long-term conditions: the role of networks in health and social care services', *Journal of Integrated Care*, **18**(1): 45–52.

Andrew, M.K., Rockwood, K. and Mitnitski, A. (2008) 'Social vulnerability, frailty and mortality in elderly people', *PloS One*, **3**(5): e2232, doi:10.1371/journal.pone.0002232.

Berkmann, L.F. and Syme, S.L. (1979) 'Social networks, host resistance and mortality: a nine-year follow-up of Alameda County residents', *American Journal of Epidemiology*, 109, 186–204.

Challis, D.J. (1981) 'The measurement of outcome in social care of the elderly', *Journal of Social Policy*, 10, 179–208.

Challis, D., Clarkson, P., Williamson, J. et al. (2004) 'The value of specialist clinical assessment of older people prior to entry to care homes', *Age and Ageing*, 33, 25–34.

Challis, D., Sutcliffe, S., Hughes, J. et al. (2009) *Supporting People with Dementia at Home*. Farnham: Ashgate.

Clarkson, P., Abendstern, M., Sutcliffe, C. et al. (2009) 'Reliability of needs assessments in the community care of older people: impact of the single assessment process in England', *Journal of Public Health*, 31, 521–9.

Clarkson, P., Hughes, J., Challis, D. et al. (2010) 'Targeting, care management and preventative services for older people: the cost-effectiveness of a pilot self-assessment approach in one local authority', *British Journal of Social Work*, 40, 2255–73.

Donaldson, C., Tarrier, N. and Burns, A. (1997) 'The impact of the symptoms of dementia on caregivers', *British Journal of Psychiatry*, 170, 62–8.

Downs, M. (1997) 'The emergence of the person in dementia research', *Ageing & Society*, 17, 597–607.

Ellis, K. (1993) *Squaring the Circle: User and Carer Participation in Needs Assessment*. Birmingham: University of Birmingham/Joseph Rowntree Foundation.

Fries, J.F. (1980) 'Aging, natural death and the compression of morbidity', *New England Journal of Medicine*, 303, 130–5.

Howse, K. (2006) *Increasing Life Expectancy and the Compression of Morbidity: A Critical Review of the Debate*, Working Paper No. 206. Oxford: Oxford Institute of Ageing.

Jorm, A.F., Henderson, A.S., Kay, D.W. and Jacomb, P.A. (1991) 'Mortality in relation to dementia, depression and social integration in an elderly community sample', *International Journal of Geriatric Psychiatry*, 6, 5–11.

Kane, R.L. and Kane, R.A. (2000) *Assessing Older Persons: Measures, Meaning and Practical Applications*. New York: Oxford University Press.

Katz, S., Ford, A.B., Moskowitz, R.W. et al. (1963) 'Studies of illness in the aged: the index of ADL', *Journal of the American Medical Association*, 183, 914–19.

Lubben, J.E. (1988) 'Assessing social networks among elderly populations', *Family and Community Health*, 11, 42–52.

Miller, P.M. and Ingham, J.G. (1976) 'Friends, confidants and symptoms', *Social Psychiatry*, 11, 51–8.

Mozley, C.G., Huxley, P., Sutcliffe, C. et al. (1999) '"Not knowing where I am doesn't mean I don't know what I like": cognitive impairment and quality of life responses in elderly people', *International Journal of Geriatric Psychiatry*, 14, 776–83.

Provan, K.G. and Milward, H.B. (1995) 'A preliminary theory of inter-organisational network effectiveness: a comparative study of four community mental health systems', *Administrative Science Quarterly*, 40, 1–33.

Rockwood, K. and Mitnitski, A. (2006) 'Limits to deficit accumulation in elderly people', *Mechanisms of Ageing and Development*, 127, 494–96.

Rockwood, K. and Mitnitski, A. (2007) 'Frailty in relation to the accumulation of deficits', *Journal of Gerontology: Medical Sciences*, 62A, 722–7.

Shaw, C. (2000) '1998-based national population projections for the United Kingdom and constituent countries', *Population Trends*, 99, 4–12.

Travis, S.S. and McAuley, W.J. (1990) 'Simple counts of the number of basic ADL dependencies for long-term care research and practice', *Health Services Research*, 25, 349–60.

Venables, D., Clarkson, P., Hughes, J. et al. (2006) 'Specialist clinical assessment of vulnerable older people: outcomes for carers from a randomised controlled trial', *Ageing & Society*, 26, 867–82.

Wenger, G.C. (1994) *Support Networks of Older People: A Guide for Practitioners*. Bangor: Centre for Social Policy Research and Development, University of Wales.

Wenger, G.C. (1997) 'Social networks and the prediction of elderly people at risk', *Aging & Mental Health*, 1, 311–20.

Wenger, G.C. and Tucker, I. (2002) 'Using network variation in practice: identification of support network type', *Health and Social Care in the Community*, 10, 28–35.

Williams, R.G., Johnston, M., Willis, L.A. and Bennett, A.E. (1976) 'Disability: a model and measurement technique', *British Journal of Preventive and Social Medicine*, 30, 71–8.

Wittenberg, R., Pickard, L., Comas-Herrera, A. et al. (1998) *Demand for Long-term Care: Projections of Long-term Care Finance for Elderly People*. Canterbury: PSSRU, University of Kent.

Research

20

Social work with older people

RHIANNON JONES

Contrary to commonly held perceptions, older age is not a period of inevitable decline, and most older people never need social work intervention, with only 15% of people over the age of 65 receiving social care support (Audit Commission, 2008). As people grow even older, however, their take-up of social work and social care support increases (Forder, 2008). It can be surmised that a person over the age of 85 is more likely to be in receipt of social care support than at any other time in their life. It is important, however, to put this statement into perspective, by noting that over 50% of people over the age of 85 are not in receipt of social care services (Phillips et al., 2006), with only 18% of people over 80 years of age living in residential care, a figure that rises to 28% for people over 90 years of age (Audit Commission, 2008).

So what are the reasons why a minority of older people may require social work intervention? Although older people are not a homogeneous group, they are more likely to warrant social work intervention if they are struggling to cope with physical frailty and impairment, ill health and/or mental health issues, such as depression and dementia, or are experiencing some form of abuse or neglect. Older people's ability to cope with these circumstances can be seriously undermined by challenging structural factors such as poverty, poor housing, social isolation, decreasing social and personal support networks, and ageism. Social workers need to recognize that older people's ability to cope may also be affected by the way they have managed traumatic events in the past, with the possibility that any unresolved trauma can return and cause additional problems to understanding and resolving the present issues (Hunt, 1997).

Social workers involve themselves in older people's lives when they no longer have the individual or collective resources to cope with, adapt to or challenge life events. Through the use of case studies, this chapter will explore some of the situations that social workers encounter when working with older people. Although social workers work in many contexts, including the voluntary and independent sectors, these case studies are all set in the statutory sector: two in a local authority multidisciplinary older people's team, one in a community mental health team, and one in a hospital social work team. These case scenarios represent a 'snapshot in time' and cannot capture the iterative nature of an assessment process. They do not aim to be comprehensive but to offer a flavour of the processes and complexities that challenge social workers working with older people.

Practice example 1   Gwyn Jones

Gwyn Jones, 90 years of age, lives on his own and so far has managed to care for and support himself independently. His neighbours, however, are becoming concerned about him as he has been seen recently at the local shops looking unkempt and asking people for money to buy food. Gwyn has also started getting regular visitors to his house. Recently, his next-door neighbour called the police because Gwyn's visitors were causing a disturbance, with a lot of shouting and banging. Although Gwyn did not want the police to do anything, they were concerned enough about his general safety and welfare to make a referral to the multidisciplinary older person's team for a section 47 assessment under the National Health Service and Community Care Act 1990.

Assessment

The first couple of times that the social worker visits, Gwyn does not allow him into the house and maintains that he is fine and does not need any support. The social worker is sufficiently concerned by Gwyn's unkempt appearance to persevere in trying to establish some form of relationship and, with the help of Gwyn's next-door neighbour, is eventually invited into the house. It transpires that Gwyn has been living alone for 10 years since the death of his learning disabled son. After Gwyn's wife died 20 years ago, he had become his son's main carer. When their son was born, 50 years ago, Gwyn and his wife had been advised by the social services department to put him into care, and since that time they have held a vehement dislike of social workers and have vowed never to let one into their house again. Gwyn's relationship with the current social worker is fragile but after three more visits, the social worker is able to piece together enough information to enable him to complete a full assessment of Gwyn's needs.

The assessment highlights the fact that Gwyn has been self-caring but recently his arthritis has made it more difficult for him to look after himself, to go out shopping or to see friends. He says that he has been feeling increasingly isolated and has not been eating very well. He is also developing sores on his legs from sitting too close to his gas fire. During the financial assessment, the social worker finds out that Gwyn has had a lot of money go missing, and this has caused him to run up debts in relation to his bills. Probing further, the social worker finds out that Gwyn's two nephews and a niece have started visiting him, and that he gives them money on a regular basis for doing his shopping. He says that they have a tendency to visit him in the evening

Practice

when he is very tired and at times forgetful, so he is unsure how much money he is giving them and how much money he has misplaced. The social worker noticed early on in their relationship that Gwyn is more mentally alert in the mornings and had arranged his subsequent visits to complement this strength. Gwyn goes on to disclose to the social worker that his relatives can be quite intimidating if he 'short-changes' them. When the social worker inquires about whether they have ever physically hurt him, Gwyn emphatically states that he does not want the social worker to investigate the situation any further. On the whole, Gwyn likes his relatives' visits as he has been lonely recently, and he feels obliged to make sure that they are not out of pocket.

On his last visit to Gwyn, the social worker tells him that the manager of the older people's team will consider the assessment and will decide how much support they can finance. Gwyn tells the social worker that he will make no promises about accepting help, and he emphasizes again that he does not want anyone 'scaring off' his relatives.

Intervention

The social worker seeks advice from the local authority adult protection officer who confirms that, in England, a service user who has mental capacity has to give permission for any investigation of suspected abuse to take place. The social worker feels that, in spite of some forgetfulness, Gwyn has the capacity to make his own mind up about whether or not he wants the suspected financial abuse to be investigated. He bases this decision on a combination of how Gwyn has been able to give a good account of himself during his period of assessment, information from the neighbours, and the fact that Gwyn's forgetfulness may well be caused by poor diet, stress and isolation and could therefore be addressed. Through discussions with the adult protection officer, the social worker understands that, although Gwyn's decision needs to be respected, there also needs to be positive intervention in order to reduce his vulnerability and minimize the risk of abuse.

Due to the safeguarding issue highlighted in the social worker's assessment of Gwyn's needs, Gwyn is given an individual budget that will buy him an adequate support package within his home as well as enable him to address his social isolation. There is enough money within the individual budget to employ a broker, should Gwyn decide that he does not want to organize the care package himself. The social worker talks through the options with Gwyn and encourages Gwyn to have a broker, because this would help to minimize the amount of money Gwyn would have to handle himself and lessen his vulnerability to possible abuse by his relatives. Although Gwyn thinks it is a good idea, he is anxious about having strangers coming into his house and asks the social worker to inquire whether his next-door neighbour would like the job of being his carer. His next-door neighbour agrees to cook him a meal once a day for four days, and Gwyn agrees to be taken out for a meal the other days to places in the community that he used to visit such as the local café, the church and luncheon club. The social worker will liaise with the broker in terms of setting up an account with a taxi firm for these trips.

The issue of Gwyn's shopping is a difficult matter to resolve as he is worried about upsetting his relatives if someone else does it for him; he is concerned that they will no longer visit him. The social worker offers to meet his relatives to propose a compromise that the shopping is split between them and the next-door neighbour who will shop for the meals that she is intending to cook for Gwyn. Gwyn agrees to this and to a weekly visit by the district nurse who will dress and monitor his leg sores.

What happens next?

A few months later, the social worker undertakes a review visit and finds Gwyn well and having put on some weight. Gwyn has established a good relationship with the district nursing service, has increased his social network and re-established contact with friends. Gwyn's relatives do not visit as often as they used to, but this does not upset him as much as he thought it would. Both Gwyn and his next-door neighbour say that money is still going missing and usually coincides with visits from his relatives. As Gwyn now has a trusted person in his life, he could agree that his neighbour might apply for lasting power of attorney to make decisions on his behalf if and when he no longer wants to or has the capacity to. This could offer him further protection from his relatives.

Practice example 2   Abdul Khan

Abdul Khan, 72 years of age, lives alone and is currently in receipt of a care package, having been referred to the community mental health team for a section 47 assessment under the National Health Service and Community Care Act 1990 12 months ago. Abdul was assessed by a consultant psychiatrist four years ago and was diagnosed as having dementia of the Alzheimer's type. His support workers and the community mental health nurses are concerned that Abdul's cognitive ability has deteriorated to an extent that the current package of care is not now sufficient to support him living at home. A referral is made to the social worker in the team for a reassessment of the situation.

Assessment

Initially, the social worker checks the records for the current level of care; it is made up of support with meals, shopping, cleaning and personal hygiene, together with a twice-daily call from the support worker. Abdul's two daughters, who live nearby, call in every evening, and neighbours try to support him when he goes out for a walk in the neighbourhood and gets 'lost'. Additionally, the community mental health nurse monitors his mental health by calling in twice a month.

The social worker then liaises with all the people who make up Abdul's support network, including the health and social care workers, relatives and neighbours.

Practice

There is general concern over the level of day-to-day risks that Abdul encounters, as he quite often refuses to let people help him and at times does not allow the support workers into the house. He is neglecting his self-care and diet, burning saucepans on the cooker and the house is often cold. Amna, Abdul's youngest daughter, feels that her father would be better off in residential care as she thinks the risks are now getting too great.

During their first meeting, the social worker notices that, initially, Abdul appears to give a good account of how he manages, what he eats, who visits him, what he buys at the shop and what time he goes to bed. It is only when the discussion continues that the social worker realizes that although Abdul's conversation is quite plausible, it is also repetitive; specific probing of certain topics results in Abdul's conversation becoming vague and generalized.

There were a couple of incidents during the social worker's visit that highlighted the impaired nature of Abdul's short-term memory: he had to be prompted that he was going to put the fire on and to be reminded of the social worker's name. Abdul does not seem to react when the social worker talks about the support workers, but he smiles and becomes cheerful when the discussion comes round to his daughters who he says he loves very much. The social worker introduces the topic of extra help and support, and the possibility of Abdul going somewhere for the day or even for a short break. In response, Abdul becomes animated, saying that he does not want any changes and wants to carry on living in his house. The social worker asks Abdul if he would be in agreement for the social worker to return and to have his daughters present so that any future plans could be discussed. Abdul agrees to this, but continues to stress that he will not leave his house. On returning to the office, the social worker contacts Abdul's daughters to arrange a meeting.

Intervention

It becomes clear during their meeting with the social worker that Abdul's daughters disagree about their father's future care. Amna is adamant that her father should have 24-hour supervision and that his wishes should be disregarded because he does not remember or understand what is being said. Anvar, Abdul's eldest daughter, supports her father's wishes to remain in his home, because she feels that it is full of memories for him and changes would be distressing and might make his confusion worse. Abdul is clearly distressed witnessing this disagreement, and becomes anxious when Amna starts asking him questions that he has difficulty in answering. The social worker explains to both daughters that there is now legislation (Mental Capacity Act 2005) stating that everyone is assumed to have the mental capacity to make decisions for themselves, and that it is unlawful to assume that someone like Abdul lacks capacity to make decisions because he has dementia. The social worker explains that the next step in this difficult situation will be to carry out an assessment of Abdul's mental capacity.

The social worker feels that although it is not a requirement of the assessment for more than one professional to be involved, it would be useful to include the community mental health nurse. Over a couple of visits, Abdul conveys to both workers the importance and meaning of his home. He talks about it with warmth, spontaneously discusses his memories of his wife and how his daughters were born and brought up in it. He shows them many photographs and both workers feel that his home gives him a sense of stability and familiarity in what must be a frightening time in his life when he is losing his memory. The social worker also takes Abdul to see a residential home, but all the time during the visit he keeps asking to be taken home, saying that he does not want to live in such a place. Both workers bear in mind the 2005 Act's emphasis that assessing someone's capacity must be done on a decision-specific basis: applied to Abdul's situation; it means that Abdul may be able to make a decision about where he wants to live, but more complex decisions – such as assessing the level of risk – may not be fully understood. It is a difficult decision for the two workers, but both feel that Abdul has the capacity at the moment to make the decision to live at home and that this must be respected, despite the considerable risks arising from his cognitive impairment. When the decision is conveyed to the daughters, both workers state that the situation needs to be closely monitored. The youngest daughter seems to accept the decision, albeit reluctantly.

The social worker concludes that the existing care package should remain in place, but with the support workers asked to encourage Abdul to come out shopping with them to see if this might lessen the number of times he goes out on his own. The social worker refers Abdul to the occupational therapist for an assessment on the use of assistive technology to increase his safety within the home. People in Abdul's support network agree to monitor the situation carefully for any changes, such as Abdul changing his views about supportive accommodation, or in case the risks and/ or his cognitive impairment increase.

What happens next?

If the risks and/or Abdul's cognitive impairment increase, then a reassessment of his mental capacity would take place; in such a case, a decision might well be taken that Abdul no longer has the capacity to make the decision to live at home. If this was the case, there would be a meeting involving all members of his support network to decide, in Abdul's best interests, whether he was able to carry on living

> **Making connexions**
> Family relationships are significant in the lives of Gwyn Jones and Abdul Khan. How does the social worker deal with the background presence of Gwyn's relatives and the disagreement between Abdul's two daughters? What knowledge and skills does the worker draw on?

at home with additional support or whether he must move to residential care. An independent mental capacity advocate could be brought in to represent Abdul's own best interests if his daughters continue to disagree over his future.

Practice example 3 | Harriet Williams

Harriet Williams, 82 years of age, has been taken to the A&E department of her local hospital, having collapsed at the bus stop after visiting her husband in the hospital. She was admitted onto an acute medical ward for assessment, diagnosed as having breathing problems due to a chest infection and trans-ferred to a 'care of the elderly' medical ward for treatment. On arrival on the ward, Harriet anxiously explains to the nurse in charge that Gerald, her 85-year-old husband, is confused and there are plans to discharge him in a couple of days. She says that he will not be able to cope on his own as she provides all his care. The ward sends the hospital social worker a section 2 noti-fication (Community Care (Delayed Discharges etc.) Act 2003) asking for an assessment of Harriet's situation.

Assessment

The social worker's first task is to brief herself on Gerald's situation. This she does by liaising with the nursing staff and the consultant responsible for Gerald's care. They confirm that he has been successfully treated for a urinary infection and is medically fit to be discharged tomorrow. No referral had been made by the ward to the social worker because Harriet had been adamant that she could cope with his care and did not want any services. Gerald's medical notes state that due to his memory loss and difficulty in communicating, he needs supervision with all activities of daily living. The social worker starts negotiating with the consultant to delay discharging Gerald, saying that he is unsafe to be at home on his own. The consultant is only prepared to delay discharge by one day because Gerald is 'blocking' a bed on an acute medical ward. Before leaving the ward to go and see Harriet, the social worker introduces herself to Gerald. He is repeatedly asking where he is, saying that he misses his wife and feels frightened. The social worker tries to reassure Gerald but he does not under-stand what she is trying to do. Before leaving the ward, the social worker raises her concerns with ward staff about Gerald's psychological state and the level of care he would need to live safely at home on his own.

It is Harriet's first time as a hospital inpatient and her first contact with a social worker. The social worker explains the need to get as much information from Harriet as possible so that a full assessment of her situation can be carried out. Harriet is finding it difficult to talk due to her breathlessness and the lack of privacy on the ward. The social worker reassures Harriet by telling her to take her time, and also lets Harriet know that she has seen Gerald. Harriet tells the social worker that she has been Gerald's main carer for six years and gets some support from her neighbour. They have no family living nearby and, until recently, had a good friendship network. Gerald's increasingly erratic behaviour has put off many of their friends from visit-ing, and Harriet feels more and more isolated.

As she gets used to talking to the social worker, Harriet confides that although she wants to carry on looking after her husband, she has been finding it increasingly stressful and feels that she has been neglecting her own health and needs. Harriet said that she had been visiting Gerald every day since he came into hospital and had become exhausted. The ward staff had kept mentioning that Gerald might be better off in a home and that is why Harriet did not want them to contact the social worker. She also feels that strangers in her home would be an intrusion and could upset Gerald. As the assessment progresses, the social worker finds out that Gerald's mental health has never been properly assessed and that his confusion and memory loss have been attributed to his age.

As the social worker carefully shifts the focus of the assessment to Harriet's own needs when she is discharged, both feel it would be helpful to ask a member of medical staff to explain her diagnosis and treatment. The registrar confirms that Harriet's chest infection is being treated with a course of intravenous antibiotics and it is hoped that she would make a full recovery and be discharged in a week or so. Harriet and the social worker agree that the priority at the moment is Gerald and how best to support his needs if he is to be discharged in a couple of days.

Intervention

The social worker convinces the medical consultant that Gerald needs a psychogeriatrician assessment by pointing out that his mental health has never been formally assessed. With nursing staff support, the social worker also points out that it would not be possible to provide a sufficiently intensive care package at such short notice to support Gerald's needs to a level of acceptable risk. The urgent referral to the psychogeriatrician is responded to in the next few days and although it serves to delay Gerald's discharge, his lack of contact with anything familiar – in particular his lack of contact with Harriet – is having a detrimental effect on his mental health: he is becoming more confused and fearful. The psychogeriatrician concludes that it would be better for Gerald to be assessed over a period of time and arranges for him to be transferred to the psychiatric ward for older people.

The social worker keeps Harriet up to date with Gerald's assessment and transfer, and although Harriet is anxious about how he will settle on the new ward, she also feels relieved that she is going to have some time to fully recover before having him back home. After completing Harriet's assessment of need under section 47 of the National Health Service and Community Care Act 1990, together with an in-depth financial assessment, the social worker secures an individual budget from her manager that buys Harriet a short-term care package for 10 days from when she is discharged. Harriet decides that she does not have the energy to arrange her own care package and wants the social worker to arrange it. They agree that she should have a support worker call twice a day and help with her shopping. The social worker also suggests a volunteer driver to take Harriet to see Gerald once she feels up to visiting him. In response to receiving a section 5 notification (Community Care (Delayed Discharges etc.) Act 2003) of Harriet's discharge date, the social worker contacts the various agencies concerned and lets Harriet's neighbours know that she will be home the next day.

Practice

The social worker contacts the community mental health team who cover the psychiatric ward for older people and updates the social worker concerned about the Williams' situation. Both agree that the type of support that Gerald and Harriet would benefit from in the long term depends on the outcome of Gerald's psychiatric assessment.

What happens next?

It is the community mental health social worker who will take over from here and will liaise with Gerald and Harriet about support that will be appropriate and relevant to their needs. This will involve further assessments such as an assessment of needs, a carer's assessment and a financial assessment to highlight any benefits that could be claimed. If Gerald's psychiatric assessment results in a specific diagnosis, such as dementia, then the social worker's role will be to make the Williams aware of any specialist support and care, facilitate their practical needs, explore the possibility of respite care, and offer an appropriate therapeutic response such as counselling and reminiscence work.

Practice example 4   Sean Maguire

Sean Maguire, 75 years of age, was diagnosed a month ago with Parkinson's disease and is the main carer for his 78-year-old partner Mick Heaney, who is in the later stages of lung cancer. Sean visits the GP because he is feeling depressed, tired and is having difficulty sleeping. During the consultation, he confides that he is finding caring for Mick very stressful and does not feel he is coping at all well. It transpires that during Mick's last admission into hospital, the discharge planning had tended to focus on support for Mick's health needs. Neither of the men had considered contact with a social worker to be necessary. With Sean's agreement, the GP contacts the local authority to refer Sean for a carer's assessment under the Carers and Disabled Children Act 2000.

Assessment

On her first visit, the social worker spends some time with Sean on his own discussing his needs as a carer. Sean highlights his main areas of concern; they include his own health, his finances and his ability to cope emotionally with the imminent death of someone he loves very dearly. Sean is unsure how he will cope without Mick, who has been part of his life for over 40 years. Sean says that they do have a small network of good friends but some of them have their own problems and some live a good distance away, making frequent contact difficult. Sean says that although Mick is coping well at the moment and is able to be up most of the day, he tires easily and trips out are onerous. Sean says he misses being able to visit his friends and stay out as long as he wants. He says that when he is out, he is always rushing to get back, anxious not to leave Mick on his own for too long.

Sean talks at length about his own recent diagnosis of Parkinson's disease, and says that although he generally feels quite well at the moment, the stress and worry over Mick is taking its toll on his own health – he is not sleeping very well, is feeling very tired at times and depressed. Sean says that it is impossible to know what is linked to his Parkinson's and what is linked to the situation with Mick. At the moment, Sean feels that they are getting enough help through the GP and the district nursing service who have requested various assistive technologies for when Mick's health starts to deteriorate. Sean confides to the social worker that it would be nice to have some help with some household tasks so that he could put his energy into Mick, but he says that he worries about the finances, as neither of them have much savings and rely on their state pension for day-to-day living expenses.

Even though the referral for an assessment is for Sean, the social worker is acutely aware that their needs are interrelated. She feels that Mick would benefit from an assessment of need under section 47 of the National Health Service and Community Care Act 1990, not because it would necessarily result in meeting the eligibility criteria for services (DH, 2010), but because an assessment can be a service in its own right and it would ensure Mick's awareness of the type of support and options available for the future.

On a further visit, the social worker spends time talking to Mick about his situation. Mick confirms Sean's view that at the moment he is well supported and feels that his current practical needs are being adequately met by the input from the health services. The social worker is mindful that Mick's situation and needs could change fairly rapidly. When she tries to engage him in a discussion about his future, she finds that he is reluctant to think about any issues in depth other than the fact that he does not want to go back into hospital for further treatment and wants to die at home. She arranges to call back the following week to have a discussion with Mick and Sean together about the range of support options so that Mick's wishes can become a reality.

Intervention

The social worker recognizes that her role not only involves giving advice about future support options but also allows her to offer therapeutic support, by enabling both Mick and Sean to express their feelings. With this in mind, the social worker negotiates with her manager to be allocated the time to undertake a series of visits to Mick and Sean. She successfully puts the case forward that she has a lot of direct work to accomplish with them but needs the time to carry it out sensitively and at a reasonable pace. The social worker also liaises with the hospice social worker who gives her information on the availability of specialist cancer support in the area, the range of hospice services and the referral process.

On the social worker's next visit to see Mick and Sean, she lets them know what she has agreed with her manager in terms of what support she can offer and asks if they are in agreement. Sean agrees immediately and Mick, although hesitant, agrees that he needs to talk more about what he is facing. His view has been changed because the

Practice

doctor had to up his pain control a couple of days ago. The social worker discusses with Mick and Sean the importance of talking to them together about the future support options and also being able to recognize their individual needs. It is agreed that Mick and Sean will have time on each visit to speak to the social worker separately.

Over a period of a month, working together, a lot of practical support is sorted out in relation to finances, by ensuring that all the benefits they are entitled to are claimed for and specialist funding agencies, such as the Macmillan Cancer Support, are approached for any one-off large expenditure on items to aid Mick's comfort. The social worker introduces them to the concept of continuing healthcare funding for when Mick becomes so ill as to need care provided by a qualified nurse. They are given the name of a social worker for future contact at the local hospital who is part of a team of social workers set up to undertake assessments for such funding. Other practical issues include making sure that their wills are up to date and that Mick's wish to have no further treatment is formally known by creating an advance decision (Mental Capacity Act 2005). Discussions with the social worker enable Mick to talk privately to Sean about how he wants to die at home, who he wants to see, things he wants to do before he dies, and what he wants at his funeral.

What happens next?

The social worker gives Sean a contact for a local carers groups as well as an online support group for people newly diagnosed with Parkinson's disease. A volunteer is found from their local Age UK agency (formed in 2009 by the joining together of Age Concern and Help the Aged) to sit with Mick for an afternoon and evening when Sean goes out to visit friends. With Mick's permission, the social worker asks his GP to make a referral to the local hospice so that Mick can make use of their daycare and volunteer facilities. The social worker puts the case forward to the GP that Mick has opted for palliative care as opposed to treatment, and that support from the hospice would help to maintain as high a quality of life for Mick as possible. The GP confirms that Mick has a poor prognosis of less than six months to live and makes the referral to the hospice.

Before concluding her work with Mick and Sean, the social worker obtains Mick's permission to refer him for continuing emotional and practical support to the hospice social worker.

In conclusion

As can be seen from these four case studies, social work intervention in an older person's life is usually preceded by a transition in circumstances, which has caused a disruption in how the older person is able to cope. Although the case studies highlight a range of issues and challenges that face some older people, a number of common themes regarding social work practice can be identified.

Social work practice involves challenging ageism (Phillipson, 2002). For example, as highlighted in the case of Harriet's husband Gerald, memory loss and confusion are often incorrectly attributed to the ageing process, resulting in many older people being denied a proper assessment. This denial often obscures a treatable condition and supports the ageist view of assuming that all confused older people have a dementia. If a diagnosis of dementia is reached, the assessment is also able to determine the kind of dementia an older person is experiencing (Marshall and Tibbs, 2006); this helps to challenge the 'lumping together' of people with dementia. Contrary to the diversity, variability and range of 'older age' reflected in the case studies, older people are often regarded as a homogeneous group and responded to in a uniform way. In each of the case studies, it was important for the social worker to hold a holistic view of ageing so that someone such as Abdul is regarded not just in terms of his dementia but also in relation to his history and biography. In Mick's situation, the social worker advocated for palliative care, the ethos of which supports the notion of holistic care. Many older people experience end of life care in a fragmented and frightening way by being responded to in a routine and nonspecialist way (Help the Aged, 2005).

The legislative context highlighted in the case studies is complex and has advantages and disadvantages for older people. In each case study, the service users were assessed using the National Health Service and Community Care Act 1990 but not all, for example Mick, met the eligibility criteria for support. With older people's needs having to be at least at a substantial level to receive support, social workers need to emphasize the difficulties and lack of abilities of service users. Social workers who want to adopt an empowering 'strengths' approach to assessment run the risk of failing to procure any money for support services. A lot of preventive work required for 'lower' level needs is also not being undertaken. Harriet, for example, may have benefited from some earlier preventive intervention, and although she was given short-term support when leaving hospital, the assessment process had to take place in the unaccommodating context of the Community Care (Delayed Discharges etc.) Act 2003. In relation to Gwyn, the nonstatutory nature of safeguarding adults within England made the social worker's role to protect very difficult. Although Gwyn refused an investigation, his support package did result in lessening the financial abuse. In Abdul's situation, the Mental Capacity Act 2005 protected him from stereotypical assumptions about his capacity and allowed the social worker to focus on his abilities, rights and wishes. This Act has been helpful in enshrining good practice by starting from an assumption of capacity and is viewed as a friend to the person with dementia (Dwyer, 2009).

The move towards personalization – through individual budgets, self-assessment and being able to choose who provides the support – presents a challenging context within which to work with older people. From the case studies, it can be seen that Gwyn benefited from the flexibility of being able to employ his neighbour; and Mick, in the future, may be able to ensure that his support positively respects his relationship with Sean. There are older people, however – such as Abdul and Harriet – who, at a time of crisis, feel unable, for whatever reason, to make informed choices about the management and organization of their care.

Practice

There is also a danger that for many older people personalization will result in a loss of contact with a social worker; and its focus on practical services serves to support the ageist notion that older people's problems only require a practical response devoid of any therapeutic and emotional support. Research on community care with older people points to the fact that 'the psychological and emotional needs of service users are often ignored in favour of practical and physical matters instead of interventions being holistically based' (Dwyer, 2009, p. 277). All the case studies highlight the way that assessment can create 'therapeutic windows of opportunity' (Marshall and Tibbs, 2006, p. 128), where the work can become more focused on emotional issues. For example, the assessment process enabled Harriet and Sean to discuss their feelings about struggling as carers, Gwyn to discuss his loneliness, Mick to discuss his feelings about facing death, and Abdul to reminisce and engage positively with his memories of the past. Social workers need to use the skills of counselling and active listening through the tool of assessment to enable older people to reach painful and difficult decisions.

As seen in the case studies, older people with complex problems often need multidisciplinary intervention and therefore the social worker needs the skills of negotiation and communication to work effectively with other professionals. There is often an advocacy role for the social worker, for example in the case of Harriet's husband and Mick, where the social workers used their knowledge of the healthcare system to negotiate a service on behalf of the older person. The social workers in the case studies all needed to work hard to engage the service user; knowledge of a person's biography, such as Gwyn's, enables the social worker to place in context and understand any reluctance on the part of the service user to engage with them. The social worker, as in the situation with Abdul, also needs the skill to cope with the many and possibly conflicting perspectives of a situation.

In conclusion, social work with older people should be about ascertaining the needs, strengths, risks and resources of a given situation and responding in a way that encourages either the maintenance or re-establishment of the important aspects of an older person's life. This task needs to be accomplished using a value base that challenges ageism and respects an older person's biography and history.

Acknowledgements

Thanks to the following practitioners who gave me their time to talk about their work with older people:

Louise Adlington, social worker, older people's team, Whiston Hospital, Whiston

Peter Holcroft, student, MA in Social Work, Manchester Metropolitan University

Noel Pine, mental health social worker, community mental health team for later life, central Manchester

Ellen Saunders, adults social work team manager, Federation of Jewish Services, Prestwich, Manchester

Further reading

■ McDonald, A. (2010) *Social Work with Older People.* Cambridge: Polity.

Social work processes, methods and interventions are the focus of this text and there are useful case examples, together with a summary statement of key lessons for each chapter.

■ Ray, M., Bernard, M. and Phillips, J. (2009) *Critical Issues in Social Work with Older People.* Basingstoke: Palgrave Macmillan.

Challenging text where issues concerning older people are viewed from a critical gerontological perspective.

■ Tanner, D. and Harris, J. (2008) *Working with Older People.* London: Routledge/ Community Care.

Comprehensive text covering theory, policy, skills and values within the area of social work with older people.

References

Audit Commission (2008) *Don't Stop Me Now.* London: Audit Commission.

DH (Department of Health) (2010) *Fair Access to Care Services: Prioritising Need in the Context of Putting People First: A Whole System Approach to Eligibility for Social Care – Guidance on Eligibility Criteria for Adult Social Care, England.* London: DH.

Dwyer, S. (2009) 'The good news and the bad news for frail older people', *Practice,* **21**(4): 273–89.

Forder, J. (2008) *The Costs of Addressing Age Discrimination in Social Care,* PSSRU Discussion Paper 2538. Canterbury: PSSRU.

Help the Aged (2005) *Dying in Older Age: Reflections and Experiences from an Older Person's Perspective.* London: Help the Aged.

Hunt, L. (1997) 'The past in the present: an introduction to trauma (re)emerging in old age', in L. Hunt, M. Marshall and C. Rowlings (eds) *Past Trauma in Late Life: European Perspectives on Therapeutic Work with Older People.* London: Jessica Kingsley.

Marshall, M. and Tibbs, M. (2006) *Social Work and People with Dementia: Partnerships, Practice and Persistence.* Bristol: BASW/Policy Press.

Phillips, J., Ray, M. and Marshal, M. (2006) *Social Work with Older People* (4th edn). Basingstoke: Palgrave Macmillan.

Phillipson, C. (2002) 'The frailty of old age', in M. Davies (ed.) *The Blackwell Companion to Social Work* (2nd edn). Oxford: Blackwell.

Practice

Name index

Subject index